T0214645

Lecture Notes in Computer Science　11792

More information about this series at http://www.springer.com/series/7409

Yuhua Luo (Ed.)

Cooperative Design, Visualization, and Engineering

16th International Conference, CDVE 2019
Mallorca, Spain, October 6–9, 2019
Proceedings

 Springer

Editor
Yuhua Luo 🆔
University of Balearic Islands
Palma de Mallorca, Spain

ISSN 0302-9743   ISSN 1611-3349   (electronic)
Lecture Notes in Computer Science
ISBN 978-3-030-30948-0   ISBN 978-3-030-30949-7   (eBook)
https://doi.org/10.1007/978-3-030-30949-7

LNCS Sublibrary: SL3 – Information Systems and Applications, incl. Internet/Web, and HCI

This Springer imprint is published by the registered company Springer Nature Switzerland AG
The registered company address is: Gewerbestrasse 11, 6330 Cham, Switzerland

Preface

This book contains the papers presented at the 16th International Conference on Cooperative Design, Visualization, and Engineering (CDVE 2019). The conference was held in Mallorca, Spain, during October 6–9, 2019.

The papers presented in this proceedings book reflect the important application areas and great potential of the CDVE technology. The achievement, progress, and future challenges are reported in areas such as aerospace engineering, remote medical monitoring, automatic machine monitoring, cooperative personal data analytics, mobile banking, remote cooperative art performance management, etc. Authors also present new findings and methodologies in their papers by addressing traditional areas such as architecture, civil engineering and construction, cooperative learning, enterprise management, etc. This gives the readers a fresh look of how the CDVE technology is shaping our industry and daily life.

Space craft design is a typical application scenario of cooperative design and concurrent engineering. There are some papers included in this volume that contribute to the topic concerning sharing of product information and concurrent engineering session management for the space crafts. One paper discusses the spacecraft interface and data management in concurrent engineering sessions which is a key process in designing new space crafts. A shared system model is provided for the engineers to exchange design information during the cooperative design. Among many issues, structural decomposition of the system and the analysis of design drivers such as the mass or power consumption of the spacecraft have attracted attention. This paper discusses the state of the art of the topic and derives a generic approach for it. The approach is customized and implemented in the virtual satellite application and directly applied to the practical study.

Recently, remote medical monitoring is an active research and development field all over the world. Some authors in this volume report on their proposal and development of a platform to realize this task. Their platform allows for the monitoring of a patient's health parameters using connected objects (blood pressure monitor, thermometer, glucometer, etc.) – a group of IoT's which can communicate with the remote platform efficiently. The central server can trigger alerts according to the real data with thresholds predefined by the medical teams. Low-Power Wide Area Network is used to offer a cost-effective alternative, which is less expensive in terms of energy than cellular networks. This is particularly suitable for transmitting small amounts of data from sensors as well as energy efficient for battery powered objects over long distances.

Along the same line of using IoT technology, there is another paper concerning the use of a machine learning approach for condition monitoring and automated diagnosis for spinning manufacturing machines. The special feature here is that the machines can keep running when the monitoring and diagnosis are being performed. Real-time data sensing and signal processing are performed via the industrial IoT. The controlled sensor network can be tailored for different critical components of the same type of machines. Back propagation neural network based multi-sensor performance assessment and prediction strategy are developed for this intelligent maintenance and diagnostic system.

Collaborative knowledge discovery is an approach by which people with no data analytics expertise could benefit from an analysis of their own personal data by experts. To facilitate effective collaboration between data owners and knowledge discovery experts, the authors of a paper in this volume have developed a software platform that uses a domain ontology to represent knowledge relevant to the execution of the collaborative knowledge discovery process. Their ontology provides classes representing the collaborators and datasets. Their ontology can specify the privacy constraints that describes the precise extent of personal data sharing with a given collaborator. A client-server software platform is developed by the authors with the function to initiate collaborations, invite experts, create datasets and share them with experts, and perform the data visualization. The collaboration operations include the creation, modification, and deletion of users in the underlying ontology and the propagation of ontology changes to related clients connected to the server.

New applications of CDVE technology reflected in this volume include mobile banking, management of remote art performance, etc. More traditional applications such as in architecture, engineering and construction, cooperative learning, etc. have also shown their progress.

The papers in this volume reflect the more practical aspects of cooperative design, visualization, and engineering that contribute to the advancement of technology and social services. It is not only shaping our daily life, but also the way in which we conduct our business and social activities.

I would like to express my sincere thanks to all the authors for submitting their papers to the CDVE 2019 conference and for their contribution to technological development and service to society. I would also like to thank our volunteer reviewers, Program Committee members, and Organization Committee members for their contributions. My special thanks go to our Program Committee chair Professor Dieter Roller at the University of Stuttgart, Germany for his consistent support of this conference. The success of this year's conference would not have been possible without their generous support.

October 2019   Yuhua Luo

Organization

Conference Chair

Yuhua Luo   University of Balearic Islands, Spain

International Program Committee

Program Chair

Dieter Roller   University of Stuttgart, Germany

Members

Conrad Boton
Jose Alfredo Costa
Alma Leora Culén
Peter Demian
Susan Finger
Sebastia Galmes
Halin Gilles
Figen Gül
Shuangxi Huang
Tony Huang
Claudia-Lavinia Ignat
Ursula Kirschner

Jean-Christophe Lapayre
Pierre Leclercq
Jang Ho Lee
Jaime Lloret
Kwan-Liu Ma
Mary Lou Maher
Manuel Ortega
Juan Carlos Preciado
Niko Salonen
Chengzheng Sun
Thomas Tamisier
Nobuyoshi Yabuki

Organization Committee

Chair

Sebastia Galmes   University of Balearic Islands, Spain

Members

Tomeu Estrany
Takayuki Fujimoto
Alex Garcia
Guofeng Qin
Pilar Fuster
Linan Zhu

Reviewers

Veronika Bolshakova
Conrad Boton
Weiwei Cai
Jose Alfredo Costa
Alma Leora Culén
Peter Demian
Tomeu Estrany
Hongfei Fan
Susan Finger
Takayuki Fujimoto
Pilar Fuster
Sebastia Galmes
Alex Garcia
Halin Gilles
Henri-Jean Gless
Figen Gül

Shuangxi Huang
Tony Huang
Claudia-Lavinia Ignat
Ursula Kirschner
Jean-Christophe Lapayre
Pierre Leclercq
Jaime Lloret
Kwan-Liu Ma
Mary Lou Maher
Manuel Ortega
Juan Carlos Preciado
Guofeng Qin
Niko Salonen
Chengzheng Sun
Thomas Tamisier
Nobuyoshi Yabuki

Contents

A Domain Ontology and Software Platform for Collaborative Personal Data Analytics

Lauri Tuovinen[1,2]([⊠]) and Alan F. Smeaton[1]

[1] Insight Centre for Data Analytics, Dublin City University, Dublin, Ireland
lauri.tuovinen@oulu.fi, alan.smeaton@dcu.ie
[2] Biomimetics and Intelligent Systems Group, University of Oulu, Oulu, Finland

Abstract. Collaborative knowledge discovery is a promising approach by which people with no data analytics expertise could benefit from an analysis of their own personal data by experts. To facilitate effective collaboration between data owners and knowledge discovery experts, we have developed a software platform that uses a domain ontology to represent knowledge relevant to the execution of the collaborative knowledge discovery process. The ontology provides classes representing the main elements of collaborations: collaborators and datasets. Furthermore, the ontology enables the specification of privacy constraints that determine the precise extent to which a given dataset of personal data is shared with a given collaborator. We have developed a client-server software platform that enables users to initiate collaborations, invite experts to join them, create datasets and share them with experts, and create visualisations of data. The collaborations are mediated through the creation, modification and deletion of individuals in the underlying ontology and the propagation of ontology changes to each client connected to the server.

Keywords: Knowledge discovery · Data analytics ·
Collaborative systems · Domain ontologies · Personal data

1 Introduction

Collection of self-tracking data using various consumer-oriented wearable devices such as fitness trackers and sleep trackers is becoming increasingly commonplace. These devices and the software applications bundled with them provide the user with basic information such as steps taken, calories expended and hours slept. However by applying knowledge discovery from data (KDD), it would be

The work of Lauri Tuovinen is funded by the European Union's Horizon 2020 research and innovation programme under the Marie Skłodowska-Curie grant agreement number 746837. The Insight Centre is funded by Science Foundation Ireland under grant number SFI/12/RC/2289, and is co-funded under the European Regional Development Fund.

Y. Luo (Ed.): CDVE 2019, LNCS 11792, pp. 1–10, 2019.
https://doi.org/10.1007/978-3-030-30949-7_1

possible for a user to extract additional knowledge from their own data, but most people lack the knowledge and data analytics skills needed in order to carry out such analyses. To get around this problem, the data owner could collaborate remotely with a KDD expert who has those required skills using a software platform designed to support this type of collaboration. There are such platforms available, but none are specifically intended for use by non-expert individuals to extract knowledge from their personal data with the help of expert collaborators.

Supporting collaborative KDD in this special case introduces requirements that need to be taken into account in the design of the collaboration platform. Our work particularly focuses on supporting the data owner in the task of negotiating the terms of the collaboration with the KDD expert. Initially, we examined the process of establishing the boundaries of how much data the data owner will share with the expert; these are determined by a number of factors, including the data owner's personal privacy preferences, the objectives of the collaboration and the level of trust existing between the data owner and the expert. The software platform should help the data owner set boundaries that represent an acceptable trade-off between potentially conflicting requirements.

The solution we developed is based on a domain ontology representing the core concepts of collaborative KDD. The software platform uses the ontology as a knowledge base where all known information about past and ongoing collaborations is recorded. A user of the platform can create new collaborations, invite other users to join them, create new datasets composed of their own personal data and share them with collaborators including experts. When a request is made to share a dataset, the owner of the dataset can attach privacy constraints allowing the requester to access only some of the data included. Expert collaborators can use the software platform to share their analysis results and attach visualisations making it easier for the expert to explain their significance.

The main contributions of the paper are:

- A domain ontology representing collaborations, collaborators, datasets, privacy constraints and visualisations;
- A software implementation that uses the ontology to facilitate collaboration via data sharing.

The results reported in this paper refine and give a more concrete form to ideas originally discussed in [17], where the ontology was presented as a standalone artifact and tested using a reasoner to show that certain inferences concerning e.g. the scope of privacy constraints are made correctly. In the current paper, the ontology is put to practice by using it as a key component in a collaborative KDD software platform, where it provides the shared data structure in which the state of a collaboration is stored and which the participants of the collaboration can synchronously edit. Additionally, this version of the ontology includes classes and properties that were not present in [17], having to do with the representation of datasets, expertise, collaboration invitations, data requests and visualisations.

The remainder of the paper is organised as follows: Sect. 2 discusses the motivation for our work and reviews related research. Section 3 presents the classes of the ontology and the relationships among them. Section 4 describes the implementation of the software platform. Section 5 presents a critical discussion of the results and identifies key issues to be addressed by future work. Section 6 concludes the paper.

2   Background and Motivation

It is widely recognised that personal data constitutes a valuable resource for companies that control large quantities of it, and because of this, companies are willing to provide services free of charge in exchange for being allowed to collect and use it. Trading personal data for access to services is one example of how individuals can benefit from their own personal data, but it is not the only option. With the rising popularity of self-tracking products, an increasing number of people have access to a steadily accumulating database of physiological data about themselves, and this data is potentially valuable to them, although there are problems arising from uncertainties concerning the accuracy of the data and limitations concerning the ability of the people to control it [18].

The application or cloud service by which the user of a self-tracking device has access to their own data may already have some data analysis capabilities, but for many requirements the only option is to export the data and use another application to analyze it. For example, some users may wish to combine data from a sleep tracking application and a food intake logger, or to combine a tracker for their exercise level or step counter with a digital weighing machine. Others may wish to see long-term trends in their time spent online, or seasonal variations in their time commuting to work. Some services make it convenient to export personal data in a portable format such as CSV, but this does not help unless the user has the skills required to do the desired analysis. For most users this means that in order to extract knowledge hidden in their own data, they need to collaborate with someone who does have those skills.

The kind of collaboration we support involves an online software platform capable of bringing together people who have data with people who have data analysis skills regardless of where they are physically located. Using the platform, a person who has collected self-tracking data can find a KDD expert with the required skill set, negotiate with the expert to agree on the terms of the collaboration, collaboratively analyze the data and evaluate the results. Collaborative KDD platforms such as KDDVM [5] and LabBook [9] already exist, but to the best of our knowledge there are none that specifically target the sub-domain of personal analytics.

What makes personal analytics an interesting special case of collaborative KDD are the unique requirements that arise from the sensitive nature of the data and from the key role of non-expert participants in the collaboration. The rationale for proposing an ontology-based platform for facilitating such collaborations is that a comprehensive domain ontology would address many of these requirements. One major requirement, namely providing the ability to find expert collaborators, is already addressed by existing systems; the KDDVM platform uses an ontology named TeamOnto [4] to represent expertise, whereas LabBook has an underlying metadata graph that is functionally similar to an ontology.

Another purpose for which KDD ontologies can be used is to provide intelligent assistance in the composition of KDD workflows, which would be particularly important when dealing with a user who is not well versed in the application of KDD tools. KDDesigner [3], the workflow design tool of the KDDVM platform, uses the KDDONTO ontology [2] to support this, although it is unclear whether it is intended that even a complete novice should be able to use the tool to create workflows. Other recently proposed KDD ontologies include the KD ontology of [19], the data mining workflow ontology DMWF [11], the data mining optimisation ontology DMOP [10], the OntoDM family of ontologies [14–16] and the unnamed big data ontology of [12].

A part of the collaborative KDD process that is notably less supported by existing solutions is negotiation of the terms of the collaboration. Supporting this part would be important in personal analytics because it is arguably here that the data owner will have the most substantial impact on the outcome of the collaboration, and also because the data owner's expected low level of expertise may make it difficult to understand all the implications of what is being agreed. We hypothesise that a domain ontology could be used for this purpose as well, both as a knowledge base for intelligent assistance and as a way of representing and enforcing the results of the negotiation.

Our main concern at this point and in this paper is the negotiation of privacy constraints, where participants establish the boundaries of data sharing in the collaboration. A negotiation is necessary because the boundaries are not simply a matter of the data owners specifying their personal privacy preferences: there are multiple points of view to take into account and between these there may be conflicts that need to be resolved. Ontology-based approaches to privacy protection have been proposed in e.g. [1,6–8], but the idea of creating privacy policies through a process of negotiation is mostly absent in these related works, as is that of data owners working in cooperation with data analysts. Our work can thus be viewed as filling a gap at the intersection of the domains of knowledge discovery, collaboration and privacy.

3   Ontology Classes and Properties

In the discussion below, the names of ontology classes are written with initial capitals. Additionally, when mentioned for the first time, the names are written in boldface. The names of object properties, when mentioned for the first time, are written in italics. The Protégé ontology development environment [13] was used to develop the ontology. The seven core classes of the ontology as used by the software platform are:

- **Collaboration**, representing a collaborative KDD project;
- **Collaborator**, representing a person participating in a Collaboration;
- **Dataset**, representing a collection of personal data used in Collaboration;
- **DataItem**, representing an individual item of data, such as a single numeric value;
- **DataRequest**, representing a request to share a given dataset;

- **PrivacyConstraint**, representing a constraint specified when a DataRequest is granted;
- **Visualisation**, representing a graphical representation of some data, usually the result of some data analysis by an expert.

A Collaboration may have any number of Collaborators participating in it, signified by the *hasParticipant* property. The Collaborator who starts a Collaboration is designated the leader, signified by the *isLeaderOf* property, and has the ability to add new participants. Similarly, a Collaboration may have any number of Datasets involved in it, signified by the *hasDataset* property. The Collaborator who creates a Dataset is designated the owner, signified by the *controls* property, and has the ability to determine how the Dataset is shared. The data owner role is represented by the Collaborator subclass **DataOwner**.

A Collaborator who is an expert in some areas has one or more **Expertise** individuals attached to it via the *hasExpertise* property. Once a suitable expert has been identified, an **Invitation** can be created by the leader of the Collaboration to request that the expert join it. The Invitation is linked to the Collaboration, the sending Collaborator and the receiving Collaborator by the *isForCollaboration, wasCreatedBy* and *isForCollaborator* properties, respectively. The expert role is represented by the Collaborator subclass **Expert**.

The Dataset class has three subclasses, **DataColumn**, **DataMatrix** and **DataCollection**. These are organised in a hierarchy where a DataCollection may have any number of DataMatrices as subsets, and a DataMatrix (essentially a table) in turn may have any number of DataColumns, which are typed (represented by the **DataType** class and the *hasDataType* property) and ordered one-dimensional collections of DataItems. The inclusion of a DataItem in a Dataset is signified by the *contains* property and the inclusion of a Dataset in another Dataset by the transitive *hasSubset* property. A Dataset is inferred via a property chain to contain all DataItems contained by its subsets.

A DataRequest targets a specific Dataset in a specific Collaboration, signified by the *isForDataset* and isForCollaboration properties, respectively. The Collaborator who created the request is connected to it via the wasCreatedBy property. The owner of the requested Dataset can grant the request, deny it or grant it with constraints. If the data owner specifies constraints, the PrivacyConstraint individuals are attached to the DataRequest via the *respondsTo* property. Each PrivacyConstraint has a scope, i.e. a specific set of DataItems that it applies to. The *appliesTo* property connects a PrivacyConstraint to each DataItem in its scope; if a given DataItem is found to be in the scope of a PrivacyConstraint, then it is not shared with the requesting Collaborator.

In practice, the scope is generally specified in terms of a **DataGrouping**, which is either a Dataset or a **DataCategory**. DataCategories can be used to group together DataItems that are not members of the same Dataset but are otherwise related; for example, it might be desirable to specify a PrivacyConstraint applying to all DataItems representing location data regardless of which Dataset they are included in. The *hasInstance* property connects a DataCategory to each DataItem belonging to it, and the *hasSubcategory* property signifies that a given DataCategory subsumes another DataCategory under it. The *has-Scope* property is used to specify the DataGrouping that a PrivacyConstraint applies to; the individual DataItems in the scope of the PrivacyConstraint can then be inferred via property chains.

When a Collaborator creates a Visualisation of a Dataset, the ontology individual is linked to the Collaborator, the Dataset and the Collaboration by the wasCreatedBy, isForDataset and isForCollaboration properties, respectively. The details of the Visualisation are controlled by parameters attached to the individual as data properties; the parameters are specific to the type of the Visualisation and consist of all the information required to reproduce its appearance as designed by its creator. The ontology classes described above and the relationships among them are illustrated in Fig. 1, where arrows with a solid line denote subclass-superclass relationships, while those with a dashed line denote object properties. For the sake of clarity, the ontology is presented in two parts and some classes and properties are omitted.

The ontology additionally specifies certain classes and properties that are not yet used by the software platform but have been tested in Protégé. The classes **AnalysisTask** and **AnalysisMethod** are intended to enable expert collaborators to specify the KDD operations to be carried out in terms of their inputs and outputs; the output Datasets are linked to the inputs via the transitive *isDerivativeOf* property, which enables the owners of the original input Datasets to exert control over the derivatives as well. For the data owners, the classes **AccessRestriction** and **ProtectionMethod** enable the specification of PrivacyConstraints that do not simply block access to data but transform it in some way to render it less sensitive. The **UtilityReduction** class represents the negative effect that a given ProtectionMethod has on the utility of a given AnalysisMethod. Further details on the ontology and these five classes in particular can be found in [17], but the reader should note that the current paper extends the ontology from the version described there; most notably, the classes Expertise, Invitation, DataRequest and Visualisation as well as the subclasses of Dataset only exist in the current version.

4   Software Architecture and Implementation

The software platform is a client-server system implemented in Java using the Apache MINA network application framework. The server component maintains a user database and a master copy of the ontology; when a client logs in to the server, the client downloads the ontology from the server and sets up a local copy. The OWL API and the JFact reasoner are used to process the ontology. Any modifications made by the client, such as creation of a new collaboration or dataset, are first applied to the local copy, then sent to the server, applied to the master copy and sent to other clients.

When a data owner initiates a collaboration, a corresponding Collaboration individual is created and added to the ontology. When the owner creates a new dataset, initially a DataCollection individual is created. The owner can then

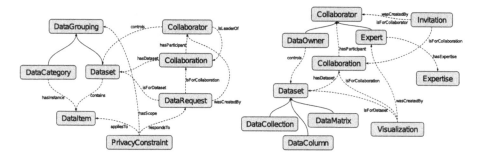

Fig. 1. The classes and object properties of the collaborative KDD ontology.

import data into the dataset from a CSV file and the software will generate DataMatrix, DataColumn and DataItem individuals according to the contents of the imported file. The data itself will be kept locally on the client host and not uploaded to the server until it is shared with another collaborator. Apache Commons CSV is used to process CSV files.

To invite an expert to join the collaboration, the data owner first performs an expert search by specifying some keywords characterising the desired expertise. The software then uses a simple algorithm to generate a list of experts ranked according to how closely their expertise matches the query. Once the data owner has selected an expert to invite, an Invitation individual is added to the ontology, triggering a notification in the client used by the expert in question. If the invitation is accepted, the expert will then be added as a participant.

Data sharing begins with the expert requesting it, which causes a DataRequest individual to be added to the ontology and triggers a notification in the client used by the data owner. The owner can then review the request and specify how much of the data will be shared. If the owner chooses to grant the request but deny access to some subsets, PrivacyConstraint individuals corresponding to these subsets will be created and added to the ontology, causing the data items in these subsets to be unavailable to the expert.

Once a data request has been granted, the data will be uploaded to the server and the expert's client notified. After the expert's client has downloaded the data, it will have a copy of the dataset that is identical to the one held by the data owner, with the exception of data items blocked by privacy constraints. The expert can then export the dataset and use a KDD tool of his/her choice such as Tableau or Python to analyze it because that is the environment the expert will be familiar with. The results of the analysis can be shared with the data owner via the same mechanism used by the owner to share the input data.

To illustrate some analysis results, the expert has the option of attaching visualisations and descriptive analysis to the result dataset. Visualisations are created by launching a dialog that allows the expert to specify the parameters of the visualisation. Once a visualisation has been created and saved, it becomes visible to other users participating in the collaboration and can be viewed by those who have access to the underlying data. When a user views a visualisation, the client reproduces it based on the parameters attached to the corresponding Visualisation individual as data properties. The visualisations are rendered using the XChart library. Some screenshots of the software can be seen in Fig. 2, showing a collaboration between a user and an expert who is analysing long-term step count data looking for regular and repeating patterns.

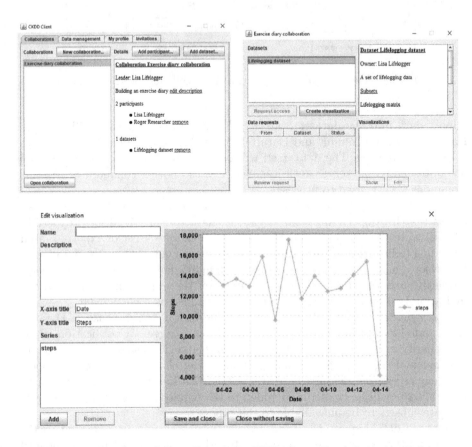

Fig. 2. Some screenshots of the collaborative KDD client. Top left: main window, top right: collaboration window, bottom: visualisation window.

5   Discussion and Future Work

The ontology was originally designed with the idea that the underlying knowledge base of the collaboration platform should enable the resolution of privacy conflicts by suggesting transformations that achieve an acceptable trade-off between the information content of the data and the privacy preferences of the data owner. This goal is reflected in the classes and properties described briefly at the end of Sect. 3. The details of this, such as how to represent and quantify utility reductions, are a topic for future research, as are connections between our ontology and related ones such as those cited in Sect. 2.

The software platform demonstrates the feasibility of the concept of using an ontology to mediate collaboration for knowledge discovery from personal data. The ontology functions as a shared view of the state of the collaboration that each collaborator can observe and modify, and the propagation of modifications through the server component ensures that the collaborators remain synchronised with one another. As we continue to refine and expand the ontology, new functionality will be added to the software accordingly.

The scenario we implicitly assume when discussing the software, involving one data owner, one expert and one dataset, is simplistic and not necessarily representative of the kind of real-world collaborations the ontology and software can support. It could even be argued that under these assumptions the software makes it unnecessarily complicated to execute the scenario by requiring data requests to be submitted before any data can be shared. However, to avoid imposing unwanted restrictions on the number of datasets and collaborators, it is important to provide data owners with the means to manage multiple datasets and to deal with the data requirements of multiple expert partners. Multiple data owners in the same collaboration is also a possibility we take into consideration.

6   Conclusion

In this paper we presented an ontology-based software platform for collaborative knowledge discovery from personal data. The software enables individuals with no data analytics expertise to collaborate with analytics experts for the purpose of extracting useful knowledge from their own personal data, such as what can be collected using wearable activity and sleep trackers. The underlying ontology represents knowledge about domain concepts such as collaborations, collaborators and datasets, and the collaborations are mediated by using the ontology as a shared view that each collaborator can modify. The software supports data sharing, privacy constraints and visualisations, serving as a proof of concept for the ontology-based approach to collaboration. Future work includes conducting user tests and expanding the data analytics and privacy preservation functionality of the software.

References

1. Barhamgi, M., Perera, C., Ghedira, C., Benslimane, D.: User-centric privacy engineering for the Internet of Things. IEEE Cloud Comput. **5**(5), 47–57 (2018)
2. Diamantini, C., Potena, D., Storti, E.: KDDONTO: an ontology for discovery and composition of KDD algorithms. In: Third Generation Data Mining: Towards Service-Oriented Knowledge Discovery (SoKD 2009), pp. 13–24 (2009)
3. Diamantini, C., Potena, D., Storti, E.: A semantic-aided designer for knowledge discovery. In: 2011 International Conference on Collaboration Technologies and Systems (CTS), pp. 86–93 (2011)

4. Diamantini, C., Potena, D., Storti, E.: Semantically-supported team building in a KDD virtual environment. In: 2012 International Conference on Collaboration Technologies and Systems (CTS), pp. 45–52 (2012)
5. Diamantini, C., Potena, D., Storti, E.: Collaborative management of a repository of KDD processes. Int. J. Metadata Semant. Ontol. 9(4), 299–311 (2014)
6. Gharib, M., Giorgini, P., Mylopoulos, J.: Towards an ontology for privacy requirements via a systematic literaturel review. In: International Conference on Conceptual Modeling, pp. 193–208 (2017)
7. Ghorbel, A., Ghorbel, M., Jmaiel, M.: PRIARMOR: an IaaS solution for low-level privacy enforcement in the cloud. In: 2017 IEEE 26th International Conference on Enabling Technologies: Infrastructure for Collaborative Enterprises (WETICE), pp. 119–124 (2017)
8. Hartmann, S., Ma, H., Vechsamutvaree, P.: Providing ontology-based privacy-aware data access through web services. In: Jeusfeld, M.A., Karlapalem, K. (eds.) ER 2015. LNCS, vol. 9382, pp. 74–85. Springer, Cham (2015). https://doi.org/10.1007/978-3-319-25747-1_8
9. Kandogan, E., et al.: LabBook: metadata-driven social collaborative data analysis. In: 2015 IEEE International Conference on Big Data (Big Data), pp. 431–440 (2015)
10. Keet, C.M., et al.: The data mining optimization ontology. Web Semant. Sci. Serv. Agents World Wide Web 32, 43–53 (2015)
11. Kietz, J.-U., Serban, F., Fischer, S., Bernstein, A.: "Semantics Inside!" but let's not tell the data miners: intelligent support for data mining. In: Presutti, V., d'Amato, C., Gandon, F., d'Aquin, M., Staab, S., Tordai, A. (eds.) ESWC 2014. LNCS, vol. 8465, pp. 706–720. Springer, Cham (2014). https://doi.org/10.1007/978-3-319-07443-6_47
12. Kumara, B.T.G.S., Paik, I., Zhang, J., Siriweera, T.H.A.S., Koswatte, K.R.C.: Ontology-based workflow generation for intelligent big data analytics. In: 2015 IEEE International Conference on Web Services, pp. 495–502 (2015)
13. Musen, M.A.: The Protégé project: a look back and a look forward. AI Matters 1(4), 4–12 (2015)
14. Panov, P., Soldatova, L., Džeroski, S.: OntoDM-KDD: ontology for representing the knowledge discovery process. In: Fürnkranz, J., Hüllermeier, E., Higuchi, T. (eds.) DS 2013. LNCS (LNAI), vol. 8140, pp. 126–140. Springer, Heidelberg (2013). https://doi.org/10.1007/978-3-642-40897-7_9
15. Panov, P., Soldatova, L., Džeroski, S.: Ontology of core data mining entities. Data Min. Knowl. Disc. 28(5), 1222–1265 (2014)
16. Panov, P., Soldatova, L.N., Džeroski, S.: Generic ontology of datatypes. Inf. Sci. 329, 900–920 (2016)
17. Tuovinen, L., Smeaton, A.F.: Ontology-based negotiation and enforcement of privacy constraints in collaborative knowledge discovery. Presentation at the 2nd International Workshop on Personal Analytics and Privacy (PAP 2018) (2018). http://kdd.di.unito.it/pap2018/papers/PAP_2018_paper_2.pdf. Accessed 13 May 2019
18. Tuovinen, L., Smeaton, A.F.: Unlocking the black box of wearable intelligence: ethical considerations and social impact. In: 2019 IEEE Congress on Evolutionary Computation (2019)
19. Žáková, M., Křemen, P., Železný, F., Lavrač, N.: Automating knowledge discovery workflow composition through ontology-based planning. IEEE Trans. Autom. Sci. Eng. 8(2), 253–264 (2011)

Modeling Users Behavior in Groupware Applications

Sergio Salomón[1](✉), Rafael Duque[2], Jose Luis Montaña[2], and Luis Tenés[1]

[1] Axpe Consulting Cantabria SL, Camargo, Spain
{ssalomong,ltenesc}@axpecantabria.com
[2] Departamento MATESCO, Universidad de Cantabria, Santander, Spain
{rafael.duque,joseluis.montana}@unican.es

Abstract. Groupware systems support collaborative work of users that share common objectives. An analysis of the behavior of these work teams can provide useful information to discover users' requirements. This paper presents a method that processes groupware user interactions and generates behavior models. The method is applied in a case study that analyzes the collaboration and interaction supported by CollBets, a groupware application for smartphones that supports collaborative betting.

Keywords: Groupware systems · Group behavior ·
Human-computer interaction · Data visualization

1 Introduction

The proliferation of mobile devices and wireless communication have led to a context in which users can easily take advantage of collaborative software. Groupware systems refer to software that supports multiple users collaborating on related tasks [12]. These systems can include features that support communication between group members, workspaces in which artifacts are built collaboratively and coordination mechanisms to organize common activities. The software developers should have accurate knowledge of the tasks to be supported by the groupware system and the collaborative interactions between the group members to be automated [6]. This knowledge can be generated not only through the traditional elicitation requirements techniques (interviews, questionnaires, observations, etc.) [18] but also through automatic collaboration and interaction analysis processes [5]. The main goal of these analysis processes is to study the interactions performed by the users of the groupware system and to provide information on the collaborative behavior of the groups. These analysis processes can be performed automatically by software tools to know the behavior of the groups interacting with a prototype of the groupware system under development and in this way to provide an idea of the degree of adaptation of the system to the users. Task analysis [13] is one of the first stages of the user-centered design

© Springer Nature Switzerland AG 2019
Y. Luo (Ed.): CDVE 2019, LNCS 11792, pp. 11–21, 2019.
https://doi.org/10.1007/978-3-030-30949-7_2

process and has the purpose of specifying the actions of the user to be supported by the groupware system. Therefore, a model of the users' behavior allows us to detect problems related to task analysis procedures that do not generate a suitable actions specification. Recent research works have focused on analysis processes that output a set of variables (fluency of communication, degree of coordination, etc.)[14]. However, these works do not provide global models that show the interchange of collaborative interactions between the users.

In this article, we propose a methodology to develop the analysis of interaction emerging from groupware systems with the ultimate purpose of generating representative group behavior models. These models use graphs to sequence patterns of actions that group members follow in their work process. Also, the models include a specific notation to indicate the purpose of each action performed by the users (communication, coordination of access common spaces, etc). The objective is to provide graphical representations that software developers could use to easily obtain real knowledge about the groupware usage made by its users. The phases of our method are the following: first, the records of user interaction (log repositories) of the system are processed to identify similar behaviors; then, users are clustered in groups with similar behavior; for each cluster, a probabilistic model is used to represent the patterns of the respective group behavior; finally, this model is enhanced with knowledge about the performed actions in order to obtain more informative data visualization.

This paper includes five additional sections. Section 2 reviews the research proposals to analyze the behavior of users of groupware systems. Section 3 describes our method to model users behaviors of groupware systems. Section 4 presents a case study that applies the method to analyze the interaction and collaboration of users from a collaborative sports betting smartphone app.

2   Related Works

The user-centered design process involves the constant construction of prototypes that are evaluated to verify that they meet the user requirements [4]. In the case of groupware systems, this verification consists in testing that the collaborative behavior of the users is facilitated [10]. The processes of analysis of collaboration and interaction study traces of log with the actions performed by the users to characterize the collective processes and that developers can evaluate the prototypes under development [9].

The output of interaction analysis can be a set of variables (participation, speed, performance, etc.) whose values provide an idea of the collaboration between team members [11]. This quantitative approach was applied by [3] in an academic environment to verify the collaborative process supported by groupware, the individual performance of each user and the artifacts built in shared workspaces. Although this analysis approach can be automated with software tools [14], these outputs lack of relevant information on the shared workspaces which are never accessed, the actions sequence patterns of the users or the collaborative interactions which are useless for the team members.

Workflow mining [1] applies techniques that process event logs to infer workflow models that represent the user collaboration. These models show the interchange of interactions between users to achieve a common goal. These techniques must approach the problem of generating models that summarize event logs with a high number of activities [17]. The two main solutions for this problem are to filter out infrequent activities [7] or to define clusters of users [19], each of one represents patterns that orchestrate the collaboration. The resulting models can detect users behaviors that are unexpected for the groupware developers.

To sum up, it can be observed that an initial group of work focuses on analyzing collaboration and interaction through variables that quantify several dimensions of the users' activities. The second group of research works generates models that represent the sequence of actions performed by the users to achieve a common goal. In order to fill the gap between these two groups of works, we propose a method that generates models of groupware users behaviors and analyses these models to infer variables that evaluate the prototype under development.

3 Method

The objective of the proposed method is to analyze user interaction in collaborative environments. To this end, the method follows several differentiated steps. First, we process the interaction data of the groupware system. Next, we build a user representation by means of the user activity in data. Then, we compare those representations to get a similarity measure between users and cluster those users in representative profiles. Finally, using the defined profiles we generate behavior models enhanced with action and task knowledge.

3.1 Interaction Data

For the interaction analysis, we exploit the logs of user actions in a groupware system. In these, each record is generally formed at least by a user identifier (u), an action identifier (a) and a timestamp value of the moment of the interaction (t). Then, we refer to the set of different possible actions in the system as $\mathcal{A} = \{a_1, \ldots, a_m\}$ and the transition time between two consecutive actions a, a' of the user u as $dt_u(a, a')$. The transition times are classified in different discrete time intervals $\{I_1, \ldots, I_H\}$ to replace the continuous time values. There are multiple strategies to create such discrete intervals, as it is shown in [16]: by fixed size values, by means of data distribution or by means of the data density. In this case, the best segmentation strategy depends on the specific application.

3.2 User Profiles

After the data preprocessing, we generate user representations by their sequence of actions in order to measure the similarity between users. Then, we can group together in the same cluster users that behave similarly.

We employ a weighted finite automaton [8] to generate the user representation by means of the user behavior. This Markov-like structure is a generative model that compacts the user activity as a stochastic process. Formally, a **weighted automaton** is defined as $\mathcal{M} = (Q, S, in, out, W)$ where:

- Σ is a finite set of symbols;
- Q is a finite set of states;
- the functions in, out give the weight distributions of initial and final states;
- W is the weight function, where $W_s(q, p)$ gives us the weight for the transition from state $q \in Q$ to state $p \in Q$ with symbol $s \in \Sigma$.

In our case, we will use the established intervals of the transition times as symbols $\Sigma = \{I_1, \ldots, I_H\}$, the states will be the actions of the system $Q = \{a_1, \ldots, a_n\}$, and we will not use the in and out functions in our methodology. $W_I^u(a_i, a_j)$ will be the weight of the transition from action a_i to action a_j in a time interval I for the user u. To compute such function, we utilize the frequencies of transitions in the data, as shown in the following formula.

$$W_I^u(a_i, a_j) = count_I^u(a_i, a_j)/a_i, a_j \in Q,\ I \in \Sigma$$

where $count_I^u(a_i, a_j)$ is the number of sequences (a_i, a_j) that appeared for user u with a transition time within interval I.

Once we generate these user models, we can compute the distance between W functions to obtain the similarity between users (as the components Q and Σ will be the same to all users). To this end, we transformed the weight function into a user vector $\boldsymbol{u}$ as shown next.

$$\boldsymbol{u} = (W_I^u(a_1, a_1), W_I^u(a_1, a_2), \ldots, W_I^u(a_n, a_{n-1}), W_I^u(a_n, a_n))\ \forall I \in \mathcal{I}$$

We use the Euclidean distance to compare the user vectors, so more similar users will have a smaller distance. Then, we compute the clustering of users with the K-means++ algorithm [2]. Through this algorithm, we minimize the within-cluster sum of square (WCSS) distances to obtain clusters of users with similar behavior. Also, this algorithm initializes the cluster centers in such a way that a better approximation to the optimum result is guaranteed. As we need to choose a suitable number of clusters k, we use the Silhouette score [15], along with the final WCSS value after K-means converge, within a reasonable range for k to the specific application. The Silhouette score considers the intra-cluster distance, as WCSS, and between clusters distance as well to evaluate the clustering results.

3.3   Behavior Models

We model the user profile behavior for each extracted cluster, using again the weighted automaton model. However, for the behavior model each cluster C defines an automaton, so the patterns of all users in the cluster are captured. Therefore, we redefine the weight function W as shown in the next formula. This function can be represented as a likelihood function using Maximum Likelihood Estimation (MLE) principle and additive smoothing.

$$W_I^C(a_i, a_j) = \sum_{u \in C} count_I^u(a_i, a_j) \ /a_i, a_j \in Q, \ I \in \Sigma$$

The previous model allows us to analyze the relevant sequence of actions emerging in a representative profile. We improved this model with knowledge specific of system actions and with a task model specifying the action spaces and effects. First, we include a classification of the actions depending on the result in the collaborative task process. The actions supported by the groupware system are classified according to the following taxonomy [9].

- Instrumental actions (A_{inst}): They modify a shared artifact in a common workspace.
- Communicative actions (A_{comm}): The users perform these actions to interchange messages. These actions are usually supported by chats, forums, emails or video conference tools.
- Protocol-based actions (A_{prot}): They enable users to coordinate tasks and access common spaces. For example, these actions can be supported by voting tools.
- Cognitive actions (A_{cogn}): These actions do not imply interaction with other group members. For example, a user makes a personal copy of a shared file.

Lastly, we defined a task model representation as a tree hierarchy using the action taxonomy and the analyzed system structure. This task model is composed of the following elements:

- The root of the model will represent the system itself.
- In the first level, all the children nodes from the root will represent the different spaces in which the system is divided.
- The nodes of next level will present types of actions that each space supports. From the previous taxonomy, those can be A_{inst}, A_{comm}, A_{prot} and A_{cogn}.
- The final level of the structure will show the different actions of the system $A = \{a_1, \ldots, a_m\}$. These leaf nodes will also contain information about their effect on the task development (when there is any); for example, if the action solves the task in question.
- The weights of the edges represent the number of interactions performed within the connected subtree structure.

4 Case Study

This proposal to use behavior models to analyze the collaboration and interaction supported by groupware was applied in a case study. CollBets [19] is a groupware system for smartphones that supports collaborative betting. CollBets was used by 31 users in this case study. These users were grouped into 9 groups of 3 users and a group of 4 users. CollBets (see Fig. 1) includes the following spaces:

- *Structured chat*: It supports communicative actions to exchange messages between group members.

- *Proposals* space: This space includes a voting tool to decide if a bet proposal is rejected or accepted by the user.
- *New bet* space: The user accesses this space to propose a bet to the group.
- *Tutorial* space: It provides guidance on the usage of the system.
- *New group* space: It provides features to form a new group of users that will collaborate in making bets.
- *My bets* space: It lists the bets made previously by the user.

Fig. 1. *Main user* interface of CollBets, *proposal* space and *structured chat*.

Also, CollBets presents the actions shown in Table 1, which are classified according to the taxonomy described in the methodology section. In this case, we classified the actions from the structured chat as communicative since those allow users to exchange messages, the actions from the proposals space as protocol-based since they served to come to an agreement to decide a bet, as well as the actions from new group space that allow deciding the composition of a group collaboratively. All actions to access a space along the tutorial are classified as cognitive. The action for sending a proposal is instrumental since it modifies (creates) a shared artifact (a bet).

We process the log records of the groupware system. The CollBets data contains the variables of user identifier, group identifier within the user collaborates, identifier of the action performed and timestamp of the interaction. Besides these, we compute the transition times between actions and classified those lengths into 4 different intervals according to the data distribution and the application domain. The resulting intervals are $I_1 = [0s, 46s]$, $I_2 = [47_s, 106s]$, $I_3 = [107s, 296s]$ and $I_4 = [297s, \infty s)$.

Next, we generate the 31 user vectors and apply the *K-means++* clustering algorithm. For the selection of a suitable number of clusters, we observe the evolution of the WCSS and Silhouette score values for $k = 2, \ldots, 16$, presented in the Fig. 2. We notice that $k = 5$ is the best value for both WCSS, following the

Table 1. Actions in the groupware system *CollBets*.

Action	Space	Description	Type
a_1	Structured chat	Access to this space	Cognitive
a_2	Structured chat	Send a free message	Communicative
a_3	Structured chat	Send a "Why..." message	Communicative
a_4	Structured chat	Send a "Because" message	Communicative
a_5	Structured chat	Send a "I think that" message	Communicative
a_6	Structured chat	Send a "I don't agree" message	Communicative
a_7	Structured chat	Send a "The best team is" message	Communicative
a_8	Structured chat	Send a "My vote will be" message	Communicative
a_9	Proposals	Access to this space	Cognitive
a_{10}	Proposals	Reject a proposal	Protocol-based
a_{11}	Proposals	Accept a proposal	Protocol-based
a_{12}	Proposals	A proposal was accepted by the group	Cognitive
a_{13}	Proposals	A proposal was rejected by the group	Cognitive
a_{14}	My bets	Access to this space	Cognitive
a_{15}	Tutorial	Access to this space	Cognitive
a_{16}	New bet	See sport events	Cognitive
a_{17}	New group	New Name	Protocol-based
a_{18}	New group	Add a person	Protocol-based
a_{19}	New group	Select a group	Protocol-based
a_{20}	New group	Rename a group	Protocol-based
a_{21}	New group	Send an invitation	Protocol-based
a_{22}	New group	Accept an invitation	Protocol-based
a_{23}	New group	Reject an invitation	Protocol-based
a_{24}	New bet	Access to this space	Cognitive
a_{25}	New bet	Send a proposal	Instrumental

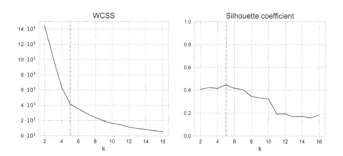

Fig. 2. Clustering evaluation for different k sizes.

Elbow criterion, and Silhouette score, as it is the maximum value. Therefore, we identified 5 different clusters, symbolizing representative user profiles, with 18, 9, 2, 1 and 1 users respectively. Last two clusters can be considered as outliers.

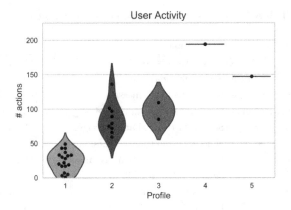

Fig. 3. User activity exhibited by the users in each cluster.

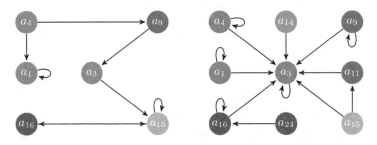

Fig. 4. Relevant patterns captured in the weighted automata of profiles 1 and 2.

When we analyze the extracted user profiles, we observe several differences that characterize them. For example, if we pay attention to the volume of user activity (see Fig. 3), it is noticeable that one of the profiles gather users with less activity, while the two outlier clusters present the two most active users in the dataset.

Once we generate the behavior models, we can conduct an in-depth analysis of the profile differences displayed in their respective behaviors. We visualize the profile patterns captured in the weighted automaton and the functionality usage represented on our task model. Comparing the weighted automata of profiles 1 and 2 shown in Fig. 4, we see different relevant patterns of actions (e.g., *my bets* space is less used by profile 1). When we analyze the task models, as can be seen in Fig. 5, we observe different tools employed (e.g., profile 1 do not use any protocol-based action in the *proposals* space)

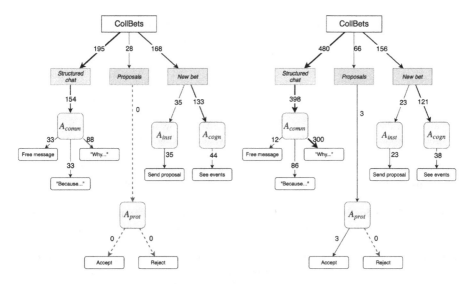

Fig. 5. Fragments of the task models for profiles 1 and 2.

5 Conclusions

User behavior models provide useful information to understand the requirements of groupware systems during the software development process. These models enable developers to understand the interactions between group members and how they use different prototypes of the system under development. This paper has described a method that automates the task of generating user behavior models.

In the proposed methodology, we performed a preprocessing phase on inter-action data registered in logs of a groupware system. With this data, we generate user models in the formed of weighted finite automata representing their activity and behavior. Next, we cluster all users into distinct profiles according to the similarity between the user models. These representative profiles allow a concise interaction analysis considering only the relevant displayed conducts. Finally, we build behavior models using the weighted automata structure enriched with system-specific knowledge by means of an action taxonomy and a task model.

We apply our methodology in a case study of a groupware application, Coll-Bets, where several users collaborate to decide sports bets. In this experimentation, we show the results that our method can provide through the detection of user profiles and the analysis of their interaction and behavior. We think that this methodology can help in the development and improvement of an application, as it shows how users interact and how they make use of the analyzed system.

Acknowledgments. The authors want to acknowledge the financial support from FEDER (Fondo Europeo de Desarrollo Regional) and The Government of Cantabria for the project 2018/INN/9 within the program INNOVA 2018.

References

1. van der Aalst, W., Weijters, T., Maruster, L.: Workflow mining: discovering process models from event logs. IEEE Trans. Knowl. Data Eng. **16**(9), 1128–1142 (2004)
2. Arthur, D., Vassilvitskii, S.: K-means++: the advantages of careful seeding. In: Proceedings of the Eighteenth Annual ACM-SIAM Symposium on Discrete Algorithms, SODA 2007, pp. 1027–1035. Society for Industrial and Applied Mathematics, Philadelphia (2007)
3. Bravo, C., Redondo, M.A., Verdejo, M.F., Ortega, M.: A framework for process-solution analysis in collaborative learning environments. Int. J. Hum.-Comput. Stud. **66**(11), 812–832 (2008)
4. Chilana, P.K., Ko, A.J., Wobbrock, J.: From user-centered to adoption-centered design: a case study of an HCI research innovation becoming a product. In: Proceedings of the 33rd Annual ACM Conference on Human Factors in Computing Systems, CHI 2015, pp. 1749–1758. ACM, New York (2015)
5. Chounta, I.A., Avouris, N.: Towards a time series approach for the classification and evaluation of collaborative activities. Comput. Inform. **34**(3), 588–614 (2015)
6. Collazos, C.A., Gutiérrez, F.L., Gallardo, J., Ortega, M., Fardoun, H.M., Molina, A.I.: Descriptive theory of awareness for groupware development. J. Ambient Intell. Humaniz. Comput. (2018)
7. Conforti, R., Rosa, M.L., ter Hofstede, A.H.M.: Filtering out infrequent behavior from business process event logs. IEEE Trans. Knowl. Data Eng. **29**(2), 300–314 (2017)
8. Droste, M., Kuich, W., Vogler, H.: Handbook of Weighted Automata, 1st edn. Springer, Heidelberg (2009). https://doi.org/10.1007/978-3-642-01492-5
9. Duque, R., Bravo, C., Ortega, M.: An ontological approach to automating collaboration and interaction analysis in groupware systems. Knowl.-Based Syst. **37**, 211–229 (2013)
10. Ehrlich, K.: Designing groupware applications: a work-centered design approach (Chap. 10). In: Beaudouin-Lafon, M. (ed.) CSCW. Wiley (1998). In: Smith, D.E. (ed.) Knowledge, Groupware and the Internet, pp. 137–170. Butterworth-Heinemann, Boston (2000)
11. Merono-Cerdan, A.L.: Groupware uses and influence on performance in SMEs. J. Comput. Inf. Syst. **48**(4), 87–96 (2008)
12. Olson, G.M., Olson, J.S.: Groupware and computer-supported cooperative work. In: Jacko, J.A., Sears, A. (eds.) The Human-Computer Interaction Handbook, pp. 583–595. L. Erlbaum Associates Inc., Hillsdale (2003)
13. Pinelle, D., Gutwin, C.: Group task analysis for groupware usability evaluations. In: Proceedings Tenth IEEE International Workshop on Enabling Technologies: Infrastructure for Collaborative Enterprises, WET ICE 2001, pp. 102–107, June 2001
14. Pinelle, D., Gutwin, C.: A review of groupware evaluations. In: Proceedings of the 9th IEEE International Workshops on Enabling Technologies: Infrastructure for Collaborative Enterprises, WETICE 2000, pp. 86–91. IEEE Computer Society, Washington, DC (2000)

15. Rousseeuw, P.J.: Silhouettes: a graphical aid to the interpretation and validation of cluster analysis. J. Comput. Appl. Math. **20**, 53–65 (1987). https://doi.org/10.1016/0377-0427(87)90125-7

16. Salomón, S., Tîrnăucă, C., Duque, R., Montaña, J.L.: User identification from mobility traces. J. Ambient Intell. Humani. Comput. (2018)

17. Tax, N., Sidorova, N., van der Aalst, W.M.P.: Discovering more precise process models from event logs by filtering out chaotic activities. J. Intell. Inf. Syst. **52**(1), 107–139 (2019)

18. Teruel, M.A., Navarro, E., López-Jaquero, V., Simarro, F.M., González, P.: A comprehensive framework for modeling requirements of CSCW systems. J. Softw. Evol. Process **29**(5), e1858 (2017)

19. Tîrnăucă, C., Duque, R., Montaña, J.L.: User interaction modeling and profile extraction in interactive systems: a groupware application case study. Sensors **17**(7), 1669 (2017)

Cellular Automata Epidemic (CAE) Model for Language Development Prediction

Hangyao Tu$^{(\boxtimes)}$, Wanliang Wang, Yanwei Zhao, and Lingyan Zhang

ZheJiang University of Technology, Hangzhou 310014, ZheJiang, China
lewieyao@126.com

Abstract. This paper proposes a cellular-automata-epidemic (CAE) model which is a combination of cellular-automata and epidemic model for predicting the language development in 50 years. In this model, three factors are considered: the international trade, global tourism and social communication. The Principal Component Analysis (PCA) is used to calculate scores which rank the effect of languages. The language which learned by people are chose by the roulette algorithm. The result shows that Bengali, Punjabi languages will fall out of top 10 and the language of French and German will get into the top 10. We believe that this work will contribute to the construction of linguistic disciplines and the development of languages.

Keywords: Language development · Prediction · CAE model · Social group behavior

1 Introduction

The primary function of language is communication, which is a social phenomenon in essence. There are currently about 6900 languages on the earth, and more than half of the world's people regard one of the following ten languages as their native languages: Chinese, Spanish, English, Hindi, Arabic, Bengali, Portuguese, Russian, Punjabi, and Japanese [1]. However, the total number of speakers of a language may increase or decrease over time because of a variety of influences, such as the language used or promoted by the government in a country, the language used in schools, social pressures, migration and assimilation of cultural groups, and immigration and emigration with countries that speak other languages.

2 Related Work

At present, scholars have carried out a lot of research on prediction algorithms, but there is little research on the prediction of world language development. At present, some scholars use machine learning to study language development prediction. Ying Haojian combines the grey box model with the neural network to establish the grey box neural network model. They predict the development trend of languages in the future

Y. Luo (Ed.): CDVE 2019, LNCS 11792, pp. 22–29, 2019.
https://doi.org/10.1007/978-3-030-30949-7_3

and describe the changes of its geographical distribution, which has a little effect to the construction of linguistics and the development of language [2]. This paper summarizes the experience of predecessors and proposes a prediction algorithm based on CAE model to tackle this problem.

3   Analysis of the Development Trend of Language

The number of people of various spoken languages is affected by a large number of factors. As the time goes by, the languages of people are also changing. We use the method which is a combination of cellular automata and epidemic model to establish a CAE model which aims to predicting the world language development. The specific process of this model is shown in Fig. 1 as follows:

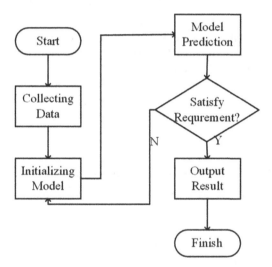

Fig. 1. Project general flow chart

Because of the impact of globalization, the impact of national economic, tourism and communication capabilities are considered for language distribution [3–5]. The comprehensive evaluation of international language influence is divided into three layers. The index data for the evaluation is shown in Table 1.

Table 1. The comprehensive index

Target layer	Standard layer	Variable layer	Unit
The comprehensive index	International trade	CO2 emission	Kt
		GDP	B$
		Per capita expenditure of medical	$
		Interest of lending	%
		Population of urban	M
		GDP per capita	$
		Ease of business	–
	Global tourism	Tourism inbound	B$
		Tourism outbound	B$
	Social communication	Internet usage	$
		Mobile phone usage	%

Above all, the integrated data are divided into three categories: international trade, global tourism and social communication. The Principal component analysis (PCA) is used to calculate scores [6, 7]. The language which plays better performance will get the lower score in these three categories. These three categories are regarded as equally important. The comprehensive score comes from the sum of International trade score, global tourism score and social communication score. Each language's scores are shown ins Table 2:

Table 2. The first 10 languages with international influence

Language	International trade	Global tourism	Social communication	Total
	Score	Score	Score	Score
English	−7.09	−5.25	−3.65	−16.0
Spanish	−1.13	0.19	−0.72	−1.66
German	0.14	−0.54	−0.07	−0.47
Japanese	0.27	−0.21	−0.18	−0.11
French	−0.17	0.31	0.02	0.16
Arabic	0.10	0.35	0.32	0.77
Portuguese	0.37	0.57	0.15	1.09
Mandarin Chinese	0.69	0.04	0.82	1.55
Russian	0.41	0.66	0.84	1.91
Malay	1.42	0.62	0.18	2.21

4   The Cellular Automata and Epidemic Model (CAE Model)

4.1   Introduction

The CAE model is a combination of cellular automata and epidemic model. The cellular automata does not have strict mathematical functions and physical equations. However, it affects the dynamical systems in cellular space with discrete time, space and state dimensions by a series of formulated rules [8, 9]. Its structure is shown in Fig. 2.

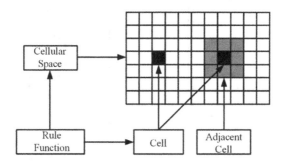

Fig. 2. The structure of cellular automata

The epidemic model divides the population into three categories. $S(t)$ is the susceptible people, which means the number of people who are not infected by epidemic at time t, $I(t)$ is the infected people, representing the number of people who have been infected at time t and can transmit the disease to the susceptible people, and $R(t)$ is the number of recovered people, the number of people who have recovered at time t and will not get the epidemic again [10].

4.2   The Hypothesis of the Model

In order to simplify the global languages distribution in the real world, the following assumptions are made for starting the construction of our model.

(1) Learners are not restricted by individual learning ability.
(2) Everyone has a chance to learn the second language.
(3) People could learn five or less languages.

4.3   Model Construction

In order to predict the changes of language in next 50 years in the world. The CAE model is established. Its flow chart is shown in Fig. 3.

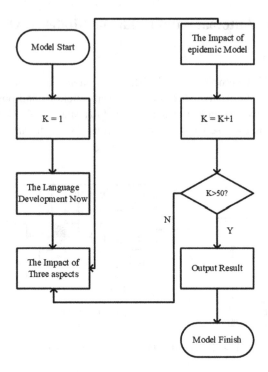

Fig. 3. The flow of constructing the EAC model

The CAE model has the following rules: (1) A cell as a language user can be changed by the influence of other languages. The language which has been learned will also change. (2) Based on the epidemic model, the language classes are regarded as diseases in this model construction process. The user of a language is regarded as an infective of the language. (3) People who are likely to learn the language are considered as susceptible, people who cannot learn the language are defined as recovered. Its corresponding mathematical relations are expressed as follows:

$$\begin{cases} P_i = S_i(t) + I_i(t) + R_i(t) \\ \frac{ds_i}{dt_i} = -\alpha_i S_i(t) I_i(t) \\ \frac{dI_i}{dt_i} = \alpha_i S_i(t) I_i(t) - \beta_i I_i(t) \\ \frac{dR_i}{dt_i} = \beta_i I_i(t) \end{cases} \tag{1}$$

The i refers to each language.

(4) The people who need to learn another language choose a famous language by roulette algorithm [11]. Roulette algorithm's main idea is that the probability of individual selection is proportional to the size of the fitness function. The language which has higher score would get higher fitness function.

The total number of languages is N. The score is normalized, the normalized score is shown as x_i.

$$x_i = \frac{score_i - score_{min}}{score_{max} - score_{min}} \tag{2}$$

The selection probability of individual x_i is

$$P(x_i) = \frac{f(x_i)}{\sum_{j=1}^{N} f(x_j)} \tag{3}$$

q_i is called the accumulation probability of individual x_i

The Roulette selection method is implemented by the following simulation process:

(1) An uniformly distributed random number r is produced in $[0, 1]$.
(2) The language x_1 is selected when $r \leq q_i$.
(3) The x_k language is selected when $q_{k-1} < r \leq q_k (2 \leq k \leq N)$.

5 Analysis and Results

Through the model, the development of various languages has successfully predicted through CAE models in 50 years. The final result is shown in Table 3:

Table 3. The top ten languages

Currently			The next 50 years		
Language	Total	Rank	Language	Total	Rank
Mandarin Chinese	109	1	English	485	1
English	98.3	2	Mandarin Chinese	431.9	2
Spanish	54.4	3	French	357.7	3
Hindustani	52.7	4	German	277.4	4
Arabic	42.2	5	Spanish	276.4	5
Bengali	26.7	6	Hindustani	189.5	6
Portuguese	26.1	7	Japanese	177.4	7
Russian	22.9	8	Portuguese	39	8
Punjabi	14.8	9	Russian	36.4	9
Japanese	12.9	10	Arabic	36	10

Through Table 3, we can find that the users of the two languages Bengali, Punjabi would be out of the top ten list. The language user numbers of French and German would enter the top ten list.

Above all, the difficulty of language learning is not considered in this study and we assume that the development trend of each country remains stable. The countries which use French and German as their native languages have strong economic strength, mature tourism industry and sound communication technology. These factors will increase the two language's users greatly. However, the country that uses Bengali as its native language has a large population base, but the overall level of development is not as good as other developed countries. By the simulation process, they will fall out from the top ten.

6 Conclusion

In fact, any top ten language is less likely to be replaced in 50 years. Because the first 10 of these languages are mature, and they become the official language of each country which has a large number of population. On the other hand, in the 6900 languages in the world, the number of use of some languages will gradually diminish, and even replaced by others.

In the hypothetical ideal condition, although a person's learning ability, language environment and learning time are limited, people could learn more than 5 languages. It also suggests that the native speakers' probability of learning other languages will be greatly increasing. Therefore, native languages will not be replaced by other languages. What's more, with more and more people learning second foreign languages, the native language of those countries which will be in a leading level of development will be more popular. In the future, we will consider these factors and raise the learning rate of people in developed countries and other part of the world. By doing so, we could improve the overall performance of our model.

Acknowledgement. This work is supported by National Natural Science Foundation of China (No. 61873240). The data used to support the findings of this study are available from the corresponding authors upon request.

References

1. Bo, C.: Social constructivism of language and meaning. Chin. Soc. Sci. (10), 121–142 (2014)
2. Ying, H., Jiang, X., Li, J.: Language trends of gray box neural network model from the perspective of language learning. Knowl. Econ. (14), 178–180 (2018)
3. Zhang, Q.: Globalization of economy and industrial engineering development. In: Proceedings of the Seventh International Conference on Industrial Engineering and Engineering Management, pp. 13–19 (2000)
4. Giulianotti, R., Robertson, R.: Sport and globalization: transnational dimensions. Glob. Netw. 7(2), 107–112 (2007)
5. Steinbock, D.: Globalization of wireless value system: from geographic to strategic advantages. Telecommun. Policy 27(3–4), 207–235 (2003)
6. Poekaew, P., Champrasert, P.: Adaptive-PCA: an event-based data aggregation using principal component analysis for WSNs. In: 2015 International Conference on Smart Sensors and Application, pp. 50–55 (2015)

7. Xiao, X., Zhou, Y.: Two-dimensional quaternion PCA and sparse PCA. IEEE Trans. Neural Netw. Learn. Syst. (2018)
8. Uguz, S., Akin, H.: On the irreversibility of moore cellular automata over the ternary field and image application. Appl. Math. Model. **40**(17–18), 8017–8032 (2016)
9. Wei, J., You, L.: The study of state prediction method based on ARIMA model and cellular automata. J. Inf. Comput. Sci. **9**(16), 4945–4952 (2012)
10. Barrett, C.L., et al.: A scalable data management tool to support epidemiological modeling of large urban regions. In: Kovács, L., Fuhr, N., Meghini, C. (eds.) ECDL 2007. LNCS, vol. 4675, pp. 546–548. Springer, Heidelberg (2007). https://doi.org/10.1007/978-3-540-74851-9_65
11. Lipowski, A.: Roulette-wheel selection via stochastic acceptance. Physica A **391**(6), 2193–2196 (2012)

EECR: Energy-Efficient Cooperative Routing for EM-Based Nanonetworks

Xin-Wei Yao$^{(\boxtimes)}$, Ye-Chen-Ge Wu, Yuan Yao$^{(\boxtimes)}$, Chu-Feng Qi, and Wei Huang

College of Computer Science and Technology, Zhejiang University of Technology,
Hangzhou 310023, China
{xwyao,ycgwu,yaoyuan,qichufeng,huangwei}@zjut.edu.cn

Abstract. Nanonetworks, which are composed of interacting nanonodes, have significant potential in many areas and applications. However, reliable communication is extremely challenging in electromagnetic (EM) nanonetworks as a result of limited transmission power, constrained nanonode capabilities, and severe path losses in terahertz band communications. In this paper, we propose a cooperative communication model for hierarchical cluster-based nanonetworks. In each cluster, there is a nano-controller that acts as a cluster head and several nanonodes that cooperatively forward packets to the nano-controller. Based on the cooperative communication model, an energy-efficient cooperative routing algorithm with optimal link cost is proposed for the nanonetworks. We first formulate the energy cost of cooperative communication between two nanonodes with a two-stage transmission strategy, as only statistical knowledge about the channel is currently available. Using the energy cost formulation, we can then establish cooperative communication transmission with optimal energy consumption. The results of the study show that the cooperative routing scheme can effectively reduce energy consumption compared to noncooperative routing schemes, thus showing great potential for use in cooperative communication schemes to enhance the performance of the nanonetwork.

Keywords: EM-based nanonetwork · Energy-efficient routing · Cooperative routing

1 Introduction

Recent advances in nanotechnology have enabled the development of nanoscale devices that are able to perform simple operations [10]. Owing to the introduction of miniature graphene-based antennas [2], these nanomachines are capable of communicating with each other over short distances and achieving high transmission rates in the terahertz frequency band [3,4]. A nanonetwork may be composed of several to thousands of nanonodes. Some characteristics of the nanonetworks are similar to ad-hoc networks: they have the ability to be reconfigured and are self-organizing. Hence, communications involving nanonetworks

© Springer Nature Switzerland AG 2019
Y. Luo (Ed.): CDVE 2019, LNCS 11792, pp. 30–38, 2019.
https://doi.org/10.1007/978-3-030-30949-7_4

tend to develop in the direction of ad-hoc networks. However, some restrictions of nanonodes [8] such as computing resource and energy, combined with the high density of nanonodes, lead to different network architectures and protocol design issues [5,6]. The main goal in designing network protocols is to maintain connectivity and improve the lifetime of the nanonetwork while sustaining simplicity [13].

Nanonetworks have more restrictions than traditional wireless networks due to the nanoscale size of nanonodes, and the designing of routing protocols involves new challenges. First, owing to the high path loss of the terahertz band and the limited energy storage capacity of the nanonodes, the transmission range of the nanonodes is greatly limited. This fact illustrates the need for a multi-hop routing algorithm to allow the nanonodes to transmit packets from source to destination [11]. Second, as a result of the limited size of the nanonodes, the energy capacities of the batteries of the nanonodes are limited. Therefore, energy harvesting nanosystems have been introduced to solve the energy problems of nanonodes, such as piezoelectric nanogenerators [9,12]. Each time a packet is sent, the nanonodes consume a lot of energy; therefore, the residual energy of the nanonode fluctuates greatly with time. Therefore, the routing protocols of nanonetworks should be energy efficient and be able to adapt to the dynamic energy state of the nanonodes. Third, the nanoscale size of the nanonodes limits the computational capability and resources. Hence, the nanonodes cannot perform complex operations or store large amounts of data.

Cooperative communication can effectively reduce energy consumption by allowing the nodes to collaborate with each other. In cooperative communications, the nodes help each other transmit messages. Cooperative communication has been well studied in traditional wireless networks and has great potential in nanonetworks as well [1]. In nanonetworks, cooperative transmission can also effectively reduce energy consumption, reduce fluctuations in the residual energy of the nanonodes, and improve the performance of the nanonetwork.

The present work proposes an energy-efficient cooperative routing (EECR) scheme for nanonetworks. Recent studies have shown that nanonetworks based on hierarchical cluster architectures achieve complex calculations in the routing path selection via nano-controllers [7]. A nano-controller is a nanoscale device with more advanced capabilities than a nanonode and coordinates the nanonodes by gathering the data they communicate [2]. We first formulate the energy cost of cooperative communication between two nanonodes with a two-stage transmission strategy, as only the statistical knowledge about the channel is available. Using the energy cost formulation, we can then establish a cooperative communication transmission scheme with optimal energy consumption.

The remainder of this paper is organized as follows. The system models are given in Sect. 2. Section 3 introduces the proposed EECR scheme. Evaluation via simulations are presented in Sect. 4. Finally, the conclusion is given in Sect. 5.

2   System Model

In the system model, one cluster of a nanonetwork consists of a nano-controller and several nanonodes randomly distributed in an area. We assume that the nanonodes can adjust their transmission power and that multiple nanonodes can coordinate their transmissions at the physical layer to form a cooperative link.

2.1   Channel Model

In the transmission of a sender nanonode t_k and a receiver nanonode r_k, s_t denotes the transmitted signal in nanonode t_k, and s_r denotes the received signals at the nanonode r_k. The sender t_i is able to adjust its transmission power p_i and that the maximum power is P_{max}. Let η_r denote the noise received at r_k, where η_r is assumed to be a zero-mean complex Gaussian random variable. The received signal at the receiver r_k is expressed as follows

$$s_r = \sqrt{\frac{p_i}{d_{tr}^\alpha}} h_{tr} s_t + \eta_r \tag{1}$$

where d_{tr} is the distance between the sender and the receiver nanonodes t_k and r_k, α is the path-loss exponent, h_{tr} is the complex channel gain between t_k and r_k modeled as $h_{tr} = |h_{tr}|\, e^{r^{\theta_{tr}}}$, where $|h_{tr}|$ is the channel gain magnitude, and θ_{tr} is the phase.

Let γ_{tr} denote the signal-to-noise-ratio (SNR) at receiver r_k due to nanonode t_k transmitting with power p_i; then

$$\gamma_{tr} = \frac{1}{P_\eta} \frac{p_i}{d_{tr}^\alpha} |h_{tr}|^2 \tag{2}$$

where P_η is the Gaussian noise.

2.2   Cooperation Model

In this routing scheme, the transmission between the sender t_k and receiver r_k considers a two-stage cooperation model. First, t_k broadcasts the packet with transmission power P_b. Every nanonode $t_i (i \neq k)$ will join the transmission to form a cooperative nanonode set $T_k = \{t_1, \ldots, t_m\}$ if all the following conditions are satisfied:

1. Nanonode t_i is within the transmission range of nanonode t_k.
2. Nanonode t_i has enough energy to cooperate in transmitting the message.
3. $d_{ti}, d_{ir} < d_{tr}$, where d_{ti} is the distance between the sender t_k and nanonode t_i, d_{ir} is the distance between nanonode t_i and the receiver r_k, and d_{tr} is the distance between the sender t_k and the receiver r_k.

The cooperative nanonodes in the T_k cooperate in the transmission using a power allocation vector $\mathbf{p} = (p_1, \ldots, p_m)$.

3   Energy-Efficient Cooperative Routing (EECR)

3.1   Cooperative Transmission

Consider a transmission from nanonode t_k to nanonode r_k; let m denote the size of the cooperative set T_k, and n denote the number of cooperative nanonodes, where $n = 0, 1, 2, \ldots, m$. For n cooperative nanonodes

$$P_b = \max\{P_{t1}, P_{t2}, \cdots P_{tn}\} \tag{3}$$

where P_b is the broadcast cost to reach n cooperative nanonodes. Then, the total cost is given by

$$C_{tr} = \min_{n=0}^{m} P_n^C \tag{4}$$

where P_n^C is the cooperative transmission cost from the $n+1$ (include the sender t_k) nanonodes to nanonode r_k. Then, the total cooperative cost is given by

$$P_n^C = P_b + \sum_{i=1}^{n} P_i \tag{5}$$

where P_i is the cost of each cooperative nanonode, and P_{tn} is the required transmission power for transmission from nanonode t_k to cooperative nanonode t_n. Considering the limited computing resource of the nano-controller, we set the transmission power of the cooperative nanonodes to the same values to reduce computational complexity. Hence, the total cooperative transmission cost P_n^C can be obtained by solving the following optimization problem:

$$\min_{\mathbf{P}} P_n^C = P_b + nP_i$$

$$\text{s.t.} \mathbf{P} \leq P_{max},$$

$$\frac{1}{P_\eta} \left(\sum_{i=1}^{n} \sqrt{P_i/d_{ir}^\alpha} + \sqrt{P_b/d_{tr}^\alpha} \right)^2 \geq \gamma_{req} \tag{6}$$

where $\mathbf{P} = [P_b, P_i]^T$, d_{tr} is the distance from nanonode t_k to nanonode t_r, d_{ir} is the distance from cooperative nanonode t_i to nanonode t_r, α is the path-loss exponent, and P_η is the Gaussian noise. γ_{req} indicates the required SNR of the receiving nanonode r_k to decode the signal.

Because n is discrete and bounded, one can use an exhaustive search scheme to find the optimal n that minimize C_{tr}. Let $\mathbf{P}^{opt} = \left[P_b^{opt}, P_i^{opt} \right]^T$ denote the optimal solution. Then, the optimal energy cost for the cooperative transmission is given by

$$P_n^C = P_b^{opt} + nP_i^{opt} \tag{7}$$

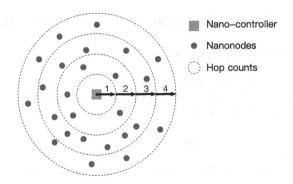

Fig. 1. Nanonodes achieve the minimum hop counts to the nano-controller in the setup phase.

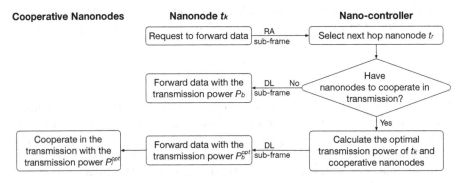

Fig. 2. Block scheme of the cooperative routing algorithm involving a nanonode t_i and the nano-controller.

3.2   Data Packet Routing

In nanonetworks, the communication between a nanonode and the nano-controller follow a dynamic time division multiple access (TDMA) scheduling [8] rule. With TDMA scheduling, complex calculations can be performed by the nano-controller, so the nano-controller can select routing paths for the nanonodes. In TDMA scheduling, a time-frame structure is divided into four subframes: random access (RA), downlink (DL), uplink (UL), and multihop (MH). The nano-controller sends commands to the nanonodes in the DL subframe. The UL subframe is used by the nanonode to directly transfer data to the nano-controller. The MH subframe is used for data transmission between the nanonodes.

In terms of general setup, several nanonodes are assumed to be spread over a square area following a random layout, where a nano-controller is deployed at the center of that area. The nano-controller first broadcasts an initialization packet. Each nanonode t_i forwards the initialization packet using maximum transmission power p_{max} to get the minimum hop counts h_i to the nano-controller, as shown in Fig. 1.

The energy-efficient cooperative routing scheme involves the following steps, as summarized through the block scheme shown in Fig. 2:

1. A nanonode t_k sends a request to the nano-controller to transmit data within RA subframe.
2. The nano-controller selects the next hop nanonode r_k from the neighbor of t_k, which has a smaller number of hop counts to the nano-controller and has the maximal remaining energy.
3. If there is no nanonode that can cooperate in transmission, nanonode t_k forward the data with transmission power P_b so that r_i can decode the data.
4. The nano-controller calculates the optimal transmission power P_b^{opt} and P_i^{opt} for t_k and the cooperative nanonodes in the cooperative routing process.
5. Nanonode t_k and the cooperative nanonodes forward the data to nanonode r_k with the optimal transmission power P_b^{opt} and P_i^{opt}.

4   Performance Evaluation

In this section we present evaluations of the performance of the proposed EECR. Particularly, the EECR is compared to the energy-efficient non-cooperative (EENR) routing scheme. NS-3 is a discrete event network simulator for internet systems that can be used for simulation of network performance. To evaluate and compare the performance of the routing schemes, we developed a simulation module in NS-3 to implement these schemes.

4.1   Simulation Parameters

The simulations consider a uniform random layout that fill a fixed, square area, with dimensions 10×10 cm^2. For simulation purposes, we consider maximum transmission power $P_{max} = 100$ nW, path-loss exponent $\alpha = 2$, noise power $P_\eta = 1$, and SNR threshold $\gamma_{req} = 10$. Considering the high density of nanonodes in the nanonetworks, the packet time to live (TTL) is set to 50 hops. Nanonodes do not process the packets that have been forwarded, but consider their storage capacity; each nanomachine stores information for at most 20 received packets.

The size of the network usually has a large impact on the performance of the routing protocols, so we simulated for different densities of nanonetworks. Regarding the energy harvesting process of the nanonodes, the energy harvest speed is affected by the environment; for example, there will be large differences between a windless environment and a windy environment. Hence, we simulated at different energy harvesting speeds.

During the comparisons of the two schemes, all simulation parameters were identical for all the routing algorithms. Each nanonode randomly starts sending packets within 10 s, sending one packet every 10 s, and sending a total of 10 packets. The simulations are conducted with different densities of nanonodes and energy harvesting speeds. The simulations for every set of parameters was repeated for 30 different network topologies, and we logged the average energy cost and successful packet arrival rates.

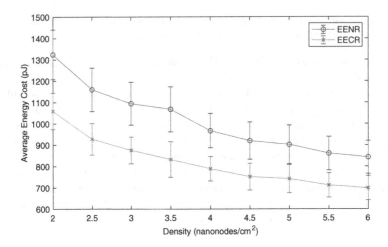

Fig. 3. Average energy cost of each packet for different densities of nanonodes.

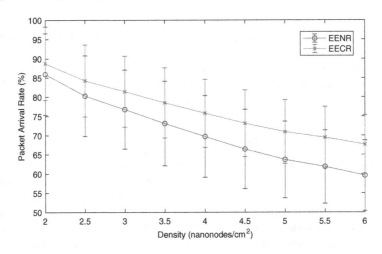

Fig. 4. Packet arrival rate of each packet for different densities of nanonodes.

4.2   Simulation Results with Different Densities of Nanonodes

The simulations with different densities of nanonodes are presented in Figs. 3 and 4. Here, the average energy harvesting speed is 120 pJ/s.

Figure 3 is plotted to observe the average energy cost of each packet for different densities of nanonodes. The EECR scheme reduces about 20% of the energy cost over the EENR scheme, and the energy costs in both the schemes decrease as the nanonode density increases. This is because in each hop transmission, the energy consumed by the EECR scheme is less than or equal to the energy consumed by the EENR scheme. The reason for this is that an increase in the average transmission hop count results in lower energy consumption.

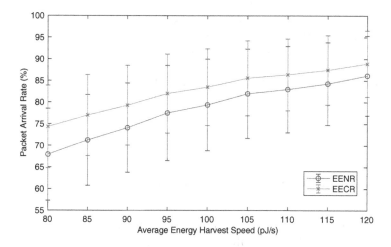

Fig. 5. Packet arrival rate of each packet for different energy harvest speeds.

As shown in Fig. 4, the packet arrival rate of the EECR scheme is higher than that of the EENR scheme. Moreover, as the density of the nanonodes increases, the packet arrival rates of the EECR and EENR gradually decrease. The reason for this is that when the density of the nanonodes is large, the energy of the nanonodes is not sufficient to forward these many packets.

4.3   Simulation Results with Different Energy Harvest Speeds

The results of simulations with different energy harvest speeds are presented in Fig. 5. Here, the density of the nanonodes is 2 nodes/cm^2.

In Fig. 5, the packet arrival rate is investigated with different energy harvesting speeds. The packet arrival rate of the EECR is higher than that of the EENR. It can also be seen that the packet arrival rates of the two routing schemes increase with the energy harvesting speed. The reason for this is that the nanonodes are able to forward more packets for greater energy harvesting speeds.

5   Conclusion

Cooperative transmission in wireless networks has been extensively studied and explores cross-layer optimization designs to fully utilize the benefits of cooperative data transmission. In this study, we investigated cooperative transmission and introduced the EECR scheme for nanonetworks by targeting cooperative transmissions in nanonetworks. Comprehensively, the simulation results indicate that the proposed EECR scheme can significantly reduce energy consumption and achieve better performance compared to the noncooperative scheme. In the simulations with different densities of nanonodes and energy harvest speeds, the

EECR exhibits lower energy consumption and higher packet arrival rates than the EENR. Cooperative transmission has great potential in nanonetworks and requires better cooperative routing schemes to support it.

Acknowledgment. This work was supported by the National Natural Science Foundation of China under Grant No. 61772471 and 61771430, and the Natural Science Foundation of Zhejiang Province under Grant No. Q19F030028.

References

1. Abbasi, Q.H., Nasir, A.A., Yang, K., Qaraqe, K.A., Alomainy, A.: Cooperative in-vivo nano-network communication at terahertz frequencies. IEEE Access **5**, 8642–8647 (2017)
2. Akyildiz, I.F., Jornet, J.M.: Electromagnetic wireless nanosensor networks. Nano Commun. Netw. **1**(1), 3–19 (2010)
3. Boronin, P., Petrov, V., Moltchanov, D., Koucheryavy, Y., Jornet, J.M.: Capacity and throughput analysis of nanoscale machine communication through transparency windows in the terahertz band. Nano Commun. Netw. **5**(3), 72–82 (2014)
4. Jornet, J.M., Akyildiz, I.F.: Channel modeling and capacity analysis for electromagnetic wireless nanonetworks in the terahertz band. IEEE Trans. Wirel. Commun. **10**(10), 3211–3221 (2011)
5. Liaskos, C., Tsioliaridou, A.: A promise of realizable, ultra-scalable communications at nano-scale: a multi-modal nano-machine architecture. IEEE Trans. Comput. **64**(5), 1282–1295 (2015)
6. Pierobon, M., Akyildiz, I.F.: Diffusion-based noise analysis for molecular communication in nanonetworks. IEEE Trans. Signal Process. **59**(6), 2532–2547 (2011)
7. Pierobon, M., Jornet, J.M., Akkari, N., Almasri, S., Akyildiz, I.F.: A routing framework for energy harvesting wireless nanosensor networks in the terahertz band. Wireless Netw. **20**(5), 1169–1183 (2014)
8. Wang, P., Jornet, J.M., Malik, M.A., Akkari, N., Akyildiz, I.F.: Energy and spectrum-aware MAC protocol for perpetual wireless nanosensor networks in the terahertz band. Ad Hoc Netw. **11**(8), 2541–2555 (2013)
9. Xu, S., Hansen, B.J., Wang, Z.L.: Piezoelectric-nanowire-enabled power source for driving wireless microelectronics. Nature Commun. **1**, 93 (2010)
10. Yao, X.W., Ma, D.B., Han, C.: ECP: a probing-based error control strategy for THz-based nanonetworks with energy harvesting. IEEE Access **7**, 25616–25626 (2019)
11. Yao, X.W., Wang, C.C., Wang, W.L., Jornet, J.M.: On the achievable throughput of energy-harvesting nanonetworks in the terahertz band. IEEE Sens. J. **18**(2), 902–912 (2018)
12. Yao, X.W., Wang, W.L., Yang, S.H.: Joint parameter optimization for perpetual nanonetworks and maximum network capacity. IEEE Trans. Mol. Biol. Multi-Scale Commun. **1**(4), 321–330 (2015)
13. Yao, X.W., Wu, Y.C.G., Huang, W.: Routing techniques in wireless nanonetworks: a survey. Nano Commun. Netw. **21**, 100250 (2019). https://doi.org/10.1016/j.nancom.2019.100250

Cardiovascular System Monitoring via Wireless Nanosensor Networks

Sebastià Galmés[✉][iD]

University of Balearic Islands, 07122 Palma, Spain
sebastia.galmes@uib.es

Abstract. This paper explores the capabilities of wireless nanosensor networks to monitor biological or chemical agents in human blood. Wireless nanosensor networks constitute the nanoscale version of wireless sensor networks. However, advances in the former cannot be accomplished by simply downscaling the technological developments achieved for the latter. This is due to several reasons: firstly, the communication paradigms proposed for nanonetworks, namely electromagnetic waves in the terahertz band and molecular signals, entail unprecedented challenges that need to be carefully addressed; additionally, new protocol designs are required as a result of the more severe resource restrictions imposed by nanonodes in comparison to wireless sensor nodes. Under these assumptions, this work-in-progress paper addresses the main technical issues involved in the development of a communication mechanism for a nanosensor network deployed in the human cardiovascular system.

Keywords: Wireless nanosensor network · Wireless sensor network · Electromagnetic communication · Molecular communication · Diffusion process

1 Introduction

One of the most prominent applications envisioned for wireless nanosensor networks (WNNs) is human health monitoring [2]. WNNs constitute the nanoscale version of the well-known wireless sensor networks (WSNs), but unfortunately this does not mean that a simple top-down approach can be applied to extrapolate the advances in one technology to the other one. In effect, downscaling the mechanisms developed for WSNs is not feasible because of the qualitative changes required by the intrinsic characteristics of WNNs:

– Firstly, the new communication paradigms proposed for nanonetworks bring up new challenges that deserve careful treatment. One of these paradigms is electromagnetic communication (EM) in the terahertz band, which has been fostered by recent advances in the development of electronic nanocomponents (nanobatteries, nanomemories, logical nanocircuits and nanoantennas). However, EM radiation in the region of nanoscale wavelengths is subject to severe molecular absorption, fact that limits the range of communications to

© Springer Nature Switzerland AG 2019
Y. Luo (Ed.): CDVE 2019, LNCS 11792, pp. 39–44, 2019.
https://doi.org/10.1007/978-3-030-30949-7_5

unprecedented small values; accordingly, WNNs are expected to be characterized by very dense deployments, which in turn will cause excessive redundant multihop paths and packet collisions. Another communication paradigm relies on the use of molecules as information carriers. Still in its infancy, molecular communication (MC) is perceived as a promising alternative inspired on the chemical and biological processes that already take place in living organisms. Though advances are taking place regarding transmitter and receiver designs, as well as channel characterization and encoding, the main drawback of MC is the large and random propagation delays which lead to undesired memory effects and very limited transmission rates.

- Secondly, nanonodes are expected to exhibit substantially more severe restrictions than wireless sensor nodes in terms of sensing, processing, data storing, data communication and actuation capabilities, fact that demands for new strategies in protocol design. The resulting protocols either are sustained by minimal amounts of resources in nanonodes or transfer the required resources to specialized devices like nanocontrollers.

This paper describes the work-in-progress focused on the development of a WNN devoted to monitoring chemical agents in human blood, in particular biomarkers revealing incipient cancer. It is commonly accepted that the best alternatives to fight against cancer are prevention or early detection. Regular blood tests can be efficient mechanisms to detect cancer in its early stages, but it is also frequent that they can only reveal advanced spread or metastasis. In order to avoid such situations, continuous monitoring becomes necessary. To achieve this goal, a WNN permanently deployed at strategical locations in the cardiovascular system may provide the necessary information to quickly detect incipient cancer. Another contribution of this nature is [3], though it proposes a WNN that is set up for clinical test only and consists of mobile nanonodes that are injected at one specific site of the cardiovascular system.

Specifically, this paper discusses the main technical issues involved in the development of a communication mechanism for a continuous monitoring WNN deployed in human blood. Some of these issues have already been addressed in previous works, whereas the rest remain to be investigated.

The rest of this work-in-progress paper is organized as follows. In Sect. 2, the system under consideration is described and the general problem is formulated. Section 3 proposes a cross link-network layer mechanism to support the robust and efficient transmission of information along the veins of the human systemic circuit. Finally, in Sect. 4 the main conclusions and pending research issues are drawn.

2   System Architecture

As stated in [1], the cardiovascular system is divided into the pulmonary circuit and the systemic circuit. The pulmonary circuit is composed by arteries and veins that transport blood between the heart and the lungs. This circuit starts at the right ventricle and ends at the left atrium. On the other hand, the systemic circuit is made up of arteries that carry oxygenated blood and nutrients from the left ventricle to all other organs and tissues, and veins that return deoxygenated blood to the right atrium. Figure 1 shows the main distribution routes within the systemic circuit that carry deoxygenated blood, where the nanosensor network is assumed to be deployed (replicated networks could be deployed for the oxygenated blood streams within the systemic circuit and for the pulmonary circuit). As it can be noticed, the network encompasses two types of devices: nanonodes, which have sensing and molecular transmission and reception capabilities, and nanointerfaces, which have sensing, molecular reception and electromagnetic transmission capabilities. Basically, nanonodes are designed to count specific biomarkers and regularly transmit the cumulative data to the next nanonode along the circuit; nanointerfaces have the same sensing ability as nanonodes, but they are designed to receive molecular data from the previous nanonode and to wirelessly report the overall count to an on-body attached register or a wearable device like a clinical watch or similar.

Nanonodes and nanointerfaces perform computing and communication tasks in a cooperative manner. The basic operation of nanonodes is as follows. Let X_{ij} be the amount of biomarkers detected by a nanonode i that is tributary of nanointerface j, and let Y_{ij} be the data transmitted by such nanonode. We assume that $j = \{1, \ldots NI\}$, with NI the number of nanointerfaces (two in Fig. 1) and $i = \{1, \ldots t(j)\}$, with $t(j)$ the total number of tributaries of nanointerface j. Then, the following equation holds:

$$Y_{ij} = Y_{i-1j} + X_{ij} \tag{1}$$

Figure 2 shows the system architecture that illustrates how this equation is implemented. As it can be noticed, Y_{i-1j} is transmitted molecularly to the next nanonode i, if $i < t(j)$, or nanointerface j if $i = t(j)$. The latter performs the following operation:

$$Y_j = Y_{t(j)j} + X_j \tag{2}$$

The cumulative sum Y_j is transmitted via EM communication to the wearable device. This device adds up the data received from all nanointerfaces, and compares it to some predefined threshold. Let S be the total amount of biomarkers detected, and Th the threshold. The final formulation of the problem requires the definition of a biomarker population. As a first step, let us assume that the generation of biomarkers obeys a non-homogeneous Poisson process of rate $\lambda = \lambda(t)$, where $\lambda > 0$ indicates the presence of a malignant tumor. Then, assuming that the threshold is selected so as to ensure early diagnosis, the design objective is to satisfy the following equation, where G denotes a predefined guarantee:

$$prob(S \geq Th/\lambda > 0) \geq G \tag{3}$$

A false alarm condition should also be imposed:

$$prob(S \geq Th/\lambda = 0) \leq FA \tag{4}$$

Here, $1 - FA$ is the guarantee that a false alarm will not take place.

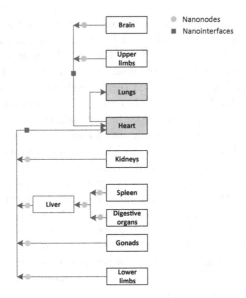

Fig. 1. Schematic view of the main distribution routes for deoxygenated blood within the systemic circuit.

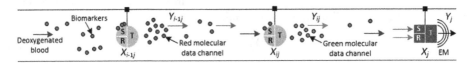

Fig. 2. Illustration of the basic computing and communication operations along a blood vessel.

3   Protocol Design

In shared transmission media, the MAC protocol is responsible for allowing that any given node monopolizes the use of the communication channel for transmission during a limited amount of time. Depending on the location of the destination, the communication path may require multiple hops over intermediate nodes. Moreover, it is possible that there exist multiple multihop paths between origin and destination, in which case it is the routing protocol that selects the best path according to some pre-established criteria. However, the particular deployment topology of the network under consideration (recall Fig. 2), as well as the fact that the shared medium is a one-way circulating fluid, simplify the design of the two protocols up to the fact that a single cross-layer solution can be adopted. Next, the main features of the proposed cardiovascular WNN are listed:

- The transmission medium is bloodstream, which circulates at about 1–2 meters per second in humans. Accordingly, a molecular channel model with drift is adopted to characterize the transport of data between two points. A channel with drift benefits the propagation delay, but it precludes from transmitting feedback information (like acknowledgments). However, fortunately this is not a significant drawback in the current application, because data sent by nanonodes are continuously refreshed.

- Nanonodes are deployed at fixed locations along the blood vessels, fact that recommends the use of a linear multihop tree to route the packets towards the corresponding nanointerface.
- The number of nanonodes is relatively small. Thus, using a colored rule for discriminating hops along a path is feasible. This means using different types of molecular carriers for different hops, in such a way that collisions are avoided.

Though the above features introduce significant design simplifications, there are still two drawbacks from the communication point of view that require detailed analysis: memory effects and symbol synchronization.

Memory effects are inherent to the molecular channel. Since molecules randomly diffuse into the environment until they eventually reach the next-hop nanonode, it is possible that molecules from previous symbols are received during the current symbol, and thus they interfere the detection process. In essence, this problem can be overcome by tuning the symbol rate according to the transmission distance, with the ultimate goal of reducing the memory level, that is, the number of previous interfering symbols. The detailed analysis is provided in [4] for a communication channel without drift and two encoding schemes, namely M-level MOSK (MOlecular Shift Keying) and M-level CSK (Concentration Shift Keying).

On the other hand, to ensure reliable transmission between nanonodes it is necessary that the receiver is able to recognize each symbol within the transmitted message. In conventional communication systems, this is achieved by embedding the clock signal into the data signal. In this way, both transmitter and receiver are synchronized in spite of the relative drift between their internal clocks. In contrast, synchronization in molecular channels is still one of the main challenges. Several synchronization mechanisms have been recently proposed for nanonetworks, which can be grouped into five categories: collective pattern-based techniques, two-way message exchange, one-way message exchange, blind synchronization and partially-untimed schemes. A detailed review of these categories is provided in [5]. However, aside from leading to very small symbol rates, the synchronization mechanisms currently proposed are very complex and/or they require two-way message exchanges, which is unfeasible in molecular channels with drift. To avoid these limitations, in [5] a molecular version of the conventional asynchronous communication protocol is proposed. It is assumed that both transmitter and receiver have their own clocks, but they are not synchronized. The basic idea is that the transmitter initiates the communication via a special symbol called beacon, and then transmits a short sequence of data symbols in such a way that the relative drift between clocks does not lead to symbol misalignment. Note that the use of short messages is consistent with the health application being considered here. The work presented in [5] assumes an M-level

MOSK encoding scheme and a molecular channel without drift and with any level of memory.

4   Conclusions and Further Research

This paper describes the work-in-progress focused on the development of a WNN to monitor specific chemical or biological agents, like carcinogenic cells, in the human cardiovascular system. A specific subsystem has been considered, which is the systemic circuit (veins side), and a cross link-network layered solution has been proposed for the communication along the main distribution routes of deoxygenated blood. Several contributions have been reported, which in turn reveal pending research: the characterization of memory effects and the development of an asynchronous communication protocol for a molecular channel with drift. In addition, the formulated design objectives, namely guarantees on early detection and false alarm avoidance, require the statistical characterization of variables X and Y introduced in the paper. Finally, a single-hop architecture could be considered, as it would entail some advantages, like a simplified design of nanonodes without receiver subsystems, though at the expense of some disadvantages: more complex nanointerfaces and very long communication paths. From the robustness point of view, the single-hop architecture would avoid the multiple single points of failure represented by nanonodes in the multihop architecture.

References

1. Martini, F.H., Bartholomew, E.F.: Essentials of Anatomy and Physiology. Pearson Education Limited, London (2017)
2. Akyildiz, I.F., Pierobon, M., Balasubramaniam, S.: Moving forward with molecular communication: from theory to human health applications. Proc. IEEE **107**(5), 858–865 (2019)
3. Mosayeb, R., Ahmadzadeh, A., Wicke, W., Jamali, V., Schober, R., Nasiri-Kenari, M.: Early cancer detection in blood vessels using mobile nanosensors. IEEE Trans. Nanobiosci. **18**(2), 103–116 (2019)
4. Galmés, S., Atakan, B.: Performance analysis of molecular communications with memory. IEEE Trans. Commun. **64**(9), 3786–3793 (2016)
5. Galmés, S., Atakan, B.: Effects of framing errors on the performance of molecular communications with memory. IEEE Trans. Commun. (submitted)

Computer Vision Approach for Indoor Location Recognition Within an Augmented Reality Mobile Application

Gabriele Minneci[1]([✉]), Alice Schweigkofler[2], Carmen Marcher[1,2],
Gabriele Pasetti Monizza[2], Tammam Tillo[1], and Dominik T. Matt[1,2]

[1] Free University of Bolzano, Bolzano, Italy
`gabriele.minneci@gmail.com`
[2] Fraunhofer Italia Research, Bolzano, Italy

Abstract. The Building Industry (BI) lacks in sharing information among different and heterogeneous stakeholders. With the advent of new technologies such as mobile devices, IoT and Industry 4.0 different approaches have been introduced, but it is still an open research field. The present essay aims at moving a step forward using augmented reality connected with the Building Information Modelling (BIM) methodology enhancing the effectiveness of process in the BI.

The authors improved the Fraunhofer Italia's AR4Construction (AR4C) mobile application, that lets construction workers visualize the BIM model of a building on site in augmented reality and interact with its design information. The main purpose of this study consists in studying and developing an indoor location functionality for the AR4C application. The research focuses on understanding the starting point and the orientation of the user, through the application of 3D mathematical structures and computer vision methods.

The result is a core module for an indoor location functionality. We have evaluated distances and orientation errors, analyzing the results according to the implementation strategy. In conclusion, possible improvements have been analyzed within this paper, which offers a first approach for visualization-only based frameworks aiming at indoor location and navigation and using BIM models as a starting point.

Keywords: Method · Applications for total life cycle support: from conceptual design to manufacturing and construction

1 Introduction

The Building Industry (BI) is an information-based industry marked by heterogeneous stakeholders and a need of exchanging accurate information in order to reach maximum efficiency and effectiveness. The lack of information sharing represents the main cause of poor performance [1]. Therefore, coordination and problem solving of challenges given by different type of stakeholders and collaborators are key to improve the construction processes [2].

© Springer Nature Switzerland AG 2019
Y. Luo (Ed.): CDVE 2019, LNCS 11792, pp. 45–53, 2019.
https://doi.org/10.1007/978-3-030-30949-7_6

In order to tackle this problem, the Augmented Reality for Construction (AR4C) project aims at developing tools for the management of technical information in a dynamic and intelligent manner, thus improving communication among stakeholders in the BI. This research specifically aims at developing a mobile application for digital transfer of building information from the design phase to the construction site, and for the entire life-cycle of the building, using Augmented Reality (AR) and exploiting an Indoor Positioning System (IPS). The application allows to visualize the whole, or just some parts (e.g. windows or walls), of the 3D BIM model "in-place" while walking through the real building. In addition to this, the application allows to extract relevant information and make the BIM model interactive. A first version of the AR4C application was already developed [1], where the basic functionalities have been implemented.

This paper focuses on the study and implementation of Computer Vision (CV) methods aiming at understanding the environment and positioning the user in a 3D model of a building. The main purpose is to integrate an indoor location core functionality in the already developed application AR4C using Computer Vision approaches.

This paper is structured as follows: Sect. 2 presents the state of the art on applications belonging to the research fields BIM, AR, CV and IPS for the resolution of specific issues of the BI. Section 3 presents the approach used developing the indoor location system. The results of the accuracy of this system are described in Sect. 4. Section 5 contains final remarks and offers inspiration for further discussion.

2 State of Art

The BIM methodology permits to use in an intelligent manner 3D models together with the project digital data throughout the entire building's life cycle. The improvement of the sharing information process can enhance communication and collaboration among stakeholders. Moreover, a BIM model can be integrated with or within other technologies to better access and manage information. Several studies were conducted, in order to integrate the BIM methodology from network-based systems [3] through the AR adoption for 3D visualization of the model [4]. The augmented reality integration with mobile devices has been already considered by several studies [5] because it gives high level of flexibility. Moreover, AR provides 3D representation and orientation in space and time, which are helpful for an easier and faster understanding of technical issues by the different stakeholders [6, 7].

AR is improving every year, either regarding the user's accessibility (ARCore, ARkit, Vuforia) or the technological aspect. It is demonstrated that AR can be useful in many fields [2, 8]. In particular, the Building Industry needs an improvement in management and collaboration between the stakeholders, since it is still based on paper-processes [1, 2]. Smart glasses technology has been introduced as a support for the construction process [9], but it needs further research and use cases on available devices. Smartphones and tablets are a good starting point for prototyping and analyzing the functionalities that a smart glass-based system can provide. Jiao et al. [3] proposes an integrated cloud AR framework focused on the stakeholder's collaboration and information sharing. This system merges the BIM model information with a cloud system, where photos taken by the users are processed.

Computer Vision has been used in the field of the BI mostly with the aim of developing solutions for the improvement of the construction workflow and for the increase of the work safety. Karsh et al. [4] use on-site images, Incremental SfM algorithm and a detailed BIM model of the building to visualize and analyze a construction process. The user can explore the site directly on the field and check information about each single BIM element of the building. Memarzadeh et al. [10] detects workers and construction machines from a 2D video stream, focusing on 3D location of resources. Park et al. [11] use a fixed stereo camera system to track different objects in a construction site around 40 m distance. The main aim of this research is to develop a system for merging BIM information capabilities with the AR potential for user experience and CV techniques for analyzing the environment (location and object recognition).

Indoor location is still an open research field and there isn't a winning approach yet, but it depends on the objectives and constraints of each project [12]. Vision analysis uses the embedded RGB camera on a device or a pre-installed camera in the building, to analyze and recognize elements in video frames. Different techniques can be used to recognize elements from a camera video-stream: edge detection [13], SIFT, SURF, SfM, SLAM [14] represent some examples, as well as Visual SLAMif if only the camera information is used [15]. The state of the art of indoor location with CV techniques is based on marks previously placed in the building and recognized by the application: QR codes, specific images or elements in the area are pre-selected and used as fixed starting point [5]. So far, there has not been any research that aims at locating the position of a user or agent basing on the 3D model of the building. Our research is focused on using the BIM model of the building to track the user's indoor position.

3   Development

We based our work on the new ARCore framework and exploited the sensors available on commercial smartphones. We have used the Huawei P20 smartphone, where we deployed the AR4C application implemented with Unity. The accuracy of our results has been tested calculating the distance error and the orientation error of the virtual camera compared to the real position of the smartphone in the building.

3.1   Initial Position

At the start scene, the user is shown the 2D map of the building, through which he can indicate approximately his position with a touch. Therefore, the active camera is moved to the touched position, with an arbitrary rotation of (0, 0, 0). Here, the user starts the process for the indoor location.

The most challenging activity of the project was to capture the starting point and orientation of the smartphone (i.e. of the user). As we decided to exclude GPS and the internal compass of the smartphone because of their inaccuracy, the adopted approach consists in the comparison between the detected real surfaces and the BIM model. The system generates two types of planes: planes detected from the real building by the ARCore framework (AR planes) and planes created from the BIM model (BIM planes). An algorithm gathers, organizes and compares the planes of these two "worlds" in order to properly align them.

The development process is divided into two parts: (i) the geometry module for the detection and generation of 3D planes in the selected building area (Sect. 3.2) and (ii) the comparison and location module for the alignment of the real and the virtual world (Sect. 3.3).

3.2 Geometry Module

The core of the IPS consists in the management of the geometrical planes. The algorithm generates and manages for the AR planes and the BIM planes a common structure. This permits an easy and fast comparison between the real world (AR planes) and the virtual world (BIM planes). Each plane contains the following information:

- ID unity plane object;
- A list of points belonging to the plane;
- The geometrical center of the plane;
- The normal vector of the plane: (a, b, c);
- The coefficients for the plane's mathematical equation: $ax + by + cz + d = 0$;
- Horizontal or vertical type of plane.

An AR plane (Fig. 1) is created from the information given by the planes detected by ARCore. The user is asked to move across the selected building area using the smartphone to detect different surfaces within the area itself. Translucent and glazed elements as well as uniform surfaces are not easy to detect. Concrete or wooden elements are instead optimal for detection.

Fig. 1. ARCore planes detection (left) and 3D Unity model for the BIM planes creation (right).

A BIM plane (Fig. 1) is calculated through the bounds of each Unity object of the BIM model. This method has been chosen because of a limitation on the geometrical information of the building model in Unity.

3.3   Planes Comparison and Location

A module called "comparer class" is responsible for the comparison of the planes from the two worlds. This module gathers the two groups of planes, which are filtered by better performance, and then it compares the remaining ones in a loop until it finds enough matchings between the two worlds. The information acquired at the end of this process is used for location. If the comparison output is correct, the user will experience the virtual world aligned with the real one.

4   Results

Different tests were made in order to evaluate the level of efficacy of the developed IPS. Tests investigate the solution accuracy, i.e. the precision in terms of distance and orientation of the overlap between the 3D model and the real environment. We have analyzed the results according to the following parameters (Table 1).

Table 1. Values of each parameter.

Parameter	Definition	Value 1	Value 2	Value 3
TotalAR	Number of detected planes	A: 3-4	B: 5-6-7	C: 8-9
OffsetRadius	Sphere radius to define a boundary for selecting BIM planes around the user	1 m	2 m	3 m
DistanceError	Maximum distance error for which AR planes and BIM planes are considered aligned	0.12 m	0.2 m	0.35 m
AngleError	Maximum angle error for which two planes are considered parallel or perpendicular	0.1 rad	0.2 rad	0.3 rad
MatchPercentage	Minimum number of planes that the algorithm needs to match to find an acceptable solution	50%	80%	100%

In case of no solutions, raw data are cleaned, and the remaining data are organized according to the number of found solutions. These are grouped by the TotalAR parameter (Table 2). The analysis focused on group B, which appears the most probable scenario in a real case because of the number of planes detected by the user. The number of detected planes defines the probability of finding a solution: the more the better.

Table 2. Number of solutions according to the total tests, grouped by the AR groups.

AR group	TotalAR	Number of solutions	Number of tests	Percentage
A	3-4	11	74	15%
B	5-6-7	49	128	38%
C	8-9	20	31	64%

4.1 Distance and Orientation Error

Results are grouped in the minimum (blue), average (red) and maximum (yellow) error rate, which is calculated for each AR group (A, B, C). Figure 2 shows the results of the distance error for the B group. The x-axis shows different combinations of the considered parameters identified by an index. These different combinations are explained in Table 3. The y-axis shows, in meters, the distance error. Some combinations of parameters gave just one solution as a result, and this unique solution is shown in the table as the average value.

Table 3. Combinations of parameters for test phase.

Index	1	2	3	4	5	6	7	8	9	10	2	3
OffsetRadius	1	1	3	1	2	3	1	3	1	1	2	3
DistanceError	0.12	0.2	0.2	0.2	0.2	0.2	0.35	0.35	0.2	0.2	0.2	0.2
AngleError	0.1	0.1	0.1	0.2	0.1	0.1	0.1	0.1	0.2	0.2	0.2	0.2
MatchPercentage	80	50	80	100	50	80	80	80	50	80	50	80

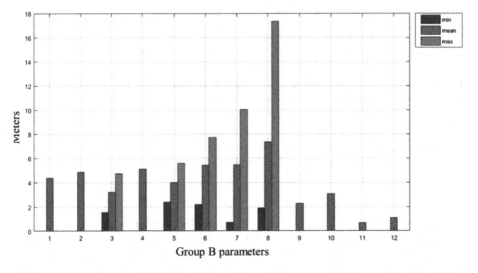

Fig. 2. Min (blue), average (red) and max (yellow) distance error of group B. (Color figure online)

The minimum error in which a solution has been found is with a DistanceError value of 0.12 m. The second value (i.e. 0.2 m) approximates the distance error found during the implementation and debug of the system. It is important so specify here, that the BIM model also contains an error percentage compared to the real word: 0.35 m was the maximum error found. This measure defines the third value of the DistanceError parameter.

Tests with the parameter AngleError = 0.3 provided no results and the solutions that needed 100% of matched planes were few. The DistanceError = 0.35 m had the worst results in all the groups. Taking this value, we can find solutions only when the AngleError is 0.1. The OffsetRadius does not affect the solution in group B and C. On the contrary, in group A the OffsetRadius is always 3 m. In this case, there are less AR planes detected.

Similarly, the orientation error has been calculated. Figure 3 shows different values of the orientation error for the same groups of parameters. The user position is referred to an XYZ frame of reference. The X and Z axes always show an error in the range of [−4; 4] degrees. The orientation around the X and Z axes is linked with the pose of the device i.e. the axes values and the position are related by internal calculations. The system keeps the visual model correctly aligned on those axes. Therefore, the user and the BIM model are always well oriented with respect to the floor. The error found regards the Y axis. The maximum error is 180°, because the objects can be rotated in both directions. Therefore, the final data are shown in the range of [0; 180] degrees in absolute form. The specific 180° value is of great importance, because it means that the plane has been identified "correctly" but it is just flipped. Most of the errors is around 0° or 180° and the most common error is the flipping. This occurs especially in group B. Any correlation between group parameters and their error cannot be found, as the available data are not sufficient to create a significant statistic.

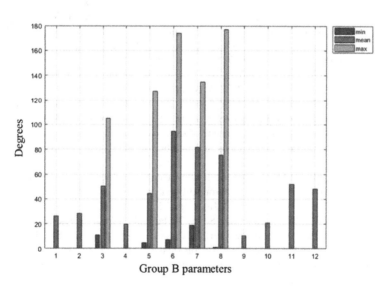

Fig. 3. Min (blue), average (red) and max (yellow) orientation error of group B. (Color figure online)

5   Discussion and Conclusion

This work aims at creating a core module as a starting point for future implementations. The research focus is to develop a new method, which uses computer vision and image processing approaches related to the indoor location, starting from BIM models. As for hardware, this research exploits only an RGB camera and sensors integrated in commercial smartphones. Considering this, the current results cannot be compared yet with the current state of the art.

As expected, the detection of 3-4 planes is not enough to locate the user: the application needs to achieve more information about the surroundings for a correct and complete indoor location of the user. The limit values of the parameters (i.e. AngleError = 0.3, DistanceError = 0.35 m, MatchPercentage = 100%) did not provide as good results as expected. Most of the tests with these values did not lead to any solutions at all. Therefore, there is a clear correlation between the parameters above and the comparison output. The error rate between the BIM model and the real building can bend results.

The evaluation focused on understanding the correlation between the parameters and the provided solutions. Moreover, research on system accuracy should be carried out after the implementation of more functionalities. A future functionality should be the choice of the best option among the solutions provided by their comparison.

References

1. Schweigkofler, A., Monizza, G.P., Domi, E., Popescu, A., Ratajczak, J., Marcher, C., Riedl, M., Matt, D.: Development of a digital platform based on the integration of augmented reality and BIM for the management of information in construction processes. In: Chiabert, P., Bouras, A., Noël, F., Ríos, J. (eds.) PLM 2018. IAICT, vol. 540, pp. 46–55. Springer, Cham (2018). https://doi.org/10.1007/978-3-030-01614-2_5
2. Fernandez-Carames, T.M., Fraga-Lamas, P.: A review on human-centered IoT connected smart labels for the industry 4.0. IEEE Access **6**, 25939–25957 (2018)
3. Jiao, Y., Zhang, S., Li, Y., Wang, Y., Yang, B.: Towards cloud augmented reality for construction application by BIM and SNS integration. Autom. Constr. **33**, 37–47 (2013)
4. Karsch, K., Golparvar-Fard, M., Forsyth, D.: Constructaide: analysing and visualizing construction sites through photographs and building models. ACM Trans. Graph. (TOG) **33**(6), 176 (2014)
5. Fusco, G., Coughlan, J.M.: Indoor localization using computer vision and visual-inertial odometry. In: Miesenberger, K., Kouroupetroglou, G. (eds.) ICCHP 2018. LNCS, vol. 10897, pp. 86–93. Springer, Cham (2018). https://doi.org/10.1007/978-3-319-94274-2_13
6. Knoth, L., Mittlbock, M., Vockner, B.: Smart 3D building infrastructures: linking GIS with other domains. ISPRS Ann. Photogrammetry Remote Sens. Spatial Inf. Sci. **4**, 187 (2016)
7. Moloney, J.: Augmented reality visualisation of the built environment to support design decision making. In: Tenth International Conference on Information Visualisation (IV 2006), pp. 687–692, July 2006
8. Fraga-Lamas, P., Fernandez-Carames, T.M., Blanco-Novoa, O., Vilar-Montesinos, M.A.: A review on industrial augmented reality systems for the industry 4.0 shipyard. IEEE Access **6**, 13358–13375 (2018)
9. Moon, S., Seo, J.: Integration of smart glass technology for information exchange at construction sites. In: ISARC. Proceedings of the International Symposium on Automation and Robotics in Construction, vol. 32, p. 1 (2015)
10. Memarzadeh, M., Golparvar-Fard, M., Niebles, J.C.: Automated 2D detection of construction equipment and workers from site video streams using histograms of oriented gradients and colours. Autom. Constr. **32**, 24–37 (2013)

11. Park, M.W., Koch, C., Brilakis, I.: Three-dimensional tracking of construction resources using an on-site camera system. J. Comput. Civil Eng. **26**(4), 541–549 (2011)
12. Microsoft. 2017 Microsoft indoor localization competition (2017)
13. Marr, D., Hildreth, E.: Theory of edge detection. Proc. R. Soc. Lond. B **207**(1167), 187–217 (1980)
14. Durrant-Whyte, H., Bailey, T.: Simultaneous localization and mapping: part i. IEEE Robot. Autom. Mag. **13**(2), 99–110 (2006)
15. Fuentes-Pacheco, J., Ruiz-Ascencio, J., Rendon-Mancha, J.M.: Visual simultaneous localization and mapping: a survey. Artif. Intell. Rev. **43**(1), 55–81 (2015)

Spacecraft Interface Management in Concurrent Engineering Sessions

Philipp M. Fischer[1]([✉]) [iD], Caroline Lange[2] [iD], Volker Maiwald[2] [iD],
Sascha Müller[1] [iD], Andrii Kovalov[1] [iD], Janis Häseker[2], Thomas Gärtner[2] [iD],
and Andreas Gerndt[1] [iD]

[1] DLR (German Aerospace Center),
Software for Space Systems and Interactive Visualization,
Lilienthalplatz 7, 38108 Brunswick, Germany
{philipp.fischer,sa.mueller,andrii.kovalov,andreas.gerndt}@dlr.de
[2] DLR (German Aerospace Center), Institute of Space Systems,
Robert-Hooke-Str. 7, 28359 Bremen, Germany
{caroline.lange,volker.maiwald,janis.haeseker,thomas.gaertner}@dlr.de

Abstract. This paper contributes to the topic of spacecraft interface and data rate management in Concurrent Engineering (CE) sessions. At DLR, CE is used together with a CE process for designing new spacecraft. The software Virtual Satellite supports this process. It provides a shared system model to the engineers to exchange design information. Until today, it supports the structural decomposition of the system and the analysis of design drivers such as the mass or power consumption of the spacecraft. During one of the S2TEP studies for a multi-mission platform it was required to have a closer look to power and data interfaces. This paper discusses the state of the art to this topic and derives a generic approach to it. This approach is customized and finally implemented in Virtual Satellite and directly applied in the S2TEP study.

Keywords: Model Based Systems Engineering ·
Interface Management · Concurrent Engineering ·
Spacecraft engineering

1 Introduction

Interface management is an essential part of spacecraft development. Traditionally, it has not been part of early design studies in Concurrent Engineering (CE) sessions. The presented work is based on hands-on results of the S2TEP project and the novelty of introducing interface modeling into DLR's concurrent engineering process supported by the software Virtual Satellite 4.

At DLR, new spacecraft and missions are designed and studied within the Concurrent Engineering Facility (CEF) in Bremen. The major design drivers analyzed in such a study are the overall mass, typically constrained by the launch mass, as well as the power budget of the system. Besides these two aspects, the

Y. Luo (Ed.): CDVE 2019, LNCS 11792, pp. 54–63, 2019.
https://doi.org/10.1007/978-3-030-30949-7_7

engineers define the functional structure of the spacecraft including a selection of components to fulfill functional requirements. This process is supported by a data-model which is implemented by DLR's software Virtual Satellite. The data-model is used to share and directly analyze system information entered by the engineers [6].

Even though analyzing the aforementioned design drivers produces a good first estimate of the spacecraft, some studies require inspecting other critical areas. One of them is about data rates of communication interfaces between components. To ensure reliable communication between, for example, the On-Board Computer (OBC) and other spacecraft components, an estimate of how much data is transferred on which interface is needed. This information is directly affecting the OBC sizing and the design of communication links. At DLR, this requires the here presented extension to the modeling capabilities provided by Virtual Satellite.

This paper discusses the current state of the art of CE and the data model at DLR. It continues on looking to other approaches dealing with interfaces and data rates including other existing data models and tools. The displayed work then elaborates on the requirements of the engineering use cases of estimating data rates, and defines the new interface extension to the data-model. The paper also provides implementation details to the extension in Virtual Satellite. The discussion finalizes on providing results of the S2TEP project where this new interface extension has been actually used.

2   Related Work to CE Process and Data Modeling

The preliminary design study of a spacecraft for a new mission is often conducted in CEFs such as the one at the Institute of Space Systems in Bremen. Here, the CE studies follow a well-defined process. It defines several aspects of a study, e.g: How many engineers from which domain have to be invited? What type of data model to use for information exchange? Which information has to be gathered at which time? [6].

At DLR such a study is supported by a Model Based Systems Engineering (MBSE) process. It requires inviting around twelve engineers from design critical domains. They discuss the design for usually one to sometimes three weeks. The design is shared in a common system model. This system model is provided by Virtual Satellite. The underlying Conceptual Data Model (CDM) provides modeling capabilities for actually creating the system model. An intrinsic rights management assigns ownership of modeled spacecraft components to responsible engineers. This rights management helps keeping the system model consistent. [6] Virtual Satellite constantly analyzes the system model and provides instant feedback to the engineers [2].

2.1   System Modeling During Concurrent Engineering Studies

During a CE study, the engineers start decomposing the system within the first days. The data-model provides a hierarchical structure of spacecraft components to support this task. The components are grouped in functional domains. As shown in Fig. 1, the spacecraft is separated into functional groups of e.g. On-Board Data Handling (OBDH) and Power Management (PWR). Here the engineers can define the components they want to use. Additionally, they are assigned to their components using the intrinsic rights management. As an example, only the PWR engineer is allowed to change information on power components, but no one else. Contrary, all engineers can read all information from all other engineers [6].

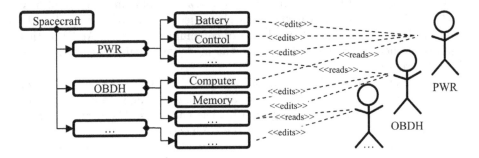

Fig. 1. Structural decomposition and ownership assignment

Information associated with the components is stored in parameters and calculations. The engineers set a parameter such as maximum power by providing a value and a unit. Provided calculations make use of these parameters to e.g. let Virtual Satellite automatically calculate the average power consumption of a component. By convention there are parameters with a special meaning such as the parameter *unit_quantity*. This parameter defines how often the component is built into the spacecraft, whereas *mode_duration* and *duty_cycle* represent the time a spacecraft remains in a specific system mode and how much of that time a component is active. The parameter *unit_active* is important for calculating the power consumptions in case of redundancies, when not all components are turned on at the same time. [6] Visualizing the inputs and outputs of such calculations similar to UML block/interface diagrams was successfully shown in previous work [14]. A language called ICML was proposed to model signals and messages in the frame of interfaces [7].

Virtual Satellite 4 is the latest development. It is intended to support the whole lifecycle of a spacecraft. Since it is impossible to foresee all upcoming requirements on a data-model, it allows extending the data-model along the lifecycle. The Generic System Engineering Language (GSEL) allows defining new concepts for such a CDM extension. Concepts are activated when needed. A concept may contain new structural elements for decomposition, new parameters to store information and calculations to process them. The parameters are defined using an extended version of engineering categories [5]. These categories are similar to the type-object and dynamic-template pattern [8,11]. Engineers can define a category together with properties. These categories can then be instantiated on individual components at run-time, where the engineers can now define the value of the properties [13]. Based on an Eclipse and EMF infrastructure, new concepts can be shipped with additional implemented functionality and installed as new plug-ins [5].

2.2 Related Data-Models for CE and Interface Management

The Open Concurrent Design Tool (OCDT) is developed by the European Space Agency (ESA). It is developed for the use in CE and in ESA's Concurrent Design Facility (CDF) in particular. It provides a CDM called Space Engineering Information Model (SEIM) including capabilities for structural decomposition as well as storing information in parameters. A set of recommended parameters is defined under the name Space Engineering Reference Data Library (SERDL). Calculations are done in external tools such as Microsoft Excel. They can exchange information with the data-model by a generic REST API [3,9].

Virtual Spacecraft Design (VSD) is another tool developed by ESA. It is designed for introducing MBSE into later project phases. It provides capabilities for hierarchical breakdown and structuring of the system, as well as adding components. On top of that, it offers configuration control mechanisms. [4] Information is stored in predefined objects such as state machines or interfaces. Designing functional electrical architecture is well supported by VSD. It allows defining *InterfaceEnds* on components and *Interfaces* connecting the *InterfaceEnds*. Individual information can be stored in engineering categories [13].

SysML provides functionality to model block-diagrams together with ports and interfaces. Blocks within a block-diagram can be defined once and then reused and nested into other blocks, thus allowing a hierarchical decomposition. The blocks can communicate to other blocks through ports. There are different types of ports such as standard ports and flow ports [12]. Standard ports can either provide or consume a service. Signals and data flows should be modeled using flow ports. There is no clear cut definition when to use which one [15].

2.3 Existing Approaches for Interface Design in S2TEP

S2TEP was a project to build a small satellite platform. The platform has been intended to be reused for several missions equipped with different payloads. [1] Such a multi-mission platform requires accurate design on the interface between spacecraft-bus and payload. The analysis of the interface focuses on functional electrical architecture. This comprises data interfaces and power interfaces. In S2TEP a special version of Virtual Satellite was initially used for later design phases after CE studies [10]. In order to handle the interface design at that time, the CDM got extended using the GSEL. The extension provides modeling capabilities for *InterfaceEnds* which can be assigned to some component e.g. an OBC. Additionally *Interfaces* allow point-to-point connections from one *InterfaceEnd* to another. *InterfaceEnds* can be refined by assigning a type. A validator proofs that both *InterfaceEnd* on an *Interface* are of the same kind [5].

3   Defining a New Methodology to CE Interface Modeling

The newly defined methodology is based on the presented work, which shows that modeling interfaces by itself is a well-researched topic. Nevertheless, introducing it for CE studies and introducing such modeling capabilities into the CDM is raising new implications and requirements such as:

1. The model has to obey the rights management and ownership on CDM level.
2. The modeling effort needs to be small to support agility of the studies.
3. The model needs to be precise enough to capture the important information.

3.1   Obeying Ownership on CDM Level

The CDM, as it has been introduced, requires that the information generated by an engineer is stored under their individual rights. Thus, others can only use it but not change it. Therefore engineers should define the connections offered by their components. Hence, the information artifact of offered connections need to be contained in the components. How these components relate to each other, meaning how they are finally connected, is not necessarily information of the same engineer. This could be modeled by someone else who is allowed to use, but not to alter the connections. Therefore, the modeling artifact for actual connections has to reference the connections on the components.

3.2   Conserving Agility for Interface Modeling

The amount of time available during a CE study is limited. The engineers' main task is designing a spacecraft and not the model. This is reflected e.g. by the implicit decomposition using the *unit_quantity* parameter. A similar approach for interfaces is recommended. First, it will create a similar work-flow. Second, it will reduce modeling effort. Third, it will avoid data ambiguities in case of changes to interfaces. Meaning a change is applied to one interface with e.g a *unit_quantity* of 4, rather than changing individual instances of it four times.

3.3   Deriving Interface Types of Interest

Different to signals and messages addressed with ICML, the two main types of interfaces identified in S2TEP are the power and data interfaces similar to VSD. The power engineer is interested in voltage ranges and power consumptions to size their sub-system correctly. The data engineer is interested in correct connection of types and comparison of data rates to match interface capacities.

The power consumption is already analyzed within Virtual Satellite, but power interfaces still need to be added together with parameters defining the voltage range. In early design iterations, this information helps the engineer to summarize the components with their power demands. In later iterations, the engineer can connect all components to the power sub-system and analyze whether required voltage levels and power consumptions match the sources.

The data interfaces are required for analyzing if data links provide the correct capacities. Further, it is of interest whether they are compliant to each other. This means that e.g. a CAN bus should only be connected to another CAN bus interface. The various different types need to be defined per project since some restrict their usage to a subset. Some other projects may introduce special ones, e.g. wireless interfaces. Similar to the power engineer, it is of interest which component is providing how much data. Therefore, new parameters have to be defined to store this information. The data rates depend on the quantity of the component and on how much data the component produces while it is turned on. To now verify capacities it is necessary to not only provide point-to-point interfaces such as in VSD or existing implementations of Virtual Satellite but also bus interfaces. Very often, multiple components are connected to e.g. one CAN bus. Still, other interfaces such as RS485 may require point-to-point connection from an OBC to a component. In the RS485 example, it is of main concern that the types are matching.

Storing the above discussed information in the data-model, it can be used to either automatically validate certain requirements or to read and analyze the data using the Virtual Satellite apps. The apps are a tool where engineers can access and analyze the data-model writing their own Java based programs. The advantage is, that changes to the analysis can be done by the engineers themselves during the CE studies. There is no need to build a new version of Virtual Satellite. To make such analysis-apps work correctly and to create a common understanding, a precise implementation and semantic definition of the model extension is required.

4   CDM Implementation for Interface Modeling in CE

Figure 2 shows the important aspects of the extension to the data-model. Similar to VSD or SysML the extension provides ports which are called *InterfaceEnds*. Two specific ones for data and power are derived from the common abstract class. The abstract class contains the attribute *quantity* reflecting the amount of a given *InterfaceEnd* instantiated on a component. The *PowerInterfaceEnd* contains three attributes defining voltage ranges. The *DataInterfaceEnds* can be typed with an instance of *DataInterfaceType* similar to the interface description in SysML. Two different sets of interfaces are derived from the abstract class: *PointToPointInterface* and *BusInterface*. The first one connects exactly two *InterfaceEnds* while the second connects to a minimum of two.

The engineers can now use these new types for modeling *InterfaceEnds* to their component. There is no clear cut definition where the *Interfaces* should be modeled. One possibility is to provide a harness component for that purpose. The other alternative is that e.g. the PWR engineer takes care of modeling them and adding the relevant interfaces to some of the PWR components. To model the redundancy of interfaces, there is also no clear cut answer. One possibility is to model the *InterfaceEnds* and *Interfaces* twice. Attention has to be paid to the analysis of e.g. a redundant power interface, since it is not necessarily said that

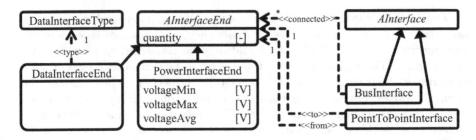

Fig. 2. Data-model extension for modeling interfaces

the power has to be provided twice but most likely once on either the nominal or redundant *Interface*. Unfortunately, this leaves room for ambiguities.

Alongside these new types, new parameters and calculations for defining the data rates are introduced based on the GSEL. The parameters are shown in Table 1 providing a short overview to their abbreviation, meaning, and if their values are manually entered (M) or a calculated (C). The corresponding calculations are shown in the following equations:

Table 1. New component parameters introduced for data rate calculations

Abbreviation	M/C	Meaning
DDutyCycle	M	Amount of time the comp. produces data when on
DUnitOn	M	Amount of data produced for one comp. turned on
DUnitStby	M	Amount of data produced for one comp. in stand by
DUnitOnWMrg	C	Amount of data plus the comp. design margin
DUnitStbyWMrg	C	Amount of data plus the comp. design margin
DUnitAvgWithMrg	C	Average amount of data with margin
DAvgWithMrg	C	Average amount of data multiplied for all comp.

$$DUnitOnWMrg = DUnitOn + (DUnitOn * mrgMaturity) \tag{1}$$
$$DUnitStbyWMrg = DUnitStby + (DUnitStby * mrgMaturity) \tag{2}$$
$$DCombDutyCycle = ComponentPwr.dutyCycle * dutyCycle \tag{3}$$
$$DUnitAvgWMrg = DUnitOnWMrg * DCombDutyCycle+ \tag{4}$$
$$DUnitStbyWMrg * (1 - DCombDutyCycle) \tag{5}$$
$$DAvgWMrg = DUnitAvgWMrg * ComponentPwr.activeUnits \tag{6}$$

These equations are similar to the already existing power calculations. The maturity of the component used is defined in the general parameters of Virtual Satellite. The combined duty cycle needs special attention. It makes additional use of the duty cycle from the power parameters. The reason for this is, that the component will only produce data in a limited time while it is turned on.

5   Application in the S2TEP CE System Model

The above implementation has been developed during one of the S2TEP CE studies in 2018. During this study, the engineers decided to further investigate power and data interfaces. Based on the engineers' requirements, the above presented implementation has been developed and installed to Virtual Satellite. Once this new CDM extension had been used to model the first interfaces, the app engine of Virtual Satellite had been used to summarize the information and to condense it into Excel sheets.

Figure 3 shows Virtual Satellite with the original S2TEP data set. The hierarchical decomposition is on the left. It presents *DataInterfaceEnds* (DIE) for the PCDU component. One of the DIEs is named nominal, the other is named redundant following the aforementioned concept. Both of them are typed as CAN bus. These types are defined beforehand in the *DataInterfaceTypeCollection* (DITC) which is a new structural element introduced by the concept. Nevertheless, the purpose of that element is solely for data organization and has no further semantic meaning for the modeled system.

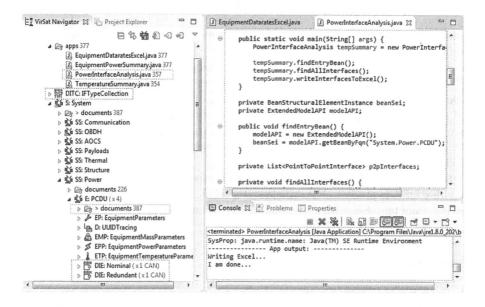

Fig. 3. Virtual Satellite 4 executing an app summarizing power interfaces

The right hand side of Fig. 3 shows an app that has been implemented. Executing it, it collects all available *Interfaces* and *InterfaceEnds* and creates and overview which is stored in an Excel file. The Excel file is located in the documents folder and is therefore shared across the whole study group. It can be generated regularly during the study based on the latest information of all domain experts. Hence, it provides better insight into the current design e.g. when comparing voltage levels of power interfaces.

6   Summary

The work described here contributes to the question of introducing data and power interface modeling into CE studies. Looking to the state of the art, analyzing interfaces and data rates is not particularly new. Also Virtual Satellite provides some functionality for later design phases already. Other projects such as VSD from ESA address functional electrical architecture with interfaces but no data rates in particular. Still all of them, together with SysML ports and connections, have their share to the answer given here.

An important aspect is that Virtual Satellite and the data-model is tailored to the CEF process. One of the critical aspects during CE studies is time. Therefore, the data-model has to be simple to use for the engineers. As a consequence, multiple components of the same type are not explicitly modeled but indirectly reflected in a parameter stating their amount. This means that introducing interfaces should not result in extensive extra modeling effort.

The resulting extension to the CDM delivers the following parts: A new engineering category with parameters to define data rates per component, calculations that make use of these parameters, and new types such as *DataInterfaceEnds* and *PointToPointInterfaces* to actually model connections of components. Already existing concepts such as calculations of power parameters have been adopted as much as possible.

This new extension has actually been developed during one of the S2TEP CE studies and integrated into Virtual Satellite. The new types and categories have been used by the engineers to model data and interface information about the system. The PWR and OBDH engineer summarized this information for sizing their components using Virtual Satellite's app engine. This demonstrates the general flexibility of Virtual Satellite allowing to introduce new concepts quickly, even during a CE session.

Finally, this implementation is a successful extension to what Virtual Satellite provides for CE studies. Nevertheless, the topic of interfaces can be complex leaving room for ambiguities e.g. when talking about redundancies. These aspects should be addressed in future work.

References

1. Dannemann, F., Jetzschmann, M., Lange, C.: Enabling technologies and processes for space missions - the S2TEP platform. In: 69th International Astronautical Congress (IAC), Bremen, Germany, October 2018
2. Deshmukh, M., Schaus, V., Fischer, P.M., Quantius, D., Maiwald, V., Gerndt, A.: Decision support tool for concurrent engineering in space mission design. In: Stjepandic, J., Rock, G., Bil, C. (eds.) Concurrent Engineering Approaches for Sustainable Product Development in a Multi-Disciplinary Environment, vol. 1, pp. 497–508. Springer, London (2013). https://doi.org/10.1007/978-1-4471-4426-7_43
3. ESA: OCDT community portal. https://ocdt.esa.int/. Accessed 20 Apr 2016
4. ESA: Virtual spacecraft design, April 2013. http://www.vsd-project.org/. Accessed 20 Apr 2016

5. Fischer, P.M., Lüdtke, D., Lange, C., Roshani, F.C., Dannemann, F., Gerndt, A.: Implementing model-based system engineering for the whole lifecycle of a spacecraft. CEAS Space J. **9**(3), 351–365 (2017). https://doi.org/10.1007/s12567-017-0166-4

6. Fischer, P.M., Deshmukh, M., Maiwald, V., Quantius, D., Gomez, A.M., Gerndt, A.: Conceptual data model: a foundation for successful concurrent engineering. Concurrent Eng. Res. Appl. **26**(1), 55–76 (2018). https://doi.org/10.1177/1063293X17734592

7. Gianni, D., Schaus, V., D'Ambrogio, A., Gerndt, A., Lisi, M., de Simone, P.: Model-based interface engineering in concurrent engineering facilities: motivations and possible applications to systems and service systems engineering. In: 6th International Conference on Systems & Concurrent Engineering for Space Applications (SECESA), Stuttgart, Germany, October 2014

8. Johnson, R., Woolf, B.: Type object. In: Pattern Languages of Program Design, vol. 3, pp. 47–65. Addison-Wesley Longman Publishing Co., Inc., Boston (1997)

9. de Koning, H.P., Gerené, S., Ferreira, I., Pickering, A., Beyer, F., Vennekens, J.: Open concurrent design tool - ESA community open source - ready to go! (2014). http://esaconferencebureau.com/docs/default-source/14c08_docs/open-concurrent-design-tool--esa-community-open-source-ready-to-go!.pdf. Accessed 27 Jan 2017

10. Lange, C., Grundmann, J.T., Kretzenbacher, M., Fischer, P.M.: Systematic reuse and platforming: application examples for enhancing reuse with model-based systems engineering methods in space systems development. Concurrent Eng. Res. Appl. **26**(1), 77–92 (2018). https://doi.org/10.1177/1063293X17736358

11. Lyardet, F.D.: The dynamic template pattern. In: The 4th Pattern Languages of Programming Conference, Monticello, Illinois, USA (1997)

12. OMG: System modelling language - version 1.5. Technical report, Object Management Group OMG (2017)

13. Rey, J.: Modeling with VSEE: Definition of guidelines and exploitation of the models - YGT final report, August 2013. http://www.vsd-project.org/download/documents/YGT%20final%20report%20Rey%20V2.pdf. Accessed 19 July 2016

14. Schaus, V., Müller, J., Deshmukh, M., Braukhane, A., Gerndt, A.: Bidirectional graphical modelling supporting concurrent spacecraft design. In: 6th International Conference on Systems & Concurrent Engineering for Space Applications (SECESA). Stuttgart, Germany, October 2014

15. Weilkiens, T.: Systems Engineering mit SysML/UML: Modellierung, Analyse, Design. dpunkt.verlag GmbH, Heidelberg (2006)

Enhancing Automation in the Construction Equipment Industry Through Implementation of BIM

Christoph Paul Schimanski[1,2](✉) , Carmen Marcher[1,2](✉) ,
Giovanni Toller[2](✉), Gabriele Pasetti Monizza[2](✉) ,
and Dominik T. Matt[1,2](✉)

[1] Faculty of Science and Technology, Free University of Bozen-Bolzano,
Bolzano, Italy
christophpaul.schimanski@natec.unibz.it,
christoph.schimanski@fraunhofer.it.it
[2] Fraunhofer Italia Research, Bolzano, Italy

Abstract. Building Information Modeling (BIM) is becoming increasingly important in the construction industry and affects almost all stakeholders from building owners, planners and contractors to building operators. However, little importance is given in the academic debate to the relationship between BIM and construction equipment providers. This raises the question how the BIM method can be used to generate benefits in this sector. The presenting researchers, in cooperation with a local construction equipment provider, have selected its container construction division as a case study and analyzed how current processes can be streamlined and automated with the help of BIM. In this context, new automation processes, BIM-object libraries and add-ins for one of the most common BIM authoring software have been developed. Through this modular design approach, a flexible and lean BIM-based Configure-to-Order production system is created. This study presents the conceptual development of this BIM-based production system for construction equipment providers considering both methodological examinations and functioning software prototypes. The BIM-based production system is currently tested by the industry partner in pilot projects and preliminary findings are presented in this study.

Keywords: BIM · Configure-to-Order · Industry 4.0 ·
Lean production system design · Algorithms

1 Introduction

Digitization and automation can be considered as potential key for productivity enhancement in construction [1]. Building Information Modeling (BIM) in this regard takes the role of a representative of industry 4.0 in construction [2, 3]. BIM models describe physical and functional properties of buildings and therefore consist of both geometric and semantic data. The BIM data exchange between the individual project stakeholders is mainly carried out via the neutral exchange format of the Industry Foundation Classes (IFC). This is a data structure based on the EXPRESS modeling

© Springer Nature Switzerland AG 2019
Y. Luo (Ed.): CDVE 2019, LNCS 11792, pp. 64–73, 2019.
https://doi.org/10.1007/978-3-030-30949-7_8

language. However, the EXPRESS schema offers few possibilities for effective data retrieval and manipulation, so that simple and user-friendly data processing in the non-proprietary IFC format remains difficult [4].

In this study, we will show that BIM data querying techniques based on Visual Programming Languages (VPL) have the potential to fill this gap. We will further work out that such techniques can constitute a valuable instrument for BIM data manipulation which is suitable also for construction equipment providers (CEP).

The construction equipment company which cooperated in this study can be defined as a Configure-to-Order (CTO) driven service provider which designs and configures container facilities in response to individual customer requests. The container themselves are composed of a modular precast system varying in size and panel configuration. We will demonstrate how BIM data in such a CTO-environment can be structured and used to allow for efficient and automized work preparation for the assembly of the final product. By doing so, this study contributes to answering the research question of *how the BIM approach can be effectively used in the construction equipment industry*.

2   State of the Art

2.1   BIM for the Construction Equipment Industry

Feng and Hsu [5] propose a framework for automatized planning of scaffolding systems which is based on an ontology model from the perspective of material management. They make use of VPL scripts to generate scaffolding objects automatically within a BIM environment. The quantity take-offs are then transferred to a MS Access database which is used to manage the material supply chain. At this stage of their research, prototypical implementations are limited to one single scaffolding type.

Other literature deals with BIM-supported crane selection and crane setup as well as site layout planning [6, 7]. Ji et al. [6] consider standards and normative regulations as well as expert interviews for defining criteria for tower crane planning based on optimization models. BIM-models are used as a visual support for disclosing e.g. potential crane collisions, whilst the meta-data in BIM models is not explicitly deployed. Abbott et al. [7] on the other hand focus on mobile crane applications. As a function of changing locations of use, the authors emphasize the importance of appropriate selection of mobile cranes to avoid accidents on site. To prevent reliance solely on the experience of site engineers, they propose a framework for crane selection leveraging BIM models in terms of both determining best fitting cranes and controlling the selection through 3D representation.

Jahr and Borrmann [8] describe the utilization of BIM to select and configure the equipment for construction sites in a more holistic way. In their study, construction equipment refers to seven different classes comprising - amongst others - construction machinery, office facilities and site security (e.g. fences). The focus is the creation of a rule-based knowledge inference system which helps to identify the most adequate equipment and to accelerate the planning process relying on BIM information. However, applying their approach result in meta-data regarding optimized selections, whilst 3D-representations of the selected site equipment as BIM objects are not available.

2.2   VPL Applications in the Construction Domain

A VPL is generally defined as formal language whose syntax and semantics are presented in a visual way, which makes it more amenable to Non-IT experts [4]. In principal however, visual programming has the same objective as coding-based programming using high-level languages such as Java or C#, which is to define algorithms for reading and/or manipulation of data [9]. Usually, VPL make use of canvas as working planes, where the user can place a variety of functions and variables defined in available libraries. These elements are depicted graphically as blocks representing nodes in a program. Like graph theory, these blocks are linked by simply directed edges representing data flow between two blocks, whilst the arguments within a node work as in a text-based code [9]. Figure 1 shows an example for a VPL condition statement.

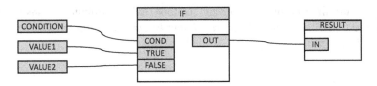

Fig. 1. VPL principle [10]

Previous and current research in the field of BIM programming based on VPL is mainly dealing with the integration of environmental sensor data such as light, humidity or CO_2-sensors with BIM-models [11], or the development of automated code checking algorithms which aim at streamlining the verification process of BIM-models according to legal requirements [12]. In a similar context, other researchers deal with the automation of holistic compliance checking processes in BIM models by making use of VPL [13]. In addition to code checking applications, the authors also analyzed automated test procedures regarding e.g. owner's specifications and general project requirements. Another example of retrieving and manipulating BIM data by means of VPL is described in [14]. They propose a framework to automate model data retrieval to support billing and payment processes during the execution phase.

Contrary to BIM data retrieval, other studies focus on VPL as enablers of generative and parametric design techniques (GPT) in architecture and engineering design. With this regard, the work of Pasetti Monizza et al. [2] is an example of GPT applied to the improvement of process efficiency in manufacturing of timber structures, whilst Bonilla Castro and García Alvarado [15] focus on the thermal design of buildings.

The studies listed are all examples on how to apply VPL for BIM applications in the context of design and execution processes. However, besides the earlier mentioned example of automated scaffolding planning [5], there are hardly any examples of VPL-BIM applications with focus on CEP. To us, this appears to be a gap in research in the area of BIM programming for CEP, since VPL constitute a promising approach to use BIM models in a tailor-made way. Taking this into account, we will make use of VPL techniques in a BIM environment to streamline and automate current processes of a local industry partner representing a CEP. The selected research methodology, the case study as well as preliminary findings are described in the following paragraphs.

3   Research Methodology

In this study we will follow a combined research approach consisting of Design Science Research (DSR) and Action Research (AR). As DSR and AR are in principle compatible as found in [16], both approaches are pursued in a mutually supportive manner. More in detail, DSR is interested in constructing new artefacts based on a distinct problem-solving hypothesis to solve a certain a problem, whilst AR is more concerned about understanding reality. Reality with this regard could refer to the same problem as addressed in DSR but understanding insights with respect to this problem are gained by causing practical interventions and observing the outcomes. In this sense, DSR can deliver artefacts which are introduced into practice by AR to test the hypothesis for solving the stated problem (Fig. 2).

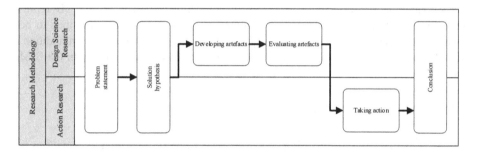

Fig. 2. Research methodology

Regarding the problem statement of this study, the above presented research question will be re-formulated to *"the construction equipment industry lacks in exploiting BIM data"*. The hypothesis for a potential solution then is, that targeted retrieval and application of BIM data can be used beneficially for process automation in the work preparation phase in this sector. To test this hypothesis, we have developed concrete artefacts for testing purposes in a pilot project with respect to DSR which are namely: (1) The definition of new BIM-based processes, (2) a BIM object library for containers, (3) BIM-based software tools and (4) a virtual container warehouse (VCW).

4   Conducting the Research

4.1   Starting Point

The case study was carried out together with a local company in South Tyrol, whose core business is the rental of construction machinery and equipment. The department of container constructions of this company was selected to start the investigations.

First, the current processes were recorded and graphically visualized in the form of process maps in BPMN notation. In the course of this process analysis, weak points were identified, possible improvement measures were worked out and discussed with the responsible employees. Through this approach, starting points were located within the current process in which a BIM implementation and process adjustments could potentially lead to shorter durations, more automation and less resource demand. The found improvement measures refer mainly to the phases of bid creation and work preparation. More in detail, the current process is characterized by customer requirements for a container facility being created in 2D using Autodesk AutoCAD®. The drawings are printed out and afterwards, an employee physically must enter the container warehouse and check which container could fit best - i.e. which container has the least modification effort to meet the requirements of the drawing. After manual selection, the container ID is written down manually on the 2D printout and later transferred to AutoCAD®. For each container ID there exist also 2D plans (floor plan and views), which must also be manually updated for all containers, since its configuration has changed.

In contrast, the target picture of the BIM-based process is shaped in such a way that the bid drawing is created with BIM-capable modeling software, so that 3D representations and required meta-data can become part of it. The meta-data is then to be used to automate the process of selecting containers from the warehouse. In addition, all 2D plans for the assigned containers are to be derived automatically from the BIM model.

4.2 Development of Artefacts

BIM-Based Process Optimization. An BIM object library for Autodesk Revit® was created, which in the future will form the basis for the creation of the bid drawing with all customer requirements. The meta-data of these requirements will then be transferred with the help of VPL to an Excel based tool, that we called *Container Manager*. Within the Container Manager, the available containers are imported from the VCW, the existing container configurations are compared with the customer requirements and an optimal container assignment is proposed with regard to minimum modification costs. After the containers have been assigned within the Container Manager, the information about the container IDs is fed back into the drawing using another VPL script. All 2D plans of the containers can then be automatically created, again with the help of a VPL script. The VPL scripts were implemented as add-ins for Autodesk Revit® with the free extension Dynamo®. The software selection was based on the existing software suites of the industry partner, but underlying logic and algorithms can be repeated with other suitable tools. Figure 3 illustrates the practical procedure.

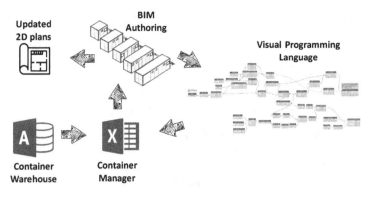

Fig. 3. BIM-based process: interplay of developed artefacts

BIM-Object Library. A total of five different container types was modelled for the object library, covering the most common applications in practice. The containers have a modular design and differ in the length of their long sides (Table 1).

Table 1. Selected container types

Container type	Length (ext.) [m]	# Panels	Width (ext.) [m]	# Panels
BM 10'	2.989	2.5	2.435	2
BM 16'	4.885	4	2.435	2
BM 20'	6.055	5	2.435	2
BM 24'	7.355	6	2.435	2
BM 30'	9.120	7	2.435	2

In the object library, the container outer dimensions represent the skeleton of the respective container type. The spaces in between are paneled. For each panel-slot different panel types can be selected (e.g. door panel, window panel or full panel). The different panel types are also part of the object library (Fig. 4).

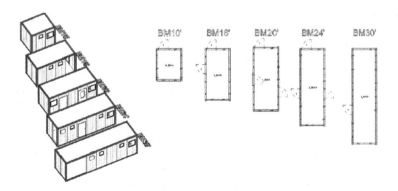

Fig. 4. BIM container object library

The panel types and their position in the container were parameterized, so that a clear comparison of drawing containers and available containers in the warehouse within the Container Manager is possible with regard to the determination of the modification effort. The parameterization therefore decides whether a panel must be installed, exchanged or entirely removed to meet the client's demand. A prerequisite for this is the digital inventory of the current container stock regarding the exact panel configuration. The latter has been realized by implementing the VCW.

Container Manager. This is a bundle of VPL-based add-ins for Autodesk Revit® that imports and exports BIM container information to an Excel workbook, where the assignment of containers available in the warehouse to the drawn containers can be done. The information regarding the available physical containers is taken from the connected database (VCW).

In order to ensure that the best possible assignment of containers can be made, a selection support has been implemented. This support functionality makes it possible to determine for each drawn container which of the containers currently in the warehouse would require the least modification effort. In addition, information about the current warehouse location and rental or sales price is available, so that a target-oriented container selection can be made, depending on which criteria are most decisive for the selection in the project (e.g. most favorable configuration vs. proximity of the warehouse).

After the assignment of container IDs, the Container Manager imports those IDs back into the BIM model and renames the corresponding drawn containers. This information enrichment is then the basis for deriving automatically 2D plans for every container ID with its new configuration.

Virtual Container Warehouse (VCW). In order to consider the fact that the industry partner's physical warehouse can be equipped with more than 300 containers and that the equipment often varies with regard to container typology and purpose (rental or sale), a digital representation of the physical warehouse making use of an MS Access database has been implemented. This database can be queried according to currently available containers and the corresponding information can be exported to MS Excel and the Container Manager where the data is available for container assignment.

4.3   Case Study

The test phase of the application of the Container Manager and the BIM object libraries embedded in the new defined processes took place on a pilot project of a container facility to be erected for a milk-distributing company in South Tyrol. This project comprised a two-story container system with a total of 28 containers of the types BM 20' (x 24) and BM 24' (x 4), whereby the type BM 24' was used exclusively as a corridor container.

This project was selected because the documentation of the work preparation in the form of plans, container assignments and the corresponding resource demand was already available as a result of the application of the traditional process (Table 2). To compare this data with the BIM approach, we re-engineered the entire project using the new tools: First the project was modelled in Autodesk Revit® making use of the BIM object library, the panels were configured accordingly and then the meta-data was exported to the Container Manager. Then the assignment of containers from the warehouse was done and the re-import of container IDs to Revit® was carried out, where the final generation of the 2D plans was triggered.

4.4   Preliminary Findings

The findings of this study obtained so far consist on the one hand of the developed artefacts. These artefacts together are ready to use and can be further examined in upcoming use cases. On the other hand, the defined BIM-based process making use of these artefacts was tested in a first pilot project: Preliminary results of measuring the impact show that the time for creation the bid drawing does not change notably but the time needed for the selection process of the right containers as well as generation of up-to-date to drawings of the new container configuration can be reduced dramatically. These results are given in Table 2.

Table 2. Comparison process duration: current state vs. BIM-based

Sub-process	Current process	BIM-based
Creation of bid drawing	2 h	2 h
Container assignment	3 h	0.5 h
Creation of 2D plans	2 h	0.1 h

5   Discussion

The use case results revealed that the added value provided by the Container Manager application is especially reflected in the time required for the assignment of the physical containers and creation of 2D plans – whilst maintaining almost the same effort in the drawing phase. The durations of work preparation could be shortened and the calculation of bid sheets for clients was partially automated, since joint use of the developed tools make it unnecessary for employees to be physically present in the container warehouse to choose the most suited container with respect to the client's needs. The selection procedure thus could be reduced significantly and the susceptibility to errors in decision-making has also been decreased. Thanks to the database connection, cost coefficients of containers and panels are linked to the selected containers. Thus, the end prices bided to clients are calculated automatically and are always accurate with respect to the bid drawing. This data-driven procedure diminishes the risk of incorrect cost estimates and thus the risk of demanding too high prices and therefore not receiving potential orders, or - vice versa - too low prices and hence selling below value. In principle, these preliminary findings can be regarded as positive and make direct application of the new BIM process recommendable.

A limitation of this study is that only one single case study has been considered so that the repetition of artefact implementation according to DSR is yet to be done.

Furthermore, other cost factors influencing the final bid sum must be considered in further research. These include, for example, labor costs and time required for installation and dismantling of panels and containers.

6 Conclusion and Outlook

This paper describes the attempt to use BIM model beneficially in the construction equipment industry making use of VPL techniques by investigating the container construction department of a local company in South Tyrol. These investigations are intended to contribute to answering the question of opportunities of BIM applications for this field of the construction industry, which is largely disregarded in literature.

To this end, a combined DSR-AR research approach was followed whose outputs in terms of artefacts such as new process definitions, BIM object libraries and add-ins for BIM-authoring software were tested in a use case scenario. Preliminary results were presented which revealed significant time savings in the bid creation and work preparation phase. These results underline the great potential of BIM applications also in the construction equipment industry. In addition, a way how BIM model information can be used with respect to individual requirements is presented by means of VPL techniques.

Currently, the evaluation of the pilot project applications is ongoing. Other parameters, which are being analyzed regarding the BIM impacts, include the automated calculation of modification and installation durations and the corresponding resource demand. The challenge in this case is the fact that, although the new BIM approach generates accurate quantities for installation tasks, these represent repetitive activities that are influenced by learning effects. This means that previously assumed linear proportional performance factors are no longer applicable and require the determination of more adequate factors to calculate durations correctly. The results of these considerations will be with the starting point for future studies.

Acknowledgements. We would like to thank the company *Niederstätter AG* in South Tyrol, Italy for the possibility the perform scientific investigations in the field of BIM for CEP through making available real-world project data and being available for interviews and in-depth process analyses.

References

1. Matt, D.T., Rauch, E.: Implementing lean in engineer-to-order manufacturing. In: Modrák, V., Semančo, P. (eds.) Handbook of Research on Design and Management of Lean Production Systems, pp. 148–172. IGI Global (2014)
2. Pasetti Monizza, G., Bendetti, C., Matt, D.T.: Parametric and Generative Design techniques in mass-production environments as effective enablers of Industry 4.0 approaches in the Building Industry. Autom. Constr. **92**, 270–285 (2018)
3. Dallasega, P., Rauch, E., Matt, D.T., Fronk, A.: Increasing productivity in ETO construction projects through a lean methodology for demand predictability. In: Proceeding of 5th International Conference on Industrial Engineering and Operations Management, IEOM 2015 (2015)

4. Preidel, C., Daum, S., Borrmann, A.: Data retrieval from building information models based on visual programming. Vis. Eng. 5 (2017). https://doi.org/10.1186/s40327-017-0055-0
5. Feng, C.W., Hsu, T.F.: Using BIM to automate information generation for assembling scaffolding - a material management approach. In: Proceedings of 34th International Symposium on Automation and Robotics Construction (2017). https://doi.org/10.22260/isarc2017/0086
6. Ji, Y., Sankaran, B., Choi, J., Leite, F.: Integrating BIM and optimization techniques for enhanced tower crane planning. Comput. Civ. Eng. **2017**(3), 67–74 (2017)
7. Abbott, E.L.S., Peng, L., Chua, D.K.H.: Using building information modelling to facilitate decision making for a mobile crane lifting plan. In: Şahin, S. (ed.) EPPM 2017. LNME, pp. 77–89. Springer, Cham (2018). https://doi.org/10.1007/978-3-319-74123-9_9
8. Jahr, K., Borrmann, A.: Semi-automated site equipment selection and configuration through formal knowledge representation and inference. Adv. Eng. Inform. **38**, 488–500 (2018). https://doi.org/10.1016/j.aei.2018.08.015
9. Pavlov, P.: Automation of information flow from Revit to BSim using Dynamo. Master thesis. Aalborg University, Denmark, p. 70 (2015). https://projekter.aau.dk/projekter/files/231026964/Dynamo_Project.pdf
10. Ritter, F., Preidel, C., Singer, D.: Visuelle Programmiersprachen im Bauwesen Stand der Technik und aktuelle Entwicklungen. In: Real Ehrlich, C.M., Blut, C. (eds.) Bauinformatik 2015 : Beiträge zum 27. Forum Bauinformatik, pp. 1–9 (2015)
11. Kensek, K.M.: Integration of Environmental Sensors with BIM: case studies using Arduino, Dynamo, and the Revit API. Inf. la Construcción **66**, e044 (2014)
12. Preidel, C., Borrmann, A., Dimyadi, J., Solihin, W.: Towards code compliance checking on the basis of a visual programming language. J. Inf. Technol. Constr. **21**, 402–421 (2016). http://www.itcon.org/2016/25. ISSN 1874-4753
13. Ghannad, P., Lee, Y.C., Dimyadi, J., Solihin, W.: Automated BIM data validation integrating open-standard schema with visual programming language. Adv. Eng. Inform. **40**, 14–28 (2019). https://doi.org/10.1016/j.aei.2019.01.006
14. Feng, C.-W., Chen, Y.-J., Yu, H.-Y.: Employing ontology and BIM to facilitate the information for subcontractor's payment requests and ledger generation. In: Proceedings of 34th International Symposium on Automation and Robotics Construction (2017). https://doi.org/10.22260/isarc2017/0109
15. Bonilla Castro, A., García Alvarado, R.: BIM-Integration of solar thermal systems in early housing design. Rev. la construcción **16**, 323–338 (2017)
16. Iivary, J., Venable, J.: Action research and design science research - Seemingly similar but decisively dissimilar. In: Proceedings of ECIS 2009, vol. 1, p. 73 (2009)

Digital Availability of Product Information for Collaborative Engineering of Spacecraft

Diana Peters[1]([✉])[iD], Philipp M. Fischer[2][iD], Philipp M. Schäfer[1][iD],
Kobkaew Opasjumruskit[1][iD], and Andreas Gerndt[2][iD]

[1] Software Systems for Digitalization, German Aerospace Center (DLR),
Mälzerstraße 3, 07745 Jena, Germany
{diana.peters,p.schaefer,kobkaew.opasjumruskit}@dlr.de
[2] Software for Space Systems and Interactive Visualization,
German Aerospace Center (DLR), Lilienthalplatz 7, 38108 Brunswick, Germany
{philipp.fischer,andreas.gerndt}@dlr.de

Abstract. In this paper, we introduce a system to collect product information from manufacturers and make it available in tools that are used for concurrent design of spacecraft. The planning of a spacecraft needs experts from different disciplines, like propulsion, power, and thermal. Since these different disciplines rely on each other there is a high need for communication between them, which is often realized by a Model-Based Systems Engineering (MBSE) process and corresponding tools. We show by comparison that the product information provided by manufacturers often does not match the information needed by MBSE tools on a syntactic or semantic level. The information from manufacturers is also currently not available in machine-readable formats. Afterwards, we present a prototype of a system that makes product information from manufacturers directly available in MBSE tools, in a machine-readable way.

Keywords: Model-Based Systems Engineering ·
Product information · Spacecraft · Concurrent engineering

1 Introduction

Complex systems cannot be realized by a single person or discipline due to the systems size and heterogeneity. The field of Systems Engineering (SE) aims to find solutions how to realize such systems successfully. One approach emerging in the SE field is Model-Based SE (MBSE), which "can be described as the formalized application of modeling principles, methods, languages, and tools to the entire lifecycle of large, complex, interdisciplinary, sociotechnical systems." [28]. By MBSE tool, we denote any software application that supports the development of a model by participants from different disciplines. The spacecraft components specified in an MBSE tool we denote as Equipment, while spacecraft components built or offered by manufacturers are denoted as products.

Y. Luo (Ed.): CDVE 2019, LNCS 11792, pp. 74–83, 2019.
https://doi.org/10.1007/978-3-030-30949-7_9

The sources of information that engineers enter in MBSE tools for spacecraft design are PDF data sheets, spreadsheets, and engineers' implicit knowledge. Even if information is stored and transmitted digitally, it is often not machine-readable and especially not automatically available in an MBSE tool. Instead, a human has to take the information from a document to enter it into another system. This manual process is both slow and error-prone. Furthermore, every manufacturer uses a different format and a different vocabulary to represent information. Sometimes, not even PDF data sheets are available—Jahnke and Martelo found, that "From the 34 found suppliers of Cubesat related hardware, 62% do publish detailed specifications and datasheets on their website." [22], which means that more than one third of the suppliers do not make this information available on their website.

As spacecraft are not anymore always one-of-a-kind products, CubeSats[1] and small series of satellites become more common. According to Lange et al. [23], it becomes also more important to reuse information from former missions. This does not only include the MBSE models themselves, but also for example spacecraft component databases, where engineers could, additionally to the information from manufacturers, also add their own data, e.g. "template components" for different size categories of spacecraft.

Jahnke and Martelo also pointed out that "[...] the task during the CE sessions of the single domain expert is shifted from actual design of the sub-system and estimation of key-parameters towards the selection of the most suiting existing solution from e.g. a database and interface cross-check to other subsystems." [22]. So it becomes more important to find a product that fits certain requirements, including interface compatibility to other products, then to design a product from scratch.

In this paper we point out the problems with the current product information exchange between manufacturer and customer, collect requirements for a system to overcome these problems, and present a prototype system that makes product information available in the in-house MBSE tool of Virtual Satellite.

2   Related Work

Several approaches exist to make the whole MBSE process or phases of it possible or easier. This includes software applications, standards, and models of space systems.

The life cycle of a space system, as described by the European Cooperation for Space Standardization (ECSS), the European Space Agency (ESA), and the National Aeronautics and Space Administration (NASA), consists of phases 0 and A through F [2][25], where in this paper we focus of the early planning phases 0 and A. Virtual Spacecraft Design (VSD) by ESA [9], Virtual Satellite by the German Aerospace Center (DLR) [14], RangeDB by Airbus Defense and Space [8], and Open Concurrent Design Tool (OCDT) [13] as well as CDP4 [1]

---

[1] CubeSats are mini satellites made of $10\,cm \times 10\,cm \times 10\,cm$ units and often use COTS (commercial off-the-shelf) products.

by RHEA Group all aim to support an MBSE process following the suggestions made by ECSS in two Technical Memorandums, ECSS-E-TM-10-23A [12] and ECSS-E-TM-10-25A [10]. These tools have an internal model of the spacecraft and its subsystems. They all require manual input of Equipment data. They all support at least either the import or export of Excel spreadsheets. Though following similar ideas and guidelines, the parameters provided by these tools, and especially the names used for those parameters, vary. Table 1 shows an overview of the mass and structure parameters of most of the mentioned MBSE tools. We selected mass and structure parameters, because those are among the most relevant parameters for the early planning phases.

Table 1. Mass and structure parameters of equipment at different MBSE tools (units in braces). The parameter names for Virtual Satellite 4 and VSD were taken from installations of the tools. OCDT and CDP4 directly implement the ParameterType concept from ECSS-E-TM-10-25. At Virtual Satellite, the margin parameters are not defined at Equipment level, but below.

MBSE Tool	Virtual Satellite 4	VSD	OCDT/CDP4
Mass	massPerUnit (kg)	Weigth [sic!] (gram)	mass (kg)
Parameters			mass margin
Structure	radius (m)		diameter (m)
Parameters	shape		shape
	sizeX (m)	Height (millimetre)	height (m)
	sizeY (m)	Length (millimetre)	length (m)
	sizeZ (m)	Width (millimetre)	width (m)

The aim of standards and formats is to provide a base for interfaces, so systems can exchange information directly, reliably, and without human interaction. For the small field of Spacecraft Onboard Interface Services the Consultative Committee for Space Data Systems (CCSDS) developed a standard for Electronic Data Sheets (EDS) [30]. EDS allow the exchange of information in a machine-readable format; no manual data transformation is necessary. Units, like "gram" or "inch" are defined in the EDS dictionary of terms, as are quantity kinds, like "massQK" or "lengthQK". But there is no definition that connects "gram" with "massQK" or that states that every physical component must have a mass.

ISO 10303 (STEP) [26] is an ISO standard for product manufacturing information, i.e., how a product is supposed to be produced, but it can be used for the whole life cycle of a product. Regarding space engineering, the technical report ECSS-E-TM-10-20A [11] lists what part of the STEP standard should be used for information exchange between which disciplines. This regards mostly computer-aided design (CAD) and physical structure contexts while other parts of the standard, like electronics, are neglected. A rather simple format to store 3D information is STL (STereoLithographie, also Standard Triangulation/Tesselation

Language) [29], which is supported by most CAD tools and used for additive manufacturing.

The specification of information exchange between manufacturers and MBSE tools does not only include technical protocols but also the information on which data is relevant in which context and what is its semantic meaning. Tailored modeling languages and tools are required to describe the semantic model of a spacecraft. Hennig et al. looked into existing languages and tools that can be used to describe Conceptual Data Models (CDMs). They conclude that none of them are ideal for this task [15]. In the same year, Ait-Ameur et al. introduced a special ontology modeling language (PLIB) for engineering in general [4]. Following their former analysis, Hennig et al. developed a conceptual data modeling language, SCDML [16], and also an ontology to describe space system design data [17]. Hoppe et al. also mentioned the benefits of ontologies and Web Ontology Language (OWL) together with the Eclipse Modeling Framework (EMF) for the MBSE process [18,19,21]. On top of that, they built the Semantic Engineering Modeling Framework (SEMF) [20]. MARVL CIP [6] is a platform that aims to support the information exchange between agencies and manufacturers across the whole life cycle of the spacecraft.

All these approaches target at the models in the MBSE process itself and sometimes at the question of how to use the same model across different phases or how to map between models of different phases. They should be taken into account to generate a "product data model" in a way that is compatible to the existing tools. But none of them can be used directly to model product data.

We looked into the previously mentioned EDS [30] and STEP [26] as potential carriers of product data. Both address the exchange of data sheet information, but they either focus on a small topic (EDS) or are used only for a certain area in practice (STEP—for 3D information). So far, no standards or practices exist to cover all relevant information for the data exchange between supplier and customer in the space sector. However, EDS and/or STEP could become a starting point for the development of a data exchange format for product data, especially with the planned new definition of the EDS standard [27].

PDF data sheets are meant to describe a product technically but there is no standard regarding the syntax or semantic of this description. There are several approaches to extract (semantic) information from data sheets, e.g. by [3,5,7,24], but we do not know of an accessible tool that performs that task reliably.

3   Methods

As CubeSats become more common and products for those are already offered in online shops, we compared the information offered by such shops with the information required by the above mentioned MBSE tools. As with the MBSE tools, we focused on parameters for mass and structure. Since the outer dimensions of CubeSats are restricted by the form factor (1U, 2U, ...), we expected to find similar presentations of the structure parameters between the different shops. Besides the parameter names we were also interested in the formats the information were offered in.

To use product information directly in MBSE tools, we see the following requirements for an exchange format:

- *machine readable* - so humans do not have to enter or copy information manually
- *uniform/standardized* - so no transformations between different formats are necessary
- *automatically comparable* - so search for a product that fits certain requirements becomes easier
- *all values for one product from a single source (optional)* - so it is not necessary to request multiple sources for the information about a single product

The results of our search and the comparison with parameters at MBSE tools are discussed in the next section.

4 Results

For each of the six CubeSat shops, the formats in which information was presented are summarized in Table 2. We were looking for information in tables (or bullet points in the format <key>:<value>), PDF data sheets, and STEP files. Shop B offered information mostly in free text[2], little in tables, and PDF or STEP files only upon request. Shop E offered parameters only in free text or in text bullet points like "Mass is ca. XYg"; Shop D offered only very few bullet points in the format <key>:<value> and STEP files only after login. None of the shops offered an API (application programming interface) to read the data—we asked all of them via e-mail. One of the shops is working on an API to request the PDF data sheets, but no machine-readable data.

Table 2. Formats of information presentation at CubeSat shops

Shop	A	B	C	D	E	F
Table on website	X	(X)	X	X	-	(X)
PDF data sheet	X	-	X	X	X	X
STEP file	X	-	-	X	X	(X)

For each shop, we picked the first search result for "solar panel" to compare the parameters presented directly by the shops (not in the data sheets of the manufacturers).

The mass and structure parameters of each shop are compared in Table 3; Shops B, E, and F did not provide any mass or structure related parameters in a table or table-like format.

---

[2] That is, running text, as opposed to bullet points, tables, or figures.

Table 3. Mass and structure parameters at CubeSat shops. Both parameters in Shop D were followed by lists with the actual values.

Shop	A	C	D
Mass Parameters	Mass	Very low solar cell mass Side solar panel weight	Mass (exact mass depends on configuration)
Structure Parameters	Nominal thickness Dimensions (PCB + Solar Cells)	Solar cells thickness PCB Thickness	Panel Thickness

Even though our sample of CubeSat shops is small, it becomes obvious that neither between the different shops nor between the shops and MBSE tools the same parameter names are used. "Mass" and "thickness" are reoccurring names, but the additional texts at the shops (see Table 3) make it clear that the semantics of those names vary (e.g., "thickness" sometimes refers to the cells only, sometimes to cells plus PCB).

5   Prototype: Product Information in MBSE Tool

We built a small prototype to make product information available in MBSE tools, including a plugin for the DLR in-house MBSE tool Virtual Satellite. Figure 1 shows an overview of the architecture.

The main component is the Product Data Hub (PDH) that consists of a crawler and a database. The database stores product information independently of manufacturers; this bridges temporary unavailability of single shops and provides a single access point for the MBSE tools. The database is filled by a crawler that request the manufacturers regularly and updates or adds entries. Here, we need only one crawler because all manufacturers provide their data in the same format. To request data from actual manufacturers (given they provide an API) would require different crawlers since currently there is no uniform data exchange format all manufacturers share.

The second component of the prototype is a manually created mockup of manufacturers that provides product information in a machine-readable way via http in a JSON (JavaScript Object Notation, a language-independent data format) format. The data format is the same for all manufacturers.

The last component of the prototype is a plugin for Virtual Satellite that enables the users to do three different things:

1. Add an *Equipment* with the values of a product in the PDH
2. Update an *Equipment* with values from a product in the PDH
3. Save an *Equipment* as product to the PDH

To add a new *Equipment* with the values of a product in the PDH, the user browses a product list provided by the plugin and selects one with fitting values (see Fig. 2). The new *Equipment* can then be used as any *Equipment* in Virtual

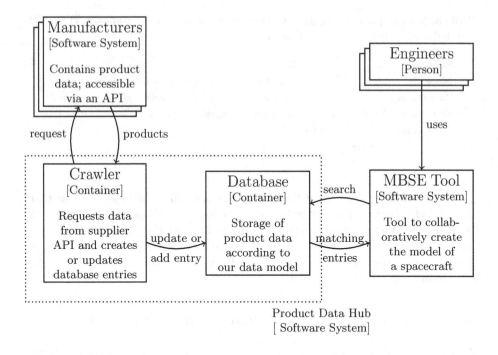

Fig. 1. Architecture of product data system

Satellite—changes at the *Equipment* have no effect on the product from which the *Equipment* was created.

The update function is rather a search function: The user specifies an *Equipment* and the plugin looks for products in the PDH that fit this specification within a range of uncertainty for all values. The range of uncertainty can be defined by the user. The user selects one product that fits the pre-specified *Equipment* and all values from the product are taken over to the *Equipment*.

The last function is to add an *Equipment* as product to the PDH. That way the user can for example define templates (e.g. for a "small battery") for which no real product from a manufacturer exists. This function can also be used to add values for products described by PDF data sheets manually.

6   Conclusion and Outlook

The comparison of parameters at MBSE tools and CubeSat shops shows that there is neither a set of parameters that is supported by everyone nor a common understanding of the semantics of the provided parameters.

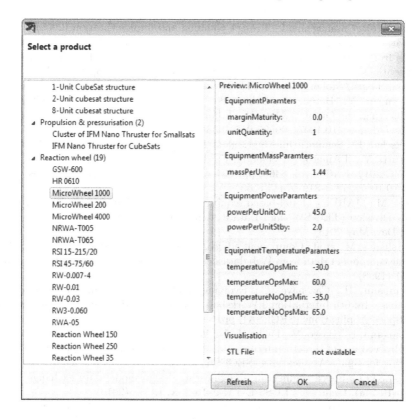

Fig. 2. Screenshot of product selection dialog in virtual satellite

Our prototype shows how product information can be exchanged between manufacturers and MBSE tools in principle. It also shows that for machine readable exchange of product information between manufacturers and MBSE tools a standardized format is needed that includes also a semantic description for each parameter. Our prototype only worked because we had control over all parts—to expand the concept, every party needs a common understanding of the exchanged information. We think that over the next years it should be possible to reach such a common understanding within the space industry, at least for parts of the information to exchange. The attempt at ESA to find a new and broader standard for EDS goes in that direction.

In the future we want to look more into semantic descriptions of space products and also in different phases of the spacecraft life cycle, since so far our focus was on the early planning phase.

References

1. Designing the Future of Your Complex Engineering Projects. https://www. rheagroup.com/cdp. Accessed 29 May 2018

2. Space project management - Project planning and implementation (2009)
3. Agrawal, R., Ho, H., Jacquenet, F., Jacquenet, M.: Mining information extraction rules from datasheets without linguistic parsing. In: Ali, M., Esposito, F. (eds.) Innovations in Applied Artificial Intelligence, pp. 510–520. Springer, Heidelberg (2005). https://doi.org/10.1007/11504894_69
4. Ait-Ameur, Y., Baron, M., Bellatreche, L., Jean, S., Sardet, E.: Ontologies in engineering: the OntoDB/OntoQL platform. Soft Comput. **21**(2), 369–389 (2015). https://doi.org/10.1007/s00500-015-1633-5
5. Barkschat, K.: Semantic information extraction on domain specific data sheets. In: Presutti, V., d'Amato, C., Gandon, F., d'Aquin, M., Staab, S., Tordai, A. (eds.) ESWC 2014. LNCS, vol. 8465, pp. 864–873. Springer, Cham (2014). https://doi.org/10.1007/978-3-319-07443-6_60
6. Bieze, M.: MARVL - Model-based requirements-verification lifecycle. Software Systems Division (TEC-SW) and Data Systems Division (TEC-ED) Final Presentation Day, May 2018
7. Castellanos, M., et al.: Component advisor: a tool for automatically extracting electronic component data from Web datasheets. In: Reuse of Web-Based Information, p. 31 (1998)
8. Eisenmann, H., Cazenave, C.: Evolving a classic SRDB into an engineering database. In: 6th International Workshop on Systems and Concurrent Engineering for Space Applications (SECESA), pp. 8–10 (2014)
9. Eisenmann, H., Basso, V., Fuchs, J., De Wilde, D.: ESA virtual spacecraft design. In: Proceedings of the 4th International Workshop on System & Concurrent Engineering for Space Applications (SECESA) (2010)
10. ESA-ESTEC: Space engineering - engineering design model data exchange (ecss-e-tm-10-25a). techreport ECSS-E-TM-E-10-25A, ECSS (2010)
11. ESA-ESTEC: Space engineering - product data exchange (ecss-e-tm-10-20a). techreport ECSS-E-TM-E-10-20A, ECSS (2010)
12. ESA-ESTEC: Space engineering - space system data repository (ecss-e-tm-10-23a). techreport ECSS-E-TM-10-23A, ECSS (2011)
13. Ferreira, I., de Koning, H.P., Gerene, S., Pickering, A., Vennekens, J., Beyer, F.: Open concurrent design tool: ESA community open source ready to go! In: 6th International Workshop on System & Concurrent Engineering for Space Applications (SECESA), October 2014
14. Fischer, P.M., Lüdtke, D., Lange, C., Roshani, F.C., Dannemann, F., Gerndt, A.: Implementing model-based system engineering for the whole lifecycle of a spacecraft. CEAS Space J. **9**(3), 351–365 (2017). https://doi.org/10.1007/s12567-017-0166-4
15. Hennig, C., Eisenmann, H., Viehl, A., Bringmann, O.: On languages for conceptual data modeling in multi-disciplinary space systems engineering. In: 2015 3rd International Conference on Model-Driven Engineering and Software Development (MODELSWARD), pp. 384–393, February 2015
16. Hennig, C., Hoppe, T., Eisenmann, H., Viehl, A., Bringmann, O.: SCDML: a language for conceptual data modeling in model-based systems engineering. In: 2016 4th International Conference on Model-Driven Engineering and Software Development (MODELSWARD), pp. 184–192, February 2016
17. Hennig, C., Viehl, A., Kämpgen, B., Eisenmann, H.: Ontology-based design of space systems. In: Groth, P., et al. (eds.) ISWC 2016. LNCS, vol. 9982, pp. 308–324. Springer, Cham (2016). https://doi.org/10.1007/978-3-319-46547-0_29

18. Hoppe, T., Eisenmann, H., Viehl, A., Bringmann, O.: Digital space systems engineering through semantic data models. In: 2017 IEEE International Conference on Software Architecture (ICSA). IEEE, April 2017. https://doi.org/10.1109/icsa.2017.35

19. Hoppe, T., Eisenmann, H., Viehl, A., Bringmann, O.: Guided systems engineering by profiled ontologies. In: 2017 IEEE International Systems Engineering Symposium (ISSE). IEEE, October 2017. https://doi.org/10.1109/syseng.2017.8088255

20. Hoppe, T., Eisenmann, H., Viehl, A., Bringmann, O.: SEMF – the semantic engineering modeling framework - bringing semantics into the eclipse modeling framework for space systems engineering. In: Proceedings of the 5th International Conference on Model-Driven Engineering and Software Development. SCITEPRESS - Science and Technology Publications (2017). https://doi.org/10.5220/0006118702930301

21. Hoppe, T., Eisenmann, H., Viehl, A., Bringmann, O.: Shifting from data handling to knowledge engineering in aerospace industry. In: 2017 IEEE International Systems Engineering Symposium (ISSE). IEEE, October 2017. https://doi.org/10.1109/syseng.2017.8088312

22. Jahnke, S.S., Martelo, A.: Special characteristics of concurrent engineering studies dealing with Cubesat missions and their impact on the CE process. In: 7th International Systems & Concurrent Engineering for Space Applications Conference (SECESA) (2016)

23. Lange, C., Grundmann, J.T., Kretzenbacher, M., Fischer, P.M.: Systematic reuse and platforming: application examples for enhancing reuse with model-based systems engineering methods in space systems development. Concurrent Eng. **26**(1), 77–92 (2018)

24. Murdaca, F., et al.: Knowledge-based information extraction from datasheets of space parts. In: 8th International Systems & Concurrent Engineering for Space Applications Conference, September 2018. https://strathprints.strath.ac.uk/65764/

25. NASA: NASA Systems Engineering Handbook. US National Aeronautics and Space Admin (2008)

26. Pratt, M.J.: Introduction to ISO 10303—the STEP standard for product data exchange. J. Comput. Inf. Sci. Eng. **1**(1), 102 (2001). https://doi.org/10.1115/1.1354995

27. Prochazka, M.: Electronic data sheets at ESA: current status and roadmap. In: Flight Software Workshop 2017, December 2017

28. Ramos, A.L., Ferreira, J.V., Barcelo, J.: Model-based systems engineering: an emerging approach for modern systems. IEEE Trans. Syst. Man Cybern. Part C (Appl. Rev.) **42**(1), 101–111 (2012). https://doi.org/10.1109/tsmcc.2011.2106495

29. Roscoe, L.E.: StereoLithography interface specification. Technical report, 3D Systems, Inc., October 1989

30. (SANA), S.A.N.A.: Spacecraft Onboard Interface Services Electronic Data Sheets and Dictionary of Terms, May 2017. https://sanaregistry.org/r/sois. Accessed 19 Feb 2018

I²PHEN: A Novel Interoperable IoT Platform for Medical Telemonitoring

A. Picard$^{(\boxtimes)}$, J.-C. Lapayre$^{(\boxtimes)}$, R. Muthada Pottayya$^{(\boxtimes)}$, and E. Garcia$^{(\boxtimes)}$

CNRS FEMTO-ST Institute, Univ. Bourgogne-Franche-Comté, DISC,
16 route de Gray, 25030 Besançon, France
{apicard3,jc.lapayre}@femto-st.fr,
{ronnie.muthada,eric.garcia}@maincare.fr

Abstract. Medical telemonitoring is an undergoing development field all over the world. We propose in this paper our novel platform I²PHEN (**I**o*T* **I***nteroperable* **P***latform for low power* **HE***alth mo***N***itoring*) that allows the monitoring of a patient's health parameters using connected objects (blood pressure monitor, thermometer, glucometer, ...) which communicate with the remote platform. The central server can then trigger alerts that were previously defined with the medical teams. For our platform we chose the LPWAN networks (Low-Power Wide Area Network) that offer a cost-effective alternative and are less expensive in terms of energy than cellular networks for transmitting small amounts of data from sensors and energy efficient battery powered objects over long distances. This field being new, and not widely used in the medical area, it is necessary to propose new solutions to remove some scientific barriers. The first obstacle is the availability and the reliability of these new networks, and more generally obtaining a better quality of service (QoS) necessary in the critical area of telemedicine: our *COMMA* first protocol is an answer. The second obstacle, and probably the most difficult, is to propose interoperable solutions in which connected objects can interact, through these new networks, with the remote platform using a local gateway: our *MARC* protocol is the answer.

Keywords: Medical telemonitoring · IoT · Interoperability · LPWAN · LoRaWan · Continua · Adaptive Data Rate

1 Introduction

Medical telemonitoring allows a health professional to remotely interpret data needed for medical follow-up of a patient [1,2]. It is intended, for example, for seniors and people with chronic diseases.

The use of telemonitoring presents several advantages for patients as well as for medical professionals in all stages of chronic diseases, beginning from the preventive stage up to the post-treatment stage [3]. It allows, among others, improving remote medical care, fostering their home support, allowing early

© Springer Nature Switzerland AG 2019
Y. Luo (Ed.): CDVE 2019, LNCS 11792, pp. 84–97, 2019.
https://doi.org/10.1007/978-3-030-30949-7_10

prevention of possible hospitalizations, Improving the coordination between the different medical team, ... The main goal of telemonitoring is to improve the quality of life of older patients and to reduce public spending through home care.

Existing platforms for patient health parameters monitoring are realized with the help of connected objects and connected medical devices (blood pressure monitor, thermometer, glucometer) which communicate with a local smartphone platform or systems like Arduino and Raspberry pi [4–7]. The server retrieving these health parameters can then trigger alerts according to a set of criteria previously defined in collaboration with the medical teams.

In this article we present our new platform I²PHEN (**I**o*T* **I**n*teroperable* **P**lat*form for low power* **HE**al*th* **mo**N*itoring*) which allows to solve the issues of health device interoperability, but also to energy saving, as well as the mobility of patients.

After this introduction, the first section of this paper presents the state of the art in this field, the next section introduces the new platform I²PHEN, followed by our two new protocols, COMMA (*COMmunication protocol for opti-Mization of trAnsmitter energy*) and MARC (*Monitoring distributed AlgoRithm using Connected health objects*).

2 State of the Art: IoT Standards

2.1 IoT Application Environments

The Internet of Things designates all physical objects connected to the Internet allowing a communication between our smart objects and their digital existence. The main evolutive factors are the energy consumption, in relation to the lifetime of batteries, and the public network coverage for objects to be connected everywhere regardless of a third-party gateway like a smartphone.

For wireless communication on a small distance, protocols such as ZigBee, Zwave and Bluetooth Low Energy (BLE) have been thought for low energy consumption in a relatively small environment, for example a house, and allow the development of Smart Homes. BLE technology, also called Bluetooth Smart is a protocol created less than 10 years ago and has very good specifications for low-power wireless communications compared to conventional Bluetooth. The design has been thought for very low power consumption devices, making it ideal for autonomous battery powered sensor nodes. Bluetooth Smart can therefore be used to communicate between relatively close local objects (less than 100 m).

For object deployment in a larger environment as well as in nature, other means of communication are employed. Cellular networks are massively used around the world to interconnect smartphones outside the home and to participate in the Internet of Things. Telephone operators offer a coverage of the territory using different cellular technologies: 2G, 3G, 4G and soon 5G. The use of 2G is particularly interesting for battery-powered sensors because it is relatively energy-efficient compared to other technologies. Initiatives are underway by the 3GPP consortium to standardize this type of connection and offer versions adapted to objects, with low energy consumption. The 5G will include a low power consumption mode. However, the key communication factor *IoT* is the arrival of Low-Power Wide-Area-Network, or LPWAN [8]: extended networks with low energy consumption. LPWANs pave the way for new wireless (radio wave) technologies designed specifically for low bit rate IoT applications. The major advantage is the very long-range communication coverage up to several tens of km while a GSM network is of the order of 1 to 2 km. Another important advantage is the very low energy consumption (an economy factor of 10 compared to Wifi or 3G) with the possibility of hibernation (asynchronous mode).

The LoRaWan and Sigfox protocols are part of LPWAN networks. They use public frequency bands: these bands can be used free of charge provided that the maximum duty cycle and the maximum transmission power are respected. These two protocols are low-power alternatives for exchanging data over a very large distance with a very low bit rate. They are ideal for exchanging small non-continuous messages between objects, or through a gateway. They cannot be applied for streaming, nor for sending images, but can be used to transmit sensors data.

2.2 Health Domain, *Continua*: An Interoperability Standard for Health Sensors

Like standard connected objects, the number of CHO (Connected Health Objects) and CMD (Connected Medical Devices) is significantly growing. Their number has risen from 46 million in 2015 to 101 million in 2018. By 2020, their number is estimated at 161 million with a market expected to reach 400 million euros [9].

It is important to distinguish CMDs from CHOs in e-health. Medical Devices (MD) are governed by the European directive 93/42CEE (26) and are subject to the label "medical device". The notion of CMD therefore simply signifies the adjunction of a connectivity to the DM [10].

The *Personal Connected Health Alliance* (PCHA) [11,12] is an international non-profit and open group of nearly 240 health care providers, and develops the Continua standard. The main goal of Continua is to facilitate and secure the integration of new models of health sensors dealing with hospital information systems and telemedicine platforms. It is the only internationally recognized standard for connected health that is supported by the European institutions (DG Health and DG Connect) and since early 2017 by the Office of the National Coordinator (ONC) in the United States. It defines the structure of the data exchanged, the means of communication, the steps in communication with objects as well as the safety of the devices. This allows a much faster and cheaper integration of new sensors (Plug & Play) provided that they comply with the Continua standard. Currently about 200 connected objects and medical devices have Continua certification.

Continua is a standard based on existing standards, such as IEEE 11073 for personal health sensors, HL7, HL7 FHIR or SNOMED CT (nomenclature of clinical terms in the medical community), as well as the PCD-01 IHE transaction (definition of profiles for heart rate, blood pressure, weight, ldots).

The PHD and IEEE 11073 standards have the concept of agents and managers. Agents are personal medical devices and are usually small inexpensive devices powered by batteries, with no display nor user interface. Managers are typically small computers or smartphones with larger computing resources and routing capabilities required to convey information autonomously from the source to the target (Fig. 1).

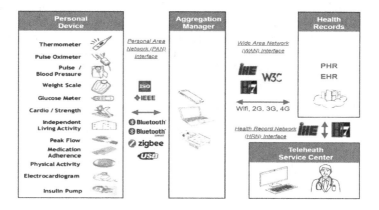

Fig. 1. Continua architecture

2.3   Communication Aspects of Health IoT

Communication Between the Object and the Local Gateway: The PHD and IEEE 11073 standards define the messages that travel between the agent and the manager, but not how these messages should be moved. Continua is a standard that includes PHD IEEE 11073 but also defines transport layers, security, ... Four transports have been defined: Bluetooth (with Health Device Profile HDP), Bluetooth Low Energy, USB Personal Healthcare Device Class and ZigBee Health Care Profile.

Communication Between the Local Gateway and the Network Core (Backend): LoRaWAN is a telecommunication protocol that enables low-speed radio communication of low-power objects communicating using LoRa technology. It is a part of the Low Power Wide Area Networks (LPWAN) [13] and it specifically allows a very long distance communication (a distance between a bridge and an equipment up to 5 km in urban areas and 15 km in rural areas), a very low energy consumption by sending a message every hour, the system consumes on average 5 µA (this corresponds to a lifetime of 5 years for a battery of 400 mAh).

It is a cost-effective and cheaper alternative to cellular networks for transmitting very small amounts of data. The LoRaWan protocol is based on spread spectrum modulation technology. LoRa, for Long Range, is the name given to the physical radio-frequency layer. Semtech's LoRa chips operate on 434 and 868 MHz frequency bands in Europe and 915 MHz for the rest of the world. These frequency bands are called ISM, ie, they are reserved for Industrial, Scientific and Medical fields. It can be used free of charge provided that you respect the maximal transmission power that is usually 25 mW for LPWAN, and the duty cycle (*limited flight time*).

The 868 MHz frequency band, used in Europe, is a European Low Power Networks (LPWAN) public bandwidth that LoRaWan uses for communication. ERC-REC-70-3E [14] defined by the CEPT (European Conference of Postal and Telecommunications Administrations) for Europe and applications by country, such as ARCEP 2014-1263 for France. This frequency band, which ranges from 865 MHz to 870 MHz, is split into 6 channels with different regulations per channel (Fig. 2).

Fig. 2. The European public frequency band 868 MHz

The first 865–688 MHz channel and the last 869.7–870 MHz channel are not used by the LoRaWAN protocol by default, but they can be extended for LoRa channels. The second channel is used by default in the LoRaWan protocol. It is on this frequency band that the 3 standardized LoRaWan sub-channels of 125 kHz each are located. It is on the width of these subbands that spread spectrum will be used during radio communication. The third channel 868.7–869.2 MHz is an area where the duty cycle is 0.1%. This area is interesting when an object emits very small amount of data per day: the risk of collision is actually lower and the reliability of communication is increased. Thus this sub-band is interesting for conserving energy or to communicate a priority message. The fourth sub-band 869.3–869.4 MHz is not usable for long-range LPWAN because the maximum power is only 10 mW, but without duty cycle it is a good area for the communication of local objects without message limitation. The 869.4–869.65 MHz channel is particularly interesting because you can communicate with 500 mW and a duty cycle of 10%. An object would not be able to use such power when running on battery power, but from the point of view of the network core it is a very good channel for downlink communications. Having a greater power will maximize the chances of the device to receive a message from the gateway, the antenna of it is often less efficient than the gateway, especially because of interference. For LoRaWAN, the duty cycle is managed on each channel. Therefore, by alternating bands 1, 2 and 6, it is possible to use up to 3% of duty cycle.

By default the operation is based on the ALOHA type for which the principle is simple: the data can be sent at any time by the transmitters and when a packet is lost due to a collision, it will be re-transmitted after a random time. The equipment therefore sends data without controlling whether the channel that it uses is available. Although several LoRa simultaneous transmissions can be processed by a single remote gateway (antenna), the nature of access to ALOHA support inevitably leads to the presence of transmission collisions and therefore loss of messages. A pre-listen (LBT) listening procedure (*Listen Before Talk*) can be used beforehand to guarantee a measured RSSI (*Received Signal Strength Indication*) of less than 90 dBm before any data transmission to significantly reduce collisions. LoRaWan also relies on the LoRaMAC protocol, which defines the interaction between nodes and remote gateways.

The ADR (*Adaptive Data Rate*) mechanism [15,16] is used to improve transmission time and energy consumption in the network. The protocol is based on the fact that LoRaWAn allows objects to individually modify transmission parameters, including Spreading Factor (*SF*), transmit power, and frequency bandwidth. The combination of these parameters makes it possible to adapt the flow rate (DR) and the transmission power (TX). The principle of the algorithm will then be to minimize these communication parameters while still ensuring exchanges between the device and the gateway. SNR (*Signal to Noise Radio*) are used by the gateway to evaluate the quality of each message exchange. By keeping a history of the SNRs on the last X communications, it is possible to evaluate the optimal transmission power to reach the remote antenna under minimal conditions. When a message is not received, for example during a change in environmental condition, the sending power is incremented step by step until the connectivity is restored. The ADR can therefore be activated when a terminal has sufficiently stable RF (*Radio Frequency*) conditions, and therefore generally useful for static devices. But it should be noted that the ADR algorithm can not be used in continuously moving systems.

In the end the adaptation of the bit rate also improves the reliability of the network in terms of performance since the messages are sent with less power, there is less chance of collisions with other messages and less chance of saturating the network by overflooding it (the more collisions and loss of messages, the more messages are sent with higher power, and more collisions will happen).

The LoRaWan protocol defines different device classes (A, B and C). This enables to setup a communication strategy per equipment in order to be the most reactive possible and more energy efficient. The A-Class is the most energy efficient. It defines that the device can send data whenever it wants and without any control. However, receiving a message is done only on receiving windows opened after emissions. Receiving windows are only opened after an emission, as this enables to notify the backend when a downlink message can be sent to be received by the device (Fig. 3).

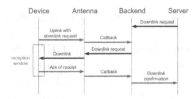

Fig. 3. Message reception by equipment with receiving window

The B-Class is based on receiving window openings at regular intervals. This requires some synchronization between the equipment and the server. This class offers a compromise between energy saving and regular downlink communication needs. The C-Class is the most energy greedy because the equipment is always listening. This allows bi-directional communications that are not scheduled at any time. However, the reception power consumption is between 10 and 11.2 mA, which reduces the battery lifetime from 400 mAh to 40 h where it could last 5 years according to Bellini [17].

Communication Between the Network Core (Backend) and the Processing Server (Medical Assessment): We use the Continua Design Guidelines, not for creating a new health device, but for receiving health data on a local gateway. This data will be sent from health devices already certified Continua (there are currently about 200) [18,19].

3   Contribution

We have just presented the state of the art on long-range and low-power networks as well as interoperability between connected medical health devices. Medical telemonitoring platforms using IoT technologies are very recent. They have appeared in the last two years in the literature [20,21] but still remain in the research field, and are not very applicable in the industry.

We have inspired ourselves on this research field to develop, from end to end, our own medical remote monitoring platform and providing additional insight on the interoperability of connected medical devices. Our research focused on the reliability of Lora networks in a mobile environment (COMMA algorithm) as well as intelligent monitoring (MARC algorithm). We will present in the platform section.

3.1   Our Novel Platform I²PHEN

In order to address the issues of interoperability of health devices, and also to save energy, and reduce costs and patient mobility, we decided to design a new mobile remote surveillance platform called I²PHEN (**I**o**T I**nteroperable **P**latform *for low power* **HE***alth mo***N***itoring*). This platform uses a local gateway to receive

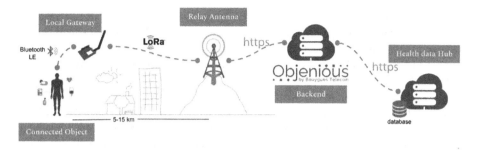

Fig. 4. I²PHEN platform architecture

data from Continua-certified connected objects as well as to transfer this data to the remote gateway. Figure 4 describes the overall architecture of the platform.

We developed our first prototype of the I²PHEN platform. We used an Arduino UNO type gateway with a USB CSR 4.0 dongle to use Bluetooth LE and exchange messages with Continua-certified connected objects. In addition we have chosen a Dragino LoRa Shield module which is a long-range transceiver compatible with Arduino. It is based on an open-source library. The LoRa Shield includes a Semtech SX1276 chip, a low-power extended-spectrum transmitter for sending LoRa messages. We use the arduino-LMIC library from IBM LMIC (LoraMAC-in-C), slightly modified to run in the Arduino environment and allowing to use the SX1276 transponders. This library makes it possible to send and receive LoRa messages at the backend server (network core) with the advantages of LoRaMAC protocol.

For the network core, we have chosen Objenious, a subsidiary of Bouygues Telecoms which offers a LoRa-compatible network with antennas located throughout the French territory. This network uses the 868 MHz frequency band. All transmitted packets will include an AppEUI field and a DevEUI field to identify the declared application and the gateway on the backbone. The latter can ignore received packets whose gateway identifier is not recognized. Finally, this gateway offers the possibility of transferring the data to our own health data hosting server without having to save it on our own.

The I²PHEN data server deals with sensible patients' health data, and must comply with the country-specific directive (in France HDS certification delivered by the french authority ASIP Santé *Agence française de la Santé Numérique*). This server stores the health data in a noSQL database of ElasticSearch type and in JSON format. In addition, on this server will be implemented an algorithm for detecting personalized alerts according to the vital parameters of the patient. We can quote the works of Hristoskova *et al.* [22] based on ontologies.

In medical telemonitoring, we need to ensure high reliability in the communication of health data, which is not necessarily the case currently with LoRa technology. That's why we have implemented several improvements to increase the reliability of communication while continuing to save energy. In addition, the properties of integrity, confidentiality and traceability will be preserved.

The gateway has three modes of operation resulting from different use cases of health devices and their degree of urgency: (1) ALL+ mode in which the gateway is permanently awake. It is therefore able to receive data from a permanently connected health device. We can thus take into consideration the health devices that constantly monitor a patient. This is called MBAN (*Medical Body Area Network*). The local gateway will also be able to receive a message from the remote gateway at any time. The use of C-class LoRaWan protocol will allow the gateway to request at any time measurements from the connected health device, to get them back in real time and to receive an analysis feedback from the server and/or the opinion of a specialist. This mode of operation has the only disadvantage of being very energy-greedy, and consequently of not being able to operate on battery. (2) ALL- mode which is based on the same operation as ALL +, except that the device is not listening permanently on LoRaWan long distance communication. However, a message will be sent every X minutes to the remote gateway for the purpose of receiving messages descending over a short time window (see principle of class A of the Sect. 2.3). This message will also guarantee to the server that the local gateway is still in operation. (3) MANUAL mode which corresponds to the situation whereby a health device is not permanently on the patient and measurements are done manually (like a tensiometer for example). At the time of manual measurement with the health device, the bridge must be woken manually. The health data can then be transferred to the latter which will transmit to the remote gateway.

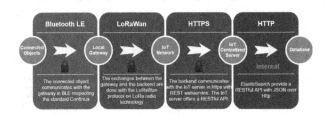

Fig. 5. The end-to-end communication

The use of a particular mode to the detriment of another is related to the different use cases of the platform according to the medical follow-up sought for the patient. For example, in the case of a blood glucose test taken twice a day by a patient with diabetes, it is advisable to use a manual mode. In the case of an automatic heart rate measurement, the ALL + mode will be strongly recommended for real-time monitoring.

To allow the awareness, the local gateway is equipped with a multi-color LED: orange during the long distance transfer and green for a few seconds once the acknowledgment of receipt received, the LED will turn red in case of connectivity problem.

The communication protocols are secured end-to-end in the I²PHEN platform. Communications established according to the Continua standard (USB,

Bluetooth, ...) are already secured. For LoRa messages, we use 128-bit AES key-based identification key management, coupled with device identification fields (DevEUI and AppEui) and an OTAA activation procedure (Over the Air) defined by LoRAWAN. Finally, between the network core and the IoT server we communicate by secure https requests. The Fig. 5 shows the different transport levels of our platform.

3.2   Two Original Protocols

Within I²PHEN we propose two new protocols that remove important obstacles in the world of Health IoTs.

COMMA (*COMmunication Protocol for OptiMization of trAnsmitter Energy*). The *ADR* algorithm allows a significant energy saving in static systems with a relatively stable environment. In the context of a constantly moving object, the ADR algorithm can not be applied because the environment changes regularly over time and the optimal calculated communication parameters can no longer be applied. However, in the daily use of the remote monitoring platform by an active person, we find that mobility is relative: individuals move regularly, but spend most of their time in known environments. For example, a given person will spend most of his time at home and then at work.

In this daily mobility, it is not recommended to disable the ADR algorithm: the idea is to do it when the object itself detects that it is moving. In addition, the LoRaWan technology is not suitable for a continuous flow of data, because of its design and its duty cycle limitation on its 868 MHz ISM frequency band, which does not allow an adaptive flow in real time. Therefore, the ADR algorithm does not allow a fast modification of the optimal parameters, because it is done incrementally, based on a history of the last 20 communications until finding the optimal parameters. If the new environmental conditions are very different from the previous ones, it can take a lot of time, and therefore cause a significant loss of energy as well as the *duty cycle*. We propose in the COMMA algorithm a faster adaptation solution of the ADR algorithm during a sudden change generated by a change of environment.

The proposed improvement is based on the use of communication histories of the different connection points of the individual (home, work, ...) in order to find a faster adaptation of the optimal communication parameters. To achieve a quick adaptation depending on the environment in which the object is located we must be able to associate a known environment encountered on a previously completed communication history. To do this, we use a multilateration technique from a LoRaWAN message received by at least 3 remote gateways to geolocate the local platform [23]. Note that the use of a GPS sensor was dropped because its energy consumption was not compatible with the expectations of the platform. The system is also able to detect a change of environment and disable the ADR in case of mobility in progress or unstable environment.

MARC (*Monitoring distributed AlgoRithm Using Connected Health Objects*). The MARC algorithm improves the patient's monitoring conditions by providing the IoT server with an artificial intelligence that allows to detect abnormal measurements or lack of measurements and trigger alerts, to retrieve back information and confirmation of receipt to the local gateway, to request new measurements, to manage the duty cycle to guarantee communication time in case of problems.

Since the algorithm is on the IoT server, it is able to know the history of patient's health data, but also the history (doctor and management team, patient medical follow-up, level of criticality and parameters for triggering an alert). The algorithm must also be able to know how the local gateways of the patients work. It is by gathering all these data that the algorithm can, when receiving a new measurement, detect if it is abnormal using ontologies [22] and triggering either:

- A request for a new measurement directly to the connected object or the patient. To send a descending message, the server contacts the network core that sends the message. In the case of an ALL- or MANUAL mode of operation, it will then be necessary to pay attention to return the message quickly after reception: in the time range where the local gateway will be listening to a descending message. It is therefore necessary to have a fast algorithm in the analysis of new measurements.
- Medical assistance (care team). In this case, a human intervention can then take place as a telephone call, or an intervention of emergency services for example.

4   Discussion

The I^{2}PHEN platform presented here is an end-to-end remote monitoring platform that spans a wide range of different technologies, standards and communication protocols. Many improvements can be made at all levels: on the platform itself (hardware and electronics), communication networks (algorithms, quality of service, or technological choice) or at the server medical data recovery level. Among these ideas, we thought about the possibility of going without a local gateway to transfer medical data to the remote gateway. Indeed, it would be possible to integrate a LoRa chip directly into the medical device. However, without the local platform, the interoperable aspect of the platform that works with all Continua-certified objects is lost, and in the case of a multi-pathological platform would lead to a multiplication of LoRa chips (and by consequence of subscriptions to networks). Moreover, the LoRaWAN technology makes it possible to create your own network freely (unlike competitors such as Sigfox or Nb-IoT ...) with remote gateways that you dispose yourself (this is among other things why this technology has been retained). This makes it easy to cover a health facility such as a hospital or a nursing home at a lower cost (around 100 euros per antenna). There is an open source network core called The Things Network which can then be used to retrieve data from antennas, manage downstream messages and manage the fleet of medical devices. The use of the free frequency band remains unchanged, their usage is still limited in time and power. If the gateways are close enough to the medical devices, the frequency band limited to 10mW but unlimited in time can be used (Fig. 2). At the end, it would be possible to create a pool of connected medical devices in a medical facility at lower cost with this technology.

For the sake of confidentiality related to this research work in collaboration with the Maincare company, we will not publish the test results in this article. The tests of the platform are presented in another article currently in finalization, in which we will present in more details the COMMA algorithm operation and its contribution in energy saving in a mobile environment.

5 Conclusion

LPWAN networks like LoRaWan are very interesting alternatives in the world of the Internet of Things. With their low energy consumption, their large ranges and their use in mobility, this makes them major players in the development of connected devices and contributes greatly to the Internet of Things in the various sectors of activity such as the environment and industry.

However, these networks also have their weaknesses, due to their limitation of use (maximum use time on the free frequency bands and very small message sizes among others), as well as their relatively low reliability (message losses due to interference or network coverage, low quality of service by default).

However, it is interesting for us to use these networks as well as their main characteristics (energy saving and mobility in particular) in the critical area of health care, and more particularly of remote monitoring. In this article, we introduced I²PHEN, a remote medical telemonitoring platform that stands out for its ability to be mobile and energy efficient using LoRaWAN technology. In order to meet the requirements of remote patient monitoring, in the critical area of health, it was necessary for us to provide sufficient quality of service to ensure the exchange of messages. The COMMA algorithm based on ADR allows this directly by the acknowledgment and retransmission of lost messages, but also indirectly by the decrease of the sending power thus generating fewer collisions.

By coupling this technology with the Continua standard proposed by the PCHA, we offer an interoperability solution to the platform. The use of the various recommendations of the standard makes it possible, among other things, to easily use several hundreds of connected medical devices that already exist on the market, to reinforce the security and to standardize the medical data collected.

The last essential brick for telemonitoring remote patients is the real-time monitoring of the medical data collected. The MARC algorithm that we developed allows us to generate alerts when abnormal values are detected, and to interact with the patient's medical circle.

In the end, we propose in this article a remote medical telemonitoring platform, I²PHEN, energy saving and mobile. This platform can meet specific needs for many patients around the world. Thanks to its mobility, it promotes continuity of care outside the home, such as work, various activities or travel times, which a conventional telemonitoring platform cannot provide. Saving energy allows to offer a less restrictive solution, avoiding daily recharges. Finally, the interoperability aspect offers a wide range of connected medical devices (blood pressure monitor, blood glucose meter, oximeter, etc.) and an easy integration of new devices. This makes it possible to propose a solution of care for the patients suffering from multipathological chronic diseases for which different measurements of constants are necessary.

The first version of I^2PHEN is in vivo test. The first results will enable us to produce publications soon.

Acknowledgement. The authors thank the French Government, the MainCare Solution Company and CNRS (French National Center for Scientific Research) for co-financing this work.

References

1. Freed, J., Lowe, C., Flodgren, G., Binks, R., Doughty, K., Kolsi, J.: Telemedicine: is it really worth it? A perspective from evidence and experience. J. Innov. Health Inform. (2018)
2. Wootton, R.: Telemedicine. Br. Med. J. **323**, 557–650 (2001)
3. Klaassen, B., et al.: Usability in telemedicine systems-a literature survey. Int. J. Med. Inform. **93**, 57–69 (2016)
4. Agarwal, S., Lau, C.T.: Remote health monitoring using mobile phones and web services. Telemed. eHealth **16**, 603–607 (2010)
5. Zhang, X.M., Zhang, N.: An open, secure and flexible platform based on internet of things and cloud computing for ambient aiding living and telemedicine. In: International Conference on Computer and Management (CAMAN), pp. 1–4 (2011)
6. Jovanov, E., et al.: A wireless body area network of intelligent motion sensors for computer assisted physical rehabilitation. J. NeuroEngineering Rehabil. **2**, 6 (2005)
7. Istepanian, H., et al.: The potential of internet of m-health things m-IoT for non-invasive glucose level sensing. In: 33rd Annual International Conference of the IEEE EMBS, pp. 5264–5266 (2011)
8. Ismail, D., et al.: Low-power wide-area networks: opportunities, challenges, and directions. In: Workshops ICDCN 2018, p. 8 (2018)
9. BI Intelligence. The global market for IoT healthcare tech will top $400 billion in 2022 (2016)
10. Surville, A.: Objets connectés et dispositifs médicaux connectés: Principaux outils disponibles à la pratique de la médecine générale en france en 2018 (2018)
11. Carroll, R., et al.: Continua: an interoperable personal healthcare ecosystem. IEEE Perv. Comput. **6**, 90–94 (2007)
12. Wartena, F., et al.: Continua: the reference architecture of a personal telehealth ecosystem. In: The 12th IEEE International Conference on e-Health Networking, Applications and Services, pp. 1–6 (2010)
13. Vangelista, L., Zanella, A., Zorzi, M.: Long-range IoT technologies: the dawn of LoRa™. In: Atanasovski, V., Leon-Garcia, A. (eds.) FABULOUS 2015. LNICST, vol. 159, pp. 51–58. Springer, Cham (2015). https://doi.org/10.1007/978-3-319-27072-2_7

14. CEPT member. Relating to the use of short range devices. ERC RECOMMEN-DATION 70–03 (2018)
15. Hauser, V., Hegr, T.: Proposal of adaptive data rate algorithm for lorawan-based infrastructure. In: International Conference on Future Internet of Things and Cloud, pp. 85–90 (2017)
16. Slabicki, M., et al.: Adaptive configuration of lora networks for dense IoT deployments. In: IFIP Network Operations and Management Symposium, pp. 1–9 (2018)
17. Bellini, B., Amaud, A.: A 5 μA wireless platform for cattle heat detection. In: 8th IEEE Latin American Symposium on Circuits & Systems (LASCAS), pp. 1–4 (2018)
18. Saha, P.: Design and implementation of continua compliant wireless medical gateway (2016)
19. Marian, B., Lothar, S.: Using continua health alliance standards. In: 12th IEEE International Conference on Mobile Data Management (2011)
20. Hayati, N., Suryanegara, M.: The IoT LoRa system design for tracking and monitoring patient with mental disorder. In: IEEE International Conference on Communication, Networks and Satellite (Comnetsat), pp. 135–139 (2017)
21. Kharel, J., et al.: Fog computing-based smart health monitoring system deploying lora wireless communication. IETE Tech. Rev. **36**, 69–82 (2018)
22. Hristoskova, A., et al.: Ontology-driven monitoring of patients vital signs enabling personalized medical detection and alert. Sensors **2014**, 1598–1628 (2014)
23. Fargas, B.C., et al.: GPS-free geolocation using LoRa in low-power WANs. In: Proceedings of 2017 Global Internet of Things Summit (GIoTS), pp. 1–6 (2017)

A New Index for Measuring Inconsistencies in Independent Component Analysis Using Multi-sensor Data

Subhajit Chakrabarty$^{(\boxtimes)}$ (iD) and Haim Levkowitz

University of Massachusetts Lowell, Lowell, MA 01854, USA
subhajitchakrabarty@hotmail.com

Abstract. In separation of source signals from signal mixtures and involving multiple sensors, an emerging useful method has been Independent Component Analysis (ICA). We examine one of the challenges of ICA – instability or inconsistency. The context of the study is ICA involving multiple sensors (time series data). Instability is said to occur when the independent components vary, each time when ICA is conducted. There is no solution to this, but there are performance indexes as attempts to quantify the problem. State-of-the-art software packages mention of the stability issue but there is no unanimity in the choice of performance indexes; the Icasso stability index and the Amari performance index are the most frequently used. Our contribution is that we propose a new index. The differentiating feature of this index is that it makes it possible for a proper comparison to be made upon repeated ICA on the same input because the new index works on the dispersion (range) of the fourth cumulants considering global maximum and minimum. Further, we test statistical significance. Future work in ICA may benefit from more consistent results and reporting of statistical significance.

Keywords: Sensor · Signal · Independent Component Analysis · Blind source separation · Data processing

1 Introduction

1.1 Independent Component Analysis

Suppose there is a cocktail party and two persons are speaking at the same time. Suppose that there are two audio sensors receiving mixtures of signals from the two sources (persons). We are required to separate the speech from each source. This is known as the Cocktail Party problem and the task is known as Blind Source Separation because we neither know the sources nor know how the signals are mixed – and we are required to separate the sources. Principal Component Analysis (PCA) can separate the mixtures into two components which will be necessarily be orthogonal to each other by PCA design, but it may not lead to the true audio sources. PCA will find directions of maximum variance. Independent Component Analysis will do a better job in this separation because it finds directions most aligned with the data. The independent components need not be orthogonal to each other, unlike principal components.

Y. Luo (Ed.): CDVE 2019, LNCS 11792, pp. 98–107, 2019.
https://doi.org/10.1007/978-3-030-30949-7_11

Another benefit of ICA is that ICA considers the true statistical independence (independence of all higher moments), while PCA considers independence only up to second moments. In PCA we maximize variance while in ICA we maximize cumulants (kurtosis) or likelihood (or mutual information or entropy). Hence, the estimated sources are uncorrelated in PCA while they are statistically independent in ICA [3, 6–8].

PCA is not without benefits and ICA has its problems. PCA preserves global covariances and leads to stable components. In ICA, a contrast function needs to be optimized because both the sources and the mixing matrix are unknown – as a result of this optimization process, the independent components may vary each time ICA is conducted. The components from ICA are not ordered (they may be permuted among themselves), unlike in PCA in which the components are ordered by variances. Apart from the problem with permuted components, the independent components are not to scale, and we cannot determine the variance. The signs can also be changed for ICA.

However, the ICA procedure includes pre-whitening (makes the covariance as the identity matrix) which could be done by PCA or other methods. Therefore, PCA and ICA are related to each other.

In ICA the objective is to find non-gaussian sources. The mixed signal may be gaussian because of the Central Limit Theorem but the sources are assumed to be non-gaussian. We now proceed to explain the formulation of ICA [3, 6–8].

Let X = sensor observation, S = source signal, A = mixing matrix. Then we have,

$$X = A * S \tag{1}$$

Let V = whitening matrix and Z = whitened matrix. Then after centering (mean = 0) and whitening (which sets covariance matrix of Z = identity matrix), we have,

$$Z = V * X \tag{2}$$

To perform de-mixing, we must find an orthogonal matrix W so that the components of $W^T Z$ may be maximum non-gaussian. If Y = estimated independent components, W = estimated de-mixing matrix, then we have,

$$Y = W^T * Z = W^T * V * X \tag{3}$$

W^T is the estimate of the de-mixing matrix (B), while $B \sim A^{-1}$. The estimated mixing matrix = $V^{-1} * W$.

We also define the global mixing- de-mixing matrix (G) as the following.

$$G = W * A \tag{4}$$

$$Y = G * S = W * A * S \tag{5}$$

In general, to find how much non-gaussian, a contrast function $\gamma(.)$ is optimized. This could be done by gradient descent (using steps of some size) or Newton methods (using derivatives). The FastICA [8] procedure uses the Newton method. The contrast function for single source, based on kurtosis, is the following:

$$\gamma_k(y) \overset{\text{def}}{=} \epsilon \frac{k^y}{\left(\sigma_y^2\right)^2} = \epsilon \frac{E\left\{\left|y^4\right|\right\} - 2E^2\left\{|y|^2\right\} - \left|E\left\{y^2\right\}\right|^2}{E^2\left\{|y|^2\right\}} \tag{6}$$

ϵ is the sign (negative or positive) and σ_y^2 is the of output $Y = W * X$.

In the real-valued case, the following functional may be considered as an orthogonal contrast for the extraction of a single source using kurtosis.

$$\gamma_k^0(y) = \left(E\{y^4\} - 3\right)^2 \tag{7}$$

1.2 Problem and Objective

As mentioned in the last section, multiple runs of the ICA over the same input signals provide different estimates of components. The following are the issues of stability.

- The extracted components can be permuted differently (no ordering)
- The components are not to scale, and variance cannot be calculated
- The components may have inconsistent sign
- The estimates may vary because of the non-deterministic nature of the algorithms. ICA may suffer from local minima (which is the case with most optimization problems).

The objective of this study is to examine the stability issues of ICA in the context of data processed by multiple sensors.

1.3 Contribution and Significance

The contribution of this work is in providing a new index for measuring the performance of ICA relating to time series. The differentiating feature of this index is that it makes it possible for a proper comparison to be made upon repeated ICA on the same input because the new index works on the dispersion (range) of the fourth cumulants. It contributes to consistency because we can also derive a matrix which is sorted by kurtosis. Further, the index permits statistical significance to be tested. Future work in ICA may benefit from more consistent results and reporting of statistical significance.

This work is significant because the results can be generalized across any time series data. So, this may apply to separation of sources for EEG, ECG, MEG, fMRI and so on in medical context, to finding sources in mixed environmental time series data, signals from space, geophysical time series, financial and economic time series and so on. Such blind source separation will involve some stability issues and our work may provide an informed basis for judgement on the performance of the ICA.

2 Background

2.1 ICA Algorithms

ICA comprises of several related algorithms and methods. The key groups of algorithms can be classified as higher order statistics (HOS) or second order statistics (SOS). SOS is also known as time-structure based. For sensor data, the main algorithms for ICA are FastICA [8], second order blind identification (SOBI), extended information-maximization (InfoMax), adaptive mixture of independent component analyzers (AMICA), algorithm for multiple unknown signals extraction (AMUSE), temporal decorrelation separation (TDSEP) and joint approximate diagonalization of eigen-matrices (JADE). We merely listed the main algorithms just to indicate the variety of algorithms which exist in this area.

For the above algorithms, broadly, there may be several choices for the methods, some of which are mentioned as follows.

Objective: Cumulant based; Maximum likelihood based.
Iterative procedure: Batch method; Adaptive method; Relative gradient.
Extraction of components: Iterative/deflationary; Joint diagonalization/symmetric/ simultaneous extraction.
Non-stationarity: Quadratic and other methods.
Pre-whitening: PCA; ZCA.
Other algorithm variants: Subspace ICA; Bayesian approaches; Semi-blind approaches.

2.2 Instability of ICA

The estimated components vary upon re-running ICA which makes it inconsistent. The mixing- de-mixing matrix (G) or the gain matrix could provide evidence of part of the inconsistencies – this we will elaborate below. Equations 4 and 5 define the mixing-de-mixing matrix.

In the ideal situation of a perfect performance of the ICA in separation of the independent components, G will simply be the permutation matrix (P). P is the matrix which has at most one element per row (and per column) as 1 and the remaining elements in the row (and column) will be 0. So, P is a permuted version of the identity matrix. An example of P is given below. In this case, P exchanges the first and third rows (or the columns) of the identity matrix.

$$\begin{matrix} 0 & 0 & 1 & 0 \\ 0 & 1 & 0 & 0 \\ 1 & 0 & 0 & 0 \\ 0 & 0 & 0 & 1 \end{matrix}$$

So, if we know how far the matrix G is from matrix P then we may have a measure (or a performance index) for evaluating the performance of ICA. But the index should consider the fact that G could be scaled. This is because as we see from Eq. 1, if the mixing (or de-mixing) matrix could be further multiplied by a diagonal matrix (scaled) and the corresponding estimate of the source be divided by the same factor, the equation remains unchanged.

However, the gain matrix cannot provide leads to understanding of the instability issues which are due to the nature of the algorithm (such as local maxima/minima) [9]. Besides, if the ICA algorithm is based on natural gradient, the gain matrix analysis becomes irrelevant. When only the de-mixing matrix is estimated, the mixing matrix is just the inverse. Again, if the ICA procedure involves Given's rotation, the issue of permutation matrix also becomes irrelevant because it is diagonalized. So, the gain matrix would have no further information.

2.3   Desired Properties of an Index (Measure) of ICA Instability

A good measure (say function f) for ICA instability may be expected to have the following properties.

P1. The measure f of X is invariant to scale, sign change and permutations. If D is a diagonal matrix, L is a sign change matrix and P is a permutation matrix, then we have,

$$f(P, D, L, X) = f(X)$$

P2. The index value will lie between 0 and 1 (normalized). A value of 0 may indicate same-source mixture while value of 1 may indicate the best separation performance possible.

$$0 \leq f(X) \leq 1$$

P3. Indexes computed upon repeating the ICA procedure should be comparable (with respect to the global maximum and minimum).
P4. Interpretation for statistical interpretation should be possible.

2.4   Measures of Instability

Broadly there are two approaches to measure the stability. The first performs resampling, clusters the independent components and measures the consistency of the clusters. The Icasso stability index (I_q) is an example of this [1]. The second type of index extracts a value from the gain matrix, G. The Amari performance index [2] is an example of this type.

The Icasso cluster quality index is defined as follows.

$$I_q(C_m) = \frac{1}{|C_m|^2} \sum_{i,j \in C_m} \sigma_{ij} - \frac{1}{|C_m||C_{-m}|} \sum_{i \in C_m} \sum_{j \in C_{-m}} \sigma_{ij}$$

In the above equation, C_m is the set of indices of components that belong to the mth cluster and $-m$ indicates that it does not belong to the mth cluster. The ideal cluster has a value of 1. If k is the number of dimensions, σ_{ij} (i, j = 1, ... k) is the absolute value of the mutual correlation coefficients, r_{ij} between the estimated independent components.

If V is the covariance matrix and W is the de-mixing matrix, then each correlation is given by one element of the matrix R, given as follows.

$$R = W * V * W^T$$

The key limitation of this index is that it resamples and clusters, both of which add their non-determinism to the results. Essentially it measures the stability of a method of clustering and does not dissect the core stability issues of ICA. However, resampling is often used in this domain [5, 9].

The Amari [2] performance index (PI) is based on the gain matrix. It has been widely used in ICA studies. In the equation below, c is the number of rows or columns. The i and j indicate the indices for row and column in the matrix G.

$$PI(G) = \frac{(\sum_{i=1}^{c} \sum_{j=1}^{c} \frac{|G_{ij}|}{\max|G_{ik}|} - 1) + (\sum_{i=1}^{c} \sum_{j=1}^{c} \frac{|G_{ij}|}{\max|G_{kj}|} - 1)}{2c}$$

The minimum value of Amari PI is 0, when we have a permutation matrix. The major benefit of this index is that it manages the scaling issue and can be normalized. However, when we perform ICA repeatedly, it results in different permuted components each time and the index values generated would not be comparable as they refer to different permuted components [9].

Other variants which work on the gain matrix are ISR (Interference to Signal ratio), which is the row-wise normalized gain matrix and its squared version, called the Inter-Channel Interference (ICI). Another index is the Minimum Distance (MD) [4] which performs linear sum assignment on the modified mixing matrix.

None of these indexes have any output which is consistent with respect to the global maximum and minimum upon repeated ICA. Though the Icasso index [1] attempts this but the clustering process adds to the instability because of the non-deterministic nature of clustering [9]. As a result, none of them satisfy P3.

3 Proposed Index

The proposed index is based on local minima and global minima. The steps are as follows.

1. Perform ICA repeatedly (say, n times). Each time calculate the maximum and minimum in the array of fourth cumulants (*cum4_array*).
2. Find the global minimum fourth cumulant and global maximum fourth cumulant from the multiple runs.
3. After find the global values, we can calculate the Stability Index (*SI*) as follows.

$$SI_i = \frac{\max_i(cum4\_array(X_i)) - \min_i(cum4\_array(X_i))}{\max_n(\max(cum4\_array(X_i))) - \min_n(\min(cum4\_array(X_i)))}$$

4. Calculate the statistical significance of the Stability Index (SI) using Mann-Whitney U test, a non-parametric test. This tests whether independent samples are drawn from the same population or not. Here application of the U test implies testing on the dispersion or range (difference between maximum and minimum) of the fourth cumulants.

The fourth cumulant is invariant to scale, sign or permutations. The unique contribution of this index is that it follows all the properties P1 to P4. It can be used to compare the performance of different ICA algorithms. It does not depend on the mixing or de-mixing matrix. It is invariant to the model.

4   Experiments and Discussion

For our experiments we used the publicly available data: CHB-MIT Scalp EEG Database (https://physionet.org/pn6/chbmit/). For example, we took the first.edf file from the first case, chb01_01. Signals were sampled at 256 samples per second with 23 EEG signals. Data is raw, not denoised. Taking a 2-dimensional view, the data is 23x921600. We performed FastICA [8] with 'symm' approach (simultaneous) and 'pow3' (kurtosis) optimization function.

None of the earlier performance measures work on global maximum and minimum, so our performance measure does not have scope of comparison. But we can compare with respect to the differentiating features of our index.

4.1   Features Observed

Firstly, the Stability Index (SI) is invariant to scale, sign and permutation because of statistical properties based on the fourth cumulant.

Secondly, if we repeat the sources (same sources) we get the same estimated signals and SI value of zero because maximum and minimum fourth cumulant will be equal. So, SI is normalized.

Thirdly, performing ICA repeatedly (to check stability performance) provided us the following results in Table 1. This kind of global values were not considered in the previous indexes on ICA, though it follows logically.

Table 1. Global values on ICA repeats

ICA repeats	Global maximum fourth cumulant	Global minimum fourth cumulant	Range
2	140.3374	0.0313	140.3061
5	141.4328	−0.0127	141.4455
10	144.2198	−0.0209	144.2407
20	145.0373	−0.0221	145.0594
50	145.2622	−0.0260	145.2882

Taking the results of the fourth cumulants obtained after performing ICA 10 times, we show the values of our Stability Index (SI) as follows. The rows refer to the results of ICA and the columns refer to the fourth cumulants of the independent components estimated (Table 2). The values of fourth cumulants shown below are rounded to whole numbers and sorted for better comparison. Here we take the global maximum as 144 to limit our analysis, though it will converge later. The last column shows the values of SI – ranging from 0.84 to 1.00 in this example.

Table 2. Sorted fourth cumulants on ICA repeats

Min																				Max	SI
0	0	1	1	1	1	2	4	5	10	15	18	19	20	21	22	23	37	78	79	138	0.96
0	0	1	1	1	2	2	4	5	10	13	18	19	22	22	22	23	36	75	78	141	0.98
0	0	1	1	1	1	2	4	5	10	14	18	19	20	21	22	23	36	78	81	136	0.94
0	0	1	1	1	1	2	5	6	10	13	18	18	19	21	21	23	37	78	79	141	0.98
0	0	1	1	1	1	2	4	5	10	18	18	18	19	21	22	23	37	78	84	121	0.84
0	0	1	1	1	1	2	4	5	10	16	18	19	20	20	21	23	37	72	78	135	0.94
0	0	1	1	1	1	2	4	5	10	16	18	19	20	20	22	23	37	78	84	132	0.92
0	0	1	1	1	2	2	4	5	10	15	18	18	19	22	23	23	36	77	78	140	0.97
0	0	1	1	1	2	2	4	5	10	16	17	18	19	22	23	23	36	77	78	141	0.98
0	0	1	1	1	1	2	4	5	10	16	18	19	19	20	21	23	36	75	78	144	1.00

For visualization, a color coding of the ordered cumulant values seem to indicate, for example, that in this case there may be six clusters. The central signal of these clusters could be found through k-medoids. Therefore, such a systematic layout may indicate the optimum number of independent components. It also makes it possible to apply various clustering methods [10] based on the fourth cumulants.

The Amari performance index [2] is uninformative here because its value for each of the ICA is close to zero (e.g. 4e−11). We also perform ICA thirty times to observe the results of the Icasso stability index [1].

It can be observed that the Icasso [1] stability index (I_q) basically shows the stability of the clustering of the components (grouping of the components in clusters). In this case (Fig. 1), many components have high index values indicating that they cluster well. I_q is based on the distance measure of correlation coefficient between

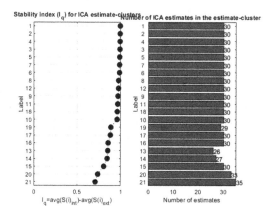

Fig. 1. Icasso stability index

components. However, our method is based on cumulants, following the theory that blind source separation can be performed (assuming at most one non-gaussian source) based on cumulants. Our method also does not have the added non-deterministic issues which come from the clustering procedure.

4.2 Statistical Significance

The statistical testing involved the Mann-Whitney U test of the sample of fourth cumulants. We use the results after performing ICA 10 times. When compared with ICA corresponding to the maximum fourth cumulant, for each of the other ICA results, Mann-Whitney U test values were found to insignificant (two-tailed at 95% significance). For the ICA with the least SI of 0.84, the p-value was 0.96012. Therefore, we can say that the ICA samples were drawn from the same population with 95% statistical significance – hence consistent. We used a non-parametric test.

5 Conclusion

Inconsistency or instability is an important limitation of ICA because the user finds it difficult to interpret the results when the results change in subsequent runs of the ICA procedure. Our Stability Index provides the user a procedure to analyze the performance of the algorithm. It can easily be adapted in case of sub-gaussian sources also. Besides it may also indicate the suitability of the hyperparameters. For example, if the stopping criterion in the estimation indicated a too-early stop then this may be reflected in low values of SI. The type of hyperparameters may also vary, such as, if natural gradient is used instead of a classical gradient. Importantly, SI is model-free; it does not depend on the mixing or de-mixing matrix which was a limitation of the Amari performance index. Besides, it is a truer performance because it can check performance against the global maximum/minimum. Arguably, this implies that it will be computationally intensive to find the global values. But this is acceptable because we are checking the performance of algorithms and estimation procedures on the data – which is a one-time activity. Once the SI is calculated and interpreted, we may know which algorithm will work best on the data.

References

1. Himberg, J., Hyvärinen, A.: ICASSO: software for investigating the reliability of ICA estimates by clustering and visualization. In: Proceedings of 2003 IEEE Workshop on Neural Networks for Signal Processing (NNSP 2003), Toulouse, France (2003)
2. Amari, S., Cichocki, A., Yang, H.H.: A new learning algorithm for blind signal separation. In: Advances in Neural Information Processing Systems, pp. 757–763 (1996)
3. Hyvärinen, A., Oja, E.: Independent component analysis: algorithms and applications. Neural Netw. 13(4–5), 411–430 (2000)

4. Ilmonen, P., Nordhausen, K., Oja, H., Ollila, E.: A new performance index for ICA: properties, computation and asymptotic analysis. In: Vigneron, V., Zarzoso, V., Moreau, E., Gribonval, R., Vincent, E. (eds.) LVA/ICA 2010. LNCS, vol. 6365, pp. 229–236. Springer, Heidelberg (2010). https://doi.org/10.1007/978-3-642-15995-4_29

5. Meinecke, F., Ziehe, A., Kawanabe, M., Müller, K.-R.: A resampling approach to estimate the stability of one-dimensional or multidimensional independent components. IEEE Trans. Biomed. Eng. **49**(12), 1514–1525 (2002)

6. Comon, P., Jutten, C.: Handbook of Blind Source Separation. Academic Press, Burlington (2010)

7. Shi, X.: Blind Signal Processing. Springer, Heidelberg (2011). https://doi.org/10.1007/978-3-642-11347-5

8. Hyvärinen, A., Oja, E.: A fast fixed-point algorithm for independent component analysis. Neural Comput. **9**, 1483–1492 (1997)

9. Chakrabarty, S., Levkowitz, H.: Denoising and stability using independent component analysis in high dimensions – visual inspection still required. In: 23rd International Conference Information Visualisation, Paris (2019)

10. Chakrabarty, S.: Clustering methods in business intelligence. In: Munoz, J.M. (ed.) Global Business Intelligence, pp. 37–50. Routledge, New York (2017)

From Sensors to BIM: Monitoring Comfort Conditions of Social Housing with the KlimaKit Model

Paola Penna[1] , Gian Luca Regis[1(✉)], Alice Schweigkofler[1],
Carmen Marcher[1,2], and Dominik Matt[1,2]

[1] Fraunhofer Italia Research, via Volta 13/a, 39100 Bolzano, BZ, Italy
gianluca.regis@fraunhofer.it
[2] Free University of Bozen-Bolzano, Piazza Universitá 5,
39100 Bolzano, BZ, Italy

Abstract. This paper describes the process for integrating the indoor comfort data collected by a monitoring system with a BIM-based model. Linking the monitored data with the BIM-based model allows to improve the visualization of the comfort parameters, that can be useful for the management of building energy system. As a case study, a residential multi-storey building, of the social housing association of the Autonomous Province of Bolzano in South Tyrol was considered. For public administration and social housing associations the creation of this comprehensive tool of information about their building stock, can be especially useful for building operation and maintenance and for the design phase in future projects. The results presented in this paper are part of an ongoing research project "Klimakit – Drive the change of the energy refurbishment market in South Tyrol. A strategy for social housing associations and public administration" [1]. The project is founded by Operational program European Fund for Regional Development EFRD 2014–2020.

Keywords: BIM · Building monitoring · Social housing ·
Retrofitting existing building

1 Introduction

The building sector represents one third of the overall energy consumption [2]. For this reason, the European Commission set a target to reduce the emission of the residential sector with 90% by 2050 [3]. In this framework, the improvement of the energy performance of the existing building stock is a priority [4]. Most retrofit projects deal with reducing the heat losses through the building envelope by insulating the opaque envelope and by replacing the existing windows. This has several benefits on the Indoor Environmental Quality (IEQ), resulting from increased indoor temperatures, homogeneous surface temperatures and a reduction of the risk of asymmetric radiant discomfort. However, the potential drawbacks of the application of Energy Efficient Measures (EEMs) are often neglected. These are mainly related to two aspects: the indoor air quality and the overheating risk during the summer season. The improvement of the building air tightness minimizes the air infiltration rate and if the building is not sufficiently ventilated it could compromise the indoor air quality [5–7] and consequently the occupants' health. The reduction of this infiltration rate also affects the risk of overheating. In fact, in high insulated buildings a small energy input significantly raises the internal temperature and if the extra heat it is not dissipated by ventilation, the indoor livability is compromised [8]. As reported by [9–11], buildings, which underwent deep energy renovations, are now facing overheating issues. This could undermine the benefit of the retrofit itself, increasing the cooling needs. Since social hosing buildings are particularly affected by the problem of poor IEQ, as underlined by [12], the application of a monitoring system for measuring indoor air quality after energy renovation is particularly important [13].

This paper presents the process for integrating the indoor comfort data collected by a multiple sensors system with a BIM-based model. Linking the monitored data with the BIM-based model allows to improve the visualization of the comfort parameters, that is useful for the management of a building energy system. Moreover it allows to integrate different types of information, related to building elements as well as IEQ, in digital form in a unique model. The process of integrating the multi sensors data into BIM has been tested and validated on a case study. The results presented in this paper are part of an ongoing research project "Klimakit – Drive the change of the energy refurbishment market in South Tyrol. A strategy for social housing associations and public administration". The project is founded by Operational program European Fund for Regional Development EFRD 2014–2020.

1.1 State of the Art

Over the last decades, the Architecture Engineering and Construction industry has undergone thorough process of digitalization. In particular, the Building Information Modelling (BIM) gained a growing interest. The BIM methodology allows to approach building design in a cooperative working environment: it enhances communication and collaboration among key stakeholders, it increases productivity and improves the overall quality of the final product. Considering the intrinsic complexity of the retrofit of existing buildings, the application of BIM methodology for these projects seems to be a promising field to investigate. One of the main advantages of BIM-based model is the possibility to integrate different types of information, of different building elements in a unique model. For example, integrating thermal properties data in the building elements can be particularly useful to automatically define the energy performance of a building and to evaluate retrofit alternatives [14, 15], but also to support the process of energy labelling [16]. The BIM-based model can help facility management work by providing information on the building condition [17]. [18] created a Heritage-BIM web-portal to share information about no-fines concrete buildings that can be useful for homeowners, designers, consultants, and councils, since there is currently little accurate information. Few works investigate the benefit of linking BIM with monitoring information. [19] evaluates the potential for using BIM as a tool to support the visualization and management of a building's performance, demonstrating a method for capturing, collection and linking of data stored across the currently disparate BIM and Building Management System (BMS) data environments. [20] integrates a wireless sensor network with a BIM-based model to monitor and assess IEQ, by measuring temperature and humidity in a subway. In this paper, the data from monitoring system have been integrated into a BIM-based model to automatically visualize the indoor comfort conditions and integrate different types of information in a unique digital model.

2   From Sensors to BIM

In this section an overview of the process of linking the data from the sensors with the BIM-based model is illustrated. The integration of the comfort data, derived from multiple sensors, into the BIM model allows to automatically combine the monitored data with the related geometrical space into the model, to easily visualize the fulfillment of certain level of IEQ and to create a comprehensive database of information in a unique model, that can be useful for management and maintenance. In this work, this process has been tested and validated on a multi-storey residential building of the social housing association of the Autonomous Province of Bolzano (IPES). The building has eight storeys: a basement with parks and cellars and seven upper storeys with 36 apartments of about 90 m^2. It was built in the '70s and it has been energy refurbished in 2015. The opaque envelope has been externally insulated (16 cm of mineral wool on the walls and 10 cm of extruded polystyrene on the flat roof) and the windows substituted with triple glazing system and improved wood-frame. The energy consumptions of the building have been reduced and they are about 25 kWh/m^2, label C according to CasaClima protocol [21]. In order to verify the indoor comfort condition after the energy refurbishment, some of the most representative apartments have been equipped with a monitoring system.

2.1   Monitoring System

The monitoring system, composed by different sensors located in different apartments, aims at store information about air quality and thermal comfort parameters. The architecture of monitoring system has been defined by Eurac Research, part of research team in the project. In particular, the following parameters have been monitored: temperature, humidity, CO_2 concentrations, brightness and presence.

Table 1. Range and measurement accuracy of the sensors.

Comfort parameters	Range	Accuracy	Unit of meas.
Air temperature	−40–+60	±0.3	°C
Relative humidity	0–100%	±1%	%
CO_2 concentration	0–10'000	100 ppm + 5%	ppm
Illumination level	0–65'535	3	lux
Presence	–	5–6 m (130° angle)	seconds

Table 1 reports the range and the accuracy of measurement of each sensor. The sensors have been installed in the living rooms of the flats since they represent a key space for monitoring comfort conditions. The monitoring system is composed by two levels, summarized in Fig. 1. The first ones is related to the sensors' system itself for monitoring air quality and indoor comfort conditions. The second ones concerns the data storage. The architecture of the sensors' system is a "star type", where all sensors communicate with a gateway server (receiver). The communication protocol between the gateway and the sensors is LoRaWAN (Low Power WAN Protocol for Internet of Things) type. As shown in Fig. 1, sensors sends the data to the gateway approximately every five minutes. The data collected by sensors are saved on the data storage of the gateway itself and sent every 10 min on a cloud storage driver, in a Structured Query Language (SQL) database.

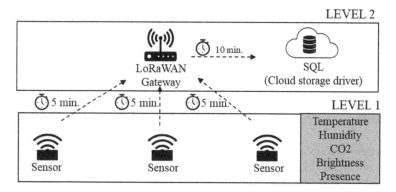

Fig. 1. Structure of the monitoring system.

2.2 Linking Data from Sensors to BIM

From the documentation received in paper form, a model of the monitored building has been created within a BIM software. It was decided to use Autodesk Revit [22] for the modelling part with a Level of Development (LOD) 200, which means a simplified representation of spaces and systems. This LOD is sufficient to integrate the comfort parameters into the geometrical spaces of the building in a cooperative way, moreover an accurate representation of the building would have taken significant time. The process of data transfer is described in Fig. 2.

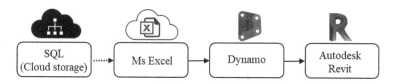

Fig. 2. Process of data transfer from sensors to BIM-based model.

For linking the monitoring data to BIM-based model, has been created a Python script who select the monitoring data from SQL database and report them on Excel file. The Python script is created using "pandas" and "squlite3" Python's libraries. The Python script select only the last measured data for each apartment from SQL database and, after the formatting the values, create an Excel file who reports the data of the monitored parameters. In this way, the automatic creation of the Excel file speeds up compilation and avoids distraction errors.

Having the monitoring data in MS Excel format allows to easily extract the data in a compatible format with Dynamo [23] and to process additional calculations that could be useful for future developments of the project (i.e. calculation of mean temperature during a day). Dynamo identifies the name of the monitoring parameters from the first line of the Excel spreadsheet and it creates within the BIM-based model, for each monitored apartment, the same parameters. The related values extracted from the Excel file columns are automatically assigned into the BIM-based model. This allow to read the last readings values of air temperature, humidity, CO_2 concentration levels, illumination level and occupants' presence, offering the opportunity of fast information retrieval on IEQ in a spatial manner. An extra parameter is created on the building model where the time of measurement is reported, in this way is possible to define which is the time of the last monitoring data reading.

3   Results

This process of coupling the data from monitoring system with BIM-based model allows to automatically integrate the information derived from different sensors in a digital model, that make the visualization of the indoor comfort conditions in different apartments of the building easier. Figure 3 shows how the data are visualized on the BIM Model as properties of the Revit room. Moreover, in Dynamo for each parameter a range of values has been set. Within this range, the comfort parameters are considered acceptable. Table 2 reports the comfort range considered for each parameter according to [24, 25]. If one of the monitored comfort parameters assumes a value outside the comfort range, the parameter is automatically highlighted on the room tag. As shown in Fig. 3, the relative humidity and the CO_2 concentrations for the monitored apartment are respectively too low and too high.

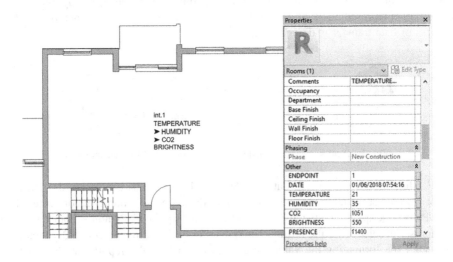

Fig. 3. Comfort parameters' readings within the BIM-based model

This means that the air into the flat is too dry and this could lead to respiratory long term-effects for the occupants. The high CO_2 concentrations means that the apartment is not sufficient ventilated. Another important aspect of linking the monitoring information with the BIM-based model is the creation of a BIM database, comprehensive of different type of information easier to be visualized. This allow to create and to export schedules and sheets who reports the data of a certain date for creating measurement history.

Table 2. Comfort range for monitored parameters.

Comfort parameters	Range	Reference
Air temperature	[18–27 °C]	[24]
Relative humidity	[40–70%]	[24]
CO_2 concentration	[400–1000 ppm]	[25]
Illumination level	[100–600 lx]	[24]

4   Discussion

The process described for linking the data recorded by a monitoring system with the BIM-based model illustrates how information about IEQ can be integrated in a digital unique model. This allow the social housing association of Bolzano (IPES) to verify the comfort levels on refurbished building and prevent discomfort conditions by driving the occupant behavior (i.e. giving behavioral advices for correctly ventilating the apartment). The integration of this parameters permits an easy visualization and communication of indoor comfort, by highlighting in a spatial manner which are the parameters that creates discomfort.

Some future development of the project concerns the processing of the data within the MS Excel for aggregating useful information. For example, isolating the data of some specific period of time, defined by the BIM operator, and calculating the mean values of the comfort parameters allows to verify if some specific period of the year are more interested by discomfort conditions and this is particularly useful for the operation and management of the building.

Another future application is related to the integration of the energy consumption data on the BIM-based model. Electricity consumption of each apartment has to be included into the monitoring system and in future could also be integrated into the model.

5   Conclusions

The paper presents some outcomes of the KlimaKit project. It describes an approach to achieve improvements in managing of buildings thanks to the adoption of a BIM-process for the information management. The information collected from a monitoring system are integrated in the BIM model of the building for its management process.

The identified solution has been developed based on the needs of the social housing association of the Autonomous Province of Bolzano and exploiting an existent monitoring system.

This work aims at creating a core module as a starting point for future implementations. Indeed, for the real adoption of this process from IPES, further development are planned. Another important aspect to consider, is the fact that IPES has not yet adopted the BIM methodology for its internal procedures. This aspect limits the adoption of the Klimakit BIM-process. Anyhow, this work allows to show and to partially demonstrate the potentiality of the BIM methodology applied to existing buildings, encouraging his future embracing from the housing association of the Autonomous Province of Bolzano.

Acknowledgment. This paper has been funded by the European Regional Development Fund ERDF 2014–2020 Südtirol/Alto Adige – Axis 1 Research and Innovation, with project KlimaKit FESR1018 (CUP: B56J16001740001). The authors would like to thank IPES, the west technical Office and the Arch. Othmar Neulichedl, as well as the Institute for Renewable Energy of Eurac Research of Bolzano.

References

1. KlimaKit Project. www.klimakit.it
2. Building Performance Institute Europe (BPIE): Europe's buildings under the microscope. A country-by-country review of the energy performance of buildings. BPIE (2011). ISBN 9789491143014
3. European Commission: A roadmap for moving to a competitive low carbon economy in 2050 (2011)
4. Meijer, F., Itard, L., Sunikka, M.: Comparing European residential building stocks, performance, renovation and policy opportunities. Build. Res. Inf. **37**(5–6), 355–551 (2009)
5. Crump, D., Dengel, A., Swainson, M.: Indoor Air Quality in Highly Energy Efficient Homes - A Review. NHBC, Amersham (2009)
6. Prasauskas, T., Martuzevicius, D., Kalamees, T., Kuusk, K., Leivo, V., Haverinenshaughnessy, U.: Effects of energy retrofits on indoor air quality in three Northern European countries. Energy Procedia **96**, 253–259 (2016)
7. Földváry, V., Bekö, G., Langer, S., Arrhenius, K., Petráš, D.: Effect of energy renovation on indoor air quality in multifamily residential buildings in Slovakia. Build. Environ. **122**, 363–372 (2017)
8. Penna, P., Prada, A., Cappelletti, F., Gasparella, A.: Multi-objectives optimization of energy efficiency measures in existing buildings. Energy Build. **95**, 57–69 (2015)

9. Ozarisoy, B., Elsharkawy, H.: Assessing overheating risk and thermal comfort in state-of-the-art prototype houses that combat exacerbated climate change in UK. Energy Build. **187**, 201–217 (2019)
10. Psomas, T., Heiselberg, P., Duer, K., Bjørn, E.: Overheating risk barriers to energy renovations of single family houses: multicriteria analysis and assessment. Energy Build. **117**, 138–148 (2016)
11. Mavrogianni, A., et al.: The impact of occupancy patterns, occupant-controlled ventilation and shading on indoor overheating risk in domestic environments. Build. Environ. **78**, 183–198 (2014)
12. Patino, L.D.E., Siegel, J.A.: Indoor environmental quality in social housing: a literature review. Build. Environ. **131**, 231–241 (2018)
13. Broderick, A., Byrne, M., Armstrong, S., Sheahan, J., Coggins, A.M.: A pre and post evaluation of indoor air quality, ventilation, and thermal comfort in retrofitted co-operative social housing. Build. Environ. **122**, 126–133 (2017)
14. Habibi, S.: The promise of BIM for improving building performance. Energy Build. **153**, 525–548 (2017)
15. Ahn, K.U., Kim, Y.J., Park, C.S., Kim, I., Lee, K.: BIM interface for full vs. semi-automated building energy simulation. Energy Build. **68**, 671–678 (2014)
16. Azhar, S., Carlton, W., Olsen, D., Ahmad, I.: Building information modeling for sustainable design and LEED® rating analysis. Autom. Constr. **20**(2), 217–224 (2011)
17. Bozorgi, P.P., Gao, X., Eastman, C., Self, A.P.: Planning and developing facility management-enabled building information model (FM-enabled BIM). Autom. Constr. **87**, 22–38 (2018)
18. Sierra, F., Mahdjoubi, L., Gething, B., Mahamadu, A.M., Alzaatreh, A.: Heritage Building Information Modelling (HBIM) to make informed decisions when retrofitting. A case study. In: Creative Construction Conference Proceedings, Ljubljana, Slovenia (2018)
19. Gerrish, T., Ruikar, K., Cook, M., Johnson, M., Phillip, M., Lowry, C.: BIM application to building energy performance visualisation and management: challenges and potential. Energy Build. **144**, 218–228 (2017)
20. Marzouk, M., Abdelaty, A.: Monitoring thermal comfort in subways using building information modeling. Energy Build. **84**, 252–257 (2014)
21. Casaclima Energy Agency: Direttiva tecnica edifice esistenti e risanamento, Bolzano (2017)
22. Autodesk, Revit 2020 (2019). http://www.autodesk.co.uk/products/revit-family/overview
23. Autodesk, Dynamo 2.1.0 (2019). http://dynamobim.org/
24. CEN, EN 15251, Indoor environmental input parameters for design and assessment of energy performance of buildings addressing indoor air quality, thermal environment, lighting and acoustics (2007)
25. CEN, EN 13779, Ventilation for non-residential buildings - Performance requirements for ventilation and room-conditioning systems (2007)

Showing Ultra-High-Resolution Images in VDA-Based Scalable Displays

Tomohiro Kawanabe[1]($\boxtimes$)(iD), Jorji Nonaka[1](iD), Daisuke Sakurai[2],
Kazuma Hatta[3], Shuhei Okayama[3], and Kenji Ono[1,2](iD)

[1] RIKEN Center for Computational Science, Kobe, Japan
{tkawanabe,jorji}@riken.jp
[2] Research Institute for Information Technology, Kyushu University, Fukuoka, Japan
{sakurai.daisuke.950@m,keno@cc}.kyushu-u.ac.jp
[3] Imagica Digitalscape Co. Ltd., Tokyo, Japan
{kazuma-h,shuhei-o}@digirea.com

Abstract. For web-browser-based *scalable display systems*, we recently presented the Virtual Display Area (VDA) [1] concept, which unifies different display resolutions and tiling by abstracting the physical pixel spaces into a single software display. Web browsers, however, are generally not designed for handling images of large size, even though ultra-high-resolution images emerge especially in the HPC and big data communities. We thus present an approach to handle ultra-high-resolution images for web-based scalable display systems while keeping the principle of the VDA to achieve both the efficiency of operations and the simplicity of software design. We show the advantage of our approach by comparing its performance to that of *SAGE2*, which is the de facto standard web-based scalable display system.

Keywords: Tiled display · Scalable display · Virtual Display Area · Visualization · Cooperative work · Remote collaboration

1 Introduction

JavaScript collaborative applications on modern web browsers have replaced numerous stand-alone applications. Web-based collaboration apps have the advantage that their development can rely on a wealth of JavaScript libraries, which allow smooth access to web-related software ecosystems. This makes web-apps a competitive solution. In the past we developed a web browser based scalable display system named ChOWDER [1] utilizing the web-related software ecosystems [2]. However, web browsers are software that originally assumes interaction with a single PC user, and the applications for viewing large-scale data are not considered, and it is impossible to display large scale data, or even if it is possible, it will have problems with performance. On the other hand, to pursue extreme performance requires the development of low-layer software, which means leaving from the ecosystem described above. Therefore, we examined how

Y. Luo (Ed.): CDVE 2019, LNCS 11792, pp. 116–122, 2019.
https://doi.org/10.1007/978-3-030-30949-7_13

to make ecosystem use and scalability compatible, and developed the large-scale image display method proposed in this paper.

The rest of this paper is organized as followed. The next section discusses the advantages and disadvantages of web browser based scalable display systems. Then, the proposed large-scale image display method and a method for avoiding the above-mentioned drawbacks are described. The performance of the proposed method is then evaluated. Finally, conclusions and suggestions for future work are given.

2   Discussion

There are two major requirements to use the scalable display systems as a scientific tool.

- Browse through a wide variety of content at the same time.
- Observe the ultra-high-resolution image without reducing it.

In order to realize these items, various scalable display system realization methods have been proposed in the past [3]. DisplayCluster [4] and SAGE [5] are well known. SAGE was replaced by the web-based SAGE2 [6] in 2014, which is compared later. They presented different methods for connecting groups of displays and computers, via network and dedicated software, to act as a large display space. Although these methods have proven to be scalable, they require specific software to be installed, and as the size of the system increases, the maintenance cost will increase proportionally. Also, in recent years, graphics hardware has evolved remarkably, and when using NVIDIA Mosaic [7] and AMD EyeFinity [8], a method of connecting multiple displays to one PC to realize tiled display wall is also common. However, the multi-display drivers provided by both companies have a limitation of maximum resolution. The modern web browsers can handle content in various formats and can use the so-called kiosk mode to set the entire physical display in the content display area, so it is suitable as display software for scalable display system, and also has a high software quality, so that the maintenance cost as described above can be suppressed. The method using web browsers is also advantageous in that content rendering can be performed by display-side software (i.e., a web browser). In other words, the content server can concentrate on sending the content data itself and some metadata (e.g., position (x, y) of the content in the web browser window) to the web browser where the content should be displayed. In the case of content displayed across multiple displays (multiple web browsers), useless data is also sent, although when the content position is moved in the tiled displays, the displaying content is already on the web browsers, since it is only necessary to send location change information from the server to the browser, there is a significant advantage of the high responsiveness of the operation. This method is extremely effective in the use of the scalable display system in which a large amount of content with relatively small resolution is browsed as an overview.

However, when dealing with large-scale images that must be displayed using the entire display area, there are the following two problems.

- Exceeding the data size which the web browser can handle.
- Performance degradation due to unnecessary communication by the increase in data area that each web browser has in duplicate.

Regarding the former, according to our survey, there was a functional limitation shown in Table 1. However, this may be improved in the future (In fact, in the past there was a limitation with smaller image sizes). The latter is in a trade-off relationship with the operation response described above, but in the case of an ultra-high-resolution image that needs to be displayed using the entire tiled display space, the movement operation is not frequently performed, but rather the longer the time that taken to display the content due to the cost of communication, makes harmful effect on operability.

Table 1. Maximum displayable resolution of major web browsers

OS	Web browser	Image size (pixels)		
		16384^2	32768^2	65536^2
Windows 10	Google Chrome ver. 72	OK	OK	×
	Mozilla Firefox ver. 65	OK	OK	OK
	Microsoft Edge ver. 44	OK	×	×
Mac OS X 10.11	Google Chrome ver. 72	OK	×	×
	Mozilla Firefox ver. 60esr	OK	OK	OK
	Apple Safari ver. 11	OK	×	×

Fig. 1. A 16K-resolution image (15360 × 6480 pixels, JPEG, 86.8 MB) used for evaluation (Data courtesy of JAMSTEC and AORI/The University of Tokyo (HPCI SPIRE3) collaboration with RIKEN AICS)

We measured the time required to display an image with a resolution of 15360 × 6480 pixels, shown in Fig. 1, with ChOWDER and SAGE2 using the

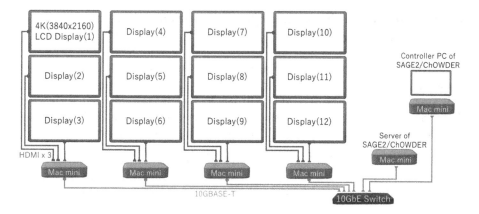

Fig. 2. System diagram of evaluation environment

evaluation equipment shown in Fig. 2, from the start of data transmission to the completion of the image displaying. The average measure time on SAGE2 was 20.53 s, and on ChOWDER was 18.00 s. Note that the results are an average of 5 measurements, and should consider an implicit error due to the manual measurement.

The data size of the image used in the evaluation was 86.8 MB, the number of displays (i.e., the number of browser windows) constituting the tiled display wall was 12, and the server delivers the image data to the entire set of displays. Consequently, approximately 1 GB (86.8 MB × 12 = 1042.6 MB) of data is transferred over the network. In either case of SAGE2 and ChOWDER, an unignorable time lag occurs. It is a negative issue that forces the user to interrupt thinking in the context of cooperative work, such as discussions and decision making. Thus we believe that improvement is needed to handle ultra-high-resolution images in a web browser based scalable display system.

In order to solve the above problems, we propose a method for dividing an ultra-high-resolution image into a plurality of image contents, registering them to the ChOWDER server, and treating them logically as one content. Dividing the content solves both of the problems described above. Although it is necessary to treat multiple contents logically as one, the Virtual Display Area (VDA), which is a key feature of ChOWDER, and has originally the concept of "layer" that can easily distinguish the contents. By taking advantage of this existing functionality, and setting the divided image contents to be in the same layer, these images will be recognized as a single image content. However, since this function requires an additional process for dividing the original image, there is a need to evaluated by including this additional step.

3 Transmission Function for Large-Scale Image Segmentation

We developed a command line program named *tileimage*, which is a JavaScript application that uses Node.js as a framework. By using this command, a large-scale image data (JPEG or PNG) will be divided by the designated number of divisions, and will be sequentially transmitted to the ChOWDER server described in the configuration file. The command is used as follows.

```
tileimage.sh [--config=configfile] imagefile
```

A sample configuration file is shown below. The values of xsplit and ysplit specify the number of divisions in the horizontal and vertical directions, respectively.

```
{
  "id": "APIUser",
  "password": "my_password",
  "url": "ws://my_ChOWDER_server:8081/v2/",
  "xsplit": 8,
  "ysplit": 8,
  "contentid": "my_content01",
  "contentgrp": "default"
}
```

The reason for the implementation as a command line program is that ultra-high-resolution images are required mainly for large scale simulation generated by HPC systems, or large scale sensing data such as weather satellite image data. They are often generated by batch programs as a post process. Therefore, it is more convenient to have the command line program for the batch processing.

4 Performance Measurements and Evaluation

We evaluated the impact of the different image division patterns, generated by the *tileimage* command, onto the performance. The obtained results are shown in Table 2. From these results, an improvement of up to 2.7 times in the display speed was observed when compared to the conventional method without the image subdivision. The 4×3 division coincided with the division patterns of

Table 2. Time required to display a 16K-resolution image using *tileimage* command (average of 5 measurements)

Division pattern	Time (s)	Division pattern	Time (s)
2×2	9.50	6×6	6.76
3×3	7.14	7×7	7.14
4×3	6.62	8×6	6.67
4×4	6.90	8×8	6.85
5×5	7.08	9×9	6.84

the display device in the present test environment, and became the fastest since there was no useless data transfer. Fundamentally, there was a tendency for speed improvement as the number of divisions increases, but there was no perceivable difference when the number of divisions is larger than 3×3. It is worth noting that the utilized network is sufficiently fast, and the amount of the transferred data is not enough to fill the network bandwidth, thus we suspect that this situation contributed to produce almost no difference even using large number of divisions. The proposed function is expected to be more effective in remote collaboration environments, with limited bandwidth, for sharing high-resolution image contents among remote locations.

5   Conclusion and Future Work

In this paper, we presented a new functionality (transmission function for large-scale image segmentation) added to the scalable display system ChOWDER. In this function, an ultra-high-resolution image to be displayed is previously divided and proper sub-images are sent to the display side in order to suppress unnecessary data transmission, and to improve the rendering speed on the display side via web browsers. We observed a speedup of about 2.7 times compared to the conventional function without image subdivision, and almost 3.1 times when compared to SAGE2. Since the transmission function is provided as a command line program, it is possible to directly transmit ultra-high-resolution images to the ChOWDER from a batch process which generates high-resolution image.

Same as the ChOWDER server, this command line program was written in JavaScript, and has also used open source libraries to implement the function, and notes that the software ecosystem is fully utilized. Since we could confirm the effectiveness of the newly added function, we are planning to add a function to register ultra-high-resolution images from the controller user interface (web browser) as well as other types of content.

References

1. Kawanabe, T., Nonaka, J., Hatta, K., Ono, K.: ChOWDER: an adaptive tiled display wall driver for dynamic remote collaboration. In: Luo, Y. (ed.) CDVE 2018. LNCS, vol. 11151, pp. 11–15. Springer, Cham (2018). https://doi.org/10.1007/978-3-030-00560-3_2
2. ChOWDER. https://github.com/SIPupstreamDesign/ChOWDER. Accessed 14 Apr 2019
3. Chung, H., Andrews, C., North, C.: A survey of software frameworks for cluster-based large high-resolution displays. IEEE Trans. Visual Comput. Graphics **20**(8), 1158–1177 (2014)
4. Johnson, G.P., Abram, G.D., Westing, B., Navrátil, P., Gaither, K.: DisplayCluster: an interactive visualization environment for tiled displays. In: 2012 IEEE International Conference on Cluster Computing, pp. 239–247. IEEE (2012)
5. Renambot, L., et al.: SAGE: the scalable adaptive graphics environment. In: Proceedings of WACE (2004). https://www.evl.uic.edu/luc/Research/papers/WACE2004.pdf

6. Marrinan, T.: SAGE2: a new approach for data intensive collaboration using scalable resolution shared displays. In: 2014 International Conference on Collaborative Computing: Networking, Applications and Worksharing (CollaborateCom), pp. 177–186. IEEE (2014)
7. NVIDIA Mosaic. https://www.nvidia.com/en-us/design-visualization/solutions/nvidia-mosaic-technology/. Accessed 14 Apr 2019
8. AMD Eyefinity. https://www.amd.com/en/technologies/eyefinity. Accessed 14 Apr 2019

Automating the Integration of 4D Models in Game Engines for a Virtual Reality-Based Construction Simulation

Simon Bourlon and Conrad Boton[(✉)] [iD]

École de technologie supérieure, 1100, rue Notre-Dame Ouest, Montreal, Canada
simon.bourlon.1@ens.etsmtl.ca, conrad.boton@etsmtl.ca

Abstract. This article is part of the first steps of a more global work in progress. It aims at automating the integration of 4D simulations in virtual reality environments, to easily generate 4D simulation alternatives in such environments. The final goal is to support collaborative constructability analysis sessions based on intuitive simulations of the construction process using BIM models. The results show that while it is possible to create 4D models in a game engine directly from a BIM model and an existing schedule, several improvements still need to be made in order to achieve the desired situation. Similar to most workflows presented in the literature, the one used in this work is not free of limitations. The evaluation of the application shows that most of the problems encountered come from the imperfect transfer of the model from the BIM software to the game engine.

Keywords: 4D simulation · Virtual Reality · Game engines ·
Building Information Modeling

1 Introduction

The Building Information Modeling (BIM) approach is increasingly being adapted in the architecture, engineering, construction and operation industry [1, 2]. 4D simulation is one of the BIM uses recognized by professionals as having the greatest benefit [3]. It consists in associating the objects of a three-dimensional model with the corresponding activities stemming from a work schedule, in order to simulate the construction process over time [4]. Several benefits may arise from the use of 4D simulation, including Analysis of constructability and activity scheduling alternatives [5, 6], communication of ideas, facilitating collaborative work and education [7–10], logistics, site development and excavation [11–13]. Despite these perceived benefits, the adoption and implementation rates of 4D simulation remain low [3]. The main reasons for this low penetration are the lack of adaptation of visualization methods and interaction techniques proposed by the current tools [4, 14].

Recent research works have proposed using Virtual Reality (VR) to overcome some of the limitations of current 4D simulation approaches, and to provide more intuitive and efficient simulation environments for practitioners [14]. 'Virtual Reality' can be referred to as "electronic simulations of environments experienced via head-mounted

© Springer Nature Switzerland AG 2019
Y. Luo (Ed.): CDVE 2019, LNCS 11792, pp. 123–132, 2019.
https://doi.org/10.1007/978-3-030-30949-7_14

eye goggles and wired clothing enabling the end user to interact in realistic three-dimensional situations" [15]. In this context, four elements have to be considered and combined: the virtual world, the immersion, the sensory feedback, and the interactivity [16].

To be able to successfully conduct a 4D simulation in VR environments, many challenges have to be addressed [14]. One of these challenges is related to the preparation and the transfer of the 4D simulation in VR environments. While the transfer of 3D models in VR environment is very well mastered and some tools are more and more proposed to transfer existing 4D models, the resulting simulation can be used only for visualization purposes as-is. However, to be helpful in most of the practitioners' usages including constructability analysis, the 4D simulation should be editable and the users should be able to automatically generate different alternatives of the simulation.

The work presented in this article aims at automating the integration of 4D models in game engines for a virtual reality-based multi-purpose construction simulation. The rest of the paper is organized in four main sections. The first section presents a literature review on Virtual Reality in architecture, engineering and construction, and the transfer of 4D simulations in VR environments. The second section reports the process of development of an application for the automated integration of 4D models in virtual reality environments. The third section proposes a discussion and the improvements track and the fourth section concludes the article.

2 Related Works

2.1 Virtual Reality in Architecture, Engineering and Construction

Using Virtual Reality in construction is not really new. In 1996, the use of VR applications in the construction industry has been investigated by Bouchlaghem et al. [17]. The investigation showed the usefulness of VR technologies both in design (for landscaping, to assess fire risk, to design lighting and interior design, etc.) and in construction (to evaluate construction scenarios, to plan and to monitor the construction processes, and to plan and layout the construction site) [17]. Berg and Vance, in 2017 [18], proposed an evaluation of the use of VR as a decision-making tool in engineering-focused businesses. The results showed that VR is now "mature, stable, and, most importantly, usable" [18]. Moreover, Virtual Reality has been presented by Issa [19] as a solution for integration in the construction industry, since "a virtual reality platform supported by knowledge-based database systems can become the main interface to construction information for every specialty throughout the construction (life) cycle of the project" [19]. The practitioners in construction generally use VR "on large complex projects and on small projects with design reuse" [20]. The use it on large complex projects, to visualize and to understand the engineering problems, with the aim to reduce uncertainty and risk [20]. In the other hand, they tend to use it on small projects with cheaper web-based equipment for more focused usages [20]. Woksepp and Olofsson [21] also assessed the applicability of VR on large construction projects. They showed that VR was useful, but need to be associated with a sufficient workflow in order to minimize waste and to improve the final result [21].

A quantitative evaluation of immersive VR systems capabilities in helping to understand virtual mockups has been proposed by Paes et al. [22]. They showed "an overall better spatial perception of the virtual model when using the immersive environment" [22] and how VR environments can "benefit current design practices by improving professionals' understanding of the spatial arrangement of the virtual model" [22]. Goulding et al. [23] proposed a prototype of an interactive VR environment, The aim is to support the learning of the challenges related to offsite construction. With the proposed system, users can identify some of the "unforeseen problems often caused by professionals' decisions, faulty work, and health and safety issues" [23].

2.2   Transferring 4D Simulations in VR Environments

Transferring 4D simulations in VR environments consists of preparing the data in an appropriate format for their suitable use in the VR systems. Usually, one uses game engines to prepare the file in the required format. Multiple game engines are available, including Unity, Quest 3D, CryEngine, Blender, Unreal, Torque 3D, etc. and it is possible to compare them regarding their functionalities and features [24, 25]. A model export workflow from Revit to Unity 3D has been proposed by the Penn State CIC Research Group [26]. It suggested to prepare the model in Revit and to export it in FBX format. Then, this FBX file should be imported and optimized in Autodesk 3DS Max. One can also use a paid script can also be used to convert Revit textures into standard material used by 3DS Max and readable by virtual reality software. Ultimately, the model can be imported as a new asset in Unity 3D.

While this is interesting, it is not adapted to the transfer of 4D simulations, as both 3D geometry and sequencing information are contained in 4D models. Broadbent [27] presented a method based on Autodesk authoring tools for the transfer of 4D models in game engines. The method proposed to export the geometry directly from Revit to 3DS Max by the use of a plugin based on the DWFx format. In the other hand, the temporal information is exported by using an XML, directly from Navisworks to 3DS Max, using a Timeline exporter plugin. It is then possible, according to Broadbent [27], to export the 4D model from 3DS Max to Unity based on FBX and Timeline files. Note that the steps of the method are only poorly described and do not provide sufficient information about how the timeline is actually transferred.

More recently, Boton [14] explored a similar workflow to transfer a 4D simulation in a VR environment. The result was not very conclusive since "all the objects start their path at 0, 0, 0 despite starting in their original locations in 3DS Max".

3 Development of an Application for the Automated Integration of 4D Models in Virtual Reality Environments

3.1 Data Preparation

The first step is to import the data that will create the 4D simulation. In the literature review, we saw that the import of the 3D model from Revit should be done in FBX format. This format allows the model to be used on Unity 3D. In order to keep the texture rendering on Unity 3D, an intermediate step was needed. It was necessary to first import the Revit model into 3DSMax and then export it in FBX format. This system made it possible not to lose visual information. However, the problem was that the tree of the elements was too complicated to manage by the code. The subobjects of the model were classified in subgroups. The code would have needed a lot of loops to recover the elements one by one. To retrieve an element in Unity from its name, it is necessary to find the "parent" GameObject and after searching among the "child" GameObjects the one who has this name. If we consider our model in full at step 0 of the tree, step 1 is then the differentiation of the stages for example, then step 2 lists the types of object present on this stage (example: ripe, doors, stairs …), this up to the level N where we find the elements named exactly as in the planning of construction. Only this would require at the code level additional iterations to at least know the value of the N scale where to look for and then go through each loop by associating the elements.

We then tested to export our model in FBX format from Naviswork. The representation of the tree was then much easier to manage. Sub-objects are not classified in subgroups. The GameObjects "child" are directly at level 1, in the case where we consider step 0 at the level of the main GameObject. The retrieval of the elements by the code was then simplified, we did not need different paths loops in search of the elements corresponding to the elements of the imported construction schedule. However, it should be noted that the rendering of textures is not optimal. The schedule is imported into Unity from an Excel file, in .csv format. Note that Unity does not take into account special characters. This requires changing one by one these elements in the text. Otherwise, it is possible to use a modification on Excel that automatically replaces all these special characters.

3.2 Automating the Generation of 4D Simulations in Unity 3D

Codes that can be used by Unity must be written in C# language. For the application, it was made the choice that all the calculations, all the functions necessary for the creation of the 4D simulation are written in the same code. Thus, the user has all the elements in a single code file from which, he can access any coding changes that may be necessary. This choice has imposed a rigour in the organization of writing to simplify reading. In this part, we present each element that constitutes this code. The chosen organization, following the constraints of this type of language, is represented in Fig. 1.

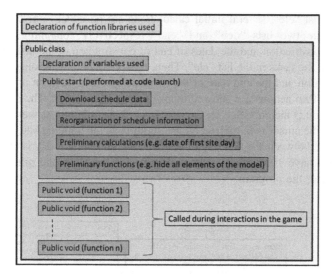

Fig. 1. Organization of the code of the application.

The first step performed at the launch of the game is the download of data related to the construction schedule. The information is to be retrieved in the "Resources" folder by means of a text file named "Planning". Then this information is reorganized in a format suitable for the following manipulations. This reorganization process is detailed in Fig. 2. The text file is transformed into a list consisting of a string list.

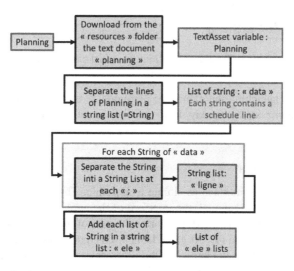

Fig. 2. Path of the program to transform the text file Planning in the list "ele".

From this list "ele", several initial calculations are possible. A first manipulation allows to create two lists "deb" and "end" respectively containing the dates of beginning of construction and the dates of end of construction of the tasks in the same order as that of the tasks in the list "ele". Then, it is possible to determine the start date of the construction and the end date of the construction. The duration of the project is then deduced. Two actions are allowed thanks to this information. The date displayed in the application is then updated on the first day of construction. As well as the length of the scale of the cursor is initialized on the duration of the building site. For example, if the difference between the first day of construction and the last day is 100 days then the cursor will have 100 possible values. Figure 3 summarizes the principles underlying this part of the program.

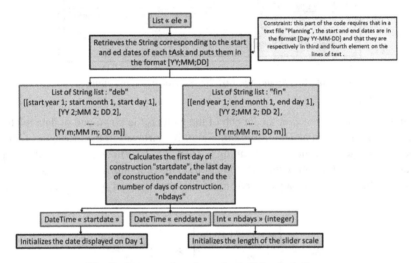

Fig. 3. Program flow from the initial calculations.

Finally, when launching the game, the 3D model is connected to the schedule and hidden as the game starts on day 1 of the site, so no element is supposed to be displayed.

3.3 The User Interface

The goal is to make an interface as simple as possible. Thus, in addition to the main window displaying the 4D model, the interface of the application is composed of four elements (Fig. 4). The first is a text, it informs the user of the date of the day of the site displayed by the application (1). At game launch, this date is initialized on the first day of the first task built. At each change on the time scale, this date is updated. Then the interface has two button type interactors. The first one displays the text "Previous day" (2) and the second displays "Next day" (3). They make it possible to modify the date of the day by making use of the previously developed interaction functions. The last element of the interface is a slider (4). This is a cursor that can be translated on the time scale. Its minimum value is the first day of construction and its maximum value on the last day of construction.

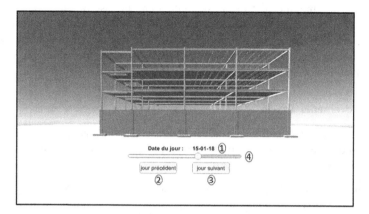

Fig. 4. User interface of the application (in French)

4 Discussion and Improvements Track

Thanks to the first-person simulation control module, the application is adapted to most virtual reality systems using Unity 3D as a game engine. This is the case of the virtual reality system named Valyz, developed by the company Realyz. The application was tested and evaluated in the Valyz environment, using multiple 4D models.

4.1 Analysis of Use and Criticisms

Several 4D models have been tested in the Valyz system. The functionalities developed in the application are present and active. The movements of the camera follow the directions given by the controller of the system. The 3D glasses can simulate the movement of the head to orient the image.

It is possible to select the construction period to display as expected in the application. However, the interface developed with the buttons, the cursor, and the display of the date is not projected. It is present on the computer screen that is connected to the Valyz system, but it is not present in the virtual environment projected on the wall. It is possible, however, for the user to interact with the buttons from the computer and this affects the displayed model. It would have been preferable for the interface to be displayed in the virtual environment so that the user can point the joystick to the interact button and manage the temporality. The problem is that in the Valyz system support software, only three-dimensional elements are displayed in the virtual environment. One of the solutions provided by computer scientists of the company marketing this system is to change the representation of the interface. In the application, the interface is created from a 2D canvas connected to the camera. The idea would be to replace each element with three-dimensional objects, for example, the buttons would be replaced by cubes also connected to the camera. The user could then interact with the object by pointing his controller. These changes require that the code be modified and that new functions be developed accordingly.

Regarding the modification of the simulation and the use of alternative schedules, the solutions proposed previously tackle the problem that the Unity application is no longer connected to the .exe file used by the software that allows to control the Valyz tool. Therefore, it is necessary to perform a new export of the file from Unity with each change, which is not optimal.

4.2   Improvements Track

A number of comments and suggestions for improvement arise from the evaluation, namely improvements in data imports, the addition of additional features related to BIM 4D, and the constraints of Unity.

Improvements in Data Imports: At the 3D model level, the FBX format is the most suitable for use in Unity. Only we saw that there was a choice to make between rendering the displayed texture and the structure of the object tree. It would be interesting to continue the search for an export system from Autodesk software in FBX format that can satisfy both a good rendering state of the model display and a structure at the same time. The tree that can be used by the developed code.

In the same way, when importing the schedule, the text file is too formally constrained. For example, the code developed assumes that the original Excel file has the following form (Column 1: Task Name; Column 2: Duration of tasks; Column 3: Start date of the tasks; and Column 4: End date of tasks).

This means that this type of file must follow a standard that is not necessarily adopted in the workplace. Only, we can notice that the code is easily modifiable if the workbook at the origin is not exactly adapted to the code. The improvement track would be to make the code more automatic, for example by first performing a function that detects in which column the useful information is located.

Regarding the link between the list of 3D elements and the scheduled task list, it could be improved by adding the use of a standard. Some, such as the Uniformat II standard, may be able to link the data more easily. It would be possible to import also in the planning a column con-holding this kind of code. For the moment, no solution has been found for this standardized code to appear in the name of the elements of the 3D model. For the editable aspect of the simulation without having to leave the game to reload a new schedule, a track of improvements would be to load in the file "Resources" several versions of the planning of construction and connected to the interface as many buttons. Thus, simply by activating a schedule by clicking on it in the interface, the application directly calculates the new simulation and therefore modifies accordingly the display of the elements constructed or not.

Additional Features Related to the 4D BIM and Constraints of Unity: One of the main features that could not be added to the application is the differentiation of the build state of each task. In our case, from the moment a task has a start date prior to today's date in the simulation, it is displayed. Otherwise, it is hidden. The idea would be to be able to have several states possible: built elements - elements in construction - elements not built. One could for example display in a normal way the constructed elements, in green the elements under construction and with a transparency effect the elements that remain to build. This was not possible because Unity 3D considers that each item from the 3D model import does not have a feature to change its appearance.

When using Unity 3D, several problems were encountered. Especially at the level of the text file corresponding to the schedule. Many characters are not allowed by the software when reading the document, such as accents or "-" that may be in the name of the tasks. It may be possible then to create an additional function that takes care of replacing or removing these characters, keeping in mind that they must still correspond to the names of the elements of the 3D model present in the tree.

5   Conclusion and Future Works

Thanks to the evolution of computer tools, it is possible to simulate and to anticipate many problems that arise on construction sites. This is all the more remarkable since the modeling software makes it possible to integrate the construction schedule. It is important for the workers to visualize the 3D model in an equivalent way. The research project reported in this paper aimed to automate the integration of 4D simulations in virtual reality environments, to easily generate 4D simulation alternatives in such environments. The work shows that it is possible to create 4D models in a game engine, directly from a BIM model and an existing schedule. However, several improvements still need to be made in order to achieve the desired situation. Future work will focus on correcting these limitations, before going further in the study of 4D models in virtual reality environments.

References

1. Sacks, R., Eastman, C., Lee, G., Teicholz, P.: BIM Handbook: A Guide to Building Information Modeling for Owners, Designers, Engineers, Contractors, and Facility Managers. Wiley, Hoboken (2018)
2. Boton, C., Forgues, D.: Practices and processes in BIM projects: an exploratory case study. In: Advances in Civil Engineering (2018)
3. Kreider, R., Messner, J., Dubler, C.: Determining the frequency and impact of applying BIM for different purposes on building projects. In: Proceedings of 6th International Conference on Innovation in Architecture, Engineering and Construction (AEC), pp. 1–10 (2010)
4. Boton, C., Kubicki, S., Halin, G.: Designing adapted visualization for collaborative 4D applications. Autom. Constr. **36**, 152–167 (2013)
5. Akinci, B., Fischer, M., Levitt, R.: Formalization and automation of time-space conflict analysis (2000)
6. Hartmann, T., Fischer, M.: Supporting the constructability review with 3D/4D models. Build. Res. Inf. **35**, 70–80 (2007)
7. Clayton, M.: Virtual construction of architecture using 3D CAD and simulation. Autom. Constr. **11**, 227–235 (2002)
8. Kang, H., Lho, B., Kim, J.: Development of web-based interactive 4D block tower model for construction planning and scheduling education. In: Proceedings of the 2004 ASEE Annual Conference and Exposition, Salt Lake City, Utah, pp. 1–10 (2004)

9. Wang, L., Messner, J.I., Leicht, R.: Assessement of 4D modeling for schedule visualization in construction engineering education. In: 24th CIB W78 Conference, Bridging ITC Knowledge to Work, Maribor, Slovenia, pp. 737–742 (2007)
10. Kubicki, S., Boton, C.: 4D-based teaching of high-rise structural principles. In: Proceedings of the CIB W78-W102 2011, Sophia Antipolis (2011)
11. Yabuki, N., Shitani, T.: A management system for cut and fill earthworks based on 4D CAD and EVMS. In: Proceedings of Computing in Civil Engineering Conference, Cancun, Mexico, pp. 1–8 (2005)
12. Shah, R.K., Dawood, N., Castro, S.: Automatic generation of progress profiles for earthwork operations using 4D visualisation model. Electron. J. Inf. Technol. Constr. 13, 491–506 (2008)
13. Boton, C., Kubicki, S., Halin, G.: The challenge of level of development in 4D/BIM simulation across AEC project lifecyle. A case study. Procedia Eng. 123, 59–67 (2015)
14. Boton, C.: Supporting constructability analysis meetings with immersive virtual reality-based collaborative BIM 4D simulation. Autom. Constr. 96, 1–15 (2018)
15. Harvey, D.: Invisible site: a virtual sho. George Coates Performance Works, San Francisco, CA, vol. 346, p. 87 (1992)
16. Sherman, W.R., Craig, A.B.: Understanding Virtual Reality: Interface, Application, and Design. Morgan Kaufmann Publishers, San Francisco (2018). ISBN 978-0128009659
17. Bouchlaghem, N.M., Liyanage, I.G.: Virtual reality applications in the UK's construction industry. http://itc.scix.net/data/works/att/w78-1996-89.content.pdf
18. Berg, L.P., Vance, J.M.: Industry use of virtual reality in product design and manufacturing: a survey. Virtual Reality 21, 1–17 (2017)
19. Issa, R.R.A.: Virtual reality: a solution to seamless technology integration in the AEC industry. In: Construction Congress VI, pp. 1007–1013. ASCE (2005)
20. Whyte, J.: Innovation and users: virtual reality in the construction sector. Constr. Manag. Econ. 21, 565–572 (2003)
21. Woksepp, S., Olofsson, T.: Credibility and applicability of virtual reality models in design and construction. Adv. Eng. Inform. 22, 520–528 (2008)
22. Paes, D., Arantes, E., Irizarry, J.: Immersive environment for improving the understanding of architectural 3D models: comparing user spatial perception between immersive and traditional virtual reality systems. Autom. Constr. 84, 292–303 (2017)
23. Goulding, J., Nadim, W., Petridis, P., Alshawi, M.: Construction industry offsite production: a virtual reality interactive training environment prototype. Adv. Eng. Inform. 26, 103–116 (2012)
24. Dickson, P.E., Block, J.E., Echevarria, G.N., Keenan, K.C.: An experience-based comparison of unity and unreal for a stand-alone 3D game development course. In: Proceedings of the 2017 ACM Conference on Innovation and Technology in Computer Science Education - ITiCSE 2017, pp. 70–75 (2017)
25. Zarrad, A.: Game engine solutions. In: Simulation and Gaming, pp. 75–87 (2018)
26. Liu, Y., Tanudjaja, G., Jiang, Z., Beck, N.: Workflow of Exporting Revit Models to Unity. State College, Pennsylvania (2016)
27. Broadbent, N.: BIM and gaming engines: how we present 4D models using our design suite and gaming engine (2011)

BIM'ShareLab: A Framework for Advanced BIM Training

Samia Ben Rajeb[1]([✉]) and Pierre Leclercq[2]([✉])

[1] Université Libre de Bruxelles, Brussels, Belgium
samia.ben.rajeb@ulb.ac.be
[2] University of Liège, Liège, Belgium
pierre.leclercq@uliege.be

Abstract. This paper presents a framework for advanced BIM training, considering the organisational changes brought by this new collaborative design strategy in companies involved in the process of a building project. The training focus concerns an extensive understanding of the impacts of BIM on current practices. The training framework is described through its 4 capsules/concepts promoted by organisational management proposed in the ShareLab between actors: awareness, sharing, common ground, cognitive and operational synchronisation. The method has been applied in 9 participative workshops and has proven to be successful with positive feedbacks from about its originality and efficiency.

Keywords: BIM building information modelling · Cooperative learning · Collaborative simulation in architecture · Engineering and construction · Cooperative user experience · ShareLab application

1 Introduction

Building Information Modelling (BIM) methods and technology aim to support joint work throughout the life cycle of the design, construction and the operation of a building. From a technical point of view, BIM deals with modelling through digital models of data relating to the building, its constraints and performance objectives. From the perspective of coordination, this information needs to be expressed and managed through a collaborative process called Building Information Management, and its integration is yet to be invented (Celnik 2014).

Many specialised courses, workshops and seminars attempt to train a diverse set of players in the construction sector. Their goal is to carry out a unified vision of the building. However, the majority of them remain limited to a technical approach to modelling. If they deal with the organisational component, they often present it as the application of rules related to management, and thereby neglect to address the impact of organisational changes caused by this unified vision.

In order to meet this need, this paper presents a framework for advanced BIM training based on the ShareLab principles (Ben Rajeb et al. 2015). Linked to the organisational dimension, this training raises the awareness of all players regarding the

© Springer Nature Switzerland AG 2019
Y. Luo (Ed.): CDVE 2019, LNCS 11792, pp. 133–141, 2019.
https://doi.org/10.1007/978-3-030-30949-7_15

real BIM stakes: beyond technological mastery, the numerical implementation of the building questions the quality of human collaborative processes before all else.

2 Origins of the BIM'ShareLab

There are three challenges associated to the implementation of BIM at the company level:

(1) guaranteeing the transition from a sequential organisation through "batches" to a collaborative process (Forgues et al. 2016);
(2) bringing technical solutions to transfer problems, and sharing numerical data (Celnik et al. 2014);
(3) considering the organisational changes at the heart of the companies involved in the life cycle of the project. This requires an extensive understanding of the impacts of BIM on current practices (Mihindu and Arayici 2008).

In this current environment, it is necessary to train, in a short period of time, all the players involved in construction in these new building model strategies. Conversely, it is important to change their way of thinking in this rapidly evolving sector. To achieve this, it is important to prepare the players to manage work teams and to face any difficulties that may result from organisational changes in a design/construction environment already disrupted by the implementation of the BIM. With this objective in mind, we propose a participative method that is intended to be integrated in BIM training. Known as the BIM'ShareLab, it is based on ShareLab principles and is intended for change management (Ben Rajeb et al. 2015) and for Serious Games, which is learning through games (Cohard 2015). The objective of this method is the constant repetition between (Fig. 1):

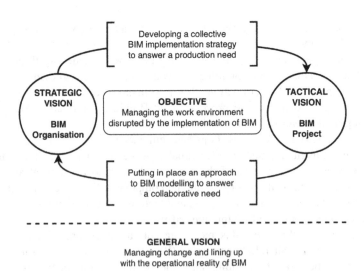

Fig. 1. Learning targeted by the BIM'ShareLab method

(a) a tactical vision for the construction of a modelling process with the optimal management of production in mind;
(b) an organisational vision of the joint construction of a collective strategy with the optimal management of collaboration in mind.

The main aim of this BIM'ShareLab is to help professionals in the construction sector to adapt to a rapidly changing environment and to align their respective visions with operational realities.

3   BIM'ShareLab Principles

The BIM'ShareLab is composed of 4 reflection capsules: 2 are participative (carried out by the learners themselves) and they are presented in the form of a game and/or a focus group; the two others are more classic (implemented by the supervisors who push the learners to ask themselves questions about their own activities and learning). These 4 reflection capsules are preceded by a moment of pooling during which participants present themselves, describe their roles in their respective firms, express their expectations of the training and define BIM in 3 to 5 words. The goal of alternating between participative and directed capsules is to address and promote conformity of different learning styles (Kolb 1984; Riding and Rayner 1998; Chevrier et al. 2000).

The succession of these 4 capsules mirrors the 4 principle concepts promoted by the model of organisational management proposed in the ShareLab (Fig. 2), namely (1) shared awareness (Carroll et al. 2003), (2) sharing (Filstad et al. 2018), (3) common ground (Murer et al. 2014) and (4) cognitive and operational synchronisation (Darses and Falzon 1996).

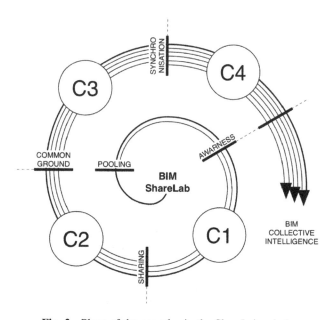

Fig. 2. Place of the capsules in the ShareLab spiral.

4   Steps of the BIM'ShareLab

The 4 steps of the BIM'ShareLab express their goals and means in the following way (Fig. 3).

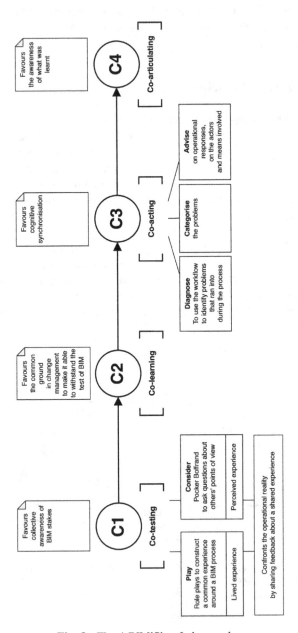

Fig. 3. The 4 BIM'ShareLab capsules.

4.1   Capsule 1: Co-testing

The goal of this first capsule is to establish a common experience between all learners (independently of their degree of knowledge of and experience with BIM). This serves as a shared example for all participants. Moreover, it illustrates each concept and theory that will be mentioned throughout the training. By way of a role play (First step: Play) then through a game of questions/answers (Step 2: Consider), this thinking and co-testing capsule allows for the first sharing of learners' feedback of their experiences between themselves and their supervisors. This promotes an initial mutual awareness of BIM stakes.

Table 1. Means used in the participative reflection C1: co-testing.

Co-testing	Participative thinking			
Step	Means	Logistics	Game leaders	Rules
1. Play: Role-playing	Role play	Management of the game – implementation – tools of production (non-BIM)	Distributor Controller	Clarification of the general rules: Rounds + End
		Management of the roles – characters: actors working in the construction sector – card with a scenario: lists the series of actions (that follow one another or occur in parallel) that need to be carried out – mission cards: describe in detail each action that needs to be carried out by the actor		Explanation of specific rules: – variations in the forms of communication – game with or without observers – game may vary depending on the number of participants
2. Consider: Sharing and giving feedback on the experiment	Series of questions	Boffrand cards Questionnaire	Questioner/tutor	Simultaneous answers to avoid the effect of influencers Round table answers with the participation managed by the questioner

From the beginning of the first capsule (Play), each role is presented to the learners in the form of Characters. Before starting the game, a card that presents the scenario is given to each learner. The scenario can be built in a way that it orders all the actions, but it can also be seen as a random and/or independent part of the actions. Thereafter, all actors are asked to sit around a table and to each choose a role. Two game leaders are chosen from the group of players: a distributor and a controller. This staging is done to immerse all the learners, with their different profiles and expertise, in a context of BIM implementation that corresponds to what they would experience. It is done without any need for numerical tools. By taking participants out of the day-to-day issues of modelling and management of information (which is often what is addressed in traditional BIM training), they are forced to confront issues linked to collaboration and information sharing. Each player must then (1) follow the scenario, and (2) execute the actions given to them by the distributor. Once the player completes his/her action, the controller verifies its proper execution, and the game continues in such a fashion until the end of the scenario.

The Micro Poker cards (Gless et al. 2017) are used in the second part of the capsule (Consider) in order to ask each learner to give their points of view about (1) their common/shared experience, (2) their respective fields of expertise and (3) their knowledge or even their opinions about what the BIM means in terms of changes in their work habits.

The more they progress in the game, the more they become aware of the fact that they need to adapt to a rapidly changing environment and to align their respective outlooks to the operational reality (Table 1).

4.2   Capsule 2: Co-learning

This second contemplative capsule's goal is to construct a common ground around organisational change management facing BIM implementation. By using the experiences from capsule 1 as a starting point, the players not only gain awareness of the fact that they will face resistance related to change, but that they will also need to answer any objections regarding: the implementation of BIM, the way the action is managed, the interoperability of the models, the way choices are made and decisions are combined, the way that resources are allocated to enable the BIM implementation etc.

The central question that the supervisor attempts to answer is how to deal with these contradictions in a work environment disrupted by the implementation of BIM. He/she finds an answer to this question through an alignment with the global vision proposed by the BIM'ShareLab (Fig. 1) and through a course managed by the teacher with the participation of the learners.

4.3   Capsule 3: Co-acting

On the basis of their previous experiences (either from their work in the field or those gained during the common C1 capsule), all participants are asked to sketch their respective work- and dataflows on a framework given to them beforehand. This chart serves as a basis for the diagnosis and identification of all the issues met during this design/construction process of a project in a BIM framework. Furthermore, it allows for another opportunity to share more precise and structured experiences between the learners, as well as cognitive synchronisation relating to they way in which the project unfolds as it pertains to the expertise of each participant. Once the issues are identified and placed (by number) on a flow chart, the learners are invited to order the issues by defined categories in relation to the origin of the issue. On the basis of this classification and that of the course given during capsule 2, the learners propose their own recommendations and attempt to improve the previous flow chart (Table 2).

Table 2. Means used in the C3 participative thinking: co-acting.

C3 Co-acting	Participative thinking	
Step	Means	Logistics
0. Charting	Workflow and dataflow	Mapping of the flow
1. Diagnosing		
2. Categorising		Categorisation chart
3. Recommending		Recommendation chart

This Co-acting capsule 3, therefore, allows participants to (1) jointly identify the types of issues, as opposed to a list of issues; (2) realise that issues associated to information sharing and collaboration management are just as frequent as those related to information modelling according to a BIM process; (3) demonstrate the influence of BIM-maturity in the way in which they should define their workflow and protocol; (4) collectively act on the workflow by considering their respective professions and proposing an action that can be dedicated and integrated to their professional context for better change management.

4.4 Capsule 4: Co-articulating

In order to promote a common awareness regarding:

- the reality in the field! As it relates to BIM implementation,
- the challenges pertaining to change resulting from BIM implementation,
- the approach needed for the integration of BIM processes in their activities (short-term) and in their firms (longer-term): toward a better management of BIM implementation,

a summary is presented to each learner in the form of photos taken, as well as elements created as a group throughout the participative thinking capsules. This expression is materialised by a collective definition, in words, of the challenges of BIM today and the medium- and long-term targets.

5   Conclusion, Validation, Limitations and Outlook

Formatted in this way, our framework has been used since 2017 in the setting of Continued Certification Programs (University of Liège, University of Louvain, Polytechnics International Tunis), in a Masters Course (Architectural Engineering, University of Liège), in Belgian professional training (Forem and IFAPME) and in customised training at the request of companies (architectural agencies, design offices in engineering and prime contracting). To this date, it has formed more than 100 learners: architects, engineers, entrepreneurs, planners, industrial draughtsmen, facility managers, quantity surveyors, etc. This method has proven to be successful and generally receives very positive feedback about its originality and efficiency.

This training continues to be developed based on the feedback given by the participants some of whom have requested if they could put it into practice in their own companies. This article, therefore, aims to formalise it in order to firmy delineate its principles, all the while allowing it to evolve and diversify in a variety of contexts.

In terms of its limitations, it is important to highlight the need to lengthen the duration of the method. It is usually limited by one-day workshop training programs. While one-day training raises awareness in the participants, it does not leave them enough time to go beyond the hypothetical scenario and use the blended experiences of all the participants in an applied setting.

Another difficulty is to adapt capsules 3 and 4 to the individual experiences of the participants. The message needs to be adapted depending on the different degrees of BIM uses – technical use or managerial use – this deals with expressing a common reflection. Different scenarios have currently been started in order to be able to effectively associate all types of BIM profiles to the training.

Along the same lines, a professional role play (characters, mission cards and scenarios) is currently being studied. Its goal is to diversify the use cases and to promote this method.

References

Ben Rajeb, S., Senciuc, A., Pluchinotta, I.: ShareLab, support for collective intelligence. In: Proceedings of the Fifth International Conference on Advanced Collaborative Networks, Systems and Applications, COLLA 2015, Malta (2015)

Carroll, J.M., Neale, D.C., Isenhour, P.L., Rosson, M.B., McCrickard, D.S.: Notification and awareness: synchronizing task-oriented collaborative activity. Int. J. Hum. Comput. Stud. **58**, 605–632 (2003)

Celnik, O., Lebègue, E.: BIM & Maquette numérique pour l'architecture, le bâtiment et la construction. Eyrolles et CSTB, Paris (2014)

Chevrier, J., Fortin, G., LeBlanc, R., Théberge, M.: Problématique de la nature du style d'apprentissage. In: Education et francophonie, vol. XXVIII (1), pp. 3–19. ACELF, Québec (2000)

Cohard, P.: L'apprentissage dans les serious games: proposition d'une typologie. Cairn.Info **3**(16), 11–40 (2015)

Darses, F., Falzon, P.: La conception collective: une approche de l'ergonomie cognitive. In: de Terssac, G., Friedberg, E. (eds.) Coopération et Conception, pp. 123–135. Toulouse, Octarès (1996)

Filstad, C., Simeonova, B., Visser, M.: Crossing power and knowledge boundaries in learning and knowledge sharing: the role of ESM. Learn. Organ. **25**(3), 159–168 (2018)

Forgues, E.-C., Carignan, V., Forgues, D., Rajeb, S.B.: A framework for improving collaboration patterns in BIM projects. In: Luo, Y. (ed.) CDVE 2016. LNCS, vol. 9929, pp. 34–42. Springer, Cham (2016). https://doi.org/10.1007/978-3-319-46771-9_5

Gless, H.-J., Hanser, D., Halin, G.: BIM-agile practices experiments in architectural design. In: Luo, Y. (ed.) CDVE 2017. LNCS, vol. 10451, pp. 135–142. Springer, Cham (2017). https://doi.org/10.1007/978-3-319-66805-5_17

Kolb, D.A.: Experiential Learning: Experience as the Source of Learning and Development. Prentice-Hall, Englewood Cliffs (1984)

Mihindu, S., Arayici, Y.: Digital construction through BIM systems will drive the re-engineering of construction business practices. In: 2008 International Conference on Visualisation, pp. 29–34 (2008)

Murer, M., Jacobsson, M., Skillgate, S., Sundström, P.: Taking things apart: reaching common ground and shared material understanding. In: Proceedings of the SIGCHI Conference on Human Factors in Computing Systems, pp. 469–472. ACM (2014)

Riding, R., Rayer, S.: Cognitive Styles and Learning Strategies. David Fulton, Londres (1998)

Implementing Mobile Technology on Construction Sites: An Ethnographic Action Research Approach

Éric St-Pierre, Conrad Boton$^{(\boxtimes)}$ ⓘ, and Gabriel Lefebvre

École de technologie supérieure, 1100, rue Notre-Dame Ouest, Montreal, Canada
conrad.boton@etsmtl.ca

Abstract. The increasing dissemination of the Building Information Modelling (BIM) approach must not overshadow the fact that many firms are still far from BIM, and are in fact just starting out on the road to adopting information technologies. This paper presents an ethnographic action research study conducted with an industrial partner that decided to implement information technologies on its construction sites, with a strong preference for home-made applications. The results suggest that firms lack the internal expertise to effectively conduct such development work. Thus, the passage of needs expressed by the firm towards the development of the application is particularly difficult and the pivotal role of the researcher was crucial in the success of the project. Multiple iterations and versions were necessary before achieving the expected goals.

Keywords: Mobile computing · Mobile cloud computing ·
Information technology for construction · Construction site ·
Ethnographic action research

1 Introduction

In the last decades, the construction industry has undergone a digital transition, manifested in particular by the growing role of information technology (IT) in practices [1–3]. In this context, the BIM approach appears to occupy an important place, and several works have shown its added value and its uses at different stages of a construction project [4]. Several studies have also shown that BIM is increasingly being disseminated in architectural, engineering and construction firms, and that the point of no return has been reached [5, 6]. However, this reality should not overshadow the fact that several firms are still far from BIM, and are in fact just beginning their adoption of information technologies [2]. The situation with general contractors and subcontractors is more challenging because the adoption of IT in the office must be accompanied by a similar adoption of mobile technologies on construction sites, in order to optimize information exchange between the office and the construction site [7].

Experiences reported in the literature show that the adoption of mobile technologies on-site can be more difficult, and poses significant challenges, due to the peculiarities and particular requirements of construction site work. Thus, the research on the subject

© Springer Nature Switzerland AG 2019
Y. Luo (Ed.): CDVE 2019, LNCS 11792, pp. 142–150, 2019.
https://doi.org/10.1007/978-3-030-30949-7_16

is often based on generic solutions [8, 9], and is limited to the study of related issues [10, 11], the link with BIM and the ability of site actors to adapt their work processes to these tools [12–15], and the study of perceived added value [16–20]. Very few studies [14] have explored the issue using a participatory approach to identify the real needs of firms, their ability to meet their own needs with their in-house resources, and the issues associated with their decisions. The research presented in this article took place at the premises of an industrial partner which decided to implement information technologies on its construction sites, with a strong preference for home-made applications. The objective of the research is to understand the internal dynamics allowing proceeding from the initial situation of the firm and the needs expressed, towards a solution adapted to the realities of its construction sites.

The article is organized into four main parts. The first part presents related works. The second part introduces the methodology. The third part presents the context and the main results. The fourth part concludes the paper and presents the future works.

2 Related Works

2.1 Information Technology in the Construction Industry

Two main flows appear in the production chain of a construction activity, as proposed by Sunke [21]: the flow of material and the flow of information, with strong interactions between the two. These flows correspond to the two major sub-processes identified by Bjork [22], namely, the information sub-process and the hardware sub-process. The material sub-process is the more tangible of the two, but needs the information sub-process, since, along with material and energy, information is the third fundamental component of sociotechnical systems [23]. Information Technology (IT) can be defined as "the use of electronic machines and programs for the processing, storage, transfer and presentation of information" [22]. The formats commonly used to represent information in construction are text documents, 2D and 3D drawings, schedules in bar chart and other formats, various diagrams and charts, tables, etc. The solutions to construction project problems are highly dependent on the experience and judgment of professionals and involve uncertainties. These barriers to applying IT in architecture, engineering and construction (AEC) lead to a challenging and interesting problem when it comes to producing an inventory of the use and the impact of IT on the industry.

Debate on the subject focuses on the premise that while demand actually exists, current technology-based solutions proposed to the industry are not adapted enough to support current needs [17, 24]. According to Bowden et al. [17], those involved in the development of such systems tend to focus on what is technically exciting and on what presents great challenges, rather than on the real needs and issues facing construction companies. Several other factors could also be raised as contributing to delays in the use of information technology; these factors can in fact be considered as barriers to adoption. Based on Bowden et al. [17], we can summarise the factors as follows: lack of leadership, resistance to change, fragmentation of the industry, difficulty of use and lack of internal competencies.

2.2 Mobile Computing for Construction Sites

According to Rebolj and Menzel (2004), because of its specific characteristics, the architecture, engineering, construction (AEC) industry is a very good field for the implementation of mobile computing. They defined mobile computing through three main components: (1) computers usable while being in motion, excluding conventional notebooks; (2) networks with enough bandwidth accessible while in motion; (3) mobile applications to support personalisation and context sensitivity [25]. Mobile information technology then includes "tablet PCs and all kinds of pocket computers [...] and wearable computers" [25], aims to enable workers to "to roam seamlessly with computing and communication functionalities in an uninterrupted way" [9]. Its deployment has been enabled in different industries by the development of "affordable mobile technologies", making it common for mobile users to "capture, store and reuse information" [17]. Rebolj and Menzel (2004) argued that mobile computing is not just another information technology, but a very important factor in construction, with the potential "to increase the effective use of IT in an integrated and holistic way" [10]. Indeed, mobile computing can "extend the boundary of information systems from site offices to actual work sites and ensure real-time data flow to and from construction work sites" [10].

Nowadays, technology has evolved dramatically, and most of the preceding issues are no longer as pertinent. Mobile cloud computing has considerably increased mobile device computing resources [26]. It combines cloud-based storage and application processing services to improve compute-intensive applications and off-device storage on mobile devices. This computing can implement multiple strategies of augmentation (storage, screen, energy, application processing) in order to alleviate the resource limitations of traditional mobile computing systems [26, 27]. It can thus significantly reduce the cost of mobile application development and execution, while greatly extending the resources and the services provided [28]. Abolfazli et al. (2014) proposed a comparison between cloud-based computing and traditional resources, showing that cloud-based systems ensure higher computational power, elasticity, user experience, reliability, security and safety. Many recent research works have explored the question of the use of mobile computing on construction sites. Some of them have studied the use of mobile apps on construction sites, focusing on the added value brought to construction projects [16–18, 20], or on extending the uses of BIM on construction sites, using mobile cloud computing [13–15].

3 Research Approach

Action research is a research approach based on the belief that it is by acting first and foremost that scientific data can be collected [29]. is a method that prioritises practice and collaboration between practitioners and researchers throughout the project process. However, it does not necessarily offer tools and techniques to allow a good understanding of the process. Ethnographic research proposes these tools and techniques for research. It was developed by anthropologists for the study of human culture, but in recent decades, it has been used as an instrument of observation for the implementation of technologies in systems. Ethnographic action research focuses on understanding the actions, thoughts and feelings of professionals, throughout their work day. This makes it possible to implement customised systems that are tailored to meet their real needs, using the ethnographic action research approach as proposed by Hartmann et al. (2009). This type of research must draw information from several sources, such as existing and completed forms, interviews, observations, reports, etc. To be possible, it requires a good integration of the researcher into the project team. After all the information is gathered, it will be possible to determine and design a platform adapted to the needs. With ethnographic action research, it is important to always be able to compare results with the initially identified needs [30].

In this research, we use the ethnographic action research principle explained above. Observations, internal documentation reviews and interviews are conducted in order to understand the business context and to identify the needs. The appropriate solutions are then proposed according to these needs, and implemented in a pilot project, to evaluate the proposals. The choice of the device was conducted in 3 steps. First, a list of requirements was established, based on the previously identified need. In the light of these requirements, the researcher prepared a shortlist of devices that potentially meet the needs. Working with the internal developers, additional criteria were then used to preselect the most appropriate devices. Finally, discussions with upper management and the operational workers led to the choice of one device.

4   Main Results

4.1   The Context

The industrial partner is a steel structure company that has been operating in the field for 40 years. It manufactures and installs steel frames, and in some cases, can offer design services. When fully operational, the firm employs close to 150 people. Although cell phones and e-mails are widely used in the firm for communication, paper is still present, and is the most used tool for management by project managers. This is also the reality for the many projects carried out by the company, which therefore leads to significant information duplication. Indeed, the use of paper is still a necessity as it allows forepersons and superintendents to do their work, including the management of incoming information from forepersons and clients (drawings, training plans, health and safety sheets, daily reports, inspection sheets, additional worksheets, etc.). The most illustrative example of the importance of paper and the duplication of information is related to management of the overtime worksheets. Once the overtime worksheets have been completed by the superintendent or the coordinator at the end of the day, the superintendent must sign them and send them to the client for approval and signature. After signing, he must scan and email them to the project manager. Then, he must place them in an envelope which will be mailed to the central office which keeps the original copies in dedicated folders. Whenever things have to be verified by the project manager before the client's signature, the process time is significantly extended.

Following the study of the internal documentation, observations of real-life experiences in the field, and interviews with stakeholders, the most important needs were identified in order to understand the current processes of the company and the review of the literature; these needs were related to information sharing and communication, access to information and simplification of existing processes, the mobility and the durability of tools, and increased productivity. More specific needs, such as those relating to the technology choice (hardware and software), helped to better guide the final decision and meet the needs of the company. Particular attention was paid to the work environment and the harsh construction site conditions. The selected hardware then had to meet the durability, strength and versatility requirements, in addition to more conventional requirements such as known operating system, and storage capacity.

4.2   Choosing the Mobile Device and Designing the Application

Ten tablets were selected and compared. The comparison elements are presented in Appendix A. Only three technologies most corresponding to the identified needs were chosen. The first was from Dell, the Latitude 7212 Rugged Extreme tablet. It meets all the needs presented above. However, it comes with a high price tag. The second is the FZ-G1 tablet, from Panasonic. Like the first tablet, it also meets all identified needs and has a slightly high price. The third one is the ET50/55 tablet from Zebra. Of the three products, it presents the most advantageous price for what it can offer as characteristics. The final choice was the Dell Latitude 7212 Rugged Extreme. The reason was simply a matter of availability. The Panasonic is more difficult to obtain and a contact at Dell facilitated communications. The final price for the technology was $3500 Canadian dollars, including a scanner module and an interchangeable battery.

The design of the application was the part that required the most effort as compared to the other aspects of the project. As a result, not all of the originally planned functionalities were included in the final solution. Four functionalities were initially selected in relation to the current context and needs: the daily job site report, time sheets for workers, overtime worksheets, and access to PDF drawings. The application was designed in three complementary and iterative phases, namely, Balsamiq mock-ups; a first development phase, with QT Creator; and a second design phase, with Delphi. The project team evaluated the results of the first version of the platform designed using QT Creator, and was not happy with the results. This first interface was then abandoned. A second attempt was made with QT Creator, using QML, a derivative of HTML that allows for more mobile-friendly applications. However, only one person in the team had knowledge of this language. This made for a difficult and time-consuming development (with QML), and once again, the decision was made to abandon the application created with QT Creator. After the failure of the first versions of the application, created with QT Creator, a decision was made to use the program with which most of the company's platforms are made, namely, Delphi. The team has advanced knowledge of Delphi, and as a result, the development of the platform could be faster. In addition, in order to have a stable application in a timely fashion, it was decided to limit the scope of the project to the daily site report requirements.

4.3 The Final Version of the Application

The development of the final version of the application was done based on the UML class diagram presented in Fig. 1. When the application is launched, the main menu is displayed. Using the three-line symbol on the top left corner, the user can navigate through the different pages of the application. Back on the team composition page, several teams can be created simply by selecting the names of the people who will compose the teams, proceeding by column. These teams will be retained in memory, so the user can quickly enter the team associated with an activity in the daily report. A person can also be removed from or added to an activity in the daily report. It was decided to compose teams in this fashion because the company's site employee database can easily be linked to the application. Consequently, when new employees are added to the human resources database, it is automatically updated.

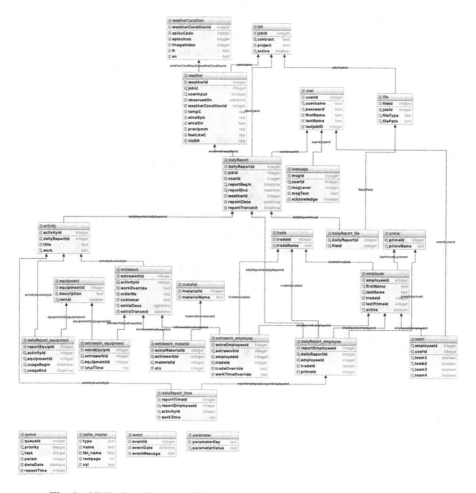

Fig. 1. UML class diagram of the data management process in the application

When a report is created, it automatically appears in the opening menu of the daily reports. Here, the date of the report is shown, along with the number of total hours worked for the day, the report status and the user who created it. The report can be modified or deleted. When entering the daily report interface, the first thing the user sees is the main menu. All reports are shown and options are provided to create a new report, or to edit or delete a selected one. The user can also navigate through time to see past reports.

Figure 2 shows how the site report interface is organised. Section marked 1 in Fig. 2 allows the user to enter the date and the time. Here, the user can also obtain information about the weather, since it can have a significant impact on the team's performance. Section 2 summarises the activities conducted during the work day. Each activity must be entered as a separate item in the application. Workers and hours can be associated to activities. On the far right, a summary of activities is found, along with associated hours. Section 3 allows the workers to author the daily report, including the daily activities and the worked hours. This allows having the right people and the right hours for the overtime worksheets (extra work). In addition, the job of each worker is indicated, as well as whether a bonus is attached to the work performed (e.g., for the group leaders). Section 4 allows the user to log all the equipment that was used during the day. This section is important for extra work, to indicate the duration of a piece of equipment usage.

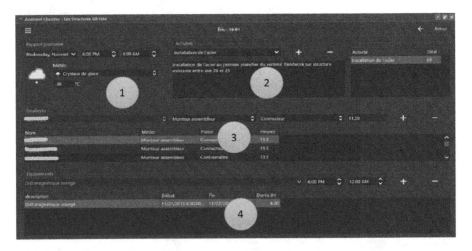

Fig. 2. Daily site report interface

5   Conclusion and Future Works

The research reported in the present paper provides a new perspective of the difficulties construction firms can face as they move to implement information technologies on their construction sites. It is very interesting to see how, despite the fact that many stable commercial applications exist, some firms prefer to rely on in-house competencies to develop their own applications. The study shows that developing such applications can be particularly challenging, with the need to have multiple iterations and failures before achieving the expected goals. In the case studied in this research, the initial needs evolved considerably throughout the application development and evaluation process. Finally, the project had to focus on only a part of the initial needs and to postpone the others for future work.

Future works will present the evaluation process of the technology and the feedbacks from the site team.

References

1. Samuelson, O., Björk, B.-C.: A longitudinal study of the adoption of IT technology in the Swedish building sector. Autom. Constr. **37**, 182–190 (2014)
2. Kubicki, S., Boton, C.: IT barometer survey in Luxembourg: first results to understand IT innovation in construction sector. In: Computing in Civil and Building Engineering, pp. 179–186. American Society of Civil Engineers, Orlando (2014)
3. Boton, C.: Use and impact of information technology in the African construction industry: a preliminary survey from Benin. In: Adjallah, K.H., Birregah, B., Abanda, H.F. (eds.) ICEASSM 2017. LNNS, vol. 72, pp. 411–418. Springer, Cham (2020). https://doi.org/10.1007/978-3-030-13697-0_31
4. Sacks, R., Eastman, C., Lee, G., Teicholz, P.: BIM Handbook: A Guide to Building Information Modeling for Owners, Designers, Engineers, Contractors, and Facility Managers. Wiley, Hoboken (2018)
5. Jung, W., Lee, G.: The status of BIM adoption on six continents. Int. J. Civ. Struct. Constr. Arch. Eng. **9**, 406–410 (2015)
6. Kassem, M., Succar, B.: Macro BIM adoption: comparative market analysis. Autom. Constr. **81**, 286–299 (2017)
7. Ahn, Y.H., Kwak, Y.H., Suk, S.J.: Contractors' transformation strategies for adopting building information modeling. J. Manag. Eng. **32**, 05015005 (2016)
8. Chen, Y., Kamara, J.M.: Using mobile computing for construction site information management. Eng. Constr. Arch. Manag. **15**, 7–20 (2008)
9. Anumba, C.J., Wang, X.: Mobile and pervasive computing in construction: an introduction. In: Mobile and Pervasive Computing in Construction, pp. 1–10 (2012)
10. Chen, Y., Kamara, J.M.: A framework for using mobile computing for information management on construction sites. Autom. Constr. **20**, 776–788 (2011)
11. Yeh, K.-C., Tsai, M.-H., Kang, S.-C.: On-site building information retrieval by using projection-based augmented reality. J. Comput. Civ. Eng. **26**, 342–355 (2012)
12. Kimoto, K., Endo, K., Iwashita, S., Fujiwara, M.: The application of PDA as mobile computing system on construction management. Autom. Constr. **14**, 500–511 (2005)
13. Davies, R., Harty, C.: Implementing "site BIM": a case study of ICT innovation on a large hospital project. Autom. Constr. **30**, 15–24 (2013)
14. Svalestuen, F., Knotten, V., Laedre, O., Professor, A.: Using building information model (BIM) devices to improve information flow and collaboration on construction sites. J. Inf. Technol. Constr. (ITcon) **22**, 204–219 (2017)
15. Park, J., Cho, Y.K., Kim, K.: Field construction management application through mobile BIM and location tracking technology. In: International Symposium on Automation and Robotics in Construction, pp. 83–89 (2016)

16. Marsh, L., Flanagan, R.: Measuring the costs and benefits of information technology in construction. Eng. Constr. Arch. Manag. **7**, 423–435 (2000)
17. Bowden, S., Dorr, A., Thorpe, T., Anumba, C.: Mobile ICT support for construction process improvement. Autom. Constr. **15**, 664–676 (2006)
18. Hasan, A., Jha, K.N., Rameezdeen, R., Ahn, S., Baroudi, B.: Perceived productivity effects of mobile ICT in construction projects. In: Mutis, I., Hartmann, T. (eds.) Advances in Informatics and Computing in Civil and Construction Engineering, pp. 165–172. Springer, Cham (2019). https://doi.org/10.1007/978-3-030-00220-6_20
19. Omar, T., Nehdi, M.L.: Data acquisition technologies for construction progress tracking. Autom. Constr. **70**, 143–155 (2016)
20. Forcada, N., Macarulla, M., Bortolini, R.: Using a mobile application to assess building accessibility in smart cities. In: eWork and eBusiness in Architecture, Engineering and Construction: ECPPM 2016: Proceedings of the 11th European Conference on Product and Process Modelling (ECPPM 2016), Limassol, Cyprus, 7–9 September 2016, p. 277 (2017)
21. Sunke, N.: Planning of construction projects: a managerial approach (2009)
22. Björk, B.-C.: Information technology in construction–domain definition and research issues. Int. J. Comput. Integr. Des. Constr. **1**, 1–16 (1999)
23. Ahmad, I.U., Russell, J.S., Abou-Zeid, A.: Information technology (IT) and integration in the construction industry. Constr. Manag. Econ. **13**, 163–171 (1995)
24. Boton, C., Kubicki, S., Halin, G.: Designing adapted visualization for collaborative 4D applications. Autom. Constr. **36**, 152–167 (2013)
25. Rebolj, D., Menzel, K.: Mobile computing in construction. J. Inf. Technol. Constr. **9**, 281–283 (2004)
26. Silverio, M., Renukappa, S., Suresh, S., Donastorg, A.: Mobile computing in the construction industry: main challenges and solutions. In: Benlamri, R., Sparer, M. (eds.) Leadership, Innovation and Entrepreneurship as Driving Forces of the Global Economy. SPBE, pp. 85–99. Springer, Cham (2017). https://doi.org/10.1007/978-3-319-43434-6_8
27. Abolfazli, S., Sanaei, Z., Ahmed, E., Gani, A., Buyya, R.: Cloud-based augmentation for mobile devices: motivation, taxonomies, and open challenges. IEEE Commun. Surv. Tutor. **16**, 337–368 (2014)
28. Ahmed, E., Gani, A., Sookhak, M., Hamid, S.H.A., Xia, F.: Application optimization in mobile cloud computing: motivation, taxonomies, and open challenges. J. Netw. Comput. Appl. **52**, 52–68 (2015)
29. Brydon-Miller, M., Greenwood, D., Maguire, P.: Editorial: Why Action Research? Action Res. **1**, 9–28 (2003)
30. Hartmann, T., Fischer, M., Haymaker, J.: Implementing information systems with project teams using ethnographic–action research. Adv. Eng. Inform. **23**, 57–67 (2009)

Many Valued Logics Supporting Establishment of a New Research Structure in an Educational Organization

Sylvia Encheva[✉] and Tom Skauge

Western Norway University of Applied Sciences,
Møllendalsveien 6-8, Post box 7030, 5020 Bergen, Norway
{sbe,tom.skauge}@hvl.no

Abstract. While most well established universities have developed their research structures based on decades of experience and adjustments, others focus on creating research clusters. Both ways however require considerable amount of time and resources. Merging educational organizations are often in need to build their research structures at faculty level without using extra time and resources. This work presents an approach facilitating development of a research structure in educational organizations.

Keywords: Cooperative decision making · Many valued logics · Research structures

1 Introduction

Expansion of research is a topic widely addressed by research communities. A number of related strategies are discussed in [3,6], and [7]. While some of the existing organizations work to attract talented researchers, others focus on centers, or clusters and creation of partnerships or collaborations.

A large number of educational organizations worldwide undergo structural changes in terms of merger. Important decisions are to be made in a relatively short period of time and more often than not with limited amount of resources. Hence the need for employing decision support systems (DSS). Quite a few free and commercial DSS are based on analytic hierarchy process (AHP), [10] and [11] or its more general form analytic network process (ANP), [12]. Well known disadvantages of such systems are related to possibilities for rank reversal, inability to handle uncertainties and inconsistencies imposed by 1 to 9 scale along with an assumption of criteria independence, [8] and [13].

While the majority of multi-criteria decision-making (MCDM) methods, [9], [15] have been developed to support individual and group decisions they are also assuming availability of potential solutions that are to be compared. They however do not assist decision makers in situations where alternative solutions ought to be build up first and ranked afterwards. In this article we propose an approach that can be used in such cases. Our model is supported by methods originating from many valued logics and data mining.

© Springer Nature Switzerland AG 2019
Y. Luo (Ed.): CDVE 2019, LNCS 11792, pp. 151–155, 2019.
https://doi.org/10.1007/978-3-030-30949-7_17

2   Related Theories

Within the field of organization theory, the idea of rational choice and rational choice systems has been criticized. Theory of the rational economic man
has been replaced by theories emphasizing lack of rationality conceptualized by
administrative man. While the economic man makes a decision based on optimization - the best alternatives given full information, the non-rational actor
makes decisions based on alternatives that are sufficient. These concepts and
theory building tasks are based om descriptive analysis - how individuals and
organizations defacto make their decisions. Such ideas however have been misin-
terpreted to also include normative ideas and guidance for how to organize new
processes of decisions. According to [4] it is a good reasons to work for, prepare
for and hope for decisions making as rational as possible. A many-valued logic
is a propositional calculus in which there are more than two truth values, [1].

Belnap's relevance logic is a four-valued logic, [2]. Its possible values are true
(T), false (F), both (B), and neither (N). The four truth values are arranged
in a logical lattice in Fig. 1. For truth tables of an operational four-valued logic
see [5]. This article provide a suggestion of how to improve rationality when
organizing research structures in universities.

For detailed overview of data mining techniques see [14].

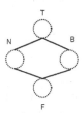

Fig. 1. Four-valued logic

3   Establishing a New Research Structure

In this scenario a faculty is aiming at establishing a new research structure.
The first step is to make a short list of research groups satisfying a number of
predefined criteria. A committee is then given the task to prepare alternative
solutions that can be used in the decision making process.

Committee members work independently of each other. They express their
opinions about the degree to which each of the suggested research groups is
satisfying any of the already selected criteria. Gradings provided by the committee members are afterwards summarized by applying four-valued logic. Our
choice of this particular type of many valued logic is an attempt to accommodate
uncertainties related to decision making. This way committee members have an

opportunity to say 'do not know', and thus apply truth degree (N) or 'a particular group satisfies a particular criterion to a degree lesser than 100%', and thus apply truth degree (B).

Committee members - a faculty member, a trade unions representative (who is also a faculty member), and a student. The model allows any number of committee members.

Criteria: (given faculty level organizing)

C1 - Support to faculty's strategy
C2 - Support to organization's strategy
C3 - Support to national strategy
C4 - Engaging the best qualified researchers
C5 - Recruitment of new faculty members into research
C6 - Involvement of students
C7 - Possibilities to obtain external fundings (i.e. assumed level sustainability)
C8 - Regional support
C9 - Support to development of new study lines

Table 1. Research groups

	C1			C2			C3			C4			C5			C6			C7			C8			C9		
	N1	B1	T1	N2	B2	T2	N3	B3	T3	N4	B4	T4	N5	B5	T5	N6	B6	T6	N7	B7	T7	N8	B8	T8	N9	B9	T9
RG1			x	x			x					x			x	x					x	x			x		
RG2	x					x			x			x	x				x		x				x		x		
RG3			x	x					x		x			x		x					x	x			x		
RG4		x		x					x			x	x				x		x					x			x
RG5	x			x			x			x					x	x				x				x		x	
RG6			x			x			x	x			x				x				x	x			x		
RG7		x				x	x			x			x				x		x			x			x		
RG8	x			x					x		x		x			x					x		x		x		
RG9		x		x			x			x			x			x					x	x					x
RG10	x			x		x		x				x			x		x		x			x			x		
RG11	x			x					x		x		x				x		x					x	x		
RG12	x			x			x					x	x			x					x	x			x		
RG13	x			x					x		x		x			x			x			x					x
RG14		x		x			x			x				x		x				x	x				x		
RG15		x				x		x		x			x			x			x					x	x		
RG16		x		x			x			x					x	x	x				x	x			x		
RG17		x				x	x					x	x					x			x	x					x
RG18		x		x					x		x		x			x					x		x				x
RG19		x	x				x			x			x			x				x			x		x		
RG20	x			x					x			x	x			x					x	x					x
RG21		x		x		x			x		x		x					x			x	x			x		
RG22	x					x			x	x			x			x			x				x		x		
RG23		x		x			x					x			x			x	x			x			x		

Table 1 has rows corresponding to research groups {RG1, ..., RGm} and columns corresponding to evaluation criteria {C1, ..., Cn}. To increase visibility we use an 'x' for obtained truth values, where 'T1' means that the corresponding research group satisfies criterion 'C1', 'B4' indicates that the corresponding research group satisfies criterion 'C4' to a certain degree, while 'N7' indicates that the degree to which the corresponding research group satisfies criterion 'C7' is not known.

Data mining techniques are first applied to the collected row data in order to filter out insignificant attributes. By this we mean attributes with missing values and or single occurrences. Classification algorithms are further on used to select sets of research groups that are to be suggested to the decision makers for reaching final conclusion.

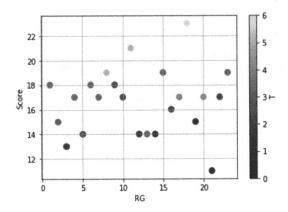

Fig. 2. Graphical representation of classification

Our classification work resulted in recommending the following five research groups RG8, RG11, RG15, RG18, and RG20. According to the degrees to which they satisfy listed criteria we can place them in two sets {RG11, RG18} and {RG8, RG15, RG23} where the groups in the first set are better than the ones in the second set. A graphical representation can be seen in Fig. 2 where a lighter color indicates larger amount of criteria with assigned truth value 'T'. Another truth value or a combination of truth values can be applied instead while making the graphical representation. Research groups are placed on the horizontal axis (RG). Their scores according to assigned truth values are placed on the vertical axis (Scores). This ranking is done on the assumption that all criteria have equal weight value.

The model allows additional tuning where all or some of the criteria are assigned different weights. Decision trees can be build to assist in another decision making process where new applications for establishment of other research groups have to be considered. Our aim is to provide support to a flexible structure that can easily accommodate new ideas and satisfy new demands.

4   Conclusion

Cooperative decision making is becoming an integral part of most business ventures. Thus the need for a variety of systems facilitating it. This article provides a suggestion about how to improve rationality when organizing research structures in universities.

Our model is an attempt to provide support for decision makers in educational organizations. It is flexible with respect to number of options, criteria, and committee members. It allows inclusion or removal of alternatives, attributes, and experts without additional cost.

References

1. Augusto, L.M.: Many-Valued Logics: A Mathematical and Computational Introduction. College Publications, London (2017)
2. Belnap, N.J.: A useful four-valued logic. In: Dunn, J.M., Epstain, G. (eds.) Modern Uses of Multiple-Valued Logic, pp. 8–37. D. Reidel Publishing Co., Dordrecht (1977)
3. Birx, D.L., Anderson-Fletcher, E., Whitney, E.: Growing an emerging research university. J. Res. Adm. **44**(1), 11–35 (2013)
4. Brunsson, N.: The Consequences of Decision-Making. Oxford University Press, Oxford (2006)
5. Ferreira, U.J.: A four valued logic. In: Meghanathan, N., et al. (eds.) NeCoM, SEAS, CMCA, CSITEC - 2017, pp. 71–84 (2017)
6. Huenneke, L.F., Stearns, D.M., Martinez, J.D., Laurila, K.: Key strategies for building research capacity of university faculty members. Innov. High. Educ. **42**(5–6), 421–435 (2017)
7. Kyvik, S., Aksnes, D.W.: Explaining the increase in publication productivity among academic staff: a generational perspective. Stud. High. Educ. **40**, 1438–1453 (2015)
8. Leskinen, P., Kangas, J.: Rank reversals in multi-criteria decision analysis with statistical modeling of ratio-scale pairwise comparisons. J. Oper. Res. Soc. **56**, 855–861 (2005)
9. Mardani, A., Jusoh, A., Zavadskas, E., Cavallaro, F., Khalifah, Z.: Sustainable and renewable energy: an overview of the application of multiple criteria decision making techniques and approaches. Sustainability **7**(10), 13947–13984 (2015)
10. Saaty, T.L.: The Analytic Hierarchy Process. McGraw Hill, New York (2000)
11. Saaty, T.L.: Decision Making for Leaders: The Analytic Hierarchy Process for Decisions in a Complex World. RWS Publications, Pittsburgh (2008)
12. Saaty, T.L., Vargas, L.G.: Decision Making with the Analytic Network Process: Economic, Political, Social and Technological Applications with Benefits, Opportunities, Costs and Risks. Springer, New York (2006). https://doi.org/10.1007/0-387-33987-6
13. Wang, X., Triantaphyllou, E.: Ranking irregularities when evaluating alternatives by using some ELECTRE methods. Omega **36**, 45–63 (2008)
14. Witten, I.H., Frank, E., Hall, M.A., Pal, C.J.: Data Mining: Practical Machine Learning Tools and Techniques (Morgan Kaufmann Series in Data Management Systems), 4th edn (2019)
15. Zakeri, S.: Ranking based on optimal points multi-criteria decision-making method. Theory Appl. Grey Syst. **9**(1), 45–69 (2018)

Distance Collaboration in Performing Arts - A Use Case and Lessons Learned

Sven Ubik[⊠], Jakub Halák, Martin Kolbe, and Jiří Melnikov

CESNET, Prague, Czech Republic
{ubik, jakub.halak, melnikov}@cesnet.cz

Abstract. We describe our experience from one of distributed concerts that we help arrange where musicians and other artists could collaborate over distance. Achieving low latency of audio and video signals sharing between participants is a critical factor. Over the past several years, we have developed a low-latency real-time system based on programmable hardware (FPGA) for audiovisual transmission. We discuss issues involved in arranging such a performance and lessons learned.

Keywords: Network performance · Low-latency audio ·
Low-latency video distance collaboration · Real-time transmissions

1 Introduction

Real-time audiovisual network transmissions allow distance collaboration in many fields. One of the most demanding areas to enable distance collaboration is performing arts. The goal is to allow people who are physically separated to play music or perform other live arts together using audiovisual network connections for mutual synchronization. Applications of such a kind of distance collaboration are in education for students in remote locations, comparative auditions or rehearsals before concerts. The network can also bring new creative possibilities, such as when people from different cultures interact together or playing together using unusual combinations of instruments, such as multiple organs or historical instruments, which are difficult to move.

Over the time, various technical means have been developed to allow people interact in real time over distance using audiovisual transmissions. Some tools have been developed specifically for education in performing arts, such as LoLa software. Then the primary consideration was minimal added latency, using components such as analog cameras providing faster response. Such systems, however, generally provide poor video quality, because the audiovisual transmission is meant for synchronization, rather than presenting to public.

On the other hand, audiovisual transmissions that are used for live television broadcast provide high quality video. The current standard format is 1080i50 or 1080i60 depending on a country. A few channels are already available in UHD-1 format (3840 × 2160 pixels). Japanese television NHK plans 2020 olympics broadcast in UHD-2 format (7680 × 4320 pixels). However, the television transmission chain exhibits much higher added latency. During "live" event broadcasts, a typical delay from the scene to a home television screen is several tens of seconds. The main reason

Y. Luo (Ed.): CDVE 2019, LNCS 11792, pp. 156–161, 2019.
https://doi.org/10.1007/978-3-030-30949-7_18

is large buffers in each hop in a transmission chain to compensate for network packet jitter and processing time in Forward Error Correction (FEC) to compensate for packet loss. In one particular example, during an open-air Czech Philharmonic orchestra concert in June 2018, audio waveforms recorded synchronously at the venue and from the TV broadcast using a mobile device were shifted by one minute (59.5 s).

For distributed performances, where artists collaborate in real time over a distance and such a performance is also presented to the audience, we need *both* small latency and high image quality at the same time, preferably from multiple cameras. In this paper, we present a possible technical solution for such a demanding distance collaboration and some experience acquired during a real event.

2 Requirements

In order to arrange a multi-site live performing arts event for an audience, we identified the following technical requirements to be met:

- Requirement R1: latency of audio max. approximately 25 ms
- Requirement R2: video quality at least 1080 lines at 60 frames per second (fps)
- Requirement R3: multiple-cameras per each site for live edit
- Requirement R4: low-latency video for musicians

Regarding R1, many previous experiments identified approx. 25 ms as a latency limit for playing together classical music [1]. Higher latency is acceptable for music with a strong beat, such as swing or popular music.

Regarding R2, due to ubiquitous television broadcast in 1080 lines resolution, people consider such a resolution as television quality visual experience. Fast hand when playing a musical instrument or body movements in dance requires a higher frame rate for smooth presentation. Current fastest cameras provide 60 fps live output.

Regarding R3, when observing remote artists through a camera view only, without an ability to freely move eyesight along the scene, it is important to provide multiple different views. This is first to better understand the scene and second to make observing the performance a richer experience. Live edit can change between, for example, a hands detail, a musician's body, a whole scene, etc.

Regarding R4, while musicians primarily use sound for synchronization, visual clues are also important, such as at the start of each movement of a music piece. Therefore, it is important to provide a separate monitor for musicians in each location, allowing them to synchronize with remote peers. First, monitors are generally faster than projectors. Second, musicians are usually situated such that they do not have a direct view at the venue projector.

3 Related Work

LoLa [2] is software developed by GARR for low-latency audio and video transmissions specifically aimed at supporting distance education in performing arts. LoLa runs on a Windows PC and needs specific hardware components, such as a particular sound card or an Ethernet adapter to maintain low latency. The added latency to audio from a sender to a receiver is approx. 6 ms. Higher buffering can be set to compensate for network jitter. For video, LoLa currently supports USB cameras from Ximea with C-mount lenses only. This means only one static and relatively low quality video per site. It is very difficult to zoom, focus or pan live such a camera during the performance.

Ultragrid [3] is open-source software for audiovisual transmissions running on a Linux or Windows PC or a Mac. It supports various video capture cards, compression codecs and works up to UHD-II resolution. Added audio delay is however higher, at the order or low tens of milliseconds and is acceptable for certain kinds of music only.

Jacktrip [4] is a command-line utility for Linux or Windows for low-latency audio transmissions. Added latency with USB sound adapters is from approx. 13 ms. It is however audio only utility with no video support.

MVTP [5] is a device based on Field Programmable Gate Array (FPGA) for low-latency audio and video transmissions developed by CESNET. Several variants exist with MVTP-Audio specifically designed for applications where audio transmissions play a key role. Both video and audio are transmitted with the added latency from a sender to a receiver under 1 ms Video transmissions use a lightweight TICO [8] codec, while audio is transmitted uncompressed. The video part supports transmission of two signals up to 1080p60 simultaneously. The network bandwidth after TICO compression is approx. 200 Mb/s for a 1080p30 signal and 400 Mb/s for a 1080p60 signal.

Several research papers presented studies on effects of latency to synchronization when playing music together, for example [1, 6, 7].

4 Design

We propose a general interconnection scheme showed in Fig. 1 for one site of a multi-site live collaborative performance. A key property is avoiding audio delays and video frame buffers where possible. A few notes about the setup follow.

- When at least approx. 400 Mb/s is available, we use MVTP devices, which provide both very low added delay (1 ms) (R1) and high-quality video (R2), which could not be provided both by other transmission means.
- When lower bandwidth is available, we use Ultragrid, which provides quality higher compression rate video codecs (R2). It can be combined with LoLa or Jacktrip for low-latency audio (R1).
- When we use SDI-embedded audio, such as in MVTP devices, we use dedicated audio embedders rather than using audio inputs on cameras or video editing devices, which generally add higher audio delay. This can be critical, delaying audio just one video frame time (approx. 16 ms for 60 fps or 33 ms for 30 fps) can make playing together impossible.
- Latency of selected monitors and projectors can be found at displaylag.com or measured with a tester available from Leo Bodnar Electronics[1]. Generally it is easy

---

[1] https://www.leobodnar.com/shop/?main_page=product_info&products_id=212.

to find low latency monitors (from approx. 3 ms) (R4) thanks to the gaming community, but low-latency projectors are nearly non-existent.

- We measured latency of various SDI and HDMI cameras using a do-it-yourself tester. As of April 2019, the fastest cameras appear to be Blackmagic URSA family with approx. 6 ms latency, being just a fraction of one frame (R4).
- For multi-site performance, we currently use a separate point-to-point transmission between a central location (which can be anywhere) and each end site. This allows highest flexibility of transmission parameters per site, as different connectivity characteristics are often available in each site.

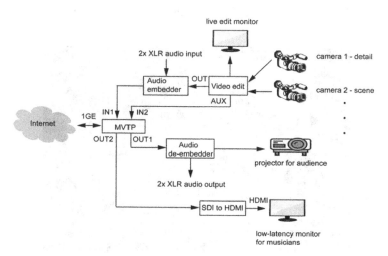

Fig. 1. Interconnection for a multi-site live collaborative performance

5 Experimental Work

Over the years, we have arranged several distributed performances in various scenarios, between different countries in several continents where various musical instruments and dance styles were involved.

The first truly television production quality distributed performance for an audience was arranged for the Vaclav Havel library in November 2018 in association with awarding the Vaclav Havel Prize for Human Rights. The appearance in the Prague location is shown in Fig. 2. The main characteristics of the event were the following:

- The concert involved two sites with musicians and also the audience in both sites. The first site was in a former church of St. Anne in Prague now used as an event space called Prague Crossroads. The second site was the hall of the Performing Arts Academy in Bratislava.
- There were four high-definition (1080p) cameras at each site (R3). We created three live edits. The first edit from cameras in Prague was used for a projection to audience in Bratislava. The second edit from cameras in Bratislava was used for a

projection to audience in Prague. The third edit was made from Prague and Bratislava edited video streams and it was used for a web-based streaming by the Czech Television.

- MVTP devices were used to transmit both video and audio (R1, R2).
- Musicians did not use headphones and also we needed to let the sound from each site to be presented by speakers to the audience on the other site. Thanks to transmissions with very low latency, no undesired feedback effects occurred (R1).
- Musicians were provided with their own monitors showing fixed, unedited view of the peer musician. A specially selected low-latency (2 ms) monitor was provided for a cellist in Prague (R4). However, in Bratislava for a pianist we had to use a small monitor placed on the piano, with approx. one frame latency.

Fig. 2. Distributed concert between Prague and Bratislava

6   Lessons Learned and Conclusion

While the musicians were satisfied with low enough latency between them, there were several interesting observations:

- A distributed nature of the performance makes it much more difficult to coordinate a rehearsal as well as the start and finish of the performance. It is very useful to maintain a parallel technical connection between supporting technical teams using instant messaging or a regular mobile phone.
- As the live edit (R3) for the television broadcast could use only previously live-edited video streams from both sites, it was important to avoid a double switch between cameras in a short time. A method that worked well was to do a site switch (between Prague and Bratislava), just after a camera switch was done on the site that was to be switched live.

- Preparation time on the site is currently longer than for television transmissions with standardized commercial equipment. The cost increase in the time of technical personnel is not significant when compared to the whole preparation time of the event that is needed also out of the venue. However, it increases the cost of venue rental and may be difficult to negotiate with the venue management.

In the future we plan to use multi-channel clock recovery on a single receiver device to accept signals from multiple remote locations. This will enable low-latency multi-site performances using fewer devices in a more cost-effective way.

References

1. Rottondi, C., Chafe, C., Allocchio, C., Sarti, A.: An overview on networked music performance technologies. IEEE Access (2016). https://doi.org/10.1109/access.2016.2628440
2. Drioli, C., Allocchio, C., Buso, N.: Networked performances and natural interaction via LOLA: low latency high quality A/V streaming system. In: Nesi, P., Santucci, R. (eds.) ECLAP 2013. LNCS, vol. 7990, pp. 240–250. Springer, Heidelberg (2013). https://doi.org/10.1007/978-3-642-40050-6_21
3. Holub, P., Matela, J., Pulec, M., Srom, M.: UltraGrid: low-latency high-quality video transmissions on commodity hardware. In: Proceedings of the 20th ACM International Conference on Multimedia (MM 2012), pp. 1457–1460. ACM, New York (2012)
4. Cáceres, J.-P., Chafe, C.: Jacktrip: under the hood of an engine for network audio. J. New Music Res. **39**(3), 183–187 (2010)
5. Friedl, A., Halák, J., Krsek, M., Ubik, S., Zejdl, P.: Low-latency transmissions for remote collaboration in post-production. In: SMPTE Annual Technical Conference and Exhibition 2012, pp. 367–377 (2012)
6. Gurevich, M., Chafe, C., Leslie, G., Tyan, S.: Simulation of networked ensemble performance with varying time delays: characterization of ensemble accuracy. In: Proceedings of the 2004 International Computer Music Conference, Miami (2004)
7. Chafe, C.: Living with net lag. In: Proceedings of the AES 43rd International Conference, Pohang, KR (2011)
8. RDD 35:2016 - SMPTE Registered Disclosure Doc - TICO Lightweight Codec Used in IP Networked or in SDI Infrastructures. RDD 35:2016, pp. 1–53, April 2016. https://doi.org/10.5594/smpte.rdd35.2016

A Cooperative Drawing Tool to Improve Children's Creativity

Yalmar Ponce Atencio[1]([⊠]) [iD], Manuel Ibarra Cabrera[2] [iD],
and Leonidas Asto Huaman[3] [iD]

[1] Universidad Nacional José María Arguedas, Andahuaylas-Apurímac, Peru
yalmar@unajma.edu.pe
[2] Universidad Nacional Micaela Bastidas de Apurímac, Abancay-Apurímac, Peru
manuelibarra@gmail.com
[3] Universidad Autonoma del Perú, Lima, Peru
astoleonidas@gmail.com

Abstract. Classroom meetings and cooperative homework typically require participants to be physically present in the room. In this setting, the whiteboard is a tool widely used to express ideas. However, nowadays it is more difficult for people to meet together in one place, particularly for young people, due to inherent risks in our current society. Therefore, virtual cooperative applications or tools are welcome. Such tools could reduce the money and time spent on cooperative classwork. Our application allows users to participate virtually through interactive drawings. The features are simple to use and allow for drawings to be made quickly, but this does not mean that drawings cannot be professional or complex. The application was implemented using open source frameworks and libraries, such as NodeJs, SocketIO, PaperJs, jQuery, and others. The results of the experiment demonstrate the high scalability and versatility of our system, the delay is low and acceptable considering that is capable of managing hundreds of objects in real time.

Keywords: Cooperative application · Virtual drawings ·
Real time interaction · Cooperative painting · Children creativity

1 Introduction

Currently, the use of virtual cooperative tools such as text editors, messaging, sharing resources, among others, has been improving productivity, since it makes remote interaction possible in a manner similar to being physically present when there are geographical difficulties. In this research work, we propose a cooperative drawing editor, where several users can collaborate in the edition of a drawing or painting. We designed the system so that it is possible to create multiple documents (scenarios), where each document can be developed or edited by working on it simultaneously with a group of users who share the document. Therefore, several work groups can create their own documents, since the

Y. Luo (Ed.): CDVE 2019, LNCS 11792, pp. 162–171, 2019.
https://doi.org/10.1007/978-3-030-30949-7_19

application is online and is accessible from any place using a web browser with internet connection. In the literature, this kind of application could be considered like a virtual whiteboard, since it can replace a whiteboard when we want to quickly design sketches or text notes, just like we would do manually on a real whiteboard. However, the application developed in this research work has been thought to be used mainly by children or students at the primary level, since it allows them to collaborate to make small drawings that are requested in their class assignments and homework. We want to emphasize that our application is quick and simple to use compared to other existing applications. It is designed to create drawings quickly, as well as to support cooperative work in real time and with the ability to simultaneously edit documents. In this research work, we do not want to compare our application with the traditional whiteboard, but rather to highlight useful features for a fast and cooperative drawing tool. Cooperative applications are a trend that can be applied in many contexts. One of the major releases in this field is the newest Visual Studio Online, which allows collaboration on implementations of code at a professional level. This type of software had already been created with various tools, but Microsoft's Visual Studio Online was the first software to be taken seriously at a professional level. The rest of the document is organized as follows: the related works are presented in the second section, the third section describes the implementation details of the application and its functions, the fourth section presents some experiments and results, as well as comparisons with similar applications; finally, the fifth section presents the conclusions and future works.

2   Related Works

Since the beginning of Web 2.0, interactive tools have been developed massively, mainly with the purpose of taking advantage of the possibility of using them wherever. This has been especially interesting since it has allowed to change the way of software development is done and the use of software, changing from the typical desktop applications to web applications. In that context, to implement a web application is currently even more complicated compared to build a desktop application, due to its inherent limitations [21]. However, in some types of applications occurs the opposite, since there are mechanisms that have been developed specifically for working on the web, such as concurrency, ubiquity, availability of information, ease, speed, etc. Sin et. al. [18] have presented how HTML5 has arrived to change the web, especially since it is now possible to develop real applications, exactly like desktop applications. In the last decade several researches were presented that include the implementation of applications with the collaborative approach, among them related to text editors [3], communication [10,20], health and medicine [1,2], chat systems [7,15], multi-player games [11], sketching [16], graphics [4,5,7,8], scheduling systems [14], sharing [19,22], real time tracking [13], education and academic systems [9], monitoring and recognition [13,23], and among others. In the case of graphical applications, allowing the user to draw some strokes or mainly handwrite over the screen or using a stylus pen. However, these approaches are still tedious or impractical processes, since that in a cooperative system, what a user changes or updates, it must be reflected to the other users in the room or document. In such a kind of applications, the resources to obtain a real time interaction are limited because depends from many conditions like, internet connexion bandwidth (upload and download), user device capabilities, among others; and we cannot think that the application can run as fast as in a local computer. Consider many elements or objects are going to add to the drawing, and it will becomes larger and more complex, and users will be adding more and more object, and the interaction becomes slower. Then, due to this fact, more and more information, every time, must be transferred and transmitted to all the user who are interacting in a document. Hence, is necessary to think on efficient data structures and algorithms to streamline this process and also ways to represent simpler and less heavy data. At this point, it is preferable, for example, to use vector formats instead of raster formats. A practical solution for this inconvenient, considering interactivity, is to use the Canvas HTML5. In [17] an approach to promote the participation of people with disabilities is presented, considering aspects such as accessibility and usability in terms of the interface, incorporating aspects of real-time communication such as chats of text, audio and video. In the work presented by Ringe et. al. [15], and previously discussed by Forster et. al. [6], they explains that this kind of applications can be useful to improve the abilities of students, since a cooperative environment makes them more productive. The work presented by Liu et. al. [12] shows that to obtain a better experience in interaction, it is important to use relatively new technologies such as websockets, since communication through the HTTP protocol can be optimized by building a dedicated web server.

3   Implementation Details

Currently, in cooperative applications, is important to use resources that allow us better flexibility, this because not only a computer could be used to run a web application, but can be used a cell phone, a SmartTv or any other device with a high definition screen and internet access. Then, in order to overcome those difficulties, it is necessary to think about building a single application that suits any device, and the way can be achieved it is by using a web browser with HTML5 support, so that the application can run in any device. Fortunately, nowadays all smart devices have the ability to run a modern web browser such as Firefox or Chrome, supporting standard resources like JavaScript, HTML5, JSON, I/O, Events, among others features. Considering that our application has a graphical interface, the interaction becomes quite slow when it is shared (multi-user) because any variation must be reflected in all connected users, then the PaperJs library based on JavaScript has been used for the management of graphics on Canvas HTML5. PaperJs is very versatile in the handling of lines and shapes, which makes the development of a graphic application easier. The application is the type of client-server and works with the software development pattern model-view-controller (MVC). The model is done in a database, which stores all the objects (Paths) created at a certain time (by the users), and a copy is done to all the users in a room or document. It allows to handle a large number of Path objects, either closed curves (shapes) or open curves (strokes).

Figure 1 shows a diagram of the proposed architecture. The first level is the client layer, which essentially executes the user interface. This proposal is platform independent, which ensures that the application can be executed by any device, with a browser and Internet connection. On the other hand, the user interface has been designed to be simpler and intuitive, so only some common tools have been considered, but it is possible to make very complete designs. The second level corresponds to the logical layer or logical level, in which the server is located. The server handles the requests of the client layer (user interface). The server is also responsible for storing and retrieving information in a database. Thus, this layer has a separate JavaScript program, which processes the functionalities of the application. The third layer is the database, in which the information about the objects that are in the scene and the users that are in the room are stored. The scene refers to the drawing area that all users share and can work cooperatively. The room refers to the group of users who share a certain scene. An Important aspect is that the application automatically creates a scene for each new access to the URL, generating two parameters in the URL, then if another user wants to enter the room that was created previously, you must add the room and scene parameters in the URL path separated by slashes.

Finally, each client connects to the server through a socket, and a socket id is assigned to each connection created between a client and the server. A socket is a bidirectional connection. The connection is maintained until the user disconnects from the application (scenario). Any data sent by the user will be loaded by the socket and a corresponding will be emitted to the server. Figure 2 shows the implemented files and the three-tier diagram.

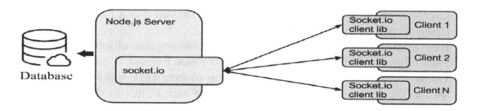

Fig. 1. The architecture used in our implementation.

3.1   Functionalities

After reviewing some similar works, it has been convenient to consider the following tools and functionalities (Fig. 3).

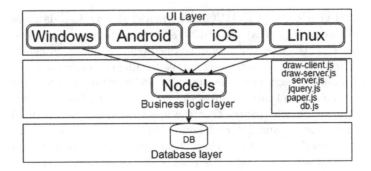

Fig. 2. Implementation source files and tier diagram.

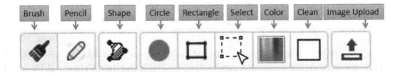

Fig. 3. The application Toolbar. (Color figure online)

- **Brush.** The brush allows to create thick lines. It creates a Path object where the Stroke is closed and have a filling color. In devices with support for stylus pen it is very useful and accurate (see Fig. 4a)).
- **Pencil.** The pencil allows to create freehand strokes, minimizing the generated points to represent a smooth stroke. The stroke is a Path object of the Stroke type without filling. In devices with pencil it is very useful and precise (see Fig. 4b).
- **Polygonal shape.** This allows to create polygonal shape objects. It is a Path object with closed Stroke and fill color (see Fig. 4c).
- **Circle.** The circle allows to create oval objects, and it is a Path object with closed Stroke and fill color (see Fig. 4d).
- **Rectangle.** The rectangle allows to create rectangular objects, and it is a Path object with closed Stroke and fill color (see Fig. 4e).
- **Color.** It allows selecting a color for the objects that will be created. In addition, it is possible to change the color of each object in the scene. This can be done by selecting the desired object and changing the color in the Color Box (see Fig. 5).
- **Upload Image.** It allows you to incorporate an image from file into the scene. This is especially useful for placing a background image and complement a drawing quickly (see Fig. 6).
- **Select.** Allows to select any created object. Later, it is possible to move, rotate, edit or delete. In addition, when an object is selected, it can also modified on its contour by moving its control points. This is very useful when is necessary to modify its shape (see Fig. 7).

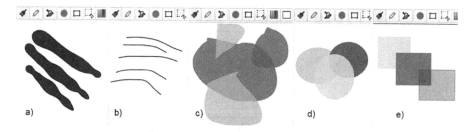

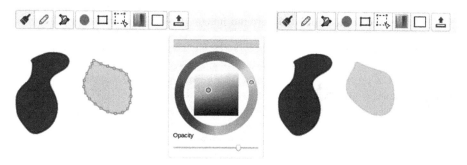

Fig. 4. The application drawing tools in action: Brush (a), Pencil (b), Shape (c), Circle (d) and Rectangle (e). (Color figure online)

Fig. 5. The color of the selected object has been changed (left). The same object, with its changed color, is reflected on the other browser (right) (Color figure online)

- **Deletion.** The application provides two type of deletions, the first one removes an object from the scene, and it can be done by pressing the 'del' key after to select the desired object to remove. The second one is for removing a point of a selected object. This can be done by selecting the desired point to remove and simultaneously pressing the 'shift' key. This is useful for refining the border or contour of a shape or stroke (see Fig. 8).
- **Clean.** It allows to remove all the objects from the scene, leaving completely empty (clear the scene).

3.2   Resources for Testing

Rapid tests were carried out with two, three and four users interacting simultaneously in a drawing. The interaction is quite fluid, without interruptions. For the tests it has been employed a Server with Intel Xeon 2.5 GHz processor, 4 Gb RAM and Ubuntu 18.04 Operating System. For the clients, different types of devices have been used:

- A desktop computer with an i7 5820K processor 3.3 GHz and 16 Gb RAM.
- A desktop computer with an i7 4770 3.0 GHz processor and 8 Gb RAM.
- A laptop computer with an i7 7500 processor 2.8 GHz and 8 Gb RAM.

Fig. 6. Uploading a background image. (Color figure online)

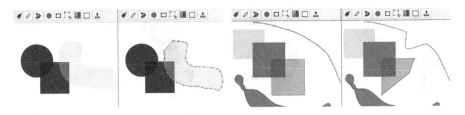

Fig. 7. The select tool. It is possible to move an object or just a control point. (Color figure online)

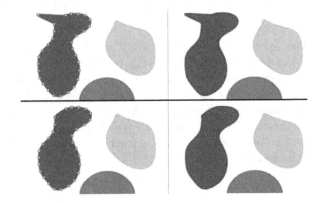

Fig. 8. The application provides deletion of objects and parts of objects. The original drawing is shown on the top-left. The modified drawing, with a point removed, is shown on the bottom. The right part (top and bottom) corresponds to a second user which is seen the changes on his browser.

- A touch-screen laptop with an Intel Atom Z8350 1.2 GHz and 4 Gb RAM.
- A smart cell-phone with an 8-Core processor and 3 Gb RAM.

Fig. 9. The first experiment was to make a drawing based on an example picture. The original picture (left) and the resultant drawing (right) made by three children. (Color figure online)

The tests were conducted using the Firefox and Chrome browsers in their last versions for each device. In the case of computers, Windows 10 Version 17134.706 operating system has been used, Linux Systems Fedora 29 and Ubuntu 18.04 have also been used.

4   Results

Some experiments, involving children and art course professors, were conducted. The first experiment consists in designing a picture that the professor left to reproduce the children. It was done by a group of children. Figure 9 shows the result. Related to the first experiment, the teacher and the three children, they said "working with the application is still a little bit difficult" because does not have all the functionalities that a commercial paint software have. A child also said "working cooperatively is heavier than work alone, because the application must be respond to more than one user that could be painting at the same place,

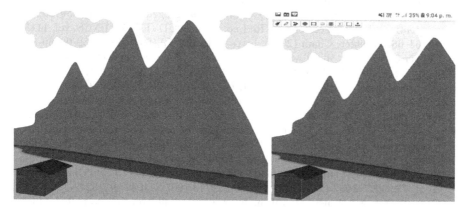

Fig. 10. A drawing made by two children, one using a computer (left) and the another using a stylus smart-phone (right). (Color figure online)

so it is confusing". Finally, all the children and the teacher agree that painting with the cooperative approach allows to paint faster than to do alone and also improves the motivation and creativity.

The second experiment was performed using different devices. The teacher asked them to make a painting. One child with a touch screen laptop with stylus pen, and the other with a stylus smart phone. Figure 10 shows the result. We also tested other collaborative painting applications such as WWW Board (https://awwapp.com) and Aggie.io (https://aggie.io.com). Both are complicated to use and less versatile to edit a drawing, even working alone, then they are less useful for cooperative purposes.

5   Conclusions and Future Work

For the future, with regard to this implementation, we consider it important to incorporate the direction handlers for control points, this in order to create designs with greater precision. It is also important to add possibilities for self suggesting strokes or basic drawings like is found in professional editors, it helps to design quickly. This feature must be similar to auto-complete in text editors. In addition, we note that it is important to incorporate the undo-redo functionality. Finally, we consider it important to deal with intersections in Path objects, this to color closed regions in a similar way to raster drawing environments.

References

1. Andrikos, C., Rassias, G., Tsanakas, P., Maglogiannis, I.: Real-time medical collaboration services over the web, vol. 2015, pp. 1393–1396 (2015). https://doi.org/10.1109/EMBC.2015.7318629
2. Andrikos, C., Rassias, G., Tsanakas, P., Maglogiannis, I.: An enhanced device-transparent real-time teleconsultation environment for radiologists. IEEE J. Biomed. Health Inform. **PP**, 1 (2018). https://doi.org/10.1109/JBHI.2018.2824312
3. Cho, B., Ng, A., Sun, C.: CoVim+CoEmacs: a heterogeneous co-editing system as a potential solution to editor war. In: Luo, Y. (ed.) CDVE 2018. LNCS, vol. 11151, pp. 64–68. Springer, Cham (2018). https://doi.org/10.1007/978-3-030-00560-3_9
4. Coppens, A., Mens, T.: Towards collaborative immersive environments for parametric modelling. In: Luo, Y. (ed.) CDVE 2018. LNCS, vol. 11151, pp. 304–307. Springer, Cham (2018). https://doi.org/10.1007/978-3-030-00560-3_44
5. Du, P., Song, Y., Deng, L.: A real-time collaborative framework for 3D design based on HTML5, pp. 215–220 (2016). https://doi.org/10.1109/CSCWD.2016.7565991
6. Forster, F., Wartig, H.: Creativity techniques for collocated teams using a web-based virtual whiteboard, pp. 7–11 (2009). https://doi.org/10.1109/ICIW.2009.9
7. Gao, L., Gao, D., Xiong, N., Lee, C.: CoWebDraw: a real-time collaborative graphical editing system supporting multi-clients based on HTML5. Multimedia Tools Appl. **77**, 5067–5082 (2017). https://doi.org/10.1007/s11042-017-5242-4
8. Gao, L., Xu, X.: A new algorithm for real-time collaborative graphical editing system based on CRDT. In: Sun, Y., Lu, T., Xie, X., Gao, L., Fan, H. (eds.) ChineseCSCW 2018. CCIS, vol. 917, pp. 201–212. Springer, Singapore (2019). https://doi.org/10.1007/978-981-13-3044-5_15

9. Ibarra, M.J., Navarro, A.F., Ibañez, V., Soto, W., Ibarra, W.: mSIREMAP: cooperative design for monitoring teacher's classes in K-12 schools. In: Luo, Y. (ed.) CDVE 2017. LNCS, vol. 10451, pp. 114–122. Springer, Cham (2017). https://doi.org/10.1007/978-3-319-66805-5_15

10. Katayama, S., Goda, T., Shiramatsu, S., Ozono, T., Shintani, T.: A fast synchronization mechanism for collaborative web applications based on HTML5, pp. 663–668 (2013). https://doi.org/10.1109/SNPD.2013.13

11. Marin, C., Cloquell, J., Luo, Y., Estrany, B.: A multiplayer game with virtual interfaces. In: Luo, Y. (ed.) CDVE 2017. LNCS, vol. 10451, pp. 94–102. Springer, Cham (2017). https://doi.org/10.1007/978-3-319-66805-5_13

12. Qigang, L., Sun, X.: Research of web real-time communication based on web socket. Int. J. Commun. Netw. Syst. Sci. **05**, 797–801 (2012). https://doi.org/10.4236/ijcns.2012.512083

13. Qin, G., Li, Q., Li, S.: Vehicle route tracking system by cooperative license plate recognition on multi-peer monitor videos. In: Luo, Y. (ed.) CDVE 2016. LNCS, vol. 9929, pp. 271–282. Springer, Cham (2016). https://doi.org/10.1007/978-3-319-46771-9_35

14. Ratajczak, J., Schimanski, C.P., Marcher, C., Riedl, M., Matt, D.T.: Mobile application for collaborative scheduling and monitoring of construction works according to lean construction methods. In: Luo, Y. (ed.) CDVE 2017. LNCS, vol. 10451, pp. 207–214. Springer, Cham (2017). https://doi.org/10.1007/978-3-319-66805-5_26

15. Ringe, S., Kedia, R., Poddar, A., Patel, S.: HTML5 based virtual whiteboard for real time interaction. Procedia Comput. Sci. **49**, 170–177 (2015). https://doi.org/10.1016/j.procs.2015.04.241

16. Sandnes, F.E., Lianguzov, Y., Rodrigues, O.V., Lieng, H., Medola, F.O., Pavel, N.: Supporting collaborative ideation through freehand sketching of 3D-shapes in 2D using colour. In: Luo, Y. (ed.) CDVE 2017. LNCS, vol. 10451, pp. 123–134. Springer, Cham (2017). https://doi.org/10.1007/978-3-319-66805-5_16

17. Santarosa, L., Conforto, D., Machado, R.: Whiteboard: synchronism, colaboration and accessibility on web 2.0, pp. 1–6 (2012)

18. Sin, D., Lawson, E., Kannoorpatti, K.: Mobile web apps - the non-programmer's alternative to native applications, pp. 8–15 (2012). https://doi.org/10.1109/HSI.2012.11

19. Ubik, S., Kubišta, J.: Scalable real-time sharing of 3D model visualizations for group collaboration. In: Luo, Y. (ed.) CDVE 2017. LNCS, vol. 10451, pp. 244–251. Springer, Cham (2017). https://doi.org/10.1007/978-3-319-66805-5_31

20. Wenzel, M., Gericke, L., Gumienny, R., Meinel, C.: Towards cross-platform collaboration - transferring real-time groupware to the browser, pp. 49–54 (2013). https://doi.org/10.1109/CSCWD.2013.6580938

21. Wilson, D., Lin, X., Longstreet, P., Sarker, S.: Web 2.0: a definition, literature review, and directions for future research (2011)

22. Wu, Y., He, F., Zhang, D., Li, X.: Service-oriented feature-based data exchange for cloud-based design and manufacturing. IEEE Trans. Serv. Comput. **11**(2), 341–353 (2018). https://doi.org/10.1109/TSC.2015.2501981

23. Liao, X., Huang, X., Huang, W.: Visualization of farm land use by classifying satellite images. In: Luo, Y. (ed.) CDVE 2018. LNCS, vol. 11151, pp. 287–290. Springer, Cham (2018). https://doi.org/10.1007/978-3-030-00560-3_40

Analysis of Instrumental Practices in Collaborative Design: Method of Identifying Needs, Means and Their Effectiveness

Gaëlle Baudoux[✉], Xaviéra Calixte[✉], and Pierre Leclercq[✉]

LUCID, Liège University, Liège, Belgium
gbaudoux@student.uliege.be,
{xaviera.calixte, pierre.leclercq}@uliege.be

Abstract. This paper presents a user-centered data collection method, concerning "means of design" and "representation supports" implemented in a collective architectural design process. Our aim is to study how these observed means and representations are adapted to agile design methods. Our method - applied on several long (3 months) architectural design processes – allows us to identify patterns of use and to consider their efficiency level brought to designers.

Keywords: Collaborative and multimode working environment ·
Architecture and engineering · Instrumented practices ·
Cooperative design analysis methodology

1 Introduction

Several fields of expertise are increasingly required in the domain of architectural design. Similarly, the constraints, which are applied at the beginning of the phases of production and in the realisation of coordination and performance, are present from the initial phases of conception. These constraints increase the number of mechanisms used in the design phase and make them more complex [1]. Are these means truly suited to the methods of design? Are they efficient for the users? Do they allow for a flexible mode of design? In order to answer these questions, this article proposes a user-centred method of data collection.

2 Latest Developments

In collaborative design, collective activity is based on 3 major types of action [2]: (1) communication: exchanging information between creators about the architectural target; (2) coordination: organising collective work; and (3) production: defining the architectural target. In this article, we associate "production" to an action achieved through the "means of design" and "communication" to one achieved through "support-representations".

Y. Luo (Ed.): CDVE 2019, LNCS 11792, pp. 172–180, 2019.
https://doi.org/10.1007/978-3-030-30949-7_20

2.1   Means of Design

What interests us is not the representation of the product in and of itself, but the type of action used to conceive the project and to produce the desired representation. We are in no way affiliated with the software used to carry-out the different actions. On the basis of Safin's work [3], we have kept 8 types of action:

(1)   Reference image: design through analogy vis-a-vis the pre-existing representations.
(2)   Paper drawing by hand: design via a graphic production by hand on paper.
(3)   Digital drawing by hand: design through a graphic production by hand on digital material.
(4)   CAD 2D: design via a two-dimensional graphic production assisted by a computer.
(5)   CAD 3D: design via a three-dimensional graphic production assisted by a computer.
(6)   Model: design through the production of a three-dimensional physical model.
(7)   CAD Parametric: parametric design assisted by a computer.
(8)   Prototype: design through static or dynamic simulations.

Hereunder, we will use the terms "means of design" or "means" when referring to these different actions of production.

2.2   Support-Representations

Under the term "support-representations", we will discuss the external representations used as a support for the discussion. As Safin highlights, "these external representations consist of all the possible representations of information (namely, the architectural target)" [3, p. 35]. They lighten the mental burden of materialising information, and thus improve the effectiveness of cognitive activities [4]. On the basis of the works of both Safin [3] and Elsen [5], we classify the different possible representations into 7 categories.

(1)   Reference image: image, sketch or photo that is not created by the creators.
(2)   Written text/keywords: words that constitute an independent representation.
(3)   Annotation: sketches or notes overlayed on a pre-existing representation.
(4)   Blueprint/sketch: symbolic production simplified by hand or on a computer.
(5)   2D plan/cut: two-dimensional graphic production in the form of a plan or a mix of objects.
(6)   2D perspective: fixed point of view on a multi-dimensional support of a three-dimensional object.
(7)   3D immersion: immersive numerical or physical three-dimensional model.

For the ease of the reader, "representation" and "support representation" will be used interchangeably.

2.3   Methods of Data Collection

Different methods of observation and analysis of the uses of architectural design have already been used in other studies. Gero [6] suggested using principles of encryption of the process to understand both the behaviour of actors and the uses of the object and tools. Other authors, such as Ericsson et Simon [7], discussed the evolution of the object and the tools independent from their uses, while Otjacques [8] retraced the uses of a tool for exchanging emails in the entire design process. Others, such as Defays [9], conducted a detailed study on a precise moment in the process which was analysed minute by minute. On the other end of the spectrum, the method suggested by Calixte allows for the observation of the uses of different tools over a long period of time [10]. None of the aforementioned methods allow for the observation of a process over a long period of time without disrupting the users.

3 Issue

Our goal is to streamline the process of design to allow for the collection of data regarding the uses of "means of design" and how they complement one another. Our research was conducted over a four-month period. To date, no other approach has been implemented in such a way. In addition, we have developed a data collection tool that is simple, fast and unobtrusive for the users. One that only intervenes at key moments to collect specifically targeted information at the heart of the design team.

4 Proposition and Methodology

Our method collects data by way of a questionnaire that is filled out by the members of the design teams who are observed at key moments during the design process. These short periods are chosen in advance and delimit the steps for the different sub-goals in the overall process of the completion of the project. For example, one of these sub-goal steps can be a presentation made to the supervisors about the structural principles or a meeting with the client about the volumetry or frontage.

The questionnaire consists of two questions. The first deals with the means of design used solely in the productive phases, and the second relates to the topic of support-representations used during the discussion between the designers in the team.

Both questions follow the same structure. They ask members of the design team:

– to cite the means and the representations used in the previous questions. The respondents are asked to indicate the means they used, in order of importance. That said, designers are free to interpret the word "importance". They could interpret it to mean importance of duration of usage, frequency, the order or impact of the design. This freedom of interpretation is crucial, as it allows the respondent to explain his/her real use of the means and the criteria that he/she finds important. It is key not to guide the respondents in their answers.
– to evaluate on a scale of 1 (very good) to 4 (very bad) the relevance of their usage as it relates to the creator's objectives. This speeds up the encoding of the data collected and it forces the respondent to take a stance. Given that the scale only has 4 levels, it is not possible for respondents to stay neutral.
– to explain, in a few words, the reasons for their evaluation or to their choice of the means and/or the representation.

- to propose an alternative option, if necessary.
- to explain in a few words, the reasons for their choice of an alternative option.

The data collected from the first question gives an understanding of the reasons behind the choices of the means and their real usage. The data from the second question allows for the identification of the needs as they relate to the task of communication between designers. The questionnaire is in paper format and does not exceed one A4 page, in order to reduce the amount of time that the designer spends on completing it. Each respondent submits one sheet with their name. This makes it possible to link the data collected from each designer during the entire design process.

Our method has, thus, 4 strengths: (1) it is immersive: data is collected during the entire process after the completion of each individual step, without interrupting the process; (2) it is centred around the user: on the one hand, the data reflects the deliberate practices and the personal opinions of the user, and on the other, it is designed for the purpose of simplicity and rapidity for the designer (less than 10 min to complete); (3) it collects information during key chosen moments: this allows for the simplification of the survey process for the designer, while covering the entire process; (4) it allows for freedom of expression: with the exception of the evaluation of the relevance, the sub-questions are open and not multiple choice. This avoids any problems linked to not understanding the suggested answers.. It also allows designers to develop their answers and thus, to go beyond the objectives of the first question.

5   Context

This method was applied in the context of an architectural workshop in the Master of Civil Architectural Engineering at the University of Liège over a four-month period, from September to December 2018. The group studied consisted of 8 teams of 3 to 4 designers, all architects and engineers. Their objective was to develop a pilot for a complex building intended for multi-purpose use: 7500 m^2 museum in an urban site. The particularity of this integrated activity resided in the liberty given to the teams in the tools that they could use.

There were 5 key moments chosen for the collection of data. Each chosen moment corresponded to the main steps of the review of the project that marked an important point in the evolution of the designed object and met a specific requirement in the deliverables and expertise (intentions, structure, budget ....).

The designers were invited to answer the paper version of the questionnaire before each review step. This protocol prevented long response times, distortions of the answers resulting from negative emotions and, more specifically, it allowed for the evaluation of the relevance of the tools.

6   Data Collected

131 questionnaires were collected in total from the experiment. Each question had 50 pieces of data, thus 6550 in total. This data covers:

- the number of uses of each means throughout the 5 sequences.
- the share of the usage of each means by the entire group of designers throughout the 5 sequences and over the entire process.
- the detail of the first, second, third, fourth and fifth mean chosen in the order of importance for each designer throughout the 5 sequences (Fig. 1).
- the average order of importance of each mean that was used throughout the 5 sequences by all the designers.
- the number of times each representation was used throughout the 5 sequences.
- the usage share of the different representations by all designers throughout the 5 sequences and in the overall process (Fig. 3).
- the average rating, of all designers, of the pertinence of the data for each means and representation used throughout the 5 sequences.
- the detail, one per designer, for each means and each representation used and their rating of their pertinence throughout the 5 sequences.
- the share allotted for each means and representation by the entire group of designers, and the different ratings given during the evaluation throughout the 5 sequences and the overall process.
- the share at different levels (designer, team, all respondents) of the different reasons for the choices of the cited usage of means and representations at each sequence and throughout the whole process.

The visualisation software Common Tools [11] was used to process the data collected. It generated different visual protocols and analysed the answers of each user, team and the entire group of designers.

7 Discussion

7.1 Feasibility

Of the 135 questionnaires that were distributed, 131 were completed. This represents a response rate of 97%. Thus, the results were representative of the group surveyed. On the scale of the design team, all the designers systematically completed the questionnaire in 6 of the 8 teams that participated. Aside from a good response rate, we were able to analyse a majority of the teams through complete data.

These numbers confirm that this method is not time intensive for the designers. This is due to the simplicity of the questions as they relate to mental energy and the rapidity of the answers (less than 10 min).

Contrary to other existing protocols that interrupt the designer in his/her activity, this data collection method perfectly slipped into the process without causing any disturbances.

Moreover, this method offers the advantage of covering many design teams at the same time during short collection periods (5 times 10 min per designer over 13 weeks). It also permits the collection of analysable data at different levels: by studying only the designer, the design team or the entire group of designers.

Its weakness lies in the respondents' understanding of the questions. Following the first completion of the survey, and after having received an explanation beforehand, it was necessary to re-explain each question and to give examples of possible answers. It should, therefore, be noted that for future use, this method of collection needs to be accompanied by a session wherein respondents are given a detailed explanation of not only the concepts and useful categories, but also the vocabulary used. It also seems necessary to give examples of possible answers on the questionnaire itself.

Lastly, certain designers did not perfectly follow protocol, as they completed the questionnaire after and not before the project review. This protocol was put in place to avoid any influence that a negative review may have on the designer's evaluation of the relevance of the means of design. From our post-experiment discussions with the respondents, it seems that negative reviews did not have an impact on their answers.

7.2   First Results

In order to prove the efficiency of this method, the writers propose to choose two types of data collected to show the way in which they can be used. The first chart (Fig. 1) details the means chosen in the order of the most important for each designer throughout the 5 sequences of the process. In the same way, we are able to obtain detailed charts for the means chosen in the order of the second, third, fourth and fifth most important for each designer throughout the 5 sequences of the process. It is, therefore, interesting to reconstitute the means chosen in order of importance for each actor in sequence 1 of the process and then in sequence 5 (Fig. 2).

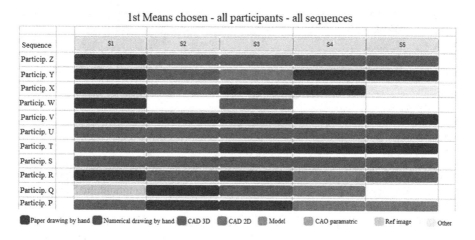

Fig. 1. Means of design chosen in order of importance.

On the basis of this data, we can identify patterns of use and how they complement one another throughout the different sequences and during the overall process. For example, two patterns that occur in sequence 1 are the series of "Paper drawing by hand – CAD3D" and "Paper drawing – Reference image". These two patterns are no longer present in the sequence 5, where we observe a series of "CAD2D – CAD3D" instead.

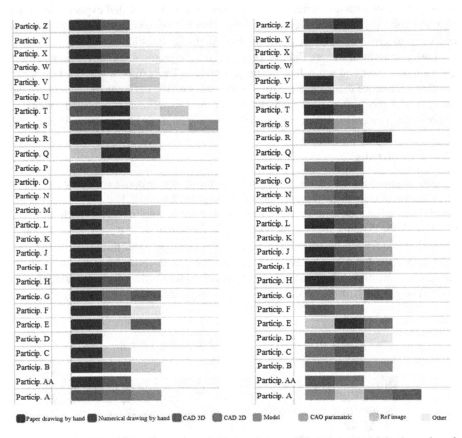

Fig. 2. Means chosen in sequence 1: on the left and in sequence 5, on the right, by order of importance.

The second chart, used to illustrate this method (Fig. 3), shows the proportion of usage of the different representations by all the respondents throughout the 5 sequences and the overall process. It can thus be seen which representations were used the most and the least in each sequence and in the overall process. Also it shows whether their uses fluctuated throughout the process. We observe, for example, that blueprints and sketches were considerably present at the beginning of the design, but they decreased with a slight, but gradual consistency throughout the process. The plans and cuts were also widely used. While they appear from the beginning of the process, they are particularly significant in the more advanced phases of design. As for the reference images, they are constantly used to support the discussion and other representatives, irrespective of the moment observed.

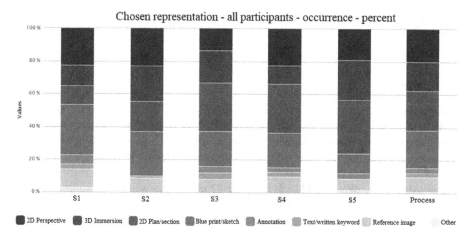

Fig. 3. Percentage between the chosen representations.

8   Conclusion

8.1   Summary

The data collection method presented in this article collects different data on the uses of means of design and support-representations throughout a four-month collective process of architectural design. It demonstrates which means are truly adapted to the methods of design and, more specifically, it shows the recurrent patterns of use. It illustrates the frequency of use, the usage, user satisfaction and the reasons for the choices of the tools.

As a result of the descriptions of the different means available to the designer, this method permits the researcher to trace their usage throughout the entire process.

Immersive and centred around the user, this method demonstrates the importance of keeping research protocol as light as possible for the designer so not to encumber their mental charge or to disturb the design process.

Aside from these patterns, the data allows us to respond to other themes such as the alteration of the means and the value-added potential of their appropriation by the user, as well as the respect of the spontaneous process of the designer in the conception phase, the efficiency of the means and the representations ….

8.2   Limitations

Three limitations were observed during this experiment. The first was the understanding of the questionnaire by the respondents. They had issues understanding the concepts and the questions. The writers' perfect understanding of the Master's workshop allowed them to identify key moments for data collection. This could prove to be more difficult in a less-controlled environment or in a professional setting.

Lastly, the designers had the same background, even if some of them had different Bachelor's degrees. The first convergent results would have likely been impacted had this not been the case.

8.3 Outlook

This work presents an initial view of the usage of the method presented in this paper.

This method appears to be equally appropriate in a larger framework with more design teams and/or more designers per team. Therefore, we plan to apply it in a professional setting beyond the pedagogical context presented in this paper.

Acknowledgements. We would like to thank the 27 students, as well as the workshop supervisors for their participation in this study.

References

1. Forgues, E.C.: Adaptation d'un modèle de maturité BIM pour les principaux intervenants de la chaîne d'approvisionnement en construction. Mémoire, Ecole de technologie supérieure de l'université du Québec, Montréal, Canada (2017)
2. Ellis, C., Wainer, J.: A conceptual model of groupware. Chapel Hill, NC (1994)
3. Safin, S.: Processus d'externalisation graphique dans les activités cognitives complexes: le cas de l'esquisse numérique en conception architecturale individuelle et collective. Ph.D. Thesis, University of Liège, Belgium (2011)
4. Kirsh, D.: Thinking with external representations. AI Soc. **25**(4), 441–454 (2010)
5. Elsen, C.: La médiation par les objets en design industriel, perspectives pour l'ingénierie de conception. Ph.D. thesis, University of Liège, Belgium (2011)
6. Gero, J.S.: Design prototypes: a knowledge representation, schema for design. AI Mag. **11**(4), 26–36 (1990)
7. Ericsson, K.A., Simon, H.A.: Protocol Analysis: Verbal Reports as Data. MIT Press, Cambridge (1993)
8. Otjacques, B.: Techniques de visualisation des informations associées à une plateforme de coopération, Ph.D. thesis, University of Namur (2008)
9. Defays, A.: Influence des communications multimodales sur le common ground. Proposition d'une méthodologie d'analyse. Ph.D. thesis, University of Liège (2013)
10. Calixte, X.: Traçabilité de l'usage des outils de conception dans un processus collaboratif. In: Séminaire de Conception Architecturale Numérique, SCAN 2018, Nantes, France (2018)
11. Ben Rajeb, S., Leclercq, P.: Instrumented analysis method for collaboration activities. In: Proceedings of the Fifth International Conference on Advanced Collaborative Networks, Systems and Applications, COLLA 2015, San Julian, Malta (2015)

Effectiveness of Color-Picking Interfaces Among Non-designers

Kristian Brathovde[1], Mads Brændeland Farner[1], Fredrik Krag Brun[1], and Frode Eika Sandnes[1,2(✉)] (iD)

[1] Oslo Metropolitan University, P.O. Box 4 St. Olavs plass, 0130 Oslo, Norway
brathovdek@gmail.com, madsfarner@gmail.com,
kragbrun@gmail.com, frodes@oslomet.no
[2] Kristiania University College, Prinsens Gate 7-9, Postboks 1190 Sentrum,
0130 Oslo, Norway

Abstract. There are relatively few studies on the effectiveness of color picking interface. This study therefore set out to measure both the efficiency in terms of task completion time and preference of four color-picking interfaces found in many design software applications including RGB, HSL, map and palette. A controlled experiment was conducted involving $n = 16$ participants without formal design training. The results show that the map and RGB interfaces were preferred by the participants while the palette interface resulted in the shortest task completion times. The HSL was the least favorable color picking interface for the given cohort of users. The results indicate that the palette, map and RGB color pickers found in entry level software probably are the most suitable for users without training in the use of colors.

Keywords: Design · Engineering · Collaboration · Color picking · HSL · RGB · Palette

1 Introduction

Color selection is a key operation in most design processes such as print and web-design, product design, interior design and design in the build environment [1]. Color selection is provided by most design-oriented software such as word-processors, graphing software, presentation software, image processing application, drawing programs, CAD/CAM, etc. Color is perceived as important to people and is deeply rooted in cultures, traditions, and personal preferences. Groups of designers collaborating in teams may often debate color choices in heated discussions.

Software application designed for general users often include color selections based on palettes, RGB-selectors and various types of two-dimensional maps, while application aimed at professional users such as designers also include the HSL model. There is no consistent name for a map and by map we mean color picking interfaces where several colors are presented in a two-dimensional space with some additional control that changes the attributes of the displayed colors. Clearly, the displayed colors are quickly accessed by a single click. It may however be more challenging to find colors that are not displayed by modifying the secondary control.

© Springer Nature Switzerland AG 2019
Y. Luo (Ed.): CDVE 2019, LNCS 11792, pp. 181–189, 2019.
https://doi.org/10.1007/978-3-030-30949-7_21

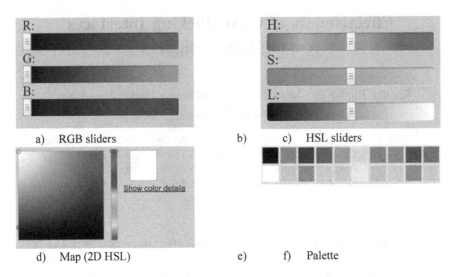

Fig. 1. Color-picking interfaces used in the experiment. (Color figure online)

Palette interfaces are similar to the color charts found in hardware stores and comprise a fixed set of predetermined colors. It thus easy to access all the colors and the palette interface is easy to understand. RGB color pickers are also common and easy to understand representing the additive model where the users control the amount of red, green and blue that is mixed into the resulting color through three sliders. The hardware centric RGB model is widely understood among computer scientists as most programming languages and html/CSS coding is done using RGB-vectors even though these technologies also support the HSL model. The HSL model is less intuitive and requires some training where the perceptual qualities of colors are controlled independently, that is hue (red, orange, yellow, green, etc.), saturation (signal red, pastel red, etc.), and lightness (dark, light, etc.) controlled using three sliders. However, once learned, the HSL model is superior to the others as it makes it easier to describe colors linguistically, facilitating collaboration and easy communication and reasoning about colors among designers in a team. The HSL representation makes it much easier to find aesthetical color schemes and adjust contrast for readability. There are also around twenty other color models used for different purposes such as CMYK for print and perceptual color spaces [2] such as CIElab which are designed to be better aligned with the human visual system.

Opinions about color models vary yet there is little empirical evidence about the effectiveness of these color models from a user perspective. This study therefore set out to gather empirical evidence about the effectiveness (productivity) and subjective preference of four common color picking interfaces in terms of task completion time.

2   Related Work

Although several approaches to computer-based color work has been proposed, that is the selecting and organizing colors [3], color picking interfaces has changed little over the years [4]. Studies on color picking interfaces have addressed topics such as its use in the build environment [1], two-handed color exploration [5] and how to specify colors as part of image retrieval queries [6]. Misue and Kitajima [7] designed a color picker based on the CIElab perceptual color space. Douglas and Kirkpatrick [8] did a thorough study of different color picking interfaces and concluded that visual feedback is more important than the color model used.

Based on interviews with designers Jalal, Maudet and Mackay [9] identified five key areas of color manipulation and proposed corresponding tools, namely the probing and tweaking individual colors, manipulating color relationships, combining color with other elements, revisiting previous color choices and revealing design process through color. Researchers have also addressed the assessment of color, for example the study by Heer and Stone [10] who proposed a probabilistic model to assess the accuracy of human naming of colors, or Luncy, Haber and Carpendale's [11] visualizations of how artists use of color have changed over time.

Much of the literature on color picking interfaces has evolved around the end result. Reinecke, Flatla and Brooks [12] addressed the situational perceivability of the chosen colors such as screen glare caused by sunlight or dimly lit screens. Others have especially focused on the higher contrast levels needed by users with low vision [13]. Webster [14] have argued for contrast requirements to be integrated into design tools and several such tools have been proposed based on the RGB-domain [15, 16] and HSL-domain [17]. Others have focused on the balancing of aesthetics and accessibility requirements [18]. Approaches to help adjust colors so that adhere to standardized minimum contrast levels have also been proposed [19] as well as visualization approaches to help designers conceptually understand contrast [20].

Some of the research has been directed towards the selection of color for data visualization purposes [21–24], for instance how to select colors that still look aesthetical when they are mixed through the stacking of transparent layers [25] or extracting aesthetic palettes from images [26, 27].

3   Method

3.1   Experimental Design

A randomized controlled experiment was set up with two independent within-subject variables, namely color setting interface and color task type. The color setting interface factor had four levels, namely RGB, HSL, map and palette. The Color task types had four levels, setting color from name (easy), setting color from name (hard), copying the color of a physical object, and setting the color from association with a physical object memory. Task completion time was measured as the dependent variable. We also measured preference as a dependent variable for the color picking interface as independent variable.

3.2 Participants

A total of 16 participants were recruited from the authors institution of which approximately two thirds were male and one third female. The participants were all students in their 20s and 30s. None of the participants were trained designers. None of the participants exhibited any signs visual impairment including color blindness. Participation was voluntary and anonymous.

3.3 Task

Each participant was asked to set four colors using the four interfaces, two of the colors were derived from linguistic names, one from association with an object from memory and one based on a physical object. The color tasks were designed such that they would not generate any follow up questions during the experiment. The colors included pink (an unsaturated red), signal green (a saturated green), the color of the sleeve of a book with a turquoise color and the yellow color in the IKEA furniture store logo. The IKEA logo was chosen as this is a visual profile that most people in the cohort were expected to be familiar with (the experiment also confirmed this).

The participant set the four colors using the four interfaces (see Fig. 1). These included RGB which comprises three sliders controlling the red, green and the blue components respectively (Fig. 1a), HSL comprising three sliders controlling the hue, saturation and lightness of a color (Fig. 1b), a two-dimensional map (Fig. 1c) and a palette showing 20 predefined colors (Fig. 1d). The map interface used was in fact an HSL interface with the saturation varying along the horizontal direction and lightness along the vertical direction (see Fig. 1c). The hue was controlled using the secondary control. The user thus had instantaneous access to all the brightness and saturation settings for a given hue. The interface presentation order was randomized to prevent any learning effects. The order of the color tasks was fixed.

The participants were also asked to rank each of the interfaces using a 10-point Likert scale displayed next to a picture of the respective color picking interface where 1 indicated a strong dislike and 10 indicating a strong preference.

3.4 Equipment

A specialized application was programmed in PhP and JavaScript for the purpose allowing the balancing of the presentation order to be automated and completion times to be measured accurately. The tests were run on a Dell XPS 9550 laptop with a 15-inch display.

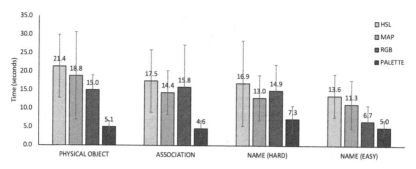

Fig. 2. Task completion time for different colors using the four interfaces. Error bars shows standard deviation. (Color figure online)

3.5 Procedure

Each participant was first briefed about the experiment. The preference survey was presented after the participants had completed all the tests. Steps were taken to keep the conditions as constant as possible for each participant. The experiment was conducted in a quiet meeting room in the authors home institutions under the same lighting conditions. The order of the color picking interfaces was balanced while the order of the color tasks was fixed. All the tests were performed using the same laptop computer and a mouse. Each session lasted approximately 10 min. The data were analyzed using JASP 0.9.1.0 [28].

4 Results

The results of the timed experiments (in seconds) are shown in Fig. 2. The results shows both a significant effect of color picking interface ($F(3, 45) = 45.710, p < .001$, $\eta^2 = .757$) and a significant effect of color setting task ($F(3, 45) = 7.938, p < .001$, $\eta^2 = .346$). Mauchly's test of sphericity indicated that the assumption of sphericity was violated for the interaction ($p < .001$). A Greenhouse-Geisser correction was therefore applied since the Greenhouse-Geisser epsilon was .340, that is, less than .75. No interaction was detected ($F(3.064, 45.964) = 2.057, p = .118$).

The results shown in Fig. 2 reveal that the palette was associated with the shortest task completion time for all the color tasks ranging from ($M = 4.6, SD = 2.1$) to ($M = 7.3, SD = 3.6$). Bonferroni post-hoc tests also revealed that the palette interface was statistically different to the other interfaces ($p < .001$). Moreover, the HSL interface was consistently the slowest interface with completion times ranging from ($M = 13.6, SD = 5.8$) to ($M = 21.4, SD = 8.5$). Post hoc tests confirms that the HSL interface was significantly different to the three other interfaces, namely RGB ($p = .013$), map ($p = .023$) and palette ($p < .001$). There is no significant difference between the map and the RGB interface in terms of completion time ($p = 1.0$).

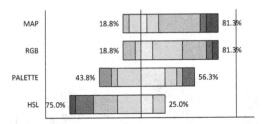

Fig. 3. Participants' subjective preferences. Orange indicate negative responses and green indicate positive responses. (Color figure online)

Figure 3 shows the participants preferences for the four color-picking interfaces suing a diverging stacked bar chart [29]. The chart reveals that most of the responses are positive for the map, RGB and palette interface while most responses are negative for the HSL interface. The map and the RGB interfaces both are the most preferred interfaces although the map interface has a higher frequency of high Likert responses. As the Likert data are of interval type a non-parametric repeated measures test was used for significance testing. The Friedman test shows that the preferences for the four color-picking interfaces are significantly different ($\chi^2(3) = 18.73, p < .001$). Connover's Post Hoc comparisons shows that the difference between two most preferred interfaces, namely the map and the RGB interfaces are not significantly different ($p = 1.0$). The least preferred interface, HSL, is significantly different to both the map interface ($p < .001$) and the RGB interface ($p < .001$). However, HSL is not significantly different to the palette interface ($p = .173$). The palette interface is significantly different from the map interface ($p = .006$) but not the RGB interface ($p = .147$).

5   Discussion

The completion times viewed in terms of task type are as excepted, namely that setting the color based on names yields the shortest completion time. Clearly the easy signal green is easier to set than the pink which require more effort in order to adjust the saturation level. The results show that the map gives a shorter completion time when setting the saturated color, perhaps because colors are simultaneously displayed at all saturation levels for a given hue while the RGB interface require multiple slider operations to achieve saturation. Similarly, the signal green is easier to set directly with a simple motion in the RGB interface while the search for green requires adjusting the secondary hue control in the map interface.

Next, setting the color via association (from memory) was the third slowest. Setting the color from the object (book cover) was the slowest. This was probably because a real object poses an absolute comparison which may require more time-consuming trial and error, while setting colors from memory does not involve such an absolute quality criterion, just simply a subjective assessment of the results.

Although Fig. 2 reveals practical differences, Bonferroni post hoc tests reveals only the easy naming task and the association tasks are significantly different ($p = .005$), as well as the easy naming task and the object naming task ($p < .001$). The lack of statistical significance was probably caused by the large variation in completion times for the different interfaces and the low number of participants.

The objective measurements are relatively consistent with the subjective measurements as the slowest interface (HSL) was also the least preferred by the participants. The RGB and the palette interfaces which were the most preferred interfaces were only ranking second and third in terms of completion times. The palette which resulted in the fastest completion times ranked as the third preferred interface with close to 50/50 distribution of positive and negative responses.

One may speculate that the high preference for the relatively inefficient RGB interfaces may be related to users' familiarity as it is found in many software applications. Note that we did not ask the participants to what degree they were familiar with the four interfaces. Users preference for the map interface may be explained by its direct manipulation. Even if users are unfamiliar with the underlying HSL model they can still find the desired color quickly. Although the palette interface was the fastest to use there were only 20 color choices which is too limited for most practical applications. The lack of choices may explain the users low ranking of the palette.

The low preference and performance results obtained with the HSL model is as expected from non-trained users. The HSL model require some basic training in color theory. For instance, it is our experience that it takes some time of computer science students to understand the purpose and benefit of the HSL model as they are often strongly attached to the RGB model. Trained designers, however, usually describe colors linguistically according to hue with saturation and brightness/lightness modifiers and are usually trained in working with colors and color harmonies. It is thus possible that the results would have been completely different with trained designers, that is, that they would both prefer and perform the tasks faster with the HSL model. Although the results suggest that the participants were unaware of the workings of the HSL model in hindsight we should have explicitly probed the participants about their practical knowledge about the RGB and HSL color models.

Another weakness of the current study is that the accuracy of the color models was not measured. In addition to perceived preference and speed of task completion it is also essential to scrutinize the results produced with the various color picking interfaces. Future work should therefore include measurements of accuracy. One may speculate that the HSL may provide the highest accuracy as it allows the designer to directly control the independent perceivable dimensions of color. With the RGB interface these dimensions are intertwined, where altering one component affects all three perceivable dimensions.

Finally, only 16 participants were recruited from a narrow student cohort. This may be a too limited source of data to make general conclusions. Clearly, a larger sample including multiple relevant cohorts would add to the power of the experiment and generalizability of the results. The current results should therefore be interpreted with some caution.

6 Conclusions

A controlled quantitative experiment was conducted to measure the effectiveness of four common color picking interfaces on a cohort of non-designers. The results show that the HSL interface was the least effective and least preferred. The users preferred the RGB and the map interfaces, but their observed performance revealed shorter task completion times with the palette color picker. Future work includes expanding the cohort to include trained designers with color theory knowledge as a between groups factor. Future work should also study the accuracy of the color picking interface as the end result often is more important than the completion time and user preferences.

References

1. Bailey, P., Manktelow, K., Olomolaiye, P.: Examination of the color selection process within digital design for the built environment. In Proceedings of Theory and Practice of Computer Graphics, pp. 193–200. IEEE (2003)
2. Robertson, P.K.: Visualizing color gamuts: a user interface for the effective use of perceptual color spaces in data displays. IEEE Comput. Graphics Appl. **8**(5), 50–64 (1988)
3. Moretti, G., Lyons, P.: Tools for the selection of color palettes. In: Proceedings of the SIGCHI-NZ Symposium on Computer-Human Interaction, pp. 13–18. ACM (2002)
4. Meier, B.J., Spalter, A.M., Karelitz, D.B.: Interactive color palette tools. IEEE Comput. Graphics Appl. **24**, 64–72 (2004)
5. Gonzalez, B., Latulipe, C.: BiCEP: bimanual color exploration plugin. In: CHI 2011 Extended Abstracts on Human Factors in Computing Systems, pp. 1483–1488. ACM (2001)
6. van den Broek, E.L., Kisters, P.M.F., Vuurpijl, L.G.: Design guidelines for a content-based image retrieval color-selection interface. In: Dutch HCI 2004, pp. 14–18. ACM (2004)
7. Misue, K., Kitajima, H.: Design tool of color schemes on the CIELAB space. In 2016 20th International Conference Information Visualization, pp. 33–38. IEEE (2016)
8. Douglas, S.A., Kirkpatrick, A.E.: Model and representation: the effect of visual feedback on human performance in a color picker interface. ACM Trans. Graphics **18**, 96–127 (1999)
9. Jalal, G., Maudet, N., Mackay, W.E.: Color portraits: from color picking to interacting with color. In: Proceedings of the 33rd Annual ACM Conference on Human Factors in Computing Systems, pp. 4207–4216. ACM (2015)
10. Heer, J., Stone, M.: Color naming models for color selection, image editing and palette design. In: Proceedings of the SIGCHI Conference on Human Factors in Computing Systems, pp. 1007–1016. ACM (2012)
11. Lynch, S., Haber, J., Carpendale, S.: Colorvis: Exploring color in digital images. Comput. Graphics **36**(6), 696–707 (2012)
12. Reinecke, K., Flatla, D.R., Brooks, C.: Enabling designers to foresee which colors users cannot see. In: Proceedings of the 2016 CHI Conference on Human Factors in Computing Systems, pp. 2693–2704. ACM (2016)
13. Troiano, L., Birtolo, C., Miranda, M.: Adapting palettes to color vision deficiencies by genetic algorithm. In: Keijzer, M. (ed.) Proceedings of the 10th Annual Conference on Genetic and Evolutionary Computation, pp. 1065–1072. ACM (2008)
14. Webster, M.: Integrating color usability components into design tools. Interactions **21**, 56–61 (2014)

15. Sandnes, F.E.: On-screen color contrast for visually impaired readers: selecting and exploring the limits of WCAG2.0 colors. In: Black, A., Lund, O., Walker, S. (eds.) Information Design: Research and Practice, pp. 405–416. Routledge, Abingdon (2016)

16. Sandnes, F.E., Zhao, A.: An interactive color picker that ensures WCAG2.0 compliant color contrast levels. Procedia-Comput. Sci. **67**, 87–94 (2015)

17. Sandnes, F.E., Zhao, A.: A contrast color selection scheme for WCAG2. 0-compliant web designs based on HSV-half-planes. In: Proceedings of SMC 2015, pp. 1233–1237. IEEE (2015)

18. Tigwell, G.W., Flatla, D.R., Archibald, N.D.: ACE: a color palette design tool for balancing aesthetics and accessibility. ACM Trans. Access. Comput. **9**, 1–32 (2017)

19. Sandnes, F.E.: An image-based visual strategy for working with color contrasts during design. In: Miesenberger, K., Kouroupetroglou, G. (eds.) ICCHP 2018. LNCS, vol. 10896, pp. 35–42. Springer, Cham (2018). https://doi.org/10.1007/978-3-319-94277-3_7

20. Sandnes, F.E.: Understanding WCAG2.0 color contrast requirements through 3D color space visualization. Stud. Health Technol. Inform. **229**, 366–375 (2016)

21. Bergman, L.D., Rogowitz, B.E., Treinish, L.A.: A rule-based tool for assisting colormap selection. In: Proceedings Visualization 1995, pp. 118–125. IEEE (1995)

22. Zhou, L., Hansen, C.D.: A survey of colormaps in visualization. IEEE Trans. Vis. Comput. Graphics **22**(8), 2051–2069 (2016)

23. Gramazio, C.C., Laidlaw, D.H., Schloss, K.B.: Colorgorical: Creating discriminable and preferable color palettes for information visualization. IEEE Trans. Vis. Comput. Graphics **23**(1), 521–530 (2017)

24. Wijffelaars, M., Vliegen, R., Van Wijk, J.J., Van Der Linden, E.J.: Generating color palettes using intuitive parameters. In: Computer Graphics Forum, vol. 27, no. 3, pp. 743–750. Blackwell Publishing Ltd, Oxford (2008)

25. Wang, L., Giesen, J., McDonnell, K.T., Zolliker, P., Mueller, K.: Color design for illustrative visualization. IEEE Trans. Vis. Comput. Graphics **14**(6), 1739–1754 (2008)

26. Phan, H.Q., Fu, H., Chan, A.B.: Color orchestra: ordering color palettes for interpolation and prediction. IEEE Trans. Vis. Comput. Graphics **24**(6), 1942–1955 (2018)

27. Lin, S., Hanrahan, P.: Modeling how people extract color themes from images. In: Proceedings of the SIGCHI Conference on Human Factors in Computing Systems, pp. 3101–3110. ACM (2013)

28. JASP Team: JASP (Version 0.9) [Computer software] (2018)

29. Robbins, N.B., Heiberger, R.M.: Plotting Likert and other rating scales. In: Proceedings of the 2011 Joint Statistical Meeting, pp. 1058–1066 (2011)

Private Security for the Cloud Mobile via a Strong Authentication Method

Imen Merdassi, Mariem Bouchaala, Cherif Ghazel$^{(\boxtimes)}$ (ID),
and Leila Saidane

Cristal Lab, National School of Computer Sciences, University of Manouba,
Manouba, Tunisia
Merdassi.Imen93@gmail.com,
bouchaala.mariem@gmail.com,
Cherif.Ghazel@email.ati.tn, Leila.Saidane@ensi.rnu.tn

Abstract. In recent years, many consumers are storing a large amount of data in the cloud, so the security of this data is very important for users and companies. The companies need to provide secure data for consumers and to offer resource access only when it is needed. For this purpose, consumers require a much higher degree of authentication, such as strong authentication, comparing with the simple couple identifier and password based identification. In this work, we will study and propose a new strong authentication security method based on One Time Password (OTP) for mobile cloud. The proposed method will be based on images selection by the users, which guarantees a secure access and authentication for services usage, while taking into account the user's preferences. We will also present and discuss experimental results, which illustrate a practical implementation of the proposed method and its benefits.

Keywords: Security · Privacy · Cloud mobile · Strong authentication · OTP

1 Introduction

Today, many common authentication methods are often used on unsecured networks, such as passwords, digital signatures, smart cards, and fingerprints. Among these methods, password authentication is considered simple and convenient for use.

Static passwords can be easily detected by hackers and must be replaced by the dynamic password system. However, since humans can remember images better than text, this is why image-based password systems are now needed to solve security authentication problems. In this context, we develop this work and our contribution, can be summarized as follows:

- We analyze security issues and requirements stack in cloud computing.
- We develop an advanced study related to security and privacy in the cloud.
- We offer a comprehensive solution to ensure this privacy security in the mobile cloud, based on strong authentication.
- We define the resulting architecture of the proposed solution with an in-depth study of the privacy security in mobile cloud based on strong authentication.

© Springer Nature Switzerland AG 2019
Y. Luo (Ed.): CDVE 2019, LNCS 11792, pp. 190–200, 2019.
https://doi.org/10.1007/978-3-030-30949-7_22

The organization of this paper follows a standard format consisting of five sections. The first section is the introduction. In the second section, we discuss related works. In Sect. 3, we discuss the preliminary concepts of cloud mobile and security. The proposed security method is defined in Sect. 4. Some experimental results and performance analysis are presented and discussed in the fifth section. Brief summary and concluding remarks are presented in the last section.

2 Related Works

In this section, we will present and discuss the traditional techniques and how images are used in different sections to provide authentication in networks for systems.

In fact, Almuairfi et al. proposed in [1] a new IPAS: Implicit Password Authentication System for non-mobile and mobile devices in which authentication information is implicitly presented to the user. This system is based on two phases; a registration phase and an authentication phase. During the registration phase, a user grants identifiers from which the server extracts keywords. Furthermore, several images containing clickable objects maybe used for representing the user personal information. During the authentication phase, the server send an image and a random keyword to the user that click on the one that represents the expected keyword.

Chen et al. introduced in [2] a new method for picture encryption, which is the combination of FRFT: Fractional Fourier Transform and WPT: Wavelet Packet Transform. During the encryption phase, the images are divided into sub bands. Some of them are randomly chosen and encrypted, using a fractional wavelet transform. During decryption, the same process is repeated, but in a reverse order. This image encryption method achieves confidentiality but it is limited to the key-space.

Chen and Zhao proposed in [3] an image authentication method based on the Hamming code technique for reducing some of the disadvantages of the previous method. The parity check bits will be produced from pixels and then will be altered in other new pixels. First, the most significant bit value of each altered pixel had to be predicted. Then, by referring to the predicted bit and its parity check bits, the corrupted pixel could be recovered. Nevertheless, by using the most significant bit, there is a probability of making an incorrect prediction.

In [4], Chan extended the work of Chang and Chan's proposal to overcome the drawbacks, or control bits parity are produced from the pixel whose bits are rearranged. The value of the most significant bit of each corrupted pixel can be determined, depending on the parity check bits. In addition, due to the reordering procedure, the recovery procedure is changed. This method has a greater ability to recover altered areas with higher quality than Chang and Chan's method.

Gurav et al. proposed in [5] a method based on graphic password authentication. In fact, during the registration phase, the user must go through an authentication process that solved many problems of the existing systems. It can be useful just the login process saving takes too much time and requires much more storage space.

Vishwakarma and Gangrade introduced in [6] an approach that system uses a random image based time synchronized OTP generation using SHA-512 algorithm and ECC method to produce encrypted OTP that will be send to users.

Cherdmuangpak et al. proposed in [7] the technique of password-based authentication built on the two-image factors that are random questions with passwords and a pre-selected image. This technique solves the problem of forgetting password by asking three random questions for each connection, which makes it difficult to exploit.

Das et al. proposed in [8] a system with five levels of security. The system introduces a combined OTP-based authentication method where image OTP is used in first level and blocks of biometric image are randomly selected in the second level of authentication. Then, the both OTP are combined using alternate merging. Hence, no random guessing can retrieve the numeric OTP that will be shared from server to user.

3 Preliminaries

3.1 Problem Statement

The most computer crimes are caused by traditional authentication such as password system. These passwords are cached on servers and on computer hard drives that may be cracked. A new alternative to the above is the third factor in the authentication phase, which uses the OTP based on images. This method is defined as following:

- Generated valid once passwords and for a short period of time.
- Each password generated by the algorithm is different from previous and next ones.
- The user is authenticated according to the OTP algorithm code received on the customer's phone.

3.2 Cloud Mobile

Mobile computing depends, through mobile devices, on the ability to use computer resources. Furthermore, mobile computing enables the execution of tasks that have been traditionally done by normal desktops. In general, mobile computing is supported by three basic concepts: software, hardware, and communication [10].

Mobile cloud computing combines the concepts of cloud computing [11] and mobile computing. This new technology makes use of the capability of data storage and data processing by using cloud computing infrastructure through the Internet.

3.3 Cloud Security

Cloud computing is a huge collection of interconnected networks with many security challenges, encompassing many technologies, including networks, operating systems, databases, virtualization, transaction management, resources planning, load balancing, concurrent access control, and memory management. As a result, the security concerns of the majority of these systems and technologies are applicable to the cloud.

This security ensures the confidentiality, integrity, authenticity and availability of information, as well as service of different layers are breach that may be raised new security concern [12].

3.4   One Time Password

The One-Time Password (OTP) is a numeric or alphanumeric string of characters, which is generated by a server automatically. The OTPs technics are not vulnerable to reply attack and have a great advantage on static password. They are valid for only one session login. So, it offers better protection than static passwords [13].

4   Proposed Security Method

In this work, we propose a new OTP based method, which built on images selected by the users. When a user makes a first registration on a website, he chooses an image easy to remember, such as images of natural landscapes, automobiles, etc.

Each time the user login, a randomly generated grid of images is displayed. The user identifies the previously selected image. A unique access code is generated by the selected image, making the authentication process more secure than using a classic method. As long as an image is a matrix whose value each element represents a discrete intensity of light [14], we have chosen to extract random numbers from the matrix of the image. These values are used as OTP, which is an important factor for the authentication. This is much easier and advantageous for the user because it must retain only a few categories to recognize the selected image.

The system architecture for the Two-factor authentication of the proposed solution has two processes, the first one is the registration process and the second is the authentication process.

4.1   Registration

In the registration phase, on the one hand, the user provides his {Id_i (identity), Pwd_i (password), IMEI (International Mobile Equipment Identity) and Nt (phone number)} to the web server. The web server forwards the message to the Cloud Authentication Server (CAS). The latter retains this data by using the LDAP server for a locally user (U_i) registration. Mainly, this phase includes the following steps:

1. The user U_i registers {Id_i, Pwd_i, IMEI, Nt} to the CAS.
2. The CAS records {Id_i, Pwd_i, IMEI, Nt} using the LDAP directory, which works as a standalone server with its own database. In addition, access to data is very fast and in a secured mode.
3. The user (U_i) registers with the image I_i of his choice.
4. The U_i securely submits {Id_i, Pwd_i, IMEI, Nt, I_i} to the CAS.
5. The CAS guards these data {Id_i, Pwd_i, IMEI, Nt, I_i}, as a piece of identification P.

4.2   Authentication

To access the cloud services, a user needs to authenticate:

1. If a user $U_{i \in [1,...,n]}$ looks to be authenticated, he should provide and send his username and password to the CAS, C_s: {Id, Pwd}, for an only limited public access to data.
2. The CAS checks the authenticity of the user by comparing if $(C_s =^? C_i)$, with C_i: {Id_i, Pwd_i} is the data selected by the user in the registration phase. If the user is identified ($C_s = C_i$), the CAS provides him a restricted access only to the public data.

During the authentication phase and to conduct the online transactions, the registered user must login with the user ID and password. However, for online financial transactions like credit/debit card transactions, it takes an extra factor like the OTP for successful authentication that is generated from an image, Fig. 1.

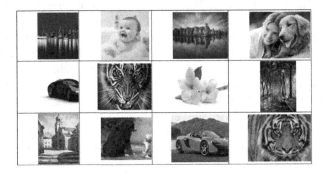

Fig. 1. A set of images displayed in the authentication phase.

3. The user U_i selects an image I_s.
4. The CAS checks the authenticity of I_s by comparing it with the sorted image then calculates the OTP using the selected image I_s.
5. The OTP_i will be provided by the CAS using the Nt and the International Mobile Equipment Identity (IMEI) provided by the CAS during the registration phase.
6. The user receives the OTP_i by phone from the CAS via the mobile network.
7. Once the OTP_i is received, U_i taps it on his computer.
8. Transfer of the OTP_s (the OTP selected by the user) to the CAS.
9. The CAS verifies the authenticity of the OTP_s: If ($OTP_i = OTP_s$) the user is authenticated, and the CAS will provide full access to the user's data. Otherwise, an error message will be generated and sent to the user.

4.3   Image Verification

The user inserts and sends C_s: {Id, Pwd} to the CAS. If $C_s = C_i$ then validates the user identity as the first factor. The user selects an image I_s, therefore, the CAS checks the authenticity of the image by comparing it with the stored image one (I_i selected during the registration phase).

The comparison of the image I_i with the selected image I_s must be done at CAS level, using the following methods, as defined by Fig. 2.

```
gray_img1 = rgb2gray(Ii);
gray_img2 = rgb2gray(Is);
binary_image1 = gray_img1 > 125;
binary_image2 = gray_img2 > 125;
[row, col] = size(binary_image1);
similar = 0;
different = 0;
```

```
for R = 1 : row
  for C = 1 : col
    if isequal(binary_image1(R,C), binary_image2(R,C))
      similar = similar + 1;
    else
      different = different + 1;
    end    end    end
total_pixels = row*col;
difference_percentage = (different / total_pixels) * 100;
    fprintf('%f%% difference between the compared images \n%d pixels being different
    to %d total pixels\n', difference_percentage, different, total_pixels )
```

Fig. 2. Algorithm for verification the selected image.

4.4   OTP Calculation

The OTP must be selected randomly using the matrix of the chosen image M_I (gray level image: I_gray). Here, the image I_s must be resized to a specified size and converted to a grayscale color image.

$$[x, y] = Size(I\_gray) \tag{1}$$

Where I_gray is the described image and x, y are the variables assigned to the maximum coordinate values of this image.

The OTP must be selected randomly using the matrix of the image described M_I (image described: I_gray), using the following methods, as defined by Fig. 3.

```
difference_percentage == 0
msize = numel I_gray);
idx = randperm (msize);
OTP = I_gray(idx(1:3));
```

Fig. 3. Algorithm of calculating of OTP.

4.5 Sending the OTP

Each user mobile has a UICC (Universal Integrated Circuit Card) which is a security element and commonly improperly called Subscriber Identity Module (SIM).

This UICC associated with the mobile terminal maybe the ideal token that can be used to achieve the strong authentication, by all as a material factor.

IMSI (International Mobile Subscriber Identity) is the unique number that is registered in the mobile SIM card and makes it possible to authenticate a terminal securely on the mobile network via the corresponding authentication mechanisms.

We consider a simplified architecture of sending the OTP using 4G method [9]. Figure 4 depicts this simplified architecture, which contains four main components: User (Smartphone), Evolved Universal Terrestrial Radio Access Network (E-UTRAN), Evolved Packet Core (EPC) and the cloud server.

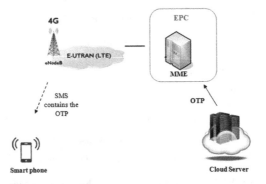

Fig. 4. Architecture of the sending of OTP.

Figure 5 presents the architecture of the proposed technique that defines two phases: the registration phase and the authentication phase, which includes the image checking step, the OTP calculation step and the OTP generation and submission step.

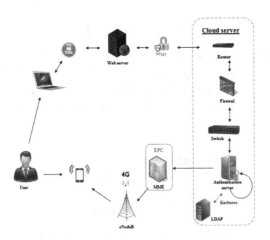

Fig. 5. Proposed technical architecture.

5   Experimental Results and Discussions

In image processing, an image is considered a mathematical function of $R \times R$ in R. Let's take the example of two images as shown in Fig. 6, with the same dimensions I_i (202×236) and I_s (202×236).

Image I_i Image I_s

Fig. 6. Images selection and comparing.

5.1   Case 1: Different Images Selection and Comparing

The execution of our algorithm shows that the two images are different: the number of different pixels is greater than zero and subsequently, the percentage of the difference between the two images is different from zero.

$$[(\text{Number of different pixels}/\text{total number of pixels}) \times 100] \qquad (2)$$

Hence, an error message should be displayed to the user (incorrect selected image) and network access will be automatically canceled by the CAS.

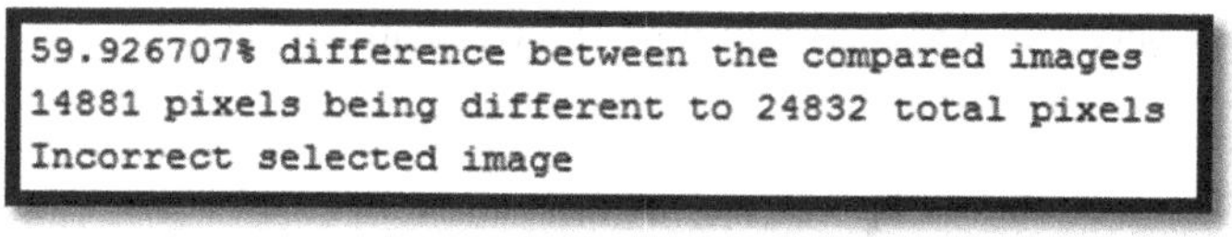

```
59.926707% difference between the compared images
14881 pixels being different to 24832 total pixels
Incorrect selected image
```

Fig. 7. Comparison result of two different images.

Figures 7 and 8 illustrate the difference between the compared images (Diff image).

$$\text{diff\_image} = \text{binary\_image1} - \text{binary\_image2} \qquad (3)$$

The two images are converted into two gray-level images (Gray img1 and Gray img2) and then two binary images (Binary img1 and Binary img2) to obtain a resulting image that contains the difference in pixels between these two compared images.

Fig. 8. Difference images selection and comparing.

5.2 Case 2: Same Images Selection and Comparing

The selected image I_i is the same as the image chosen during the authentication phase I_s. It means that there are no different pixels in these two compared images and thereafter the difference percentage is equal to zero (Fig. 9).

```
0.000000% difference between the compared images
0 pixels being different to 24832 total pixels
```

Fig. 9. Corresponding images comparison result.

Since there are no different pixels, Fig. 10 presents a difference image (Diff image) totally black which shows that the two images are perfectly corresponding then the Cloud Access Server (CAS) passes to the OTP calculation phase.

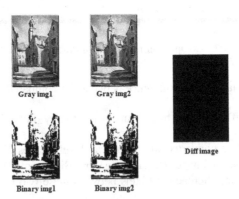

Fig. 10. Corresponding images selection and comparing.

After comparing and checking the two images and if they match, the image I must be resized to a specified dimension and converted to a grayscale color image.

As Fig. 11 shows, the OTP is selected randomly by using the matrix of the described image M (I_gray image).

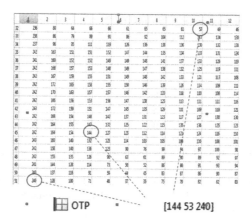

Fig. 11. Result of the calculated OTP.

Figure 12 shows the execution time of the comparison of the images and the calculation of the OTP, (a) shows the execution time of 6 times when the images are different whereas (b) presents the time of where the comparative images are identical.

When comparing the two figures we notice that the calculation of the OTP does not take a long time.

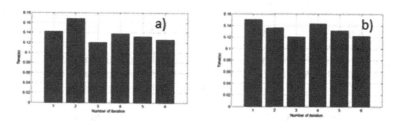

Fig. 12. Execution time of the proposed method.

6 Conclusion

Attackers are learning more and they become more sophisticated in using new fraudulent techniques to acquire confidential information. Strong authentication is developed and introduced to get rid of multiple attacks as phishing, sniffing and others. In addition, One Time Passwords (OTP) are introduced to counter these attacks. They are commonly used to authenticate a user. To generate an OTP, some simple functions like random numbers generation are also applied.

On the MATLAB platform, the efficiency of our strong authentication solution is modeled and approved based on images and code generation and usage.

References

1. Almuairfi, S., Veeraraghavan, P., Chilamkurti, N.: A novel image-based implicit password authentication system (IPAS) for mobile and non-mobile devices. Math. Comput. Model. **58** (1–2), 108–116 (2013)
2. Chen, L., Zhao, D.: Image encryption with fractional wavelet packet method. Optik (Stuttg) **119**(6), 286–291 (2008)
3. Chan, C.S., Chang, C.C.: An efficient image authentication method based on Hamming code. Pattern Recognit. **40**(2), 681–690 (2007)
4. Chan, C.S.: An image authentication method by applying Hamming code on rearranged bits. Pattern Recognit. Lett. **32**(14), 1679–1690 (2011)
5. Gurav, S.M., Gawade, L.S., Rane, P.K., Khochare, N.R.: Graphical password authentication: cloud securing scheme. In: Proceedings – International Conference on Electronic Systems, Signal Processing and Computing Technologies (ICESC 2014), pp. 479–483 (2014)
6. Vishwakarma, N., Gangrade, K.: Secure image based one time password. Int. J. Sci. Res. (IJSR) **5**(11), 680–683 (2016)
7. Cherdmuangpak, N., Anusas-amonkul, T., Limthanmaphon, B.: Two factor image-based password authentication for junior high school students. In: 14th International Joint Conference on Computer Science and Software Engineering (JCSSE), pp. 1–6 (2017)
8. Das, R., Manna, S., Dutta, S.: Secure user authentication system using image-based OTP and randomize numeric OTP based on user unique biometric image and digit repositioning scheme. In: Bhaumik, J., Chakrabarti, I., De, B.P., Bag, B., Mukherjee, S. (eds.) Communication, Devices, and Computing. LNEE, vol. 470, pp. 83–93. Springer, Singapore (2017). https://doi.org/10.1007/978-981-10-8585-7_8
9. Shaik, A., Borgaonkar, R., Asokan, N., Niemi, V., Seifert, J.: Practical attacks against privacy and availability in 4G/LTE mobile communication systems, February 2016
10. Noor, T.H., Zeadally, S., Alfazi, A., Sheng, Q.Z.: Mobile cloud computing: challenges and future research directions. J. Netw. Comput. Appl. **115**(May), 70–85 (2018). https://doi.org/10.1016/j.jnca.2018.04.018
11. Jlassai, M., Ghazel, C., Saidane, L.: A survey on quality of service in cloud computing. In: 3rd International Conference on Frontiers of Signal Processing, France, September 2017
12. Singh, A., Chatterjee, K.: Cloud security issues and challenges: a survey. J. Netw. Comput. Appl. **79**, 88–115 (2017)
13. Das, R., Chakraborty, A., Nandi, S., Dutta, S.: An approach to implement secure user authentication scheme using secret values extracted from private information and unique biometric images of user directed by randomize numeric and image based OTP. Int. J. Appl. Eng. Res. **12**(19), 8595–8601 (2017)
14. Richards, J.A., Jia, X.: Remote Sensing Digital Image Analysis (n.d.). https://www.springer.com/us/book/9783642300615

Mobile Finance with Collaborative Application of the Fintech ABCD Technologies

Lei Li[(✉)], Jingjia Qi, Libo Zhao, and Wei Jiang

Harbin Finance University, Harbin, China
lilei@hrbfu.edu.cn

Abstract. Nowadays, innovation in the financial field largely depends on the progress of technology. Artificial Intelligence, Block Chain, Cloud Computing and Data (ABCD for short) represent the modern technology frontier which has integrated and collaborated with each other. The cooperation of ABCD makes financial institutions better at sharing information, diversified innovative ways and channels, improving the degree and quality of integration between technology and finance. ABCD constitute the core of Fintech (combination of finance and technology). More importantly, it leads the pace of financial innovation, and also becomes the key weapon to obtain future development opportunities. Fintech plays a vital role in cooperative effort in marketing, risk control, auditing, investment consulting and research in the financial field. This article introduces the current situation of Fintech development and analyzes the relationship between Fintech and real economy. And shows how ABCD collaborate with each other for innovation to achieve an effective combination of finance and technology, so as to promote the development of real economy.

Keywords: Collaborative · Innovation · Finance technology · Mobile finance

1 Introduction

1.1 ABCD

- Artificial Intelligence (AI) is a branch of computer science. It attempts to understand the essence of human intelligence and simulate it in a similar way to human. The research in this field includes robots, language recognition, image recognition, natural language processing and expert systems etc.
- Block Chain is a growing list of records, called blocks, that are linked using cryptography. Each block contains a cryptographic hash of the previous block, a timestamp, and transaction data. It has wide use for distributed data storage, point-to-point transmission, consensus mechanism and encryption algorithm etc.
- Cloud Computing is dynamical computing and use virtualized resources over the Internet.
- Data in the financial technology refers to big data sets that cannot be managed and processed by conventional software tools in a certain time range.

These four technologies cooperate with each other and constitute the core of Fintech.

© Springer Nature Switzerland AG 2019
Y. Luo (Ed.): CDVE 2019, LNCS 11792, pp. 201–208, 2019.
https://doi.org/10.1007/978-3-030-30949-7_23

1.2   Fintech

Fintech is the combination of finance and technology, that is, the scientificalization of financial business. In 2016, the Financial Stability Council issued its first special report, and initially defined "Fintech". It is a financial innovation brought by technology, including new business models, applications, processes or products, which has a significant impact on financial markets, financial institutions or the way financial services provide.

With the financial system incorporating more diverse technological components, such as intelligent robots, VR, bio-verification technology, financial technology is more inclined to innovation in the application of traditional industry. In the view of some enterprises, Fintech mainly uses big data, block chains and other Internet innovation technology for risk control and platform management. From the technique point of view, the main way to develop forward for financial industry is to use technology to innovate products and services.

1.3   Current Situation of Fintech Development in China

In China, the growing development and popularization of IT and communication technology make it possible for emerging technologies to be widely used in traditional industries. The financial industry pays more attention to the innovation of products and services. The core driving force for its development is the progress and application of technology. Therefore, Fintech has arisen as they need.

At present, information processing and data analysis based on Internet technology have become the source of application in Fintech. Therefore, the main technologies of Fintech focus on cloud computing, block chains and artificial intelligence. In the future, these technologies will continue to promote the innovation of financial products and services, and further adjust the industrial structure for the traditional real economy. And build a healthy economic development ecological system. Fintech serves the real economy by promoting the combination of financial innovation and industrial innovation, guiding the real economy to carry out the transformation and upgrading the product management strategy, and providing a more scientific and efficient channel of capital allocation.

Nowadays, the main application of Fintech are as follows.

- First, the open and sharing mode of resources based on new interconnection technology. On the one hand, the sharing economy of financial technology such as cloud computing, big data and distributed technology improves the allocation and utilization efficiency of existing resources, which is conducive to the efficient flow of funds, logistics and information. On the other hand, Fintech can reduce the dependence of real economy on suppliers and provide them with more product choices and guarantees.
- The second is to use financial technology to analyze economic scenarios. Analyze the changes of consumer behavior habits and grasp the market dynamics. Financial technology and various scenarios in the real economy are integrated through the Internet and the corresponding intelligent technology. Get through the online and offline, and market customer at low cost.

- Third, technology has strong computing power. In modern competition of economy, information acquisition and processing is an important factor to obtain real economic benefits. The development of Fintech makes real economy have a strong hardware foundation in dealing with business information and specific product supply and demand information.

1.4   Relationship Between Fintech and Real Economy

The competitiveness of real economy determines the process of industrialization and modernization of a country, and is a cornerstone of its economic development. Financial support is an important material basis for the smooth development of real economy. At this stage, the extensive and in-depth application of technology in the financial industry has a great role in promoting the service of the real economy and reducing the service cost of traditional industries. To a certain extent, the development of Fintech has promoted the development of real economy, but more importantly, it is mutual promotion. The progress of Fintech has promoted the efficiency of real economy development, and the development of real economy has also provided the source of innovation for financial industry. They promote each other and lay the foundation for the sustainable development of whole social.

As shown in the Fig. 1, at present, the core technology of Fintech comes from artificial intelligence, block chain, cloud computing and big data, and coordinates with the development of technology enterprises. Technology enterprises serve the real economy directly or indirectly through financial institutions. This process has become the main path choice for Fintech to serve the real economy.

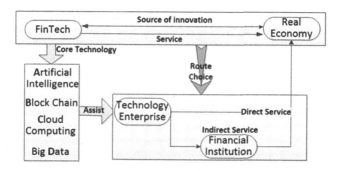

Fig. 1. The route choice of Fintech serving the real economy.

2   A Typical Scenario Using ABCD

2.1   Customer User Interface

When a client is enjoying a holiday at the seaside with the family but still worrying about the financial account, he can use the smart phone to control the flow of funds based on the ABCDs technology. A typical user interface in mobile finance is shown in Fig. 2.

There are four main application areas of this typical user interface on the smart phone.

- The first is for utility payment. The payments may include paying for mobile phone consumption to communication companies, paying for credit card, charge for water and electricity fees and so on. These services are frequent and related to everyday life closely.
- The second is for wealth management. Now many people in China do not put their spare money in bank because of the convenience of using electronic payment system. They use this new function to earn more or draw money in advance, even buy some stocks using mobile payment system as it is really very convenient. A new application field which is the mobile insurance system is getting more and more popular which can help to obtain the compensation more quickly.
- The third one is the exchange of funds. This part includes transfer money from different accounts and gets some micropayment from friends and relatives.
- The last one is for shopping and entertainment which also contains large amount of money transactions. It can be more convenient to use mobile phone than cash or credit card.

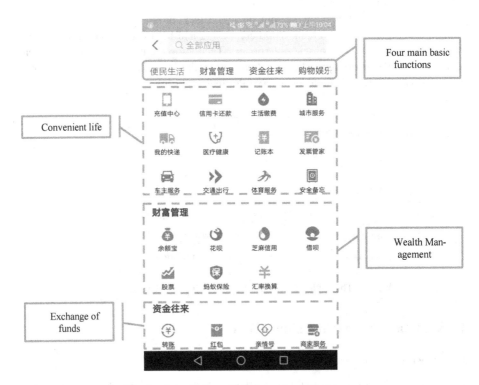

Fig. 2. A typical user interface in mobile finance.

2.2   Flow Chart of Mobile Finance Application with ABCD Technologies

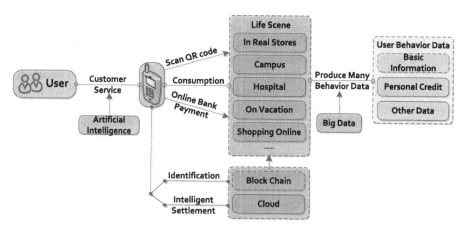

Fig. 3. Flow chart with ABCD.

In physical stores, consumers can use mobile devices to scan QR code to realize consumption rather than using cash or credit card. There is no need to get change and it becomes much more efficient. Nowadays, college students in the campus use the mobile phone apps to buy meals, school items and get other services more frequently. Universities become a big market because college students like new technologies and tend to accept new things easily (Fig. 3).

Another scenario of mobile finance is during the vacations or travels. Clients now purchase tickets and live in hotels using smart phone applications to get more efficient services.

2.3   The Function of Each Component

- A: Artificial Intelligence makes financial decision and services to be automated and more intelligent. AI helps people to get intelligent decision.
- B: The Block Chain is a mechanism to assure security, reliability and unalterable operations which can resolve the trust problem of financial transactions. Almost all scenarios in the mobile finance involves transactions. There is a need to reduce cost, improve efficiency and optimize the integrity environment.
- C: Cloud computing makes technology and resources fully utilized in a flexible way. It can resolve the problem of limited storage space, limited computing power and leave the storage and computing power in the cloud. In the finance field, the cloud is mainly used for intelligent settlement which can increase the efficiency of exchange between different banks and financial institutions.
- D: There is a huge volume of data, high growth rate and diversified information in finance field. It requires a new processing mode to have stronger storage power and process optimization ability. Big Data provides this power for the financial transactions.

3 Summary and Areas that Need to Be Improved

Financial institutions are using ABCD's collaborative innovation mechanism to lay out new markets, explore new demands and new services. Applying the mobile Internet technology and big data technology can accelerate the integration of new technology and financial industry. It can better serve the real economy of manufacturing industry, agriculture, traditional service industry and all the areas that needs financial exchange. It can dramatically raise the ability of market information response, the feedback ability of user experience, the innovation ability of platform resource construction and sharing, etc. The cooperation of ABCD makes financial institutions much better at sharing information, diversifying business channels. It supports the innovation in the financial field in a new way. However, there are still some traditional areas that need to pay special attention by applying the ABCD technology.

3.1 Inefficient Traditional Marketing Methods

The target customer of traditional banks in China is concentrated on large and middle-size state-owned enterprises or major customer groups. With the intense competition in the banking market increasingly, the target of marketing is sinking to small and medium-size enterprise and ordinary consumers. Using the traditional marketing method to treating the new market shows "clumsiness" for banks immediately which high cost, low conversion rate, low precision, and not in line with the new target market demand etc.

Big Data technology can help financial institutions to focus on the small and medium-size enterprise and small customers with low cost and high efficiency. Meet most customers who are owned little funds but large in quantities, then grasp market trends more quickly.

3.2 High Cost of Financial Risk Control

It is found that the traditional risk control process is high cost and difficult to meet the new market demand when applying it to small and medium-sized enterprises or ordinary individuals. And credit fraud is prone to occur in pre-loan and post-loan of risk management.

Block chain technology and Big Data break the information islands, and the make information share possible. By applying the two technologies it is much easier to get clients' credit information in different institutions. This can minimize the occurrence of information fraud.

3.3 Inaccurate Audit Process

The traditional internal audit process of banks includes five modules: audit preparation, data analysis, audit implementation, audit report and project summary. It needs on-site audit. There are many participants, mainly depending on the professional quality of auditors. The methods are outdated, inefficient, with poor accuracy, and stability which needs to be improved.

Artificial intelligence and big data can help to make traditional audit work to be more in well defined procedures. Human agents can free from that mechanical and inaccurate work and to be more creative.

3.4 To Meet the Growing Investment Needs

The continuous growth of the total amount of individual investable assets and the trend of digitalization of wealth management push banks to reshape their investment and financial management models. Traditional bank asset management mainly provides wealth management services to high net worth people, with high communication costs and laboring costs, low efficiency and limited coverage of customer groups.

To meet the ever growing market investment needs is a main focus for financial institutions and they can get market investment needs information quickly by using the cloud and big data technology which can cut the cost substantially.

3.5 Non-real Time Research Results

Traditional bank investment relies on manual collection, processing and analysis of data. The search method and the data acquisition are incomplete. It takes a long time to form a report. The reliability of the research results is doubtful. Many of them have a strong subjectivity and a poor stability. This leads to the risk of lacking early warning and timely adjustment.

Using artificial intelligence and big data technology, the research will be based on a massive amount of real time data which can result in more reliable and timely decisions.

4   Conclusions

Nowadays, mobile finance has become a main method of fund exchange in China. People are used to this kind of life with no cash and no card in many scenarios. Therefore, we should further develop the technologies to meet the huge demand of people, guarantee the basic transactions smooth, complete and ensure the safety of fund transactions and management. ABCD technologies coordinate together have improved and will improve further the efficiency and security of the use of funds, which will promote the real economy development.

Acknowledgment. The authors would like to thank Professor Yuhua Luo, University of Balearic Islands, Spain, for her help and support to revise this paper with patience in making this work possible.

This work is a partial result of the project "Study on Countermeasure of Financial Technology Service to the Real Economy in Heilongjiang Province" (Project number: 2018-KYYWF-019), which is from the "Heilongjiang University Fundamental Scientific Research Expenses" and the project "Exploration and Research on the Cultivation of Financial Big Data Talents" (Project number: SJGZ20170027), which is from the "Higher Education Teaching Reform Project in Heilongjiang Province".

References

1. Ye, W.: Intelligent transformation of financial technology and banking. China Finance (21), 67–68 (2017)
2. Lu, M., Yu, P.: Trends in Fintech and commercial bank innovation. Bankers (4), 127–130 (2017)
3. Wang, G., He, J.: Future and responsibility of Fintech. South. Finance (3), 14–17 (2017)
4. Philippon, T.: The Fintech opportunity. NBER Working Papers (2016)
5. Arner, D.W., Barberis, J.N., Buckley, R.P.: The evolution of Fintech: a new post-crisis paradigm? Soc. Sci. Electron. Publ. **47**(4), 1271–1319 (2015)
6. Nicoletti, B.: Financial services and Fintech. In: Nicoletti, B. (ed.) The Future of Fintech. Springer, Cham (2017). https://doi.org/10.1007/978-3-319-51415-4_2
7. Wang, Y.: Study on the influencing factors of Fintech enterprise value based on value chain. Jiaotong University, Beijing (2017)
8. Yan, Y.: Research on innovation of financing system for high-tech SMEs. Wuhan University (2011)
9. Xu, Y.: Research on the construction and operation model of regional science and technology financial service platform. Suzhou University (2015)
10. Zhang, X.: Fintech summary of research. Chin. Commer. (2), 17–20 (2017)
11. Li, S.: Subject Group of Guangzhou Branch of the People's Bank of China. Comparison and Enlightenment of Fintech Development between China and the United States. South. Finance (5), 3–9 (2017)

Collaboration and Co-creation in a General Engagement Platform to Foster Organizational Benefits During a Post-project-phase

Alina Koehler, Andreas Mladenow[(✉)], and Christine Strauss

Department of eBusiness, University of Vienna, Vienna, Austria
alina_koehler@gmx.net, {andreas.mladenow,
christine.strauss}@univie.ac.at

Abstract. This paper aims to provide a conceptual layout and design as starting point for an intra-organizational general engagement platform (GEP). Accordingly, we identify concepts and functions that are required or/and that are value generating for the development of a GEP for company-internal co-creation in post-project phases. Furthermore, we discuss pros and cons in terms of a SWOT-analysis. Results may provide a basis for further empirical studies, practical development, or/and future research in this direction.

Keywords: Crowdsourcing · Collaboration · Co-creation · Post-project phase · General engagement platform

1 Introduction

The integration and participation of the crowd in the process of new product development (NPD) and/or innovation processes, and the associated potential business value has been extensively researched [cf. e.g. 1–3]. Similarly, user-centered development and participatory design have proven to be successful in software development, just as in project management. These examples have two characteristics in common, i.e. integration and participation of users and a limit in time: the process of NPD usually is completed after a certain period of time until the product is launched; software is developed and finally installed and in use; projects are carried out and finalized after some time. Recently, in the context of service systems engineering and internal crowdsourcing a concept has been introduced, which aims at "the time after" where post-project benefits are generated by means of a so-called engagement platform (EP) [4]. While many co-creation platforms have been created with the aim of involving externals, the described engagement platform (EP) represents a prototype for internal user co-creation to support the success of socio-technical systems. An increased benefit for the company in terms of systems' efficiency and employees' satisfaction is to be expected. Therefore, the present paper draws and defines concepts and functions required for the development of an engagement platform for company-internal co-creation in the post-project phase on base of a real-world application. Against this background, in Sect. 2 the preconditions and nature of a post-project phase of a general engagement platform (GEP) is shown. Section 3 pinpoints the conceptual

© Springer Nature Switzerland AG 2019
Y. Luo (Ed.): CDVE 2019, LNCS 11792, pp. 209–218, 2019.
https://doi.org/10.1007/978-3-030-30949-7_24

and functional issues of a post-project phase. Section 4 provides a detailed discussion on the implementation and application of a GEP for post-project phases. Section 5 contains concluding remarks and a brief outlook on future research.

2 Background

According to Archibald, Filippo and Filippo, the post-project phase starts when a project passed through the go-live [5]. Following, we will consider the distinction between project-phase and post-project phase according to Archibald, Filippo and Filippo [5]. The post-project phase includes all activities in the actual usage phase, after finalizing the development and implementation phase.

The GEP will be described in terms of underlying concepts. It is supposed to foster benefits concerning (correctness in) usage, processes and work practice in the post-project phase. By doing so, they firstly focused on the principles of a sociotechnical system through selecting and enabling actors and resources to use the platform and secondly integrated underlying concepts such as the bottom-up approach, service systems engineering or crowdsourcing. Finally, a GEP allows the users to initiate, comment, proceed and implement change by jointly working together. Throughout this novel concept of an EP, benefits of different kind could be realized, e.g. in terms of an improvement of the sociocultural system or improvement of value in the project context [4].

Against this background, we evaluate the implementation and application of a GEP for the post-project phase. Therefore, it is highly important to firstly examine the underlying concepts, which define the research case's foundation and secondly examine its present findings with alternative literature. The core concepts can be divided into an organizational (bottom-up approach), societal, (internal crowd-sourcing), economic (benefits management) and technological (service system engineering) and socio-technical system) view. This analysis supports the conceptual and functional development of a GEP.

One of the fundamental concepts of Semmann and Grotherr is displayed by the usage of a bottom-up approach instead of a top-down approach when it comes to a situation in which organizational structure value generation can be improved [4]. The authors argue that such approach enforces the user co-creation by overcoming time lags and fostering emergent benefits [4]. The top-down approach engages few users, primary the management, who function as change drivers by initiating and exemplifying change downwards along an organizational hierarchy. In contrast, the bottom-up approach encourages change in the lowest hierarchy stage, which represents the lower management and the employees of a company. As those persons are especially involved in operational activities, they usually know best about actual issues with certain projects or might have already found alternative solutions, which just need to be adressed to a specific person to enable an implementation process [6]. Other authors support the argumentation concerning the benefits of a bottom-up approach in terms of change management, by disclosing survey data that shows that if change is solely initiated and executed by the top, no significant effect on an employee's willingness to support change can be determined [4]. In contrast, change that has been initiated by employees in the lower-level hierarchy, tends to find the greatest possible support among an organization's workforce [7].

Hence, internal crowdsourcing represents a very suitable approach concerning the realization of benefits of an EP [4]. The term crowdsourcing describes the especially internet-based phenomenon of finding and connecting volunteer user groups to solve a problem or a task in order to create value, which not only helps the client, but also the volunteers. Internal crowdsourcing describes the application of solving issues at an intra-organizational level by forming user groups with the organization's employees and is rather long-term oriented than external crowdsourcing [4, 8, 9]. Further, internal crowdsourcing is especially suitable for solving tasks with increased complexity, a high amount of required (tacit) knowledge, high development effort, a contextual character due to organization-centered issues or such tasks, which contain company secrets [4, 10]. Since various other authors agree that the "potential of crowdsourcing has been related to creating new ideas and innovations, solving problems effectively, lowering costs and shortening product development cycles" [11], such benefits are similarly created through internal crowdsourcing as well.

Benefits management describes the core motivation behind the research case's EP, since it aims to add value by overcoming common issues in the post-project phase. In general, the term has been defined in literature as "the process of organizing and managing, such that the potential benefits arising from the use of IT are actually realized" [12]. As the quote states it correctly, the EP from the research case does not necessarily aim for generating whole new ideas or concepts. Despite, in first place, the EP strives for adding value by making existing, but unused benefits, usable for the organization, by empowering users to become active in initializing and implementing solutions for existing problems [4].

The terms service system and sociotechnical system can be distinct from each other, although their meanings are quite similar. Böhmann, Leimeister, and Möslein state, that service systems can be defined as "complex socio-technical systems that enable value co-creation" [13]. According to Geels [14], a socio-technical system links artefacts, capital, knowledge, labor and cultural meaning not autonomously but in an organized way which pursues a specific goal. A service system can be seen as special type of socio-technical systems with focus on value creation, whereas the term service system engineering describes the actual development or execution of such service system, at which actors, resources and their respective interaction are configured in a way that especially focuses on the efficiently shared usage of resources and the maximization of the resulting value [15]. Sum agrees by perceiving a service system as an ecosystem, which unites actors, processes, tools and technologies and emphasizes that the overall aim lies in delivering value and quality to the end users of a system [16]. Since the goal of the present paper is to conceptualize an EP which fosters engagement and value for its users, especially the concept of service system engineering has to be integrated in doing so.

3 Project Phase: Conceptual and Functional Issues

This paper aims to serve a general concept of involving employees for co-creation. In order to find inspiration beyond the use case and due to the fact that post-project phase platforms still do not exist, other user co-creation platforms and co-creation forms of the project phase will be analyzed.

3.1 Conceptual Issues

Oertzen, Odekerken-Schröder, Brax, and Mager define various forms of co-creation for services based on their empirical research, in which the authors aimed for the nature of the terminology around co-creation throughout a comprehensive article screening [17]. Although the specific forms do not necessarily require a platform, they are considered to be interesting in terms of out-of-the-box idea generation and conceptual transitions for a GEP.

Based on the authors' findings, the present paper considers the terms co-ideation (idea crowdsourcing and lead user involvement) and co-design (solution crowdsourcing) as being especially useful from a framework-related perspective. Those forms will be evaluated by means of respective industry practice concerning their background situation, idea and procedure and subsequently drawings with focus on value generation for a GEP.

The term *co-ideation* stands for "co-generation of ideas" [18] as a procedure of opening the phase of idea generation to a broader (external) network of Stakeholders, which can be e.g. lead users, customers, partners or experts, who share ideas and communicate which each other within an organizational environment on respective websites. Furthermore, Oertzen et al. classified two subcategories of applying co-ideation in industry practice and named lead user involvement and idea crowdsourcing [17]. Lead user involvement has been initially developed by Eric von Hippel in 1986 and has since then been a very popular topic in research and practice. Lead users often become autonomously creative and develop own solutions or have theoretic ideas, which are important for organizations in order to identify their customers' needs. The example case of the LEGO Mindstorm, which contains modules that enable the building of programmable robots online, has in theory been developed for children. In practice, 70% of the users are adults, who have been called the LEGO Mindstorm User Group (MUG) and provide significant direct or indirect input for LEGO's product innovation processes [19, 20]. Initially, the robots only have had predefined modules to use, but as someone hacked himself into the software, LEGO let him and others process and was able to watch, how users developed whole new functions [21]. Another possibility of co-ideation is displayed by the procedure of idea crowdsourcing, as stated previously. Similar to (internal) crowdsourcing, the motivation of idea crowdsourcing rather lies in initiating new ideas than in solving current problems. For example, the energy provider E.ON launched an open idea submission contest based on a TV show, where the crowd would be able to see different E.ON products in use and was subsequently asked to submit ideas, how new services and products of the company could look like [17, 22]. Users who had the best ideas won a prize money and their ideas have been transferred to the R&D department of E.ON, in order to launch them within few years [23]. Such examples of co-ideation, displayed by different ideas from users, show how companies can work together with (internal or external) users and customers in terms of initiating, developing and improving ideas. Lead users do not have to necessarily be found outside the company, but also might be employees of the company with respective foreseeing, proactive and creative characteristics. Even though, not every practical idea of those might find proper usage, those people seem to have lead user potential and should be actively involved into the idea initiation process in the post-project phase [4]. Further, in terms of idea crowdsourcing, since a certain problem within a project has been found and formulated, a company can initiate an internal contest for their employees in order to find the best solution. An incentive does not necessarily have to be of monetary nature, but can also include extra holiday, responsibilities for interesting projects or a training.

Co-design's overall idea lies in the goal of bridging the gap between an identified need or idea and feasible solutions by engaging many actors with similar interests. Especially the respective users play an important role when it comes to knowledge, experience, concept and knowledge development. A representative example is the BMW co-creation Lab, which aimed to bring together hobbyists and experts with an ideas competition in order to develop collaboratively new design concepts [17, 18]. More specifically, within the framework of solution crowdsourcing, at which companies ask their product's or service's consumers for suitable solutions, the streaming provider Netflix invited users to improve the company's predictive accuracy concerning the probability of a user liking a proposed movie through a contest. The best solution was determined by a comparison with past data [24–26]. Since a GEP is supposed to include forming teams for designing, developing and implementing identified solutions [4], this concept can even be expanded. One good way to do so lies in arranging a fixed team structure for design and development of solution concepts, which will include conceptual experts (designers), idea/solution initiators (employees) and a knowledgeable coordinator (project lead). This structure will support at improving efficiency of collaboration, time and cost effort, value generation and learnings.

3.2   Functional Issues

A worldwide operating company, which aimed for increasingly connecting its employees concerning the purpose of more efficient knowledge transfer and innovation management built an internal platform that should enhance knowledge networking and knowledge exchange among employees especially regarding efficiently finding the "right" internal person with the required expertise [27]. Expertise and knowledge should be usable across countries and sectors while maintaining the platform as an internal means of communication in order to keep company-internal information confidential. Furthermore, the platform pursued organizational (synergies) and individual (motivation) benefits realization. The platform contains several functions, i.e. networks, news, profile pages, urgent requests, dashboard and other supporting utilities. To cross the bridge in terms of how TechnoWeb 2.0 may deliver application for a GEP, each function's purpose will be briefly discussed [27].

As a technical base, the open source software Liferay was used, which allowed the linkage with previously consisting company internal software and programs, such as the Intranet. Further, use case workshops, where the management and employees interactively develop usage scenarios for the platform and clarify potential platform issues, turned out to be very helpful for employees. Also, the possibility for employees to be able to proactively propose new functions or general functional changes in the pilot phase received very positive feedback. Overall, the expectations of the platform have been met in terms of value and benefits generation [27].

4 Post-project Phase: Development of a GEP

Subsequently, elaborated knowledge from all previous sections will be combined, in order to create a conceptual and functional idea of a GEP for the post-project phase. Since the EP is supposed to be able to contain projects of any (online) kind or any company structure, potential company-internal projects could exemplarily have either a technical (e.g., software), administrative (e.g., resource allocation system), social (e.g., employee engagement software) or financial value (e.g., accounting software).

The present section will firstly summarize discovered conceptual requirements, which have been figured out to be essential or at least value generating, when it comes to developing and implementing a GEP.

Since this paper has named and examined various concepts from several co-creation forms through practical examples, the core value/core learning of each concept will be finally summarized as depicted in Table 1.

Considering all subsequent functions of the GEP, it must be noted that those are not based on technical, but on design-related thinking and proceeding jointly combined with background knowledge based on literature findings. The functions are structured in four different subdivisions and their relating functionalities or interaction possibilities in terms of All projects (GEP), Specific Project, Project Group and Profile from a user's perspective.

Table 1. Summary and description of the core value of all discovered concepts

Concept	Core value/core learning for a GEP
Bottom-up approach	Employees are enabled to act as idea initiators and change drivers
Internal crowdsourcing	Discovering user groups, which are already there (employees) for solving tasks with increased complexity, which require a high amount of tacit knowledge, high development effort, a contextual character or tasks, which contain company secrets
Benefits management	Focus on discovering unused value/benefits and making such already existing value usable for the organization, by empowering users to become jointly active in taking care of well-known problems
Service system (Engineering)	A service system must by organized in a way that delivers maximum value and quality to the end user within an ecosystem
Sociotechnical system	The human factor is an especially important driver when it comes to securing a functioning sociotechnical system in an organization
Co-ideation	Concept is based on opening the phase of idea generation to a broader network of stakeholders, which can be e.g. lead users, consumers or customers, but also employees (internal)
Idea crowdsourcing (Co-ideation)	Fostering creative interaction with users (e.g. employees) throughout idea contests in order to use a broader group of people to come up with innovative ideas
Lead user involvement (Co-ideation)	(Internal) Lead User own valuable characteristics (proactivity, foreseeing, creativity) and have to be discovered by an organization in order to enable them to become change drivers
Co-design	Engaging different actors (e.g. users and designers) who have different knowledge but similar interests in order to bridge the gap between an identified need or idea and feasible solutions
Solution crowdsourcing (Co-design)	Users (e.g. employees) are asked to find solutions for specific issues or problems

Furthermore, it is of crucial importance to carefully embed the planned GEP into a sociotechnical system within a specific business environment. This environment not only includes technology and resources, but – even more important – people who are interested in improving processes and outcome of their environment. Therefore, stakeholders have to be analyzed in order to secure an ongoing smooth daily business in a company [14]. The present paper does not consider a special project or company, wherefore those stakeholders will be described, who generally happen to be in place in any company, and who have influence on organizational resources and company-internal values.

A SWOT-Analysis will base on the findings of the analyzed research case, but also on other real-world examples, such as the TechnoWeb 2.0 case, as described previously. This will happen throughout an internal and external analysis with respect to a distinction between Strengths, Weaknesses, Opportunities, and result in a subsequent SWOT-Matrix as depicted in Table 2.

Table 2. SWOT-Matrix of a general engagement platform

| | | Internal analysis | |
		Strengths	Weaknesses
External analysis	Opportunities	The EP contains various kind of potential concerning value creation, which just has to be set free through the usage of resources. Further, transfields and transactore synergies and value might additionally increased by embedding more projects on the EP	Since the weakness of the EP lies mainly in investing finite resources, which could be needed elsewhere with more direct return, value can be increased by putting more projects than one on the EP and increase synergies and value, which can be handed back to client projects (cycle)
	Threats	Employees might focus too much on internal projects on the EP and neglect their actual projects. This can be prevented by developing efficient trade-off regulations, which forces employees to strictly stick to a specific amount of time a month, which they can use for the EP	Especially in the beginning, when the coordination and development costs will be high, this procedure could be designed as an own project with a fixed, small project team to prevent too many resources being involved

- Strengths (internal analysis): A GEP is carefully embedded within the company's sociotechnical system, shares resources and combines different professional fields and actors which will lead to an overall value generation of different kinds. Further, the GEP enables the process of making existing but unused values usable, which leads to value generation which does not require intense development and implementation of entirely new ideas. The work on the GEP will foster team-work abilities by connecting different people from different company fields, which would not have directly been working together, reduce barriers and increase working flexibility. Those actors, who contributed in solution-finding and team-work, might be entrusted with additional tasks or projects. Additionally, the creative developing of change initiatives might disclose new talents or abilities of actors.
- Weaknesses (internal analysis): Especially in the beginning, when the GEP is developed and implemented into the company's sociotechnical system, increased coordination and resource costs will appear through the usage of finite (human) ressources that could have also been used for other (client) projects that would result in value for the company.
- Opportunities (external analysis): An adapted framework of an GEP might be applicable for any web-based projects in companies which also provides the possibility for a company to have more than one project on the GEP and additionally generate synergies between them.

- Threats (external analysis): Employees might focus too much on the GEP and neglect their actual projects.

5   Conclusion and Outlook

This paper introduces the development and design for an intra-organizational general engagement platform. The suggested concepts for co-creation, user involvement and collaboration among employees of an organization during post-project phases were derived from related applications, and were underpinned with relevant literature.

Determining adequate incentives to motivate employees to participate in such platform is one example for further work. Future research should combine methods and tools from various disciplines, such as knowledge management, systems engineering, technology transfer, and innovation management.

References

1. Mladenow, A., Bauer, C., Strauss, C.: Social crowd integration in new product development. CrowdSourcing communities nourish the open innovation paradigm. Glob. J. Flexible Syst. Manag. **15**(1), 77–86 (2014)
2. Hoyer, W.D., Chandy, R., Dorotic, M., Krafft, M., Singh, S.S.: Consumer cocreation in new product development. J. Serv. Res. **13**(3), 283–296 (2010)
3. Petersen, K.J., Handfield, R.B., Ragatz, G.L.: Supplier integration into new product development: coordinating product, process and supply chain design. J. Oper. Manag. **23**(3–4), 371–388 (2005)
4. Semmann, M., Grotherr, C.: How to empower users for co-creation – conceptualizing an engagement platform for benefits realization. In: 13th International Conference on Wirtschaftsinformatik, St. Gallen, Switzerland, pp. 91–105 (2017)
5. Archibald, R.D., Di Filippo, I., Di Filippo, D.: The six-phase comprehensive project life cycle model including the project incubation/feasibility phase and the post-project evaluation phase. PM World J. **1**(5), 1–40 (2012)
6. Kezar, A.: Bottom-up/top-down leadership: contradiction or hidden phenomenon. J. High. Educ. **83**(5), 725–760 (2012)
7. Heyden, M.L.M., Fourné, S.P.L., Koene, B.A.S., Werkman, R., Ansari, S.S.: Rethinking 'top-down' and 'bottom-up' roles of top and middle managers in organizational change: implications for employee support: TM-MM change roles and employee support. J. Manag. Stud. **54**(7), 961–985 (2017)
8. Estellés-Arolas, E., González-Ladrón-de-Guevara, F.: Towards an integrated crowdsourcing definition. J. Inf. Sci. **38**(2), 189–200 (2012)
9. Zuchowski, O., Posegga, O., Schlagwein, D., Fischbach, K.: Internal crowdsourcing: conceptual framework, structured review, and research agenda. J. Inf. Technol. **31**(2), 166–184 (2016)
10. Schlagwein, D., Bjørn-Andersen, N.: Organizational learning with crowdsourcing: the revelatory case of LEGO. J. Assoc. Inf. Syst. (JAIS) **15**(11), 754–778 (2014)
11. Simula, H., Vuori, M.: Benefits and barriers of crowdsourcing in B2B firms: generating ideas with internal and external crowds. Int. J. Innov. Manag. **16**(06), 1240011 (2012)

12. Ward, J., Elvin, R.: A new framework for managing IT-enabled business change. Inf. Syst. J. **9**(3), 197–221 (1999)
13. Böhmann, T., Leimeister, J.M., Möslein, K.: Service systems engineering: a field for future information systems research. Bus. Inf. Syst. Eng. **6**(2), 73–79 (2014)
14. Geels, F.W.: From sectoral systems of innovation to socio-technical systems. Res. Policy **3**, 6–7 (2004)
15. Alter, S.: Metamodel for service analysis and design based on an operational view of service and service systems. Serv. Sci. **4**(3), 218–235 (2012)
16. Sum, J.: Service systems engineering: framework & systems modeling, vol. 1, pp. 1–68. Institute of Technology Management, National Chung Hsing University (2014)
17. Oertzen, A.-S., Odekerken-Schröder, G., Brax, S.A., Mager, B.: Co-creating services—conceptual clarification, forms and outcomes. J. Serv. Manag. **29**(4), 641–679 (2018). https://doi.org/10.1108/JOSM-03-2017-0067
18. Russo-Spena, T., Mele, C.: "Five Co-s" in innovating: a practice-based view. J. Serv. Manag. **23**(4), 527–553 (2012)
19. Gyrd-Jones, R.I., Kornum, N.: Managing the co-created brand: value and cultural complementarity in online and offline multi-stakeholder ecosystems. J. Bus. Res. **66**(9), 1484–1493 (2013)
20. Tidd, J., Bessant, J.R.: Managing Innovation: Integrating Technological, Market and Organizational Change, 5th edn. Wiley, Chichester (2013)
21. Chesbrough, H.: Bringing open innovation to services. MIT Sloan Manag. Rev. **52**(2), 85–90 (2011)
22. Verrinder, J.: E.ON and 100% Open Launch Crowdsourcing Project (2012). https://www.research-live.com/article/news/eon-and-100open-launch-crowdsourcing-project/id/4006939
23. Harwood, R.: E.ON Innovation – and the winners are…, June 2012. (Company Website)
24. Bell, R.M., Koren, Y.: Lessons from the Netflix prize challenge. SIGKDD Explor. Newsl. **9**(2), 75–97 (2007)
25. Prpic, J., Shukla, P.P., Kietzmann, J.H., McCarthy, I.P.: How to work a crowd: developing crowd capital through crowdsourcing. Bus. Horiz. **58**(1), 77–85 (2015)
26. Zhou, Y., Wilkinson, D., Schreiber, R., Pan, R.: Large-scale parallel collaborative filtering for the Netflix prize. In: Fleischer, R., Xu, J. (eds.) AAIM 2008. LNCS, vol. 5034, pp. 337–348. Springer, Heidelberg (2008). https://doi.org/10.1007/978-3-540-68880-8_32
27. Mörl, S., Heiss, M., Richter, A.: Siemens: Wissensvernetzung mit TechnoWeb 2.0. In: Enterprise 2.0 Fallstudien-Netzwerk. München/St. Gallen/Koblenz/Frankfurt: Andrea Back, Michael Koch, Petra Schubert, Stefan Smolnik (2011). https://www.e20cases.org/files/fallstudien/e20cases-09-siemens.pdf

Decision-Making in Crowdfunding – The Value of Behavioral Issues in Collaborative Business Environments

Valerie Busse[1,2(✉)], Christine Strauss[1], and Michal Gregus[2]

[1] Department of eBusiness, University of Vienna, Vienna, Austria
valerie.busse@infinanz.de,
christine.strauss@univie.ac.at
[2] Faculty of Management, Comenius University, Bratislava, Slovakia
michal.gregusml@fm.uniba.sk

Abstract. Collaborative behavior and cooperative issues gained attention with fast growing social networks. Especially, research in the rather novel funding form, called crowdfunding is rapidly increasing. Consequently, this paper addresses behavioral issues in the highly complex decision-making processes of various actors in crowdfunding. It (i) provides a detailed overview of current literature and (ii) its major outcomes on behavioral issues, as well as (iii) indicates research gaps in the field of crowdfunding and behavior decisions in terms of collaborative business environments.

Keywords: Crowdfunding · Behavior · Social networks · Collaboration · Cooperation

1 Introduction

The way companies are doing business is characterized by massive changes due to digitization, which in B2C is determined by highly mobile, interacting, and transacting digital natives [1]. Crowdfunding is one of the most emerging digital phenomenon which tremendously expanded within recent years and represents a remarkable business stimulus. The three main actors in the crowdfunding process are the entrepreneur, the intermediary, and the crowd. In order to improve efficiency within this triadic relationship, it is necessary, that actors collaborate.

Current research addresses questions on which factors contribute to the behavioural aspects of crowdfunding seen from three different viewpoints, namely the entrepreneurial perspective, the perspective of the crowd but also the examine the viewpoint of the intermediary, i.e. the crowdfunding platform. However, research attending the topic on hand is still in a nascent stage (cf. [2]). The aim of this paper is to verify the fact, the extent and the modus of collaboration and cooperation of the three main actors in the crowdfunding process (cf. Figure 1).

The following Sect. 2 of the paper at hand explains in detail the purpose of the study and the applied procedure, which follows [3]. Section 3 presents the performed analysis and its results, which are discussed in Sect. 4.

© Springer Nature Switzerland AG 2019
Y. Luo (Ed.): CDVE 2019, LNCS 11792, pp. 219–228, 2019.
https://doi.org/10.1007/978-3-030-30949-7_25

Fig. 1. Triadic relationship of actors in crowdfunding

2 Purpose and Procedure

According to Webster and Watson "A review of prior, relevant literature is an essential feature of any academic project" [4]. Other authors such as Petticew and Robert (2005) state the relevance of a literature review by providing several advantages of using this method [5]. The method gives a detailed overview whether or not the research topic has been covered previously [4]. As a consequence, the results may imply that a potential research question is worth answering, and the issue has not been already satisfactory resolved. The benefit of putting the research on hand in the context of other related work in other or even similar research fields. Furthermore, it is essential to investigate whether a literature review in the topic area has been conducted. The following literature review methodology aims to achieve the following purpose: to provide a clear picture of existing literature, to identify gaps in current research, and to provide suggestions for further research. In order to identify possible literature reviews in the topic of decision-making and behavioral theories in crowdfunding, a broad search of literature reviews towards the research topic was conducted in Google Scholar. The searching term was limited to "crowdfunding and literature review" By screening the existing literature reviews, the most actual and suitable ones including their limitations are listed below: The main article which emerged most suitable is published by Hoegen et al. (2018) [6]. This paper provides a very detailed literature review, however, it only reviews articles from the investors perspective and excludes the decision-making process from the entrepreneurial point of view. Further research by Kaartemo considers 51 empirical studies by focusing only on articles in English language, and therefore only catches the topic in a very broad perspective [7]. Other literature reviews on the topic of crowdfunding focus either on one specific form, do not provide suitable Keywords or do not go into depth [8]. Subsequently, none of the existing literature review answers the research question on hand.

2.1 Selection of Search Resources

We have chosen five resources to perform the literature review, i.e. SpringerLink, Sciencedirect, IEEE Xplore, Wiley Online Library, and Web of Science. The choice of those five resources was guided by the effort to include technical-oriented as well as management-oriented databases.

SpringerLink: SpringerLink provides access of over 12 million scientific documents, i.e., journals, books, series, proceedings, reference works and protocols [9]. The platform has been chosen for our study not only for its size but also for reasons of scientific disciplines (i.e. management, computer science, economics, engineering, social sciences etc.). SpringerLink is an important outlet for research written in German language.

ScienceDirect: ScienceDirect is Elseviers' leading information platform [10] and provides comparable benefit for the purpose of our study like SpringerLink in terms of scientific disciplines.

IEEE Xplore: The IEEE Xplore digital library comprises technical and scientific content published by the Institute of Electrical and Electronics Engineers (IEEE). The platform offers web-access to scientific documents in the field of electronics, electrical engineering, and computer science [11].

Wiley Online Library: Wiley Online Library currently provides scientific articles among several disciplines including chemistry, computer science, law, social and behaviour science and many others [12].

Web of Science: The Web of Science is an online subscription-based scientific database that provides a comprehensive citation search. It gives access to various databases that reference cross-disciplinary research [13].

2.2   Determination of Keywords

Several terms were used to find the most relevant articles within the topic of interest. For the term "Crowdfunding" and the term "Platform", synonyms were used in order to generate more results. "Crowdsourcing" was used as a synonym for "Crowdfunding" to highlight more scores. These terms where combined with a combination of Keywords including "Attitude", "Behavior", "Entrepreneur", "Platform", "Fishbein" and "Ajzen", "E-commerce", "Consumer behavior", "Purchase motivation", "Theory of planned behavior" and "Internet pure player (IPP)". To find even more detailed related work the term "Intermediary" was used as a synonym for "Platform". Exact keywords, search terms and their combinations applied in the retrieval phase are listed in Table 1.

2.3   Determination of Inclusion and Exclusion Criteria

Crowdfunding is a relatively "young" research topic and lacks of relevant literature before 2009. For this reason the search for publications refers to the last decade, and was limited to the years between 2009 and 2019. Only those publications, which appeared in that time-window and contain the previously determined keywords, were taken into consideration. The literature review focuses on high-quality peer-reviewed research; for this reason bachelor and master-theses, industry reports, interviews, comments, and editorials were excluded from further analysis. Hence, the inclusion criteria are formulated such that peer-reviewed publications (i.e. articles, publications, conference proceedings, journal articles, books, book series, early access articles, protocols and reference work) published between 2009 and 2019 and containing the selected keywords appear in the final set of papers.

3   Analysis and Results

Table 1 provides the keywords applied in the search procedure, detailed outcomes per search resource and per keywords, as well as detailed outcomes in total (n_1), after elimination of duplicates (n_2), after screening for inclusion (n_3), and after quality assessment (n_4).

Table 1. Details of search procedure – keywords, resources and outcomes

Keywords/Resources	IEEE	SL	SD	WOL	WoS	Total
Crowdfunding + Consumer behavior	2	699	396	274	28	1399
Crowdfunding + Purchase motivation	0	300	190	167	4	661
Crowdfunding + Theory of planned behavior	0	452	255	199	3	909
Crowdfunding + Theory of reasoned action	0	536	13	285	1	835
Crowdfunding + Internet pure player (IPP) + Consumer behavior	0	0	0	0	0	0
Crowdsourcing + Consumer behavior	18	1805	969	779	38	3609
Crowdsourcing + Purchase motivation	0	624	334	333	2	1293
Crowdsourcing + Theory of planned behavior	2	1613	923	567	6	3111
Crowdsourcing + Internet pure player (IPP) + Consumer behavior	0	0	1	0	0	1
Crowdsourcing + Theory of reasoned action	0	1867	70	736	0	2673
Crowdfunding + E-commerce + Consumer behavior	0	185	107	181	1	474
Crowdsourcing + E-commerce + Consumer behavior	0	373	185	385	1	944
Crowdfunding + Attitude	2	476	249	180	24	931
Crowdfunding + Behavior	17	1089	618	421	152	2297
Crowdfunding + Fishbein + Ajzen	0	5	6	4	0	15
Crowdsourcing + Fishbein + Ajzen	0	16	30	8	0	54
Crowdfunding + Entrepreneur + Platform + Attitude	0	156	109	67	1	333
Crowdfunding + Entrepreneur + Platform + Attitude Behavior	0	112	91	55	1	259
Crowdfunding + Entrepreneur + Intermediary + Attitude + Behavior	2	0	40	24	0	66
Crowdfunding + Entrepreneur + Intermediary + Attitude + Behavior + Fishbein + Ajzen	0	0	0	0	0	0
Crowdsourcing + Entrepreneur + Platform + Attitude	0	175	123	95	0	393
Crowdsourcing + Entrepreneur + Platform + Attitude + Behavior	0	138	111	70	0	319
Crowdsourcing + Entrepreneur + Intermediary + Attitude + Behavior	0	0	30	17	0	47
Crowdsourcing + Entrepreneur + Intermediary + Attitude + Behavior + Fishbein + Ajzen	0	0	0	1	0	1
Total - n1	43	10621	4850	4848	262	20624
After elimination of duplicates - n2	37	3536	2328	597	188	6686
After screening for inclusion - n3	25	266	85	54	49	479
After quality assessment - n4	8	6	23	4	17	58

Legend: SL= SpringerLink, SD= Science Direct, WOL= Wiley Online Library WoS= Web of Science

Figure 2 depicts the reducing impact of the filtering process after each of the four steps n_1 to n_4. After those four filtering-steps n_1 to n_4 have been performed the remaining articles formed the basis for further analysis; they made up 0,28% of the entire set of retrieved publications.

Figure 3 visualizes the constant raise in the frequency of publication activities of the chosen relevant publications over time.

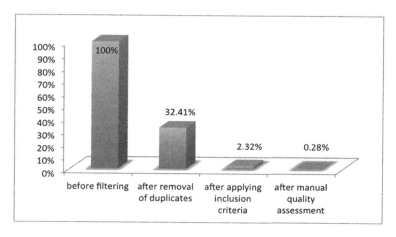

Fig. 2. Subtotals in the stepwise filtering process

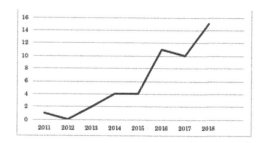

Fig. 3. Development of publications' frequency over time

4   Findings and Discussion

After performing the described stepwise filtering process we analysed 54 papers in detail (four papers had to be excluded ex-post as they turned out to be "hidden" duplicates). As shown in Table 2, the key findings from the selected relevant publications contain 46 quantitative approaches, 6 qualitative and 2 mixed approaches. Although the number of qualitative research in this field has increased since 2017, the majority of research is of quantitative nature.

Results show further that authors addressed the topic of crowdfunding from different perspectives and viewpoints. Nevertheless, most research focused either on behavioral aspects in crowdfunding, by considering the essential point of cooperation aspects of both, the web-page (in terms of usability, accessibility, easiness of navigation, security, pictures underlining the content, reviews, factors of convenience using the platform) [37, 65] or on behavioral motivation aspects of the crowd such as intrinsic motivation factors, e.g., making-the-product happen, feeling empathy for the team, previous interest in the product [38, 54]. For instance, Bi and Usman [36] showed that

Table 2. Detailed overview of relevant publications

Source	Year	Reseach Method/Design	qual.	quan.	mix	col.
[14]	2016	Preference Meta Model for Twitter Data	x		x	
[15]	2018	Multimodal Affective Responses		x		
[16]	2016	Exploratory empirical approach	x		x	
[17]	2016	Empirical analysis, linear regression	x			
[18]	2015	Stochastic actor-based models (ABMs)	x			
[19]	2017	Multipile regression analysis		x		
[20]	2016	Test hypothesis based on 264 crowdfunding campaigns from Kickstarter	x		x	
[21]	2016	In-depth interviews, inductive research approach	x		x	
[22]	2019	ELM model	x			
[6]	2018	Multidisciplinary full-text keyword search of all peer-reviewed journals in three databases	x			
[23]	2018	Crowdfunding as a model	x			
[24]	2011	IRT based liklihood ratio test		x		
[25]	2015	entity resolution (ER) algorithms		x		
[26]	2018	Three experimental studies		x		
[27]	2019	Two coding assignments		x		
[28]	2019	Experimental study	x			
[29]	2017	Campaign succes of Kickstarter projects		x		
[30]	2018	OLS regression		x		
[31]	2019	Elaboration Likelihood Model (ELM)		x		
[32]	2018	Vector Auto Regression		x		
[33]	2019	Cross-sectional analysis		x		
[34]	2018	Logistic regression models		x		
[35]	2018	GLS regression analysis		x	x	
[36]	2017	Linear regression analysis		x	x	
[37]	2016	Multiple regression analysis (MRA) and structural equation modelling		x		
[38]	2017	Exploratory factor analysis		x		
[39]	2017	Best practice summary	x			
[40]	2018	Functional data analysis (FDA)		x		
[41]	2016	Multiple linear regression		x		
[42]	2014	Unique model		x		
[43]	2017	Confirmatory factor analysis (CFA) and Partial Least Squares		x		
[44]	2016	Field studies, partial least square modeling (PLS), Smart PLS3		x		x
[45]	2017	Proposition of typology for brands	x			
[46]	2013	Case study	x			
[47]	2019	Models for landscape research		x		x
[48]	2016	Linear regression		x		
[49]	2014	Value-Added Benefits from Crowdfunders		x		x
[50]	2014	Framework of crowdfuning benefits		x		
[51]	2018	Survey, sample n=320, PLS algorithm		x		
[52]	2018	Survey, sample n=295, Spearman correlations		x		
[53]	2016	Test model (250 consumers in online panel)		x		
[54]	2018	Survey, sample n= 412, Pearson correlation, factor analysis		x		
[32]	2018	Vector Auto Regression Model		x		
[55]	2018	Descriptive statistics		x		x
[56]	2019	Conceptual model		x		x
[57]	2017	S-O-R Model		x		
[58]	2017	OLS regression		x		
[59]	2014	Survey, sample n=153		x		
[60]	2016	Survey, interviews			x	
[61]	2015	SEM	x			
[27]	2018	Three empirical studies including survey, experiment and case study			x	
[62]	2019	Statistical analysis of two different data sets		x		
[63]	2017	Time series analysis		x		
[64]	2015	Case study on Kickstarter.com		x		

Legend: qual. = qualitative, quan. = quantitative, mix= mixed method, col. = collaboration

detailed introductory words and/or videos underlining the content gives funders the impression the project may be of higher quality; in addition, a higher "like"-count and online reviews improve the perceived project quality. Results also provided evidence that the project or product type has a major influence on investment decisions [36].

However, in order to improve efficiency in the overall triadic relationship between entrepreneur, intermediary and crowd, it is essential to consider the collaboration and cooperation between intermediary and entrepreneur or the crowd as the factors appear as interactions and correlate with each other. Some authors such as Bernardes et al. aim in their study to measure the use of crowdfunding platforms in the achievement of the loyalty and satisfaction of consumers by considering product availability of different cultures [55]. This approach as well as others partly answered the research question and considered collaborative environments within the triadic relationship [14, 15, 19, 35, 36, 44, 45, 49, 55, 56, 66, 67]. It is also noticeable, that several researchers focus on one specific type of crowdfunding, i.e. mostly equity-based crowdfunding, and ignore reward-, donation- or lending-based forms. Therefore, there is no evidence that their research results can be generalized [41]. Furthermore, the review revealed that only a limited number of research applied common models to explain complex behavioral and collaborative processes [14, 34, 40].

Fan-Osuala et al. [40] used contribution patterns to forecast fundraising outcomes in crowdfunding. The authors used a two-pronged approach to build a forecast model and compared their results to other parametric and semi-parametric benchmarks. Substantial improvements could be shown [40]. However, the authors did not mention common models, which are used to explain complex collaborative behavioral motivations and decisions.

5   Conclusion

The study at hand provides an extensive search and analysis of relevant literature to gain insights on the extent and the modus of collaboration and cooperation of the three main actors in crowdfunding processes, i.e. intermediaries, entrepreneurs, and the crowd. Our study focused on behavioral issues in the decision-making processes of those main actors in crowdfunding. It provides an overview of current literature and its major results with emphasis on behavioral issues.

Concluding, a detailed framework based on comprehensive and well-known behavioural model such as the theory of reasoned action by Fishbein and Aijzen, considering cooperation and collaboration aspects among the main actors is necessary to provide a formal basis for the still partly unexplored concept of crowdfunding. It may provide evidence on behavioural interdependencies based on models, which were successfully applied in similar fields and comparable environments to explain complex behavioural interrelations. Additionally, in order to be able to formulate well-grounded design recommendations, and to provide management support for crowdfunding settings, it is necessary to consider the entire range of alternative forms of crowdfunding and to make transparent the mechanisms that stimulate collaboration from a behavioral perspective.

References

1. Brem, A., Vaiardot, E.: Revolution of innovation management: internalization and business models. In: Revolution of Innovation Management, pp. 1–13 (2017)
2. Busse, V.: Crowdfunding – an empirical study on the entrepreneurial viewpoint. In: Xhafa, F., Barolli, L., Greguš, M. (eds.) INCoS 2018. LNDECT, vol. 23, pp. 306–318. Springer, Cham (2019). https://doi.org/10.1007/978-3-319-98557-2_28
3. Ly, N.T.: Digital transformation of business models and business strategies - a systematic literature review. University of Vienna, Faculty of Business and Statistics (2018)
4. Webster, J., Watson, R.: Analyzing the past to prepare for the future: writing a literature review. MIS Q. **26**, 8–23 (2002)
5. Prettcrew, M., Roberts, H.: Systematic Reviews in Social Science. Blackwell Publishing, Hoboken (2006)
6. Hoegen, A., Steiniger, M.D., Veit, D.: How do investors decide? An interdisciplinary review of decision-making in crowdfunding. Electron. Markets **28**(3), 339–365 (2017)
7. Kaartemo, V.: The elements of a successful crowdfunding campaign: a systematic literature review of crowdfunding performance. Int. Rev. Entrepreneurship **15**(3), 1–45 (2017)
8. Kumar, S., Goyal, N.: Behavioural biases in investment decision making – a systematic literature review. Qual. Res. Financ. Markets **7**(1), 88–108 (2015)
9. Springer (2019). Retrieved from www.springer.com

10. ScienceDirect (2019). Retrieved from www.sciencedirect.com
11. IEEE (2019). Retrieved from https://ieeexplore-ieee-org.ezproxy.napier.ac.uk/Xplore/home.jsp
12. Wiley online library (2019). Retrieved from https://onlinelibrary.wiley.com
13. Web of Science (2019). Retrieved from https://apps-webofknowledge-com.ezproxy.napier.ac.uk/WOS_GeneralSearch_input.do?product=WOS&search_mode=GeneralSearch&SID=E6pdPmIFjNaByObCS6P&preferencesSaved
14. Svee, E., Zdravkovic, J.: A model-based approach for capturing consumer preferences from crowdsources: the case of Twitter, pp. 1357–2151. IEEE (2016)
15. Okada, G.: Advertisement effectiveness estimation based on crowdsourced multimodal affective responses. In: The IEEE Conference on Computer Vision and Pattern Recognition (CVPR) Workshops, pp. 1263–1271 (2018)
16. Beier, M., Wagner, K.: User Behavior in crowdfunding platforms-exploratory evidence from Switzerland. In: 49th Hawaii International Conference on System Sciences (HICSS), pp. 3584–3593 (2016)
17. Xue, J., Sun, F.: Influencing factors of equity crowdfunding financing performance - an empirical study. In: International Conference on Management Science and Engineering (ICMSE), pp. 1855–2155 (2016)
18. Posegga, O., Zylka, M.P., Fischbach, K.: Collective dynamics of crowdfunding networks. In: 48th Hawaii International Conference on System Sciences, pp. 1530–1605 (2015)
19. Xiaoyu, M., Mingru, Y., Zhang, J.: Signaling factors in overfunding: an empirical study based on Crowdcube. In: International Conference on Service Systems and Service Management, pp. 1904–2161 (2017)
20. Lins, E., Fietkiewicz, K.J., Lutz, E.: How to convince the crowd: an impression management approach. In: 49th Hawaii International Conference on System Sciences (HICSS), pp. 1530–1605 (2016)
21. Boeuf, B., Durivage, F.: Make them pay! Understanding consumer participation in crowdfunding. In: Obal, M.W., Krey, N., Bushardt, C. (eds.) Let's get engaged! crossing the threshold of marketing's engagement era. DMSPAMS, pp. 95–96. Springer, Cham (2016). https://doi.org/10.1007/978-3-319-11815-4_32
22. Xiang, D., Zhang, L., Tao, Q., Qang, Y., Ma, S.: Informational or emotional appeals in crowdfunding message strategy: an empirical investigation of backers' support decisions. J. Acad. Mark. Sci., 1–18 (2019, in print)
23. Comite, U.: Crowdfunding as a model and financing instrument in social enterprises. In: Bilgin, M.H., Danis, H., Demir, E., Can, U. (eds.) Consumer Behavior, Organizational Strategy and Financial Economics. ESBE, vol. 9, pp. 203–220. Springer, Cham (2018). https://doi.org/10.1007/978-3-319-76288-3_15
24. Behrend, T., Sharek, D., Meade, A., Wiebe, E.: The viability of crowdsourcing for survey research. Behav. Res. Methods 43(3), 1554–3528 (2011)
25. Saberi, M., Hussain, O.K., Janjua, N.K., Chang, E.: Cognition and statistical-based crowd evaluation framework for ER-in-house crowdsourcing system: inbound contact center. In: Sharaf, M.A., Cheema, M.A., Qi, J. (eds.) ADC 2015. LNCS, vol. 9093, pp. 207–219. Springer, Cham (2015). https://doi.org/10.1007/978-3-319-19548-3_17
26. Bitterl, S., Schreier, M.: When consumers become project backers: the psychological consequences of participation in crowdfunding. Int. J. Res. Mark. 35(4), 673–685 (2018)
27. Zhang, H., Chen, W.: Crowdfunding technological innovations: interaction between consumer benefits and rewards. Technovation 84, 11–20 (2019)
28. Wehnert, P., Baccarella, C., Beckmann, M.: In crowdfunding we trust? Investigating crowdfunding success as a signal for enhancing trust in sustainable product features. Technol. Forecast. Soc. Chang. 141, 128–137 (2019)

29. Zvilichovsky, D., Danzinger, S., Steinhart, Y.: Making-the-product-happen: a driver of crowdfunding participation. J. Interact. Mark. **41**, 81–93 (2018)
30. Du, Z., Li, M., Wang, K.: "The more options, the better?" Investigating the impact of the number of options on backers' decisions in reward-based crowdfunding projects. Inf. Manag. **56**(3), 429–444 (2019)
31. Liang, T., Wu, S., Huang, C.: Why funders invest in crowdfunding projects: role of trust from the dual-process perspective. Inf. Manag. **56**(1), 70–84 (2019)
32. Xiao, S., Yue, Q.: Investors' inertia behavior and their repeated decision-making in online reward-based crowdfunding market. Decis. Support Syst. **111**, 101–112 (2018)
33. Hornuf, L., Schwienbacher, A.: Market mechanisms and funding dynamics in equity crowd-funding. J. Corp. Finan. **50**, 556–574 (2018)
34. Mamonov, S., Malaga, R.: Success factors in Title III equity crowdfunding in the United States. Electron. Commer. Res. Appl. **27**, 65–73 (2018)
35. Cox, J., Nguyen, T., Thorpe, A., Ishizaka, A., Cakhar, S., Meech, L.: Being seen to care: the relationship between self-presentation and contributions to online pro-social crowdfunding campaigns. Comput. Hum. Behav. **83**, 45–55 (2018)
36. Bi, S., Lui, Z., Usman, K.: The influence of online information on investing decisions of reward-based crowdfunding. J. Bus. Res. **71**, 10–18 (2017)
37. Xu, B., Zheng, H., Xu, Y., Wang, T.: Configurational paths to sponsor satisfaction in crowdfunding. J. Bus. Res. **69**, 915–927 (2015)
38. Bretschneider, U., Leimeister, J.: Not just an ego-trip: exploring backers' motivation for funding in incentive-based crowdfunding. J. Strateg. Inf. Syst. **26**(4), 246–260 (2017)
39. Paschen, J.: Choose wisely: crowdfunding through the stages of the startup life cycle. Bus. Horiz. **60**, 179–188 (2017)
40. Fan-Osuala, O., Zantedeschi, D., Jank, W.: Using past contribution patterns to forecast fundraising outcomes in crowdfunding. Int. J. Forecast. **34**(1), 30–44 (2018)
41. Lukkarinen, A., Teich, J., Wallenius, H., Wallenius, J.: Success drivers of online equity crowdfunding campaigns. Decis. Support Syst. **87**, 26–38 (2016)
42. Bellefamme, P., Lambert, T., Schwienbacher, A.: Crowdfunding: tapping the right crowd. J. Bus. Ventur. **29**(5), 585–609 (2014)
43. Zhao, Q., Chen, C., Wang, J., Chen, P.: Determinants of backers' funding intention in crowdfunding: social exchange theory and regulatory focus. Telematics Inform. **34**(1), 370–384 (2017)
44. Maier, E.: Supply and demand on crowdlending platforms: connecting small and medium-sized enterprise borrowers and consumer investors. J. Retail. Consum. Serv. **33**, 143–153 (2016)
45. Bal, A., Weidner, K., Hana, R., Mills, A.: Crowdsourcing and brand control. Bus. Horiz. **60**(2), 219–228 (2017)
46. Martinez, M., Walton, B.: Crowdsourcing: the potential of online communities as a tool for data analysis. In: Open Innovation in the Food and Beverage Industry, pp. 332–342 (2013)
47. Bubalo, M., Zante, B., Verburg, P.: Crowdsourcing geo-information on landscape perceptions and preferences: a review. Landscape Urban Plan. **184**, 101–111 (2019)
48. Lee, J., Seao, D.: Crowdsourcing not all sourced by the crowd: an observation on the behavior of Wikipedia participants. Technovation **55**, 14–21 (2016)
49. Macht, S.: Reaping value-added benefits from crowdfunders: what can we learn from relationship marketing? Strat. Change **23**(7–8), 439–460 (2014)
50. Macht, S., Weatherston, J.: The benefits of online crowdfunding for fund-seeking business ventures. Strat. Change **23**(1–3), 1–14 (2014)

51. Datta, A., Sahaym, A., Brooks, S.: Unpacking the antecedents of crowdfunding campaign's success: the effects of social media and innovation orientation. J. Small Bus. Manag., 1–27 (2018, in print)

52. Strickland, J., Stoops, W.: Feasibility, acceptability, and validity of crowdsourcing for collecting longitudinal alcohol use data. J. Exp. Anal. Behav. **110**(1), 136–153 (2018)

53. Rodriguez, Y., Sicilia, M.: Explaining consumer's participation in crowdfuning. The mediating role of trust and social identification. In: EMAC (2016)

54. Yang, Q., Lee, Y.: An investigation of enablers and inhibitors of crowdfunding adoption: empirical evidence from startups in China. Hum. Factors Ergon. Manuf. Serv. Ind. **29**(1), 5–21 (2019)

55. Bernardes, B., Lucian, R., Nelsio, A.: Crowdfunding: analysis of satisfaction and loyalty behaviors of Brazilian consumers in the context of cultural products. Revista de Gestão e Projetos **9**(2), 65–79 (2018)

56. Ahsan, M., Cornelis, E.F.I., Baker, A.: Understanding backers' interactions with crowdfunding campaigns: co-innovators or consumers? J. Res. Mark. Entrepreneurship **20**(2), 252–272 (2018)

57. Zhang, S., Kwok, R., Liu, Z.: Reward-based crowdfunding: a study of online investment behaviors among China funders. In: 2017 2nd ACSS International Conference on the Social Sciences and Teaching Research (ACSS-SSTR 2017), pp. 9–15 (2017)

58. Zhao, L.: Hedonic value and crowdfunding project performance: a propensity score matching-based analysis. Rev. Behav. Finance **2017**, 169–186 (2017)

59. Ho, H., Lin, P., Lu, M.: Effects of online crowdfunding on consumers' perceived value and purchase intention. The Anthropologist **17**(3), 837–844 (2014)

60. Steinberger, N.: Why supporters contribute to reward-based crowdfunding. Int. J. Entrepreneurial Behav. Res. **23**(2), 336–353 (2017)

61. Kang, M., Gao, Y., Wang, T., Zheng, H.: Understanding the determinants of funders' investment intentions on crowdfunding platforms: a trust-based perspective. Ind. Manag. Data Syst. **116**(8), 1800–1819 (2016)

62. Gera, J., Kauer, H.: Dynamics of pledge behavior of crowdfunded projects. In: Crowdsourcing: Concepts, Methodologies, Tools, and Applications, pp. 1402–1418 (2019)

63. Liao, Y., Tran, T., Lee, D., Lee, K.: Understanding temporal backing patterns in online crowdfunding communities. In: Proceedings of the ACM on Web Science Conference, pp. 369–378 (2017)

64. Colombo, M., Franzoni, C.L.: Internal social capital and the attraction of early contributions in crowdfunding. Entrepreneurship Theory Pract. **39**(1), 75–100 (2015)

65. Yu, H., Shen, Z., Miao, C., An, B.: Challenges and opportunities for trust management in crowdsourcing. In: International Joint Conferences on Web Intelligence and Intelligent Agent Technology, vol. 2, pp. 486–493 (2012)

66. Mladenow, A., Bauer, C., Strauss, C.: Collaborative shopping with the crowd. In: Luo, Y. (ed.) CDVE 2015. LNCS, vol. 9320, pp. 162–169. Springer, Cham (2015). https://doi.org/10.1007/978-3-319-24132-6_19

67. Bauer, C., Mladenow, A., Strauss, C.: Fostering collaboration by location-based crowdsourcing. In: Luo, Y. (ed.) CDVE 2014. LNCS, vol. 8683, pp. 88–95. Springer, Cham (2014). https://doi.org/10.1007/978-3-319-10831-5_13

Application of Decision Support Systems for Advanced Equipment Selection in Construction

Carmen Marcher[1,2(✉)], Andrea Giusti[2(✉)],
Christoph P. Schimanski[1,2], and Dominik T. Matt[1,2]

[1] Free University of Bolzano, Piazza Università 1, 39100 Bolzano, Italy
`carmen.marcher@natec.unibz.it`
[2] Fraunhofer Italia Research, Via A.-Volta 13A, 39100 Bolzano, Italy
`carmen.marcher@fraunhofer.it`,
`andrea.giusti@fraunhofer.it`

Abstract. We consider the problem of supporting decision makers in construction projects for making the rational-best choice between the introduction of advanced technological solutions and the use of conventional approaches. The complexity, uniqueness, and uncertainty, typical of construction projects, are the main obstacles in this kind of decision problems. We propose a method for the development of decision support systems for such problems based on Bayesian decision theory. Bayesian decision theory is applied to capture and rationally solve such decision problems. We account for uncertainty and construction process specific criteria, for structuring the knowledge-base and easing the elicitation of the decision network. The applicability potential of the proposed approach is presented by means of an example application scenario.

Keywords: Decision support · Construction automation ·
Cooperative decision-making · Bayesian decision theory · Industry 4.0

1 Introduction

While the manufacturing sector is increasingly investing in Industry 4.0 [1], highlighting the potential improvements in terms of productivity and quality, the construction industry (CI) still hesitates to invest in advanced technology [2]. For this reason it is necessary to support the CI to overcome reluctance towards the adoption of advanced technological solutions [3]. Due to the uniqueness, complexity, and uncertainty, typical for construction projects, it is necessary to evaluate the available options on a project basis reflecting preferences through a cooperative contribution of domain experts [4]. Support systems for decision making can assist decision makers in the choice between available technological solutions. Mohan [4] highlighted the potential application of expert systems in the domain of equipment selection in construction execution. Hastak [5] adopted the analytical hierarchy process for defining the main criteria that have to be considered in the comparison of automated and conventional solutions in construction and developed a decision support system (DSS). Jahr and Borrmann [6] proposed a semi-automated site equipment selection by means of a

Y. Luo (Ed.): CDVE 2019, LNCS 11792, pp. 229–235, 2019.
https://doi.org/10.1007/978-3-030-30949-7_26

rule-based expert system. The adoption of Building Information Modelling (BIM) as shared knowledge base, leads to new opportunities in decision-making and has been addressed in different application areas: equipment selection [6], investment selection [7], assessment of environmental impact of design decisions [8], comparison of conventional and modular construction [9], assessment of building stocks [10].

We propose a novel method for the application of DSSs in construction that exploits Bayesian decision theory, specific criteria for structuring the knowledge-base in construction processes, as well as expert knowledge. The applicability potential is presented by means of an exemplary application scenario. The paper is structured as follows: Sect. 2 introduces the proposed approach and Sect. 3 describes its application. Section 4 discusses results and concluding remarks.

2 Proposed Approach

Our proposed approach for the application of DSSs in construction relies on Bayesian decision theory [11] and gains knowledge from different sources. Bayesian decision theory allows us to capture and rationally solve decision problems that involve uncertainty. Additionally, we consider structuring the knowledge of the problem domain according to construction specific criteria that affect the decision between automated and conventional systems. The knowledge of the problem domain is provided by the project documentation and through a cooperative contribution of domain experts. The proposed approach forsees the development of a DSS that is structured in three modules: user interface, inference engine, and a structured knowledge base.

User Interface. Within the user interface the decision maker poses a query to a rational agent, sets evidence (if any), and gets advice on the best rational decision or action.

Inference Engine. The inference engine solves queries against the structured knowledge base and gives advice to the user using Bayesian decision theory. Bayesian decision networks can be constructed as follows [12]: (1) modeling of the decision network by identifying variables, causal relations between them and defining the model structure; (2) implementing the network by eliciting probabilities and utilities; (3) testing of the model by verifying a set of known input and output values; (4) analysing the model by performing sensitivity analysis.

Knowledge Base. The knowledge is structured according to specific criteria [5]: need-based criteria (e.g. requirements in terms of the execution process), technological criteria (e.g. material handling), economic criteria (e.g. potential improvements of productivity, quality and cost), safety/risk criteria (e.g. health and safety hazards and investment risk), and project specific criteria (e.g. project constraints). The knowledge of the problem domain is collected systematically through a cooperative contribution, thus forming the basis for the elicitation of probabilities and utilities.

3 Exemplary Application

We consider the decision-making process for equipment selection in an exemplary construction project. In particular, we emulate the choice between the use of a conventional scaffold and a mast climber work platform for the façade installation at the NOI Techpark[1] in Bolzano (Italy). The façade installation was awarded through a public tender where the bidders had to address also the installation procedure. The decision problem was analysed with the project manager of the executing company that won the tender, and with a project manager of the awarding authority representing the role of the decision maker.

In the following, we adopt the usual representation of decision networks, as described in [11, 12]: (a) decision nodes (rectangles) represent problem variables and available choices; (b) chance nodes (ovals) represent random variables that may be observed to provide information (evidence), for solving the problem; (c) utility nodes (diamonds): represent the utility function to assess the expected utility for available choices; (d) arcs describe dependencies between the variables. The implementation of our exemplary case study is demonstrated using the python wrapper pyAgrum for the C++ aGrUM library for building and computing Bayesian networks [13].

3.1 Modelling of the Decision Problem

The construction of the probabilistic model concerns the elicitation of the qualitative part of the model. For this purpose, the available project documentation and tender requirements were studied. This allowed to define the set of variables of the problem domain and investigate causal relations between them in cooperation with domain experts. The model was simplified by combining and removing variables that are not directly involved in the decision. The resulting causal decision network is represented in Fig. 1. Chance nodes that have a direct impact on the utility function have been defined according to the project documentation, the requirements of the client and the executing company: Cost (CO), Productivity (P), Safety (S), Interferences (I). Within the model the choice between conventional and automated scaffold is represented by the decision node scaffold type (ST) and utility is assessed within the utility node (U). The decision is also governed by the following chance nodes: dimension (D) which refers to the external shell of the building that needs to be scaffolded; accessibility all levels (AL) which refers to the simultaneous accessibility to all levels; system adaptability (SA) which describes the adaptability to operational requirements; material handling (MH) which describes the impact on material transport; accessibility level 0 (A0) which describes the impacts in terms of accessibility at the ground floor.

3.2 Implementing the Model

The implementation refers to the definition of the quantitative part of the network, eliciting conditional probabilities (CP) and utilities (U). CP were elicited in cooperation

---

[1] https://noi.bz.it/en.

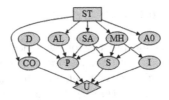

Fig. 1. Model of the decision network for the scaffold selection.

with the domain expert of the executing company, mapping his verbal statements form "certain" to "impossible" as suggested in [12]. U are defined through a cooperative contribution of domain experts, by ordering them from the worst (U = 0) to the best possible outcome (U = 1). The proposed utility function that captures the agent's preferences is defined as follows:

$$U = \beta_1 \times uCO + \beta_2 \times uP + \beta_3 \times uS + \beta_4 \times uI. \tag{1}$$

Where uCO, uP, uS and uI represent the subjective utilities as defined in Table 1 and their coefficients $\beta1$, $\beta2$, $\beta3$ and $\beta4$ (Subsect. 3.4) allow weighting of utilities.

Table 1. Utilities outcome according to the domain experts.

Cost	uCO	Productivity	uP	Safety	uS	Interferences	uI
"increased"	0	"as-usual"	0	"as-usual"	0	"as-usual"	0
"on-budget"	1	"increased"	1	"improved"	1	"reduced"	1
"reduced"	1						

The elicitation of the qualitative and quantitative information of the probabilistic model allows us to perform inference given available evidence. The most reasonable choice is computed as the one that maximizes the expected utility, as defined in Sect. 16.1 of [11].

3.3 Testing of the Model

For the verification and refinement of the model several tests were performed to check if it provides reasonable output based on evidence. For example, if we consider the simultaneous accessibility to all levels as a necessary requirement, this excludes the adoption of an automated scaffolding system. By making these considerations, different tests for various evidence settings were performed. All tests provided reasonable outputs. Figure 2 illustrates how the model is reasoning without setting any evidence. We can deduce that the elicited probabilistic model suggests that it is likely that, compared to a conventional system, the automated system will have a positive impact on interferences, safety and productivity. On the other hand, the risk of overspending increases.

3.4   Analysing the Model

After checking that the model provides reasonable output based on evidence, sensitivity analysis is performed by systematically varying the coefficients of the utility function.

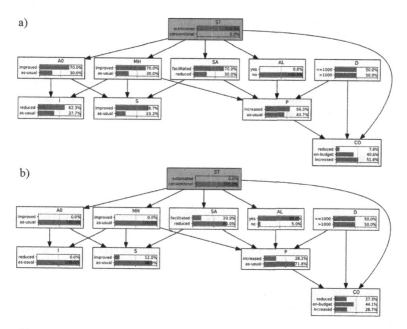

Fig. 2. Inference calculation for automated (a) and conventional solution (b).

Table 2. Sensitivity analysis for the best rational decision and MEU.

uCO	uP	uS	uI	No evidence		D > 1000 m²	
β_1	β_2	β_3	β_4	Decision	MEU	Decision	MEU
0.45	0.45	0.05	0.05	a	0.510	a	0.311
0.20	0.30	0.20	0.30	a	0.637	a	0.346

Table 2 shows the responses of the rational agent to the variations in terms of rational best decision – automated (a) or conventional (c) – and maximum expected utility (MEU) related to the case study. For example, when considering the variable dimension as the only available evidence, and an un-balanced weighing of the contributions to the utility function as defined by the domain experts, the automated scaffold system is suggested by the developed system as most rational.

4 Conclusion and Outlook

To the best knowledge of the authors, this is the first time that the application of Bayesian decision theory in construction equipment selection is performed. The exemplary case study shows the applicability potential of decision theory for equipment selection with manual construction of probabilistic networks. The manual construction of probabilistic networks is a time-consuming task that needs close collaboration with domain experts. The proposed approach will be further developed by considering data-driven modelling.

Acknowledgements. The authors gratefully acknowledge the domain experts Robert Ploner, project manager of Metall Ritten S.r.l., and Alexander Alber, project manager of the building development department of NOI S.p.a..

References

1. Rauch, E., Matt, D.T., Brown, C.A., et al.: Transfer of industry 4.0 to small and medium sized enterprises. In: Transdisciplinary Engineering Methods for Social Innovation of Industry 4.0, vol. 7, pp. 63–71 (2018). https://doi.org/10.3233/978-1-61499-898-3-63
2. Oesterreich, T.D., Teuteberg, F.: Understanding the implications of digitisation and automation in the context of Industry 4.0: a triangulation approach and elements of a research agenda for the construction industry. Comput. Ind. **83**, 121–139 (2016). https://doi.org/10.1016/j.compind.2016.09.006
3. European Commission Internal Market, Industry, Entrepreneurship and SMEs. In: Construction. https://ec.europa.eu/growth/sectors/construction_en. Accessed 4 May 2019
4. Mohan, S.: Expert systems applications in construction management and engineering. J. Constr. Eng. Manag. **116**, 87–99 (1990). https://doi.org/10.1061/(ASCE)0733-9364(1990)116:1(87)
5. Hastak, M.: Advanced automation or conventional construction process? Autom. Constr. **7**, 299–314 (1998). https://doi.org/10.1016/S0926-5805(98)00047-8
6. Jahr, K., Borrmann, A.: Semi-automated site equipment selection and configuration through formal knowledge representation and inference. Adv. Eng. Inform. **38**, 488–500 (2018). https://doi.org/10.1016/j.aei.2018.08.015
7. Nowak, P., Książek, M., Draps, M., Zawistowski, J.: Decision making with use of building information modeling. Procedia Eng. **153**, 519–526 (2016). https://doi.org/10.1016/j.proeng.2016.08.177
8. Zhu, J.Y., Deshmukh, A.: Application of Bayesian decision networks to life cycle engineering in Green design and manufacturing. Eng. Appl. Artif. Intell. **16**, 91–103 (2003). https://doi.org/10.1016/S0952-1976(03)00057-5
9. Hammad, A., Akbarnezhad, A.: Modular vs conventional construction: a multi-criteria framework approach. In: ISARC. Proceedings of the 34th International Symposium on Automation and Robotics in Construction. Vilnius Gediminas Technical University, Department of Construction Economics & Property, pp. 214–220 (2017)
10. Carbonari, A., Corneli, A., Di Giuda, G., et al.: BIM-based decision support system for the management of large building stocks. In: ISARC. Proceedings of the International Symposium on Automation and Robotics in Construction. IAARC Publications, pp. 348–355 (2018)

11. Russell, S.J., Norvig, P., Davis, E.: Artificial Intelligence: A Modern Approach, 3rd edn. Pearson Education Inc., Upper Saddle River (2016)

12. Kjærulff, U.B., Madsen, A.L.: Bayesian Networks and Influence Diagrams: A Guide to Construction and Analysis, 2nd edn. Springer, New York (2013). https://doi.org/10.1007/978-0-387-74101-7

13. Gonzales, C., Torti, L., Wuillemin, P.-H.: aGrUM: a graphical universal model framework. In: Benferhat, S., Tabia, K., Ali, M. (eds.) IEA/AIE 2017. LNCS (LNAI), vol. 10351, pp. 171–177. Springer, Cham (2017). https://doi.org/10.1007/978-3-319-60045-1_20

The Collective Construction and Management of Spatial Knowledge in Open Spaces: A Pilot Study

Domenico Camarda[✉], Giulia Mastrodonato, and Mauro Patano

Polytechnic University of Bari, Via Orabona 4, 70125 Bari, Italy
domenico.camarda@poliba.it

Abstract. Spatial environments have been largely studied over time, under different perspectives. Under a cognitivist perspective, they represent knowledge-intensive, meaningful spaces and entities that human agents relate to and adapt during their existence.

The comprehension/identification of space fundamentals by human agents can be of great interest in strategic planning, in that they may represent structures, pillars, invariant, resilient characters of the environment, on which to build/plan the layout and development of regions and towns.

Our work focuses on the potentials and problems of orientation and spatial knowledge in endogenous and exogenous agents in spaces with reduced - in particular extremely reduced - population, using a case-study experimental approach.

In particular, we are interested in the essential information for orientation in navigation and for the identification of the resources necessary to guarantee operative systems of relationship between agents and between agents and spaces.

Keywords: Knowledge management · Collective spatial cognition · Open space · Spatial variables · Environmental planning

1 Introduction

Under a cognitivist perspective, spatial environments represent knowledge-intensive, meaningful spaces and entities that human agents relate to and adapt during their existence [1]. They are intrinsically based on dynamic complexity, therefore trying to understand the typical spatial behaviours of a human agent is often hard task, inducing planning as well as managing problems in many domains [2]. Particularly experimental literature often shows that not always there is clear distinction between space 'fundamentals' and space ancillary, ornamental qualities in spatial analysis [3, 4].

The comprehension/identification of space fundamentals by human agents can be of great interest in strategic planning, in that they may represent structures, pillars,

---

The study was developed by authors as a common research work. In this framework, M. Patano wrote chapter 1, G. Mastrodonato wrote chapter 2, D. Camarda wrote chapters 3 and 4.

© Springer Nature Switzerland AG 2019
Y. Luo (Ed.): CDVE 2019, LNCS 11792, pp. 236–243, 2019.
https://doi.org/10.1007/978-3-030-30949-7_27

invariant, resilient characters of the environment, on which to build/plan the layout and development of regions and towns. The research on the spatial knowledge forms of living agents is today in progressive development, in environments of automatic computation of psychology or engineering [5]. Research on forms of spatial knowledge at the macro-scale is still limited [1, 6]. This work focuses on the potentials and problems of orientation and spatial knowledge in endogenous and exogenous agents in spaces with reduced - in particular extremely reduced - population.

The ways of progressive identification and enrichment of information during navigation in this type of space is analyzed here. In particular, we are interested in the essential information for orientation in navigation and for the identification of the resources necessary to guarantee operative systems of relationship between agents and between agents and spaces.

In this research framework, the paper is then organized as follows. A digression on the research background on spatial cognition issues follows the introduction and is carried out in chapter two. The third chapter briefly deals with the main characters of the research project where the present study is structured. Chapter four shows the experimental case study carried out here, with essential, describing methodology and discussing the results of the developed analysis. Brief concluding remarks are reported in the end, dealing with achievements, suggestions and possible follow-ups.

2 Spatial Cognition Research Background

Cybernetic and artificial intelligence studies include large reasoning about spatial cognition features, as they are important for operational planning. Rather interestingly, they put town a basic distinction between structured and unstructured spaces. Fundamentally, it parallels a similar distinction between spaces geometrically simple (elementary profiles, few unexpected events, few secondary items, few decisions required) and spaces geometrically complex (composite profiles, recurrent unexpected events, many secondary items and many decisions required) [7–9]. It is easy to understand that a robot develops movements and learns surrounding spaces more straightforwardly in simple geometries, so determining more identifiable cognitive situations. This seems rather clear, although robot agents can typify great part of reality and are able to move also in unstructured world-like human agents.

Human agents show a different situation. A reasonably recognizable space is for us geometrically simple, empty, maybe unidirectional space. This is represented, for example, by an interior corridor, long and empty, with a series of doors, windows, skylights. It consists of a point of origin and an end point, with no lateral intersections. This space could be assimilated to the arc of a graph, it is certainly simple and can be walked by the human agent with little attention.

Yet the human agent considers complex a very crowded space, with a multi-dimensional geometry that is difficult to recognize. This is, for example, an open space, like a rural area or a city fair, with an unclear form, origin, endpoint, thus demanding specific attention. A human walks casually through it, with the frequent risk of colliding with the imprecise trajectories of people, or getting lost, or losing her/his friend or child who still does not know how to move in a complex space. Such complex spaces may suggest human agents a preliminary action of memorization of characteristic landmarks with the aim of replace an incomprehensible "structure" or "geometry" [10–12].

Goodman [3] argued on a distinction between 'structure' and 'ornament', in human perceptions of complex spaces. The representation space is increasingly considered as a multiform issue, complex and intrinsically non-reducible. It also changes with time, but with features that are not always so obvious as traditionally expected [13, 14].

Such situation is even more complex, if possible, when dealing with the potentials and problems of orientation and spatial knowledge in endogenous and exogenous agents in spaces with reduced - in particular extremely reduced - population.

It is a question of identifying and experimentally analyzing variables and systems of latent variables in spaces with reduced (or non-existent) information content on the anthropic levels of spatial structuring.

It is a matter of laying the foundations - also through experimentation on human agents - of the modelling of functional (operational) cognitive systems that are suitable for these spaces.

As a general consideration, these are cognitively poorly structured spaces. However, we assume the research hypothesis that a good cognitive structuring of such large spaces of nature, hostile to itself to the intensive population, is possible when the essential (ontological) latent variables are identified. These variables are therefore investigated, which are considered quite similar to those of high-population spaces with a high degree of randomness of interactions and transformations.

From reasoning on the available literature, the work aims to analyze some experiential narratives focusing on the themes of the cognitive characterization of rural paths. In particular, the results of experiments conducted with students of the engineering school of the Polytechnic of Bari are analyzed in a modelling perspective.

A general research objective of the experimentation is to investigate the fundamental characteristics of the open space through spatial cognition by agents who navigate within open spaces themselves. Relevant data are analyzed in order to draw correlations between elements present in protocols collected by ad-hoc experimentation.

A more specific objective of the present paper is to analyze the possible dependence of spatial sensations and perceptions from the other physical and relational elements that characterize the rural open space.

3 The Case Study

Las year, an experimentation campaign was carried out with 180 students of the 2nd year of the master's degree in Building Systems, Urban Planning course. Each agent had to choose and travel a route in an open rural space, photographing elements that s/he considered to be of interest and recording sensations, perceptions and/or emotions along the way. The track, the places of interest and the notes were recorded and geo-referenced through smartphone apps and personal and residential details were reported on an online repository.

The present analysis was carried out on a reduced sample of 16 observations. This is a small part of the entire population involved, since the work of control, formatting and normalization of the great amount of data is only at the beginning. Apart from personal details, data are mostly stored on kml/kmz (Google Earth) files, from which numerical elements are then drawn out in the form of string, text and graph (Figs. 1 and 2).

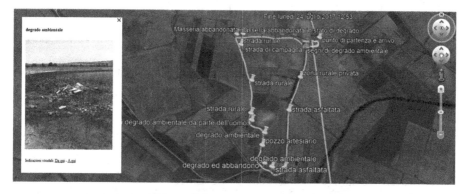

Fig. 1. Example of track with the location of photo takings

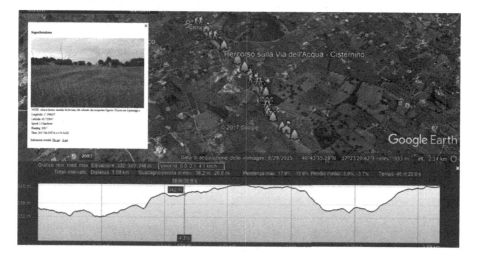

Fig. 2. Example of track with photo and note taking locations

In particular, textual notes taken by each agent along the route have been analysed by using simple data mining software Concordance, to draw out word and concept frequencies. The aggregation of textual concepts into categories has then been developed by manual ex-post analysis. In the end, the complete database is reported in Fig. 3, whereas specifications of acronyms, including the clusters of concepts grouped by synthetic categories, are reported in Fig. 4.

#	Matricola	Città di residenza	Luogo		percorso					features							
			toponimo	linea d'aria residenza - luogo (km)	altezza min (m)	dislivello (m)	lunghezza (km)	tempo impiegato	costruzioni	fauna	flora	paesaggio naturale	dissipazione e inquinamento	sensazioni, percezioni, emozioni	industrie, trasformazioni, impianti	strade
1	552201	Fasano	Cisternino	12	368,2	44,9	1,6	00:46:20	14	2	4	10	2	6		4
2	553745	Bitritto Puglia	Bitonto	15	81	26,7	2	00:42:00	14			3		4	2	5
3	555252	TRIGGIANO	Carbonara	3,3	41	15,4	0,835		10			13	3	5		1
4	555512	Laterza	Laterza	6,6	350	48,4	4,3	00:40:00	5			12	5		3	7
5	556879	Lucera	Lucera	5	192	19,8	2,82		2	1		7				4
6	556927	Rocchetta S.A. (FG)	Rocchetta	1,6	596	76	1,02	00:12:04	13		3	7				5
7	557428	Altamura	Altamura	6	308	23,4	0,8	00:29:00		1		6		1		11
8	557559	Foggia	Siponto	32	1	3	2,31		8	1		15	5	12		9
9	557604	Foggia	Segezia	14	134	208	12	00:45:12	9		1	11				10
10	557637	Martina Franca	Chiancaro	1,5	397	423	2,9	00:51:39	15	1		7	3		2	3
11	557658	Manfredonia	Amendola	18	34	39	0,617			2	1	30		2		15
12	557719	Troia	Troia	0,6	1	1	2,29					6			2	12

Fig. 3. Excerpt of the collected database (features are described through the citation frequencies of relevant words in the notes)

	LUO	linea d'aria residenza - luogo (km)
	ALT	altezza min (m)
	DIS	dislivello (m)
	LUN	lunghezza (km)
	TEM	tempo
Costruzioni, edificazioni	COS	EDILIZIA, BORGO, MASSERIA, CASALE, COSTRUZIONE, URBANI, CONVENTO, FONTANA, PIETRA, PONTE, CHIESA, EDIFICIO, MURETTI, SILOS, TORRE, VILLA, ABBEVERATOIO, ABITATO, CASA, DEPOSITO, FRANTOIO, PAESE, PORTA, POZZO, TORRI, TRULLO, ARCO, ARCO, CAPANNI, CASTELLO, FINESTRE, MANUFATTO, MARMOREE, MONASTERO, SCALA
Fauna	FAU	CAVALLI, INSETTI, ANIMALI, CANI, COLEOTTERO, DOG, FAUNA, VIPERA
Flora	FLO	VEGETAZIONE, ALBERI, PIANTA, FLORA, CIPOLLE, ERBA, FICO, FIORE, FRONDE, MORE, POMODORI, VERDURE
Paesaggio naturale	PAE	CAMPO, GRANO, RURALE, COLTIVAZIONI, TERRA, ULIVI, VIGNA, CAMPAGNA, TORRENTE, VALLE, AMBIENTALE, AMBIENTE, FLUVIALE, INCOLTO, NATURA, PAESAGGIO, AGRICOLO, AGRUMETO, BUCOLICO, FIUMETTO, PARCO, RACCOLTO, ACQUA, AMBIENTE, ARATURA, CANNETO, FILARI, MONTI, PARK, STEPPA, STERPAGLIA
Dissipazione e inquinamento	INQ	RIFIUTI, DEGRADO, ABUSIVISMO, AMIANTO, ECOMOSTRO
Sensazioni, percezioni, emozioni	SEN	ABBANDONO, LONTANANZA, VISTA, SENSAZIONE, IMMAGINE, PERICOLO, APERTO, BRUCIATA, DETURPA, INCOMPIUTO, ODORE, SECCO, SPAZI, ANTICO, BENE, BREVE, FENOMENO, GRANDI, PANORAMA, RISTORO, TEMPO, BELLO, COLORI, DISSESTATO, ESPLORARE, FORTUNA, LIBERTÀ, ORIZZONTE, PERICOLANTE, PIACEVOLE, PROSPETTIVA, RUMORE, SCORGIO, SCORGERE, SENSO, SGRADEVOLE, SUGGESTIVO, TRANQUILLITÀ, VENTICELLO, ABBAIARE, ACCIDENTATO, ACRE, AGEVOLE, APPARIVA, ARIA, ARSO, ASSENZA, BENESSERE, CALDO, CALMA, COGNITIVA, COMODO, CONFONDE, CONTRASTO, DIMENSIONI, DISMISURA, DISTESA, EFFETTO, ESALAZIONI, FATICA, GRADEVOLE, IGNOTO, ILLUMINAZIONE, LUCE, ORIENTARMI, PACE, SICUREZZA, SPENSIERATEZZA, SPERANZA, STANCHEZZA, TORRIDO
Industrie, trasformazioni, impianti	TRA	INDUSTRIALE, PALE, EOLICO, ARTIGIANALE, RECINTO, CANCELLO, ACQUEDOTTO, AZIENDA, DIGA, TRATTORE, ANTENNA, PALI, PANNELLI, PISCINA, TRALICCI
Strade	VIE	STRADA, PERCORSO, SENTIERO, ATTRAVERSARE, TRAGITTO, ASFALTO, CAMMINO, STERRATO, RAGGIUNGERE, SEGUIRE, PASSEGGIATA, SALITA, BIVIO, FERROVIA, INCROCIO, SVOLTA, CURVA, RETTILINEO, TRACCIATO, TRAFFICATA, VIAGGIO

Fig. 4. Legend of the aggregated variables

The internet portal of the experimental session, with personal details as well as relevant directions and information for respondents, is reported in Fig. 5.

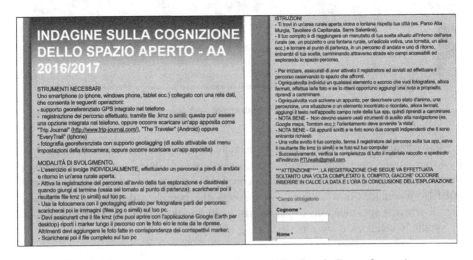

Fig. 5. The experimentation portal (powered by Google Forms features)

As previously mentioned, the specific objective of this work is to analyze the possible dependence of spatial sensations and perceptions from the other physical and relational elements that characterize the rural open space. In this framework the statistical analysis method of multiple regression analysis was used as a pilot methodological experiment. As Fig. 3 shows, some items in the database were missing. However, the regression was carried out using the Data analysis plug-in of Microsoft Excel (Italian version), which allows the interpolation of existing data to make up for missing information. Statistical results are summarized in Fig. 6.

Statistica della regressione					
R multiplo	0,982640754				
R al quadrato	0,965582851				
R al quadrato corretto	0,896748553				
Errore standard	0,751293047				
Osservazioni	16				

ANALISI VARIANZA					
	gdl	SQ	MQ	F	Significatività F
Regressione	10	79,17779379	7,917779379	14,02764147	0,004668639
Residuo	5	2,822206212	0,564441242		
Totale	15	82			

	Coefficienti	Errore standard	Stat t	Valore di significatività
Intercetta	-3,570862097	2,296282993	-1,555061858	0,180651519
LUO	0,078783236	0,033579746	2,346153427	0,065874277
ALT	-0,016870336	0,0022455	-7,512953976	0,000660929
DIS	0,026831546	0,003343132	8,025870826	0,0004855
TEM	-0,107639794	0,025144141	-4,280909603	0,007856704
COS	-0,301188845	0,088042521	-3,420947527	0,018818889
FLO	4,465275009	0,565118875	7,90147915	0,00052237
PAE	-0,053589763	0,040582835	-1,320503191	0,243879332
INQ	2,184816712	0,377690286	5,784678067	0,002172805
TRA	0,489347216	0,370403873	1,321117981	0,243689162
VIE	-0,085035897	0,05014506	-1,695798089	0,150690871

Fig. 6. The multiple regression analysis output

The above analysis leads to a synthetic regression equation:

$$Y_{SEN} = -3.57 + 0.08X_{LUO} - 0.01X_{ALT} + 0.27X_{DIS} - 0.1X_{TEM} - 0.3X_{COS}$$
$$+ 4.47X_{FLO} - 0.05X_{PAE} + 2.18X_{INQ} + 0.48X_{TRA} - 0.08X_{VIE}$$

Starting from the statistical analysis of the database, as resulting in the above regression equation, some suggestions of a certain interest emerge.

First of all, we can note that the expression of sensations and perceptions during navigation increases in relation to the quantitative variation of some features.

Particularly, the expression of sensations increases if presences of pollution and dissipation of resources appear in the route (INQ: coeff. = +2.18; p = 0.002).

It also increases in relation to the presence of floral and vegetational elements (FLO: coeff. = 4.46; p = 0.001).

It seems to increase even in relation to the distance of the route from the place of residence of the agent (LUO), as well as to the presence of industrial plants and elements of environmental transformation (TRA), but the relevant p-values are unacceptable, probably due to the small sample.

On the other hand, the expression of sensations and perceptions during navigation increases with the decrease of the presence of rural and urban buildings (COS: coeff. = 0.30, p = 0.019).

It also increases with the decrease of the time necessary to complete the route (TEM: coeff. = 0.11; p = 0.007).

Moreover, the expression of sensations and perceptions seems to decrease with increasing altitude (ALT: coeff. = −0.02; p = 0.001), but tends to increase with the increasing difference of altitude levels along the route (DIS: coeff. = +0.03; p = 0.001).

4   Conclusions

The above study seems to show outcomes of a certain suggestion, even if not completely robust and/or satisfying in statistical terms.

As a matter of facts, there are many coefficients with low numerical value, so that the investigated variables have little influence on the dependent variable - i.e., the agent's spatial sensations and perceptions along the route (SEN). Furthermore, some variables exhibit little causal dependence and in some cases observation data are missing and need to be interpolated. Concerning the aggregation of textual concepts by categories, it has been developed with a raw and hybrid approach that has possibly determined errors. In fact, while the word frequency has been collected through datamining tools, it has been subsequently contextualized and categorized manually by the analyst through ex post analysis.

Yet after carrying out the whole analysis, it was still possible to derive interesting qualitative considerations.

In fact, they seem to suggest that the perception of an open space, largely devoid of the strongly structuring elements present in confined urban spaces, still depends on some recurrent physical and landscape elements that end up giving it a cognition based latent structure.

Such suggestions can be particularly useful and interesting to support decisions regarding the management of open spaces, their valorisation during the identification processes of physical and/or identity resources for hypothesis of environmentally sustainable development of settlements, as well as for land use planning purposes.

In the current stage research, some follow-up activities seem to be important to be carried out in the next future. They will particularly aim at giving greater robustness and reliability to the analysis and develop more aware and useful considerations. First, an enlargement of the analysis to the entire sample of 180 observations will be an indispensable and significant step, also trying to include missing data with their proper values where available. Secondly, attempts will be made to integrate the statistical analysis with probabilistic inference techniques, in order to compensate statistical errors induced by the multiple regression tool.

Concerning follow-up activities, the survey carried out here will be subsequently complemented by ontological aggregative approaches, as increasing emerging in spatial cognition literature [15]. This effort is oriented to investigate the possible realization of formal models more suitable to replicate and/or to interpret the complexity of the relevant environmental system.

References

1. Proulx, M.J., Todorov, O.S., Taylor Aiken, A., de Sousa, A.A.: Where am I? Who am I? The relation between spatial cognition, social cognition and individual differences in the built environment. Front. Psychol. **7**, 64 (2016)
2. Denis, M., Loomis, J.M.: Perspectives on human spatial cognition: memory, navigation, and environmental learning. Psychol. Res. **71**, 235–239 (2007)
3. Goodman, N.: The Structure of Appearance. Harvard UP, Cambridge (1951)
4. Borri, D., Camarda, D.: Modelling space perception in urban planning: a cognitive AI-based approach. Stud. Comput. Intell. **489**, 3–9 (2013)
5. Borri, D., Camarda, D.: Spatial ontologies in multi-agent environmental planning. In: Yearwood, J., Stranieri, A. (eds.) Technologies for Supporting Reasoning Communities and Collaborative Decision Making: Cooperative Approaches, pp. 272–295. IGI Global Information Science, Hershey (2010)
6. Dolins, F.L., Mitchell, R.W.: Spatial Cognition, Spatial Perception: Mapping the Self and Space. Cambridge University Press, Cambridge (2010)
7. Georgiev, A., Allen, P.K.: Localization methods for a mobile robot in urban environments. IEEE Trans. Robot. Autom. ({TRO}) **20**, 851–864 (2004)
8. Kelly, D.M., Bischof, W.F.: Orienting in virtual environments: how are surface features and environmental geometry weighted in an orientation task? Cognition **109**, 89–104 (2008)
9. Danziger, D., Rafal, R.: The effect of visual signals on spatial decision making. Cognition **110**, 182–197 (2009)
10. de Hevia, M.D., Spelke, E.S.: Spontaneous mapping of number and space in adults and young children. Cognition **110**, 198–207 (2009)
11. Gero, J.S., Tversky, B. (eds.): Visual and Spatial Reasoning in Design. University of Sydney, Key Centre of Design Computing and Cognition, Sidney (1999)
12. Hirtle, S.C.: Neighborhoods and landmarks. In: Duckham, M., Goodchild, M.F., Worboys, M.F. (eds.) Foundations of Geographic Information Science, pp. 191–230. Taylor & Francis, London (2003)
13. Pouget, A., Ducom, J.C., Torri, J., Bavelier, D.: Multisensory spatial representations in eye-centered coordinates for reaching. Cognition **83**, B1–B11 (2002)
14. Day, S.B., Bartels, D.M.: Representation over time: the effects of temporal distance on similarity. Cognition **106**, 1504–1513 (2008)
15. Barkowsky, T., Knauff, M., Ligozat, G., Montello, D.R. (eds.): Spatial Cognition 2006. LNCS (LNAI), vol. 4387. Springer, Heidelberg (2007). https://doi.org/10.1007/978-3-540-75666-8

Machine Learning Method for Spinning Cyber-Physical Production System Subject to Condition Monitoring

Basit Farooq and Jinsong Bao[✉]

College of Mechanical Engineering, Donghua University, Shanghai, China
basitfarooq@gmail.com, bao@dhu.edu.cn

Abstract. Digitalization encapsulates the importance of machine condition monitoring which is subjected to predictive analytics for realizing significant improvements in the performance and reliability of rotating equipment i.e., spinning. This paper presents a machine learning approach for condition monitoring, based on a regularized deep neural network using automated diagnostics for spinning manufacturing. This article contributes a solution to find disturbances in a running system through real-time data sensing and signal to process via industrial internet of things. Because this controlled sensor network may comprise on different critical components of the same type of machines, therefore back propagation neural network based multi-sensor performance assessment and prediction strategy were developed for our system which worked as intelligent maintenance and diagnostic system. It is completely automatic requiring no manual extraction of handcrafted features.

Keywords: Cyber-physical production system · Condition monitoring · Machine learning · Prognostics and health management · Spinning

1 Introduction

The process of gathering data through sensors becomes relatively less expensive, which can make an automatic collection of real-time operation and condition data increasingly feasible. With the continuous development in the manufacturing industry and after the launch of industry 4.0 seamless connectivity among smart devices can allow sharing of data about performance, condition, and maintenance noncompliance. It has been estimated that by 2020, digitalization in the manufacturing sector will achieve an exceptional and remarkable milestone. Blistering evolution of smart machines and machine to machine communication connectivity and its applications allow highly controlled mechanism based monitored algorithms, tightly integrated with the internet networking and its users to improve maintenance decisions and influence.

Led by the convergent set of transformational technologies such as industrial automation, artificial intelligence, augmented reality, machine to machine communication, machine learning, internet of things, big data, cloud computing and its digitalization, the term Industry 4.0 was started in Germany where it became a preference issue for research centers and different organizations [1]. This renaissance provides new

Y. Luo (Ed.): CDVE 2019, LNCS 11792, pp. 244–253, 2019.
https://doi.org/10.1007/978-3-030-30949-7_28

possibilities for the improved productivity, performance and profitability for manufacturing, which also compels transformation of traditional structures, systems and strategies towards unprecedented possibilities and modernization i.e., Cyber physical system and industrial internet of things [2]. Until today there was a clear path for success in manufacturing but recently unmet manufacturing needs of futuristic industry or we can say the renew-new approach, transforms existing system simultaneously by adding new proposition that will make the manufacturing industries future ready.

Based on comprehensive and systematic literature research, the massively interacting systems like cyber physical production systems require higher connectivity and network feedback control loop. By condition monitoring holistic overview of information gained from different systems can be used in decisions making and only its critical aspect can be considered. Presumably any decision that we do make is based on our present knowledge about the system in hand, for a perfect system exceptional technology need to be advanced that could make such information distinguishable and effectible on time. The principal concern of writing this paper is to define the basic parameters in designing the sensor signal statistical mechanism which can provide not only the networked control system but also helps in fault detection and prevention to avoid such major breakdowns, specifically for condition monitoring purpose. So intelligent prognostics can provide the systematic approach that can continuously track health index to predict risks of unacceptable behavior overtime as well as identify exactly which components of a machines are prone to fall [3].

The remainder of the paper is structured as follows: Within Sect. 2 general spinning architecture and its different level of integration are defined. In Sect. 3, the state of the art CPPS model is presented. The outcome of the state of the art machine learning predictive analytics using condition monitoring algorithms is discussed within Sect. 4. Finally, the paper is concluded within Sect. 5.

2   General Spinning Architecture

2.1   The Process of Spinning Manufacturing

Spinning is the process of changing the fiber from a disorganized state to orderly arrangement along the longitudinal direction. It is a typical multi-process, continuous and mass production with high speed and large dynamic characteristics. The physical space of the spinning cyber-physical system is made up of people, machines, materials, methods and rings involved in yarn production. The processing of all kinds of data in physical space is continuously iteratively optimized into a knowledge base of spinning design, process, manufacturing and testing. Which improves yarn production efficiency, tracking yarn quality and reducing production cost and other aspects of great significance. Physical space and information space achieve interaction through industrial IoT constructed by various intelligent sensors, RFID, Wi-Fi, Tag and others [2] (Fig . 1).

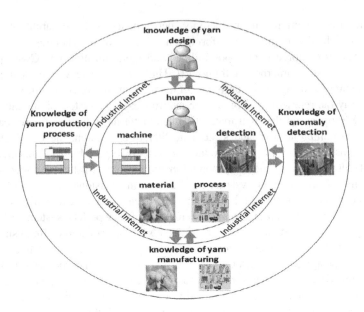

Fig. 1. The process of spinning as a cyber-physical production system

In the process of spinning, the real-time requirements of the task processing are very high. The task must be handled promptly, otherwise the process will be interrupted and the production will be stagnant, which will bring huge losses to the enterprise. Spinning is a vast area in the textile field, even you could call it the heart of the textile industry. The current spinning information space is typically deployed in remote cloud centers because cloud centers have strong computational, analytical and processing capabilities. However, with the continuous enlargement of production transformation and upgrading, the number of production equipment for spinning also upgraded.

2.2 Framework of CPPS

Based on CPPS, the smart textile industry is a highly sophisticated and integrated factory involving tight coupling between the digital twins; physical and computational components. By physicalizing the cyber and cyberizing the physical [4], computing elements ensure the system availability for the real time data processing for fault detection and identification during the yarn making operations. The designed implemented architecture works directly dependable upon computing elements (sensors, actuators), machine to machine interactions through seamlessly integration of wireless communication network and industrial internet of things; Collecting the information using sensors, analyzing them by worldwide services and interacting them with the physical world are the characteristics of this CPS system [5]. This interaction in the production environment leads to a CPPS as a part of "industry 4.0". Figure 2, shows a typical execution of predictive health monitoring and convergence of data flow between the physical world and the cyber world.

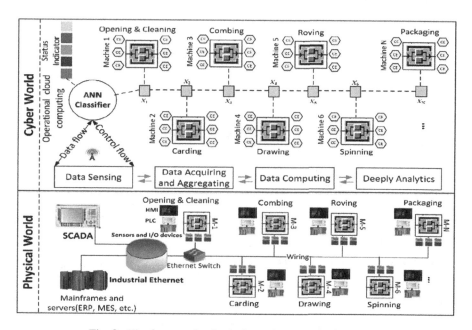

Fig. 2. The framework of spinning cyber and physical world

3   State of the Art Key Technologies of CPPS

3.1   Data-Driven Prognostics and Health Management

A connected factory floor enables real-time data generation, asset utilization and maintenance schedules that predict and detect faults to help streamline procurement. Currently most of the industrial manufacturing equipment are equipped with smart sensors to facilitate real-time monitoring, efficient controlling and data optimization. These devices monitor the health of various sub-systems or modules and allow diagnostic operations by triggering prognostic operations based on user defined thresholds. Computing elements consist of the sets of sensor and a communication device. Central processing device collects data from smart sensors and processes them, meanwhile executing various diagnostic and prognostic algorithms. However, such architecture where all or most of the processing components are reliant on a single processor is liable to various problems, the most serious being vulnerability to complete loss of functionality in case of a crash of central processing elements [6]. Furthermore, with the increase in the amount of sensor data and algorithmic complexity traditionally centralized systems become unsuitable for successful operations. In order to avoid these circumstances we attain specific mechanism free from these troubles with respect to our prognostic approach and its versatility of algorithmic implementation (Fig. 3).

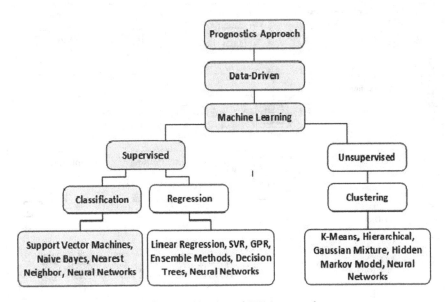

Fig. 3. Classification of PHM approach

3.2   Degraded Incipient Sensor Failure Scenarios

Smart sensor network system shows great promises for constructing powerful industrial internet of things based functions. Communication devices used for networking are characterized by anticipating, deducing, and energizing. Nonetheless, with in these interconnected objects, the detection and confinement of a failure sensor is not an obvious problem, which is our focal point to solve by designing suitable model and perfect algorithm for our system.

Figure 4, addresses the mechanism for detection, confinement and accommodation of a fallen sensor that satisfies the following attributes; capable to distinguished where a failure happened, validate the measurements of a sensor without the use of redundant computing elements, and able to detect and isolate multiple sensors fail at the same time. During the monitoring if the computing elements detects a disturbance it raises a flag alarm, depending on the availability of the resources it either switches to prognostics mode or informs the base station to perform the prognostic task. These computing elements provide the intelligent prognostics which can frequently trail the system health degradation and hypothesize the temporal behavior [7].

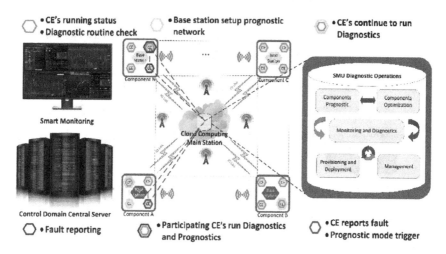

Fig. 4. Self-aware fault detection

4 Machine Learning Maintenance Approach for Condition Monitoring

4.1 Predictive Analytics Using Machine Learning

Condition monitoring can be viewed more precisely along with several aspects. Firstly we can monitor the condition of the different significant components of the spinning frames (e.g. spindles) at the most granular level, the more higher vibrational frequency the more signals provides warning signs. Secondly, monitoring can be performed by having a physical impact on the component through sensor data, and the two main types of monitoring used in our case includes intrusive and non-intrusive monitoring. Intrusive monitoring involves vibrational analysis, while on the other hand in non-intrusive monitoring ultrasonic testing, acoustic emission using power signal analysis plays its roles. Finally, fault detection and fault prediction performs prognostics and diagnostics for required monitoring, where we identifies the fault types and its detail descriptions. e.g., when it happens and where the underlying models find the disturbed patterns through the signal data that predicts future failures. The s models are established based on the machine learning method and fault diagnosis performances of these models, analyzed by PCA for different features set. Supervised learning using classification and regression models conduct online diagnosis and prognosis of each connected manufacturing machines (Fig. 5).

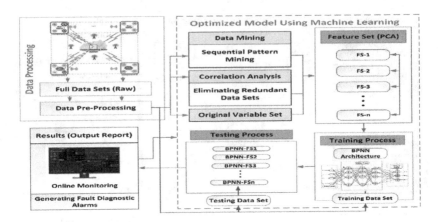

Fig. 5. Machine learning feature engineering

4.2   Case-Study

Condition monitoring algorithm development mainly focuses on classifying normal vs failure patterns and predicting the remaining useful life (RUL). After collecting bundles of raw datasets through IIoT infrastructure, it is pre-processed and irrelevant logical variables are removed, furthermore redundant feature variables were removed using correlation analysis method and sequential pattern mining technique is used to acquire optimal features variables. At last the condition indicators of fault detection model is established using optimal feature variables (Fig. 6).

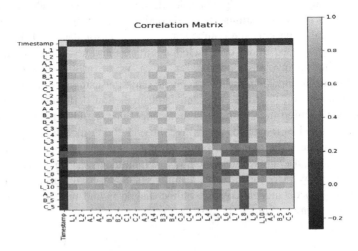

Fig. 6. Correlation analysis matrix

This reconfigurable design system is capable of detecting, diagnosing and recovering possible failures, which may occur during the real-time processing. Batch and online learning are the two implemented ways widely used to train the back-propagation algorithm for feed forward neural networks [8]. While the study shows back propagation method is used to calculate the error contribution of each neuron after a batch of data is processed. Concealing the optimized predictive maintenance algorithm, it is used to adjust the weight of each and every neuron, and completing the learning process for them. Consisting of sets of sensors with links between them, computational model works the same as the biological neural network and similarly to a biological network a neural network learning is based on multiple inputs with the desired output. The performance of the machine learning algorithm depends on multiple sensor nodes deployed in a specific area of spinning frames (Figs. 7 and 8).

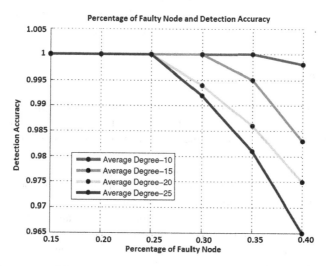

Fig. 7. Percentage of faulty nodes vs detection accuracy for 1008 spindle sensor nodes

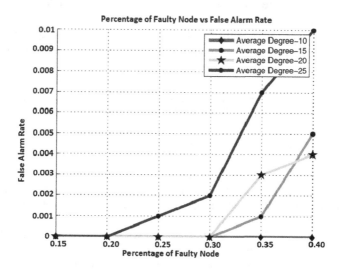

Fig. 8. Percentage of faulty nodes vs false alarm rate for 1008 spindles sensor nodes

A spinning frame consisting of 1008 sensor nodes are randomly deployed using normal distribution in a rectangular terrine of size 100 × 100 respectively for the simulation in our case. The percentages of faulty sensor nodes are introduced here are 0.15, 0.20, 0.25, 0.30, 0.35, and 0.40, respectively. A certain arrangement of the sensors suitable for multiple tasks and the machine to machine interactions classifies the different states of the equipment. Back-propagation neural network considered being supervised learning method which requires a known desired output for each input. The most applications of artificial neural network uses multi-layers perception network and train them with the back-propagation algorithm consisting of three contiguous layers [9], each layer has distinct processing elements. Subject to condition monitoring artificial neural network aims to produce more accurate equipment RUL prediction by using machine learning predictive methods.

5   Conclusions

Modernistic evolution in computational adequacy have opened opportunities for unified condition monitoring analytics, where multi-dimensional data can be used to supplement knowledgeable, predictable, cost-effective and booming decision-making. Monitoring practices, through use of machine learning techniques can inform planning resulting in lean maintenance interruption to spinning industry. This paper presented machine learning driven condition monitoring and mainly focuses on various tasks, including spindle critical rotational components failures.

In our reconfigurable fault diagnostic distributed CPPS framework, fault diagnosis models were established based on the machine learning method for condition monitoring purpose. Analyzed by PCA for different features set, Confining, event detection, and event cognizance are the tasks applied by PCA, well suited for processing datasets containing continuous and categorical variables from the computing network. At the beginning raw data is pre-processed and irrelevant logical variables are removed by applying sequential pattern mining, and redundant data variables are then eliminated using correlation analysis, after that a robust feature selection technique is proposed to extract surplus information to be trained and tested by the back propagation neural network.

Acknowledgement. This research was financially supported by the Fundamental Research Funds for the Central Universities (Grant No. 2232017A-03).

References

1. Nikolic, B., Ignjatic, J., Suzic, N., Stevanov, B., Rikalovic, A.: Predictive manufacturing systems in industry 4.0. Trends, benefits and challenges. In: Annals of DAAAM and Proceedings, vol. 28, 1 January 2017
2. Jeschke, S., Brecher, C., Meisen, T., Özdemir, D., Eschert, T.: Industrial internet of things and cyber manufacturing systems. In: Jeschke, S., Brecher, C., Song, H., Rawat, D.B. (eds.) Industrial Internet of Things. SSWT, pp. 3–19. Springer, Cham (2017). https://doi.org/10.1007/978-3-319-42559-7_1

3. Yan, R., Gao, R.X., Chen, X.: Wavelets for fault diagnosis of rotary machines: a review with applications. Signal Process. **96**, 1–15 (2014)
4. Uhlemann, T.H-J., Lehmann, C., Steinhilper, R.: The digital twin: realizing the cyber-physical production system for industry 4.0. In: Procedia CIRP, vol. 61, pp. 335–340 (2017)
5. Picard, A., Anderl, R.: The integrated component data model for smart production planning. In: Proceedings of the 19th International Seminar on High Technology, pp. 1–6, October 2014
6. Sun, C., Ma, J., Yao, Q.: On the architecture and development life cycle of secure cyber-physical systems. J. Commun. Inf. Netw. **1**(4), 1–21 (2016)
7. Saha, S., et al.: Distributed prognostic health management with gaussian process regression. In: 2010 IEEE Aerospace Conference. IEEE (2010)
8. Karaboga, D., Akay, B., Ozturk, C.: Artificial Bee Colony (ABC) Optimization algorithm for training feed-forward neural networks. In: Torra, V., Narukawa, Y., Yoshida, Y. (eds.) MDAI 2007. LNCS (LNAI), vol. 4617, pp. 318–329. Springer, Heidelberg (2007). https://doi.org/10.1007/978-3-540-73729-2_30
9. Zhang, L., et al.: Automated quality assessment of cardiac MR images using convolutional neural networks. In: Tsaftaris, S., Gooya, A., Frangi, A., Prince, J. (eds.) SASHIMI 2016. LNCS, pp. 138–145. Springer, Cham (2016). https://doi.org/10.1007/978-3-319-46630-9_14

Turbulence Enhancement for SPH Fluids Visualization

Yanrui Xu[1], Xiaojuan Ban[1(✉)], Yan Peng[2], Xiaokun wang[1],
Sinuo Liu[1], and Jing Zhou[1]

[1] School of Computer and Communication Engineering,
University of Science and Technology Beijing, Beijing, China
xuyanruiedw@me.com,{banxj,wangxiaokun}@ustb.edu.cn,
liusinuo@xs.ustb.edu.cn,ZhouJing_Me_CN@hotmail.com
[2] School of Management, Capital Normal University Beijing, Beijing, China
pengyan@cnu.edu.cn

Abstract. In this paper, we present a novel method to restore turbulence details for Smoothed Particle Hydrodynamics (SPH) using the viscosity based vorticity field as a cooperative project of numerical simulation and computer visualization. One of the major issues that hinder the accuracy of the fluid simulation is the numerical dissipation, which comes along with the discretization of space and time. Therefore unrealistic results are unavoidable. To recover kinetic energy from the numerical dissipation, we propose a vorticity refinement solver for SPH fluids without extra restriction to the time step. In our method, the vorticity field of the fluid is enhanced proportional to the loss of energy due to the viscosity force. This means our method not only can increase existing vortices but also creating additional turbulence. Compared with Biot-Savart integrals, our method is more efficient by applying stream function to recover the velocity field from the vorticity field.

Keywords: Computer graphics · Cooperative visualization ·
Smoothed Particle Hydrodynamics · Turbulence

1 Introduction

Maintaining turbulence details within reasonable computation costs is an object that has been chased for decades in every fluid simulation approach. SPH approach, a representative Lagrangian approach, is capable of simulating incompressible fluid accurately and efficiently, presenting rich details and vivid motions. Though many researches dedicated to reach the incompressible state for fluid simulation have been proposed, the numerical dissipation still remains to be resolved.

Generally, there are two types of vortex models: irrotational vortex models as well as rigid body vortex models. The rigid body vortex is the vortex that rotates likes a rigid body does, making its vorticity be twice the angular velocity

© Springer Nature Switzerland AG 2019
Y. Luo (Ed.): CDVE 2019, LNCS 11792, pp. 254–260, 2019.
https://doi.org/10.1007/978-3-030-30949-7_29

everywhere. The irrotational vortex, however, is the vortex which is vorticity-free except for the center. The velocity of irrotational vortex is inversely proportional to the distance to the center. In traditional SPH approaches, the self-rotation of the fluid particle is neglected during simulation, therefore the rotational kinetic energy of the particle is dissipated. Moreover, the dissipation gets more significant as the discretization of space is coarser. Viscosity plays an important role in the rotation of particles. However, only a few researches focused on this particular type of numerical dissipation.

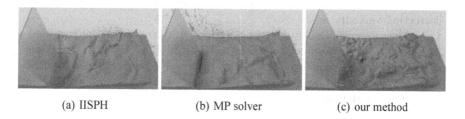

(a) IISPH   (b) MP solver   (c) our method

Fig. 1. Breaking dam collides with a board using 1.82M particles. Here we observe that only one big vortex is formed using IISPH. MP solver enhances the simulation result to some extend. Our method improves the turbulence details greatly and the surface details are richer than MP solver.

2   Related Work

2.1   Preserve Numerical Accuracy in SPH Method

Monaghan [1] first addressed the simulation of free surface flows with SPH methods and laid the foundation for the SPH fluid simulation. Bender and Koschier managed to guarantee both zero compression and divergence-free for the velocity field. We use IISPH approach as the basic algorithm for our experiments. High frequency details are likely to be smoothed out because of the numerical dissipation as Ihmsen et al. [2] pointed out. It is especially apparent when using coarse discretization [1,3,4]. So methods restoring these details are required to be developed in fluid simulation.

2.2   Restoring Turbulence in Fluid Simulation

Since high-frequency details like turbulence are very important, methods specifically for restoring turbulence details are needed. These methods can be classified into vorticity confinement methods and Lagrangian vortex methods [4].

The vorticity confinement (VC) method was first introduced by Fedkiw et al. [5]. Macklin and Muller [6] then applied it in SPH. Lentine et al. [7] improved the vorticity confinement method and successfully made it to be both energy and momentum conserving. Jang et al. [8] introduced the multilevel vorticity confinement scheme to obtain a better result.

The Lagrangian vortex method can be applied to many areas. In 2010, Weißmann [9] used it to smoke simulation. In 2014, he [10] proposed a filaments computation method to represent the vortex. Eberhardt [11] then improved this method. Zhu et al. [12] tried to simulate vortex details around moving objects. Golas et al. [13] also handled boundaries with Eulerian grid. And Zhang et al. [14] extended this work for smoke simulation using the advection-projection scheme. Bender [4] proposed micropolar fluid model which is applicable with inviscid fluid. Zhang et al. [14] introduced IVOCK method to prevent energy dissipation by correcting vorticity loss.

Our scheme is inspired by Zhang's method [14] and could be regarded as a Lagrangian vortex method. Further, neither the Biot-Savart integral nor a vector valued Poisson equation is required to be solved in our scheme. Instead, we recover velocity field from vorticity field using stream function, which greatly improves the simulation efficiency.

3   Numerical Calculations in Existing SPH Methods

Traditional Lagrangian fluid simulation methods use Navier-Stokes equations to describe the motion of the fluid which is represented by particles. The acceleration of particles is obtained by the combination of gravity, viscous force and pressure:

$$\mathbf{a} = \mathbf{a}_{pro} + \mathbf{a}_{vis} + \mathbf{a}_g = -\frac{1}{\rho}\nabla p + \nu\nabla^2\mathbf{v} + \mathbf{g} \tag{1}$$

where ρ indicates the density of the fluid, p is the pressure, ν is the kinematic viscosity, v denotes the velocity and $\mathbf{g}$ is the gravity. ∇^2 represents the Laplace operator. The viscosity term in the equation could be artificially discretized as:

$$\nabla^2\mathbf{v} = 2(d+2)\sum_j \frac{m_j}{\rho_i} \frac{\mathbf{v}_{ij}\cdot\mathbf{x}_{ij}}{|\mathbf{v}_{ij}{}^2| + 0.01h^2}\nabla W_{ij} \tag{2}$$

where $\mathbf{x}_{ij} = \mathbf{x}_i - \mathbf{x}_j$ is the distance between two particles i and j, d is the dimension. Artificial viscosity is used to avoid the instability from the original calculation.

4   Viscosity Based Vorticity Refinement

Our method restores velocity field through vorticity. Meanwhile, we also managed to avoid solving the Poisson equation through applying viscosity to refine the velocity directly.

4.1   Vorticity Adjustment in SPH System

In this method we grant vorticity for every particle as a three dimensional vector attribute. It is expressed as the rotation of the velocity field:

$$\omega = \nabla \times \mathbf{v} \tag{3}$$

The vorticity is used to describe the potential of rotation of at a specific position. In SPH, it can also be derived within the system:

$$\omega_i = \nabla \times \mathbf{v_i} = -\frac{1}{\rho_i} \sum_j m_j (\mathbf{v_i} - \mathbf{v_j}) \times \nabla_i W_{ij} \tag{4}$$

where W_{ij} is the smoothed kernel. We apply cubic spline kernel in this paper. m is the mass for each particle.

The vorticity alters and affects the trace of the particle as the velocity of a particle changes. During the movement of a fluid particle, it is affected by forces from its neighboring particles, which results in a change in velocity. It can be summarized into two cases, as is shown in Fig. 2.

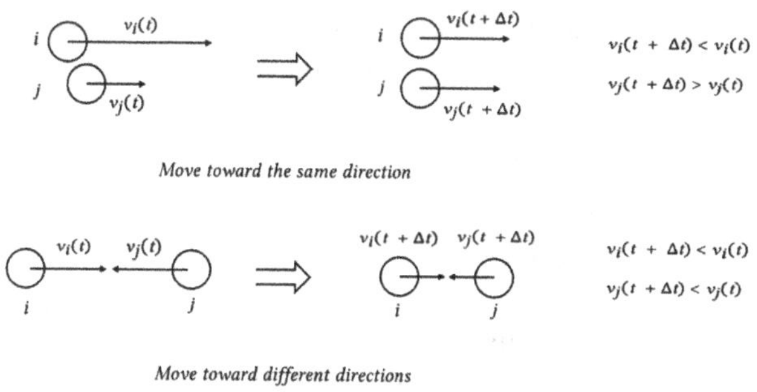

Move toward the same direction

Move toward different directions

Fig. 2. Two kinds of energy conversion: 1. Movement in the same direction: the velocity of one particle is increased, that of the other one is reduced. 2. Relative motion: Both particles' velocity is reduced.

The energy increment and the energy change rate caused by the viscosity can be expressed as:

$$R = \frac{\delta \widetilde{E}(t + \Delta t)}{E(t)} = \frac{\frac{1}{2} m \mathbf{v}_{vis}^2 (t+\Delta t) - \frac{1}{2} m \mathbf{v}^2 (t)}{\frac{1}{2} m \mathbf{v}^2 (t)} = \frac{\mathbf{v}_{vis}^2 (t + \Delta t) - \mathbf{v}^2 (t)}{\mathbf{v}^2 (t)} \tag{5}$$

where $\mathbf{v}_{vis}(t + \Delta t) = \mathbf{v}(t) + \Delta t \cdot \nu \nabla^2 \mathbf{v}(t)$ is the velocity that is only affected by the viscous force. This equation is only calculated when the particle's velocity increases, that is $\mathbf{v}_{vis}(t + \Delta t) > \mathbf{v}(t)$. The vorticity increment is represented by the following function:

$$\delta \omega = \omega \cdot \sqrt{R} \alpha \tag{6}$$

$\delta\omega$ indicates the correction of vorticity, α is the parameter to adjust the degree of vortex appearance in the system, which could be set between 0 and 1. The turbulence being recovered is rougher as α is larger.

4.2   Recover Volecity Field Using Stream Function

In the fluid simulation, the change of vorticity field affects both the magnitude and the direction of the linear velocity field. To derive the refinement of the velocity field $\delta\mathbf{v}$ from $\delta\omega$ recovered from the previous step, we use stream function to express the relationship between the linear velocity $\mathbf{v}$ and the vorticity ω:

$$\mathbf{v} = \nabla \times \psi \quad and \quad \nabla^2\psi = -\omega \tag{7}$$

Now a bridge between vorticity field and velocity field has been successfully built. By using the Helmholtz decomposition we can get:

$$\psi = \frac{1}{4\pi} \sum_j \frac{\delta\omega_j v_j}{\|\mathbf{x}_i - \mathbf{x}_j\|} \tag{8}$$

By summing up the linear velocity correction δv and the velocity $\tilde{\mathbf{v}}$ affected by the viscous force, we can obtain the refined velocity $\hat{v}$:

$$\hat{\mathbf{v}}(t + \Delta t) = \tilde{\mathbf{v}}(t + \Delta t) + \delta\mathbf{v} \tag{9}$$

5   Experiments and Discussions

We examined our vortex refinement (VR) method using several scenes and compared it with the classical IISPH approach and the micropolar (MP) solver. Both our VR solver and the MP solver were integrated with IISPH. The density error was enforced to less than 0.1%.

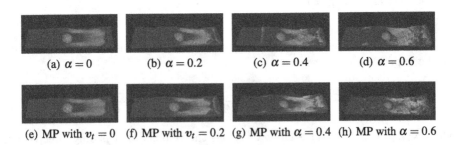

(a) $\alpha = 0$ (b) $\alpha = 0.2$ (c) $\alpha = 0.4$ (d) $\alpha = 0.6$

(e) MP with $v_t = 0$ (f) MP with $v_t = 0.2$ (g) MP with $\alpha = 0.4$ (h) MP with $\alpha = 0.6$

Fig. 3. 3D break-dam experiment using VR solver and MP solver with different control parameters. First row: VR solver. Second row: MP solver. In (h), unreasonable turbulence appears, which means the numerical calculation using MP solver with $v_t = 0.6$ is not stable enough.

To exhibit the numerical effectiveness of our approach, a dam breaking simulation is carried out. Figure 3 shows the scenario simulated with 1.072M particles using IISPH (when $\alpha = 0$ or $v_t = 0$) and our VR solver as well as the MP solver. We can see that the traditional IISPH approach is not able to exhibit turbulent effects. However both our method and the MP solver are quite effective. Compared with the MP solver, our method can still remain stable when $\alpha = 0.6$, but the numerical instability issue begins to appear in the MP solver when $v_t = 0.6$.

In order to demonstrate the stability and the effectiveness of our solver, we carried out a complex scenario shown in Fig. 4. A spinning propeller is put into the water. We find that no turbulence effect is produced or preserved using IISPH and the MP solver. On the contrary, our method adds energy in a physically reasonable way and creates vivid turbulent details on the surface. Further, the highly turbulent motion is stable in this scene, which proves the good stability of our solver.

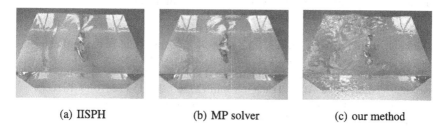

| (a) IISPH | (b) MP solver | (c) our method |

Fig. 4. A propeller interacts with 1.59M fluid particles using IISPH, MP solver, our method.

6   Conclusion

We proposed an SPH based turbulence refinement method that applies vorticity energy dissipation to restore the velocity field. Our method can reduce numerical dissipation significantly. By setting parameter with flexibility, the violence of turbulence could be altered easily. In our experiments, we exhibit that the proposed method could greatly enhance the turbulent effects. As a cooperative application, the numerical model greatly enhances both the fidelity and efficiency of the computer animation.

Acknowledgments. The authors acknowledge the financial support from the National Key Research and Development Program of China (No. 2016YFB0700500), and the National Science Foundation of China (No. 61873299, No. 61702036, No. 61572075), and Key Research Plan of Hainan Province (No. ZDYF2018139).

References

1. Monaghan, J.J.: Simulating free surface flows with sph. J. Comput. Phys. **110**(2), 399–406 (1994)
2. Ihmsen, M., Orthmann, J., Solenthaler, B., Kolb, A., Teschner, M.: SPH fluids in computer graphics
3. de Goes, F., Wallez, C., Huang, J., Pavlov, D., Desbrun, M.: Power particles: an incompressible fluid solver based on power diagrams. ACM Trans. Graph. **34**(4), 50:1–51:11 (2015)
4. Bender, J., Koschier, D., Kugelstadt, T., Weiler, M.: Turbulent micropolar SPH fluids with foam. IEEE Trans. Vis. Comput. Graph. **25**, 2284–2295 (2018)
5. Fedkiw, R., Stam, J., Jensen, H.W.: Visual simulation of smoke. In: Proceedings of the 28th Annual Conference on Computer Graphics and Interactive Techniques, pp. 15–22. ACM (2001)
6. Macklin, M., Müller, M.: Position based fluids. ACM Trans. Graph. (TOG) **32**(4), 104 (2013)
7. Lentine, M., Aanjaneya, M., Fedkiw, R.: Mass and momentum conservation for fluid simulation. In: Proceedings of the 2011 ACM SIGGRAPH/Eurographics Symposium on Computer Animation, pp. 91–100. ACM (2011)
8. Jang, T., Kim, H., Bae, J., Seo, J., Noh, J.: Multilevel vorticity confinement for water turbulence simulation. Vis. Comput. **26**(6–8), 873–881 (2010)
9. Weißmann, S., Pinkall, U.: Filament-based smoke with vortex shedding and variational reconnection. ACM Trans. Graph. (TOG) **29**, 115 (2010). Citeseer
10. Weißmann, S., Pinkall, U., Schröder, P.: Smoke rings from smoke. ACM Trans. Graph. (TOG) **33**(4), 140 (2014)
11. Pinkall, U., Thuerey, N., Eberhardt, S., Weissmann, S.: Hierarchical vorticity skeletons. In: Proceedings of the ACM SIGGRAPH/Eurographics Symposium on Computer Animation, - SCA, pp. 1–11 (2017)
12. Zhu, B., Yang, X., Fan, Y.: Creating and preserving vortical details in SPH fluid. In: Computer Graphics Forum, vol. 29, pp. 2207–2214. Wiley Online Library (2010)
13. Golas, A., Narain, R., Sewall, J., Krajcevski, P., Dubey, P., Lin, M.: Large-scale fluid simulation using velocity-vorticity domain decomposition. ACM Trans. Graph. (TOG) **31**(6), 148 (2012)
14. Zhang, X., Bridson, R., Greif, C.: Restoring the missing vorticity in advection-projection fluid solvers. ACM Trans. Graph. (TOG) **34**(4), 52 (2015)

Residual Feature Pyramid Architecture for Monocular Depth Estimation

Chunxiu Shi, Jie Chen, and Juan Chen[(⊠)]

College of Information Science and Technology,
Beijing University of Chemical Technology, Beijing 100029, China
jchen@mail.buct.edu.cn

Abstract. This paper investigates Visualization of Image Depth Information architecture of fully convolutional residual networks, based on it, residual feature pyramid network architecture for monocular image depth estimation is proposed. Firstly, the input monocular RGB image is preprocessed. Secondly, the feature pyramid structures are introduced into the fully convolutional residual networks, which realizes multi-scale feature extraction and reused, at the same time, both the number of parameters in networks and the computational complexity are greatly reduced. Finally, Experiments are done on the commonly used NYU official dataset. Experimental results show that the proposed method has advantages over many recent advanced methods. And the object outlines in our inferred depth maps are clearer and exquisite which look qualitatively better. In addition, this paper uses a simpler networks structure to realize a lower system error.

Keywords: Monocular image depth estimation · Residual feature pyramid · CNN architecture

1 Introduction

According to the number of cameras used in scene depth estimation, the visual methods are mainly divided into monocular, binocular and multi-objective [1]. Owing to fewer camera parameters are required, the depth estimation method of monocular image application is more convenient and widespread [2]. However, it is difficult for visual models to capture enough features from monocular images to infer the 3D structure of the scene. So extracting the depth information of the scene from monocular views is not easy in most cases. Therefore, the ability to estimate depth from monocular images is not only a challenging task but also a necessary technology without a direct depth sensor.

At present, Convolutional Neural Networks (CNN) is widely used in the fields of visual recognition [3], image segmentation [4], and human posture estimation [5]. In addition, it also has applications in depth estimation. In 2014, Eigen et al. [6] first proposed a depth estimation algorithm using CNN, which indicates that the Neural Network also has good performance in monocular image depth estimation. After that, a number of CNN algorithms for depth estimation are emerged, which are effectively studied by input image preprocessing, deepening network layers, changing network structures, adding multi-scale information and so on.

© Springer Nature Switzerland AG 2019
Y. Luo (Ed.): CDVE 2019, LNCS 11792, pp. 261–266, 2019.
https://doi.org/10.1007/978-3-030-30949-7_30

This paper aims to reuse low-level features on the basis of reducing the number of network layers and to obtain high-quality prediction maps by adding detailed description information. Furthermore, on the premise of maintaining or surpassing the most advanced image depth estimation algorithm, a network structure with fewer parameters, stronger real-time performance and simple structure is realized. Eventually, the effectiveness of this method is verified by testing on NYU official dataset.

2   Related Work

The common network structures in CNN include AlexNet, VGGNet, and ResNet, etc. In 2014, Eigen et al. [6] of New York University first proposed using CNN to estimate single image depth. Liu et al. [7] divide the original image into superpixels and then use Conditional Random Field (CRF) and CNN to estimate image depth [8, 9].

In recent years, the Full Convolutional Residual Network (FCRN) proposed by Laina et al. [10] in 2016 solves depth estimation as a regression problem and achieves a leading level. First, FCRN uses ResNet-50 network as feature classifier and replaces the fully connected and classification layer in ResNet with convolution layer to form full convolution networks. Then, FCRN proposed a new and more efficient up-convolution method: the feature map of the output of coding networks is directly processed through four convolution cores of different sizes ((A) 3*3, (B) 3*2, (C) 2*3 and (D) 2*2). Although their work has made breakthroughs in this field, after careful observation and analysis, the detailed information of the object in the prediction map output by FCRN is lost more, and the prediction of part of object structure outlines is imprecise.

3   Residual Feature Pyramid Networks (RFPN) for Image Depth Estimation

We proposed here an RFPN structure inspired by the structure of the depth estimation network proposed in [10] and FPN used in object detection in [11]. This paper uses ResNet, which can keep the accuracy rate unchanged while the gradient will not disappear in the deeper case. However, with the development of ResNet, the resolution of the original image decreases and detailed features of the image may be ignored. Therefore, this paper uses feature pyramid structure to involve multi-scale information, so that low-level features can be reused repeatedly. Compared with top-level features, it adds detailed feature information. Finally, under the condition of ensuring high prediction accuracy, it reduces the error of the prediction process and outputs better quality depth maps.

3.1   Feature Pyramid Networks (FPN)

Tsung-Yi Lin et al. proposed an effective and simple feature pyramid framework in [11]. This method takes a single scale image of arbitrary size as input, and outputs scaled feature maps on multiple levels by complete convolution. In the pyramid construction of Fig. 2, the bottom-top paths are used to calculate a feature hierarchy consisting of multi-scale feature maps. And the top-down paths are sampled up to improve the resolution of features. These features are finally enhanced by horizontal connection. This architecture is popular in recent research. This process is independent of the trunk convolution architecture and has been applied in multi-scale target detection based on deep learning. These advances will benefit further research in the field of monocular image processing in the future. In this paper, we propose to use it in FCRN [10].

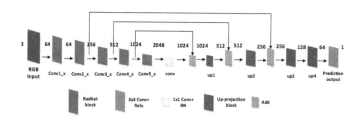

Fig. 1. Proposed networks structure.

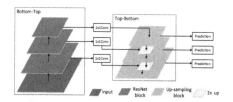

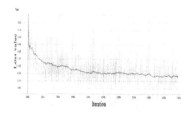

Fig. 2. Feature pyramid structure.   **Fig. 3.** The change process of loss

3.2 Residual Feature Pyramid Networks (RFPN)

It is found that the output characteristics of conv1_x, conv2_x, conv3_x and conv4_x in ResNet are only used once, so some details are ignored in the final prediction. In order to enhance the detailed features and reuse the extracted features, inspired by the structure proposed in [11], an RFPN based on small-scale datasets is proposed in this paper, which is shown in Fig. 1. The output features of ResNet block and the output of the up-sampling block are added according to the dimension values. The whole structure is divided into three parts: down-sampling, up-sampling and feature pyramid. First, the subsampling part is constructed by ResNet-50 to extract the feature of the input RGB images. Then, the feature pyramids are used to fuse the output features of each structure block of ResNet. At last, the original input resolution is restored after the up-sampling, thus the depth estimation of the monocular image is completed.

Because of the advantages and disadvantages of $\mathcal{L}_2$ and $\mathcal{L}_1$ loss functions, BerHu (reverse Huber) will be used as loss function [10, 12]. After testing, BerHu loss function can achieve better results than using $\mathcal{L}_2$ or $\mathcal{L}_1$ loss function alone. So, we use this loss function in our paper.

4   Experiments

4.1   Network Training

Experiments in this paper are all carried out on NYU Depth V2 (NYUD2) dataset [13]. In network training, pre-trained model of ResNet is loaded first, and the up-sampling components in the network are initialized at the same time. Secondly, the batch size is set to 8, and epochs are 50. The original learning rate is 1e-5 and reduced by 0.6 per 8–10 epochs. At the same time, BerHu loss function is used and Adam function is used for global optimization. The change of loss value during training is shown in Fig. 3.

4.2   Qualitative Evaluation and Quantitative Evaluation

Comparing with the advanced depth prediction methods [14, 15], we found that the detail features in the output image of each method are not as obvious as those in [10] (see the articles for details). Therefore, the forecasting graph obtained by the proposed RFPN method is compared with that in FCRN. The same RGB image is transmitted to FCRN, and the predicted results are shown in Fig. 4.

| RGB Image | Ground Truth | RFPN(ours) | FCRN |

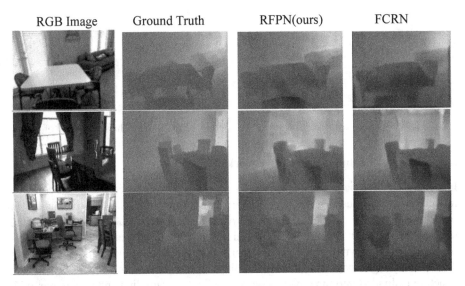

Fig. 4.   Comparison of experimental results

It can be clearly found that the introduction of feature pyramid structure makes the final output prediction image more detailed, feature information can be better reflected, and the image content is richer and more consistent with ground-truth information.

In this paper, the performance evaluation indicators of the proposed RFPN are as follows:

$$(a)\; \text{rel} = \frac{1}{N}\sum_{i=1}^{N}\frac{|D_i - D_i^*|}{D_i^*} \qquad (b)\; \text{rms} = \sqrt{\frac{1}{N}\sum_{i=1}^{N}(D_i - D_i^*)^2}$$

$$(c)\; \text{rms(log)} = \sqrt{\frac{1}{N}\sum_{i=1}^{N}(lgD_i - lgD_i^*)^2} \qquad (d)\; \%\, \text{correct} = \max\left(\frac{D_i}{D_i^*}, \frac{D_i^*}{D_i}\right) = \delta < T$$

Among them, D_i denotes the estimated depth of the first pixel in the image, D_i^* denotes the corresponding true value, N denotes the total number of pixels, and threshold precision denotes the maximum relative error of the estimated depth in the number of pixels within the specified threshold. T is the threshold, set to 1.25, 1.25^2, 1.25^3.

As can be seen from Table 1, the results are basically similar to those of other advanced methods. Compared with FCRN, the decrease of $\delta < 1.25$ is only 0.001–0.002. However, it is precise because of the introduction of the feature pyramid structure that the detailed information in the prediction graph is enhanced, and the low-level features are better reflected so that the rms and rms(log) both achieve the best results at present. Compared with Laina et al. [10], rms is reduced by 11.34% and rms (log) is reduced by 5.64%, moreover, relative error rel ranks second.

Table 1. Comparing with state-of-art results on the NYUD2 dataset. The quoted values are derived from the data reported by the authors in their respective papers.

NYU Depth v2	Error (lower is better)			Accuracy (higher is better)		
	rel	rms	rms (log)	$\delta < 1.25$	$\delta < 1.25^2$	$\delta < 1.25^3$
Eigen et al. [6]	0.215	0.907	0.285	0.611	0.887	0.971
Eigen and Fergus [15]	0.158	0.641	0.214	0.769	0.950	0.988
Laina et al. [10]	**0.127**	0.573	0.195	**0.811**	0.953	0.988
M. Moukari et al. [14]	0.159	0.592	–	0.793	**0.954**	0.989
RFPN (**Ours**)	0.142	**0.508**	**0.184**	0.809	**0.954**	**0.989**

5   Conclusions

In this paper, an RFPN is proposed for the loss of some detailed features in the depth estimation of monocular images. The experimental results show that the detailed information of the proposed RFPN structure is more abundant and the object features are clearer. In the future, we will further adjust the network model to improve image depth prediction accuracy. Secondly, we plan to expand the dataset for training, not only the official NYU data set, so as to improve the generalization ability of RFPN. In addition, we plan to apply the depth information extraction algorithm of images to the three-dimensional reconstruction of indoor robot environment, and realize modeling through visualize programmed.

References

1. Michels, J., Saxena, A., Ng, A.Y.: High-speed obstacle avoidance using monocular vision and reinforcement learning. In: Proceedings of the Twenty-First International Conference on Machine Learning, ICML, pp. 593–600. ACM, Bonn (2005)
2. Wu, B., He, Z.J., He, T.L.: Perceiving distance accurately by a directional process of integrating ground information. Nature **428**, 73–77 (2004)
3. He, K., Zhang, X., Ren, S.: Spatial pyramid pooling in deep convolutional networks for visual recognition. In: IEEE Transactions on Pattern Analysis and Machine Intelligence, vol. 37, pp. 1904–1916. IEEE (2015)
4. Chen, L.C., Papandreou, G., Kokkinos, I.: Semantic image segmentation with deep convolutional nets and fully connected CRFs. In: Computer Science, pp. 357–361 (2014)
5. Jonathan, T., Arjun, J., Yann, L.C.: Joint training of a convolutional network and a graphical model for human pose estimation. In: NIPS 2014 Proceedings of the 27th International Conference on Neural Information Processing Systems, vol.1, pp. 1799–1807 (2014)
6. Eigen, D., Pusch, C., Fergus, R.: Depth map prediction from a single image using a multi-scale deep network. In: Proceedings of the 27th International Conference on Neural Information Processing Systems, NIPS, vol. 2, pp. 2366–2374 (2014)
7. Liu, F., Shen, C., Lin, G.: Deep convolutional neural fields for depth estimation from a single image. In: 2015 IEEE Conference on Computer Vision and Pattern Recognition, CVPR. IEEE, Boston (2015)
8. Li, B., Shen, C.H., Dai, Y.C., Hengel, A.V.D., He, M.: Depth and surface normal estimation from monocular images using regression on deep features and hierarchical CRFs. In: Proceedings of the IEEE Conference on Computer Vision and Pattern Recognition, CVPR, pp. 1119–1127. IEEE, Boston (2015)
9. Wang, P., Shen, X., Lin, Z., Cohen, S., Price, B., Yuille, A.L.: Towards unified depth and semantic prediction from a single image. In: Proceedings of the IEEE Conference on Computer Vision and Pattern Recognition, CVPR, pp. 2800–2809. IEEE, Boston (2015)
10. Laina, I., Rupprecht, C., Belagiannis, V., Tombari, F., Navab, N.: Deeper depth prediction with fully convolutional residual networks. In: 2016 Fourth International Conference on 3D Vision, 3DV, pp. 239–248. IEEE, Stanford (2016)
11. Lin, T.Y., Dollar, P., Girshick, R., He, K.M., Hariharan, B., Belongie, S.: Feature pyramid networks for object detection. In: The IEEE Conference on Computer Vision and Pattern Recognition, CVPR, pp. 936–944. IEEE, Honolulu (2017)
12. Roy, A., Todorovic, S.: Monocular depth estimation using neural regression forest. In: Proceedings of the IEEE Conference on Computer Vision and Pattern Recognition, CVPR, pp. 5506–5514. IEEE, Las Vegas (2016)
13. Silberman, N., Hoiem, D., Kohli, P., Fergus, R.: Indoor segmentation and support inference from RGBD images. In: Fitzgibbon, A., Lazebnik, S., Perona, P., Sato, Y., Schmid, C. (eds.) ECCV 2012. LNCS, vol. 7576, pp. 746–760. Springer, Heidelberg (2012). https://doi.org/10.1007/978-3-642-33715-4_54
14. Moukari M., Picard S., Simon L., Jurie F.: Deep multi-scale architectures for monocular depth estimation. In: The IEEE Conference on International Conference on Image Processing, pp. 1884–2019. IEEE, Athens (2018)
15. Eigen, D., Fergus, R.: Predicting depth, surface normals and semantic labels with a common multi-scale convolutional architecture. In: 2015 IEEE International Conference on Computer Vision, ICCV, pp. 2650–2658. Santiago, Chile (2015)

FindImplant: An Online Application for Visualizing the Dental Implants from X-Ray Images

Julio Cesar Huanca Marin$^{(\boxtimes)}$ (iD) and Yalmar Ponce Atencio$^{(\boxtimes)}$ (iD)

Universidad Nacional José María Arguedas, Andahuaylas-Apurímac, Peru
{juliohuanca,yalmar}@unajma.edu.pe

Abstract. Web applications are very popular today and many fields of knowledge have been benefited, however, still there are many study fields which there are not helpful tools. In this research, we propose the implementation of a collaborating tool for identifying dental implants in X-Ray images, due the identification of dental implant images is a tedious intensive manual task. Our proposal is based on computer vision techniques such as features detection, description and matching. The query image can be obtained from X-Ray image data using an ordinary camera, like the ones found on a mobile phone. Then we extract features on the image in order to aid in the search for the best matches in the catalogue. The digital catalogue has a few hundred images of dental implants, and finding the best match takes a few seconds. The application has a high success rate and is helpful for dentists, returning the three best candidates, therefore reducing the work of a Dentist from analyzing hundreds of image to just a few.

Keywords: Dental implant X-Ray · Shape matching ·
Image descriptor · Pattern recognition ·
Medial axis of polygonal shape · Collaborative web application

1 Introduction

Over the last decades, image processing and computer vision researches have become popular tools for many applications, such as Image representation [19], image classification and retrieval [7], recognition and matching of objects [11], and many others. All the works mentioned before take advantage over the presence of stable and representative features in the image. Thus, detecting and extracting the image features are fundamental steps for achieve good results. In order to find similarities between two images is necessary to identify a set of "Points of Interest" (PoI) in each image [3]. Usually, in a first classification task, feature descriptors on a query image are compared with the features in images of a Data Set, and the image that gives maximum correspondence is considered the best match. In that case, feature descriptor matching can be

© Springer Nature Switzerland AG 2019
Y. Luo (Ed.): CDVE 2019, LNCS 11792, pp. 267–276, 2019.
https://doi.org/10.1007/978-3-030-30949-7_31

based on distance measures such as Euclidean or Mahalanobis norm. In the context of matching and recognition, the first step is identify and describe PoIs on the images. Once the descriptors are computed, they are compared to find a relationship between images, thus the keypoints are covariant to a class of transformations. Later, for each detected regions, an invariant feature vector representation (i.e., descriptor) for image data around the detected key point is built. Feature descriptors extracted from the image can be based on second-order statistics, parametric models, coefficients obtained from an image transform or a combination of them. Two kind of image features can be extracted from an image namely global features and local features. Global features (e.g., color and texture) aim to describe an image as a whole and can be interpreted as a particular property of the image involving all pixels. While, local features aim to detect key points or interest regions in an image and describe them. In this context, if the local feature algorithm detects n key points in the image, there are n vectors describing shape, color, orientation, texture, etc. The use of global colour and texture features are proven surprisingly successful for finding similar images in a database. While the local structure oriented features are considered adequate for object classification or finding other occurrences of the same object or scene [20]. Meanwhile, the global features can not distinguish foreground from background of an image, and mix information from both parts together [17].

While in the literature, a large variety of feature extraction methods have been proposed to compute reliable descriptors. Some of these feature descriptors were exclusively designed for specific applications such as shape matching [18]. Among these descriptors, the scale invariant feature transform (SIFT) descriptor [9] and the Speeded-up Robust Features (SURF) descriptor [1] (which is partly inspired in SIFT) are the most popular and widely used in most of applications.

Although, in some applications, included our case, only with using these descriptors is not possible to get good results, due to the nature of the query image, which could be of different size, different resolution, or even of different definition. Depending on what we want match or detect, we still must use additional techniques (shape matching [5,6]) in order to achieve acceptable results.

2   The Problem

We will begin explaining about the problem and what we want to do. In this section, we introduce, in detail, our problem and what the target to solve. Dentists usually have several patients with dental implants, and some of them have their dental implants broken or worn and need to change. However, there is no direct way for knowing which implant they have, because the patient might have been treated by other dentists. The only way to determine which implant is, is taking a maxillofacial X-Ray image (Fig. 1) and cut the portion that encloses the implant (Fig. 1) for analyzing it. There are many kind of dental implants, and still with a X-Ray image will be difficult to recognize which implant is, even for an experimented dentist. Therefore, do it manually if difficult and tedious.

Initially, we thought that applying an image feature descriptor (such as SURF) would be enough, however descriptors does not work very well in images

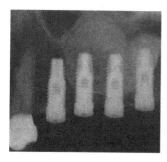

Fig. 1. A maxillofacial X-Ray (left). The Dentist seeing the maxillofacial X-Ray at a highly illuminated surface (middle). Taking a portion of the X-Ray with a cellphone camera (right).

with different global features. This is our case, where the X-Ray image have a noise background with poor definition, while the dental implant image (in the data set) is clean and have a good definition. In the next section we present some elements which were used in order to achieve the expected results.

2.1 Image Descriptors

Currently, a good approach in order to recognize some object in an more large image(scene) is by using descriptors. Descriptors has advantages and disadvantages for specific situations, and we has been tested some of them.

- **Invariant Feature Transform - SIFT.** This method extracts distinctive invariant features from images that can be used to perform reliable matching between different views of an object or scene. The features are invariant to image scale and rotation, and are shown to provide robust matching across a substantial range of affine distortion, even if there are changes in 3D viewpoint, or there is noise, and even if there is changes in illumination [9].
- **Speed-Up Robust Features - SURF.** This algorithm has been proposed by Herbert [1], which is based on SIFT [8]. SURF only works with gray-scale images, locating "Points of Interest" (PoIs) and generating Eigen-Vectors. Similar to SIFT, the PoIs remain even if the orientation of the image changes.
- **Maximally Stable External Regions - MSER.** Methodology proposed by Matas et.al. [10]. This is a robust method detecting and supporting perspective changes. Their algorithm locates extreme PoIs in the image, searching to identify connected regions from the brightness intensity. Thus, this detects edge regions with a large intensity variation.
- **Features from Accelerated Segment Test - FAST.** Is an edge detection method proposed for find PoIs in images [13]. This have not information about descriptors orientation and is highly sensitive to noise. In order to overcome their drawbacks, it uses a machine learning technique by creating a decision tree.

- **Oriented FAST and Rotated BRIEF - ORB.** This algorithm was brought up by Rublee [16]. In their paper "ORB: An efficient alternative to SIFT or SURF", as the title suggest, they present a good alternative to SIFT and SURF in computation cost, matching performance and mainly avoid problems with patents. Since, SIFT and SURF are patented and you are supposed to pay if you want to use in a commercial application.
- **Fast Library for Approximate Nearest Neighbors - FLANN.** This is a library that contains a collection of algorithms optimized for fast nearest neighbor search in large datasets and for high dimensional features [12].

Dental Implants Data Set

Although we have not used a standard data set of dental implant images (like FERET [14] for face images), we have built our own catalogue with a reasonable number of images. The Fig. 7a shows the elaborated catalogue. This catalogue have around a hundred of dental implants images, and it allows to add more dental implants. However, the images must have white background and no shadow effects.

3   Our Solution

3.1   Matching Process

Since an image consists of various information like: size, colors, definition, resolution, etc., typically, descriptors are used for searching patterns on images. In our context, specifically, is more difficult to treat, due to that X-Ray image is expected to be taken from a cell-phone camera (although it is possible to use any image file, the advantage of our proposed system is just when it is used from any mobile device with camera). Thus, using the cell-phone's camera, we can to take a picture trying to encloses only the dental implant, as illustrated at Fig. 1.

Once we have a dental implant image to query, we want find it on the dental implant images data set. This process could be made by using some algorithms to match patterns by comparing two images. This could be implemented in several ways, even using different programming languages and in different platforms. We have chosen the OpenCV library [2]. OpenCV has many examples that show how to use their implemented techniques for matching patterns in images. For implementing our matching application we, initially, have used the SURF, FLANN and ORB methods, but due to the different X-Ray image features the obtained results were not as expected. As mentioned in the above section, due to very different features in X-Ray image, the known match descriptors have not been designed to treat this kind of situations.

The Fig. 2 shows the SURF descriptor works fine if the query image have similar global features than the image on the data set. Similarly, in the Fig. 2.a-b, a rotated image is queried and the SURF descriptor matches good too.

However, querying a X-Ray image, taken from a device camera, the SURF descriptor doesn't matches (see Fig. 2.c-e). Although the queried X-Ray image, in

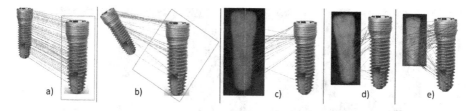

Fig. 2. The SURF descriptor searches for the correspondence of one image in another. If used, the same image but with different sizes matches correctly (a), even if the image has a different orientation matches correctly (b). However, when the image where you want to search does not have the same resolution, it can not find a match (c), even worse if the image has a rotation (d) or if the image is of different size (e).

this case, was very blurry, in general X-Ray images have different global features than the images on the data set, then, descriptors are not capable to identify objects if the query images have different features.

3.2 Improving the Matching Process

In order to overcome the mentioned drawbacks, was necessary to seek other alternatives. We have noticed that a cheap approach is to detect closed contours in the images (contours of the dental implants). Since we know that both images (the X-Ray image and the Image from the Data Set) contains uniquely a dental implant, so we can expect that the queried image will be found on the data set, or found images with similar dental implant. It is possible that the searched image does not match exactly with any image in the image set, then our application returns three possible candidates, since the comparison algorithm returns a value, so we can return three candidates with the best results. The Fig. 3 shows our proposed pipeline.

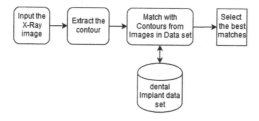

Fig. 3. Our proposed pipeline.

The first step take a picture from the desired dental implant in the X-Ray image. In the second step, the contour of the dental implant is extracted. The Fig. 4 shows this process.

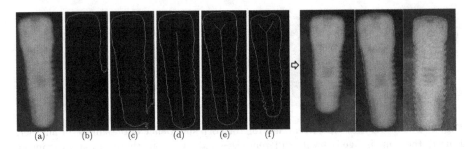

Fig. 4. (a) The input image to query. (b) Starts a contour detection process trying to wrap the desired object on the image. The medial axis line is not reached yet. (c)-(f) The implemented mechanism increases or decreases in a binary search manner in order to find a medial axis polyline, with no branches. The right side demonstrate contours detected successfully.

By knowing that the matching technique using descriptors works well only for images that have similar global features, and conversely the X-Ray images not always have the same properties, depending on several aspects, like the device camera quality, ambient illumination, X-Ray quality, etc., then, a contour extraction algorithm was implemented.

However, there is no an automatic process to do it, because it depends on the image quality and its features. We initially have processed manually, the taken X-Ray image, in order to get a desired contour (we have used some popular free software like Gimp, although there are many other applications to edit images, even for smart cell-phones).

This manual process is fairly not the best way to do the contour extraction. So we propose a naive approach in order to overcome this limitation. We refer to use the medial axis method for a polygonal shape. [4, 15].

Figure 5 shows implants identified on a small catalogue.

Fig. 5. Dental implants identified on the catalogue.

3.3   Implementing the Web Application

Since one of our goals is implement an collaborating application for dentists, which could be used from many devices, from personal computers to SmartTVs. Implement an application that have all the described features is challenge.

Thus, we have implemented two prototypes in order to experiment with our approach. Since our main target is that the application will be used wherever, we implemented a client server application, where the server is responsible for the core image based algorithms and analysis processing, while the web based application was designed to provide a friendly user interface to collect and send query images over the internet, via http protocol, to the remote server.

So we have implemented a command line application in C++, using the OpenCV library. However, the application can't be used directly from any device. Thus we have implemented a second application, which is a web application (see Figs. 7a, b and c) with a graphical user interface. This application needs an internet connection for sending a query X-Ray image, and in the background, the queried image is compared with the images on the data set (dental implant catalogue). Internally, the web application executes the command line application, which has been installed on the remote web server where our web application is hosted. The command line application runs on a computer, it receives the X-Ray image passed by the web interface, and it compares with all the images in the data set, returning the images with best matching values.

The implemented application does not run entirely in the client device, a part of it runs on the web server. It was also decided to do in this way because this process could expend a considerable time and requires some resources which not all devices have. Figure 6 shows our proposed software architecture.

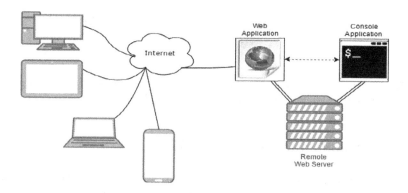

Fig. 6. Proposed software architecture.

4 Results

In order to experiment with the developed web application, we have used personal computers and other devices capable to execute a modern web browser, since our proposed system is a web application, achieving the collaboration between dentists. So, our proposed system, as mentioned above, combines two applications: a web application and a console application. Both of them run on a computer equipped with an Intel Xeon Processor and 8 GB DDR4 RAM, which is our web server.

The web application runs in all modern web browsers, and the dental cata-logue could be saw, and allows add new ones if is desired. In order to identify a dental implant, the x-ray image should be loaded and select the "identify implant" option. When the web application receives a query, it runs the console application, which is the one that really detects the dental implant and looks in the images set (catalogue) for identify it.

The developed web application has been proven using some common devices such as personal computers, laptops, cell-phones, tablets and SmartTVs. The follow Figs. 7a, b and c show our system running in a web browser in different devices.

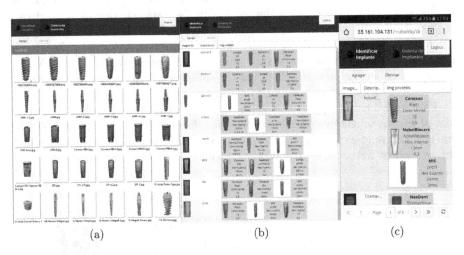

(a)   (b)   (c)

Fig. 7. (a) The system shows the catalogue of dental implants. (b) Some tests done using the system. (c) The system is running in a mobile device.

5   Conclusions and Future Works

The image processing has been evolving constantly, and has become a funda-mental tool which can be used in many different areas. In this work, we have shown a specific approach which will be used in the medical area, specifically in the dentistry area, making the dental implants will be easier to identify and recognize. Because dentists, in their daily life, could have patients with different type of dental implants, and they could need change or repair them, and for dentists, is difficult to identify between many dental implants in a catalogue. In order to automate this task we have proposed a system which consists in use of image processing and computer vision techniques.

Initially, we have presented tests comparing some descriptors and classifiers. Next, we have done some experiments where we show that using only these tools are not sufficient, so we had to use some additional techniques for preprocessing the images, more specifically detect the dental implant contour on the query image. For this purpose, we have used a medial axis technique. However, in some query images, blurred or opaque, this is still not capable to find a good match image.

For the future works, we will going to improve the contour detection module, since it is the fundamental part, and the entire system depends on it for finding the correct dental implant.

We should also mention that each image to query is compared with all images in the catalogue, and we have noticed that, if our catalogue would have thousands of images this would be impractical, so we need some efficient way to find quickly the desired image.

References

1. Bay, H., Ess, A., Tuytelaars, T., Van Gool, L.: Speeded-up robust features (SURF). Comput. Vis. Image Underst. **110**(3), 346–359 (2008). https://doi.org/10.1016/j. cviu.2007.09.014
2. Bradski, G.: Opencv library. Dr. Dobb's J. Softw. Tools **120**, 122–125 (2000)
3. Burghardt, T., Damen, D., Mayol-Cuevas, W., Mirmehdi, M.: Correspondence, matching and recognition. Int. J. Comput. Vis. **113**(3), 161–162 (2015). https:// doi.org/10.1007/s11263-015-0827-8
4. Chin, F., Snoeyink, J., Wang, C.A.: Finding the medial axis of a simple polygon in linear time. In: Staples, J., Eades, P., Katoh, N., Moffat, A. (eds.) ISAAC 1995. LNCS, vol. 1004, pp. 382–391. Springer, Heidelberg (1995). https://doi.org/10. 1007/BFb0015444
5. Flusser, J.: On the independence of rotation moment invariants. Pattern Recogn. (PR) **33**(9), 1405–1410 (2000). https://doi.org/10.1016/S0031-3203(99)00127-2. http://library.utia.cas.cz/prace/20000033.pdf
6. Hu, M.K.: Visual pattern recognition by moment invariants. IRE Trans. Inf. Theory IT **8**, 179–187 (1962)
7. Liu, S., Bai, X.: Discriminative features for image classification and retrieval. In: Image and Graphics, International Conference on 00, pp. 325–330 (2011). https:// doi.org/10.1109/ICIG.2011.149
8. Lowe, D.G.: Object recognition from local scale-invariant features. In: Proceedings of the International Conference on Computer Vision-Volume 2, vol. 2, ICCV 1999, p. 1150. IEEE Computer Society, Washington, DC (1999), http://dl.acm. org/citation.cfm?id=850924.851523
9. Lowe, D.G.: Distinctive image features from scale-invariant keypoints. Int. J. Comput. Vis. **60**, 91–110 (2004)
10. Matas, J., Chum, O., Urban, M., Pajdla, T.: Robust wide baseline stereo from maximally stable extremal regions. In: In Proceedings of the BMVC, pp. 384–393 (2002)
11. Miksik, O., Mikolajczyk, K.: Evaluation of local detectors and descriptors for fast feature matching. In: International Conference on Pattern Recognition (ICPR 2012) (2012)
12. Muja, M., Lowe, D.G.: Fast approximate nearest neighbors with automatic algorithm configuration. In: VISAPP International Conference on Computer Vision Theory and Applications, pp. 331–340 (2009)

13. Pass, G., Zabih, R., Miller, J.: Comparing images using color coherence vectors. In: Proceedings of the Fourth ACM International Conference on Multimedia, MULTI-MEDIA 1996, pp. 65–73. ACM, New York (1996). https://doi.org/10.1145/244130. 244148

14. Phillips, P.J., Moon, H., Rizvi, S.A., Rauss, P.J.: The feret evaluation methodology for face-recognition algorithms. IEEE Trans. Pattern Anal. Mach. Intell. 22(10), 1090–1104 (2000). https://doi.org/10.1109/34.879790

15. Preparata, F.P.: The medial axis of a simple polygon. In: Gruska, J. (ed.) MFCS 1977. LNCS, vol. 53, pp. 443–450. Springer, Heidelberg (1977). https://doi. org/10.1007/3-540-08353-7_166. http://dblp.uni-trier.de/db/conf/mfcs/mfcs77. html#Preparata77

16. Rublee, E., Rabaud, V., Konolige, K., Bradski, G.: ORB: an efficient alternative to sift or surf. In: Proceedings of the 2011 International Conference on Computer Vision, ICCV 2011, pp. 2564–2571. IEEE Computer Society, Washington, DC (2011). https://doi.org/10.1109/ICCV.2011.6126544

17. Tuytelaars, T., Mikolajczyk, K.: Local invariant feature detectors: a survey. Found. Trends. Comput. Graph. Vis. 3(3), 177–280 (2008). https://doi.org/10.1561/ 0600000017

18. Viola, P., Jones, M.J.: Robust real-time face detection. Int. J. Comput. Vision 57(2), 137–154 (2004). https://doi.org/10.1023/B:VISI.0000013087.49260.fb

19. Yap, P.T., Kot, A.C., Jiang, X.: Two-dimensional polar harmonic transforms for invariant image representation. IEEE Trans. Pattern Anal. Mach. Intell. 32, 1259–1270 (2009). https://doi.org/10.1109/TPAMI.2009.119

20. Zhang, S., Tian, Q., Huang, Q., Gao, W., Rui, Y.: USB: ultrashort binary descriptor for fast visual matching and retrieval. IEEE Trans. Image Process. 23(8), 3671–3683 (2014). https://doi.org/10.1109/TIP.2014.2330794

Newtrap: Improving Biodiversity Surveys by Enhanced Handling of Visual Observations

Yoanne Didry, Xavier Mestdagh, and Thomas Tamisier$^{(\boxtimes)}$

Luxembourg Institute of Science and Technology (LIST), 41, rue du Brill,
L-4422 Belvaux, Grand Duchy of Luxembourg
{yoanne.didry,thomas.tamisier}@list.lu

Abstract. Biodiversity measuring calls for massive capture of in situ fauna observations over a long period. The present research aims at reducing the cost and the bias of the measures by limiting human intervention for producing those observations. It is based on a integrated infrastructure made of an automated underwater camera trap and a collaborative visual interface to analyze, process and manage the observations. In a latter stage, the infrastructure will be complemented with full image processing and machine learning capabilities to automate as much as possible the handling and exploitation of the observations.

Keywords: Biodiversity monitoring and visualization · Camera trap · Image processing · Collaborative survey

1 Introduction

Amphibians, in particular newts, draw attention of researchers and regulatory bodies over the world as pertinent bio-indicators to assess wetland conservation status. [1] The monitoring of their status traditionally relies on massive exploitation of direct observations through life trapping such as depicted in Fig. 1, which requires a high investment of human resources, is relatively intrusive and disturbing for the fauna and suffers from several causes of potentially imperfect detection, which are in turn compensated by repeating surveys [2].

More specifically, estimating the population size of newts is based on the repeated use of a live trapping tool during a breeding season. Each sampling event requires two field trips for trap laying and trap removal. During the removal of the trap, each individual is handled individually to take a picture of the belly in a standardized position. In fact, the belly of some newt works as a human finger-print, each pattern being unique to an individual. Belly pictures from all sampling events are thus compared with the support of an *Automatic Picture Identification* (API) software [3], and the population size is estimated by capture-recapture (CR) statistical methods [4]. In addition, API software allows to measure the length, and to determine the age, gender and condition of the individuals.

Y. Luo (Ed.): CDVE 2019, LNCS 11792, pp. 277–281, 2019.
https://doi.org/10.1007/978-3-030-30949-7_32

Fig. 1. Standard methods for newt trapping Top: Dewsbury newt trap (left), bottle trap (right) Bottom: Laar newt trap (left), Ortmann's funnel trap (right)

Nowadays, the production of newt population estimates requires therefore intensive field efforts for the handling of individuals, which affects the welfare of the fauna, causes important bias in the results, and makes long-term and large scale quality data sets hardy available.

2   Improved Camera Trap Engineering

In order to improve on standard capturing methods we developed an apparatus for live observation of newts with a set of features for limiting the use of human resources. The main advance of Newtrap is to combine on the one hand an original physical design of the trap to place the newt in a standardized position with the belly fully visible, and on the other hand a powerful hardware to automate the photography of the newt. In the latest version, Newtrap embeds a Raspberry Pi card with a camera, powered through a mobile battery and Power over Ethernet (PoE). As a result, the manual handling of the animal is no longer necessary.

The Newtrap prototype is depicted in Fig. 2. Disposed below the surface, Newtrap attracts into it and release in water newts trough four gates in different directions. The body of Newtrap is a tunnel where the newt is forced into the best position to identify the features of its body. A camera looks into the tunnel and is triggered by the motion of individuals. Newtrap is then able to automate the production of ventral images (colour or near-infrared) without any newt handling.

Additionally, whereas the extraction of any characteristics of the observations required hitherto a manual playback of videos, it is possible to determine directly

Fig. 2. Newtrap prototype: overview with 4 gates - shooting glass tunnel - example of captured image

from the images taken through Newtrap the species, sex, size, and even identity of the newt, as well as the exact date and time of the observations.

3   Collaborative and Visual Interpretation of Observations

As the position of the newt and the shooting conditions are standardized, Newtrap reduces the noise in the observations and eases many more subsequent steps such as image tagging, survey encoding, species monitoring, and capture-recapture. Newtrap is thus complemented with Newtrap Manager, a web application especially designed for the observations produced through Newtrap, dedicated to support the collaborative work of environmentalists in the management of observation sites and the annotation of images and videos. Basic meta data include sampling location, device used, responsible of the observations and some additional information such as vegetation percentage, water depth, or scheduled working period. Figure 3 shows the main page for site management in Newtrap Manager.

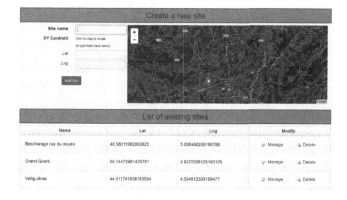

Fig. 3. Newtrap Manager

With a view to a more advanced prototype, Newtrap manager is being used to prepare high quality data for the implementation of efficient automatic image processing functionalities. In this regard, we obtained in one season more than 3000 high quality annotated pictures, ready for classification using advanced machine learning technique.

The first task in image processing consists in selecting images displaying a unique and complete view of a single newt among the database of raw observations released by Newtrap. We achieved this task satisfactorily by relying on supervised learning techniques, notably Support Vector Machines (SVM) based on feature vectors computed in the shape of Histogram of Oriented Gradients (HOG) [5] described in the picture below (Fig. 4).

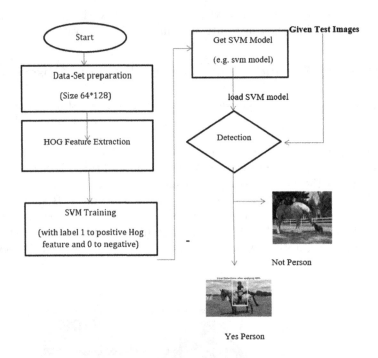

Fig. 4. Supervised learning using feature vectors

Further tasks concern the classification of ventral images released by Newtrap for determining species and gender of the 4 newt species commonly monitoring for biodiversity survey: Triturus cristatus, ichthyosaura alpestris, lissotriton vulgaris and lissotriton helveticus. Additionally, patterns shown on the belly of the Triturus cristatus will be used for the recognition of individuals.

As a first classification trial we focused on the recognition of the gender, on a subset of 1162 males and 796 females images, in different resolutions, split in 80% training and 20% test sets. We applied convolutional neural network (CNN) with 3 layers: convolutional later, pooling layer and fully connected layer. The convolution layer is the core building block of the neural network, the pooling layer replaces the output of the network at certain locations by deriving a summary statistic of nearby outputs and the fully connected layer maps the representation between the input and the output.

The main advantage of CNN is to rely on models pre-trained on large data sets, and use transfer learning to customize the models to the final goal. We tested both MobileNet V2 [6] and Inception V3 [7] pre-trained models developed at Google with a huge dataset of 1000 classes of web images. We freezed the convolutional base created at the first step and used it as a feature extractor, added a classifier on top of it and trained the top-level classifier. The training process hence forces the weights to be tuned from generic features maps to features associated specifically to our dataset. Using Tensorflow and Keras (python), we obtained $+/-75\%$ accuracy with images resized at a resolution of 128×128, and raised to $+/-85\%$ accuracy with a resolution of 256×256.

4 Conclusion

Since ever, amphibians are the subject of abundant attentions and research projects due to the important role they play in ecosystems and their sensitivity to environmental changes. Newtrap is an enhanced infrastructure made of an improved newt camera trap and associated software for processing observations, which allows detecting the presence of species without stress, and optimizing the use of reference methods for population estimates. Compared to traditional biodiversity monitoring methods, the approach proposed by Newtrap aims to be cheaper by reducing human resource, faster by avoiding manual handling of animals, while delivering high resolution time series and more independent observations. Over the next seasons, the infrastructure will be used intensively to produce a catalogue of reference images in view of complementing Newtrap with the automated processing of the observations based on image processing and machine learning.

References

1. Dornelas, M., et al.: Quantifying temporal change in biodiversity: challenges and opportunities. Proc. R. Soc. B: Biol. Sci. **280**(1750), 20121931 (2012)
2. Drechsler, A., et al.: Ortmann's funnel trap-a highly efficient tool for monitoring amphibian species. Herpetol. Notes **3**, 13–21 (2010)
3. Mathe, M., et al.: Comparison of photo-matching algorithms commonly used for photographic capture-recapture studies. Ecol. Evol. **7**, 5861–5872 (2017)
4. Snoopy: Portable software for capture-recapture surveys. https://prezi.com/xqoogmni0ymu/snoopy
5. Dalal, N., Triggs, B. Histograms of oriented gradients for human detection. In: International Conference on Computer Vision and Pattern Recognition. IEEE Computer Society (2005)
6. https://towardsdatascience.com/review-mobilenetv2-light-weight-model-image-classification-8febb490e61c
7. https://software.intel.com/en-us/articles/inception-v3-deep-convolutional-architecture-for-classifying-acute-myeloidlymphoblastic

Author Index

Printed in the United States
By Bookmasters